THE VIEW FROM BELOW

THE VIEW FROM BELOW

Urban Politics and Social Policy

SUSAN S. FAINSTEIN
*Livingston College, Rutgers University
and Center for Policy Research*

NORMAN I. FAINSTEIN
*Columbia University
and Center for Policy Research*

LITTLE, BROWN AND COMPANY   *Boston*

Contents

THE VIEW FROM BELOW

Introduction: Urban Politics —
The View from Below

The evolution of American society may yet reduce its central cities to the status of historical curiosities no longer essential to its economy and culture. Already our national highways permit travel from one suburban or rural area to another without driving on city streets. The passenger train, with its great downtown stations, has become a vestigial system to which the federal government pays symbolic respect while shifting investment elsewhere. The city is unnecessary to the functioning of airplanes and airports if not a hazard to flight safety. The development of electronic communications means that our industrial and financial institutions can function effectively in low density suburban areas or even thousands of miles apart; businessmen can deal with each other electronically while their firms' computer banks exchange millions of bits of information in a matter of seconds. Although the shops and colorful street life of a few city neighborhoods like Greenwich Village or the North End of Boston are specifically urban, our national cultural institutions need not remain in the city at all. The cinema is already suburbanized. So, too, are sports. Perhaps symphony orchestras, ballets, and theaters can also leave the old cities. Indeed, of all our national firms and institutions, the only ones not likely to desert the central cities are the Greyhound and Trailways terminals. Poor people travel by bus, and the poor may well comprise a majority of our urban population. Blacks, Puerto Ricans, Mexican-Americans, and recent migrants from rural areas and from abroad will typically be left in the city. And the city will be left to them.

The passing of the city might be lamented by a small number of Americans who, contrary to our national tradition, highly value urban life. But to many more of us such a course of events would be tragic because of the implications of both its circumstances and final result. The circumstances under which more affluent people leave the central cities to the poor are already clear. They include residential integration, crime and the fear of crime, decaying housing, and inadequate public services. Suburbs are attractive not only because of their green space and low-density housing, but also because of their social and racial homogeneity. In short, the cities may become superfluous to the mainstream of our society because a higher quality of day-to-day life can be purchased else-

1

where by those who can afford it. At the same time, the cities will become more financially impoverished. Their governments cannot reverse
the physical and institutional decay, despite the increasing intensity of
political attack from the urban poor. The cities become the locus of major
social conflict, while the middle class moves out and is better able to
ignore the poor and *their* cities. The decline of the cities is thus not only
a matter of natural or social evolution, but also an indication of tensions
and contradictions in the entire society.

Present developments may well result in cities with residential populations that are very largely poor and nonwhite. Poverty will be physically encapsulated, removed from the lifespace of most Americans and
perhaps from their consciousness as well. This does not mean that inner-
city residents will gain complete control of their local governments. Non-
residents will still have a personal stake in holding on to their civil service
jobs. Policemen, firemen, schoolteachers, social workers, and others who
provide services to city clients will continue to be recruited from populations significantly different from those they are purportedly serving. Urban
bureaucracies will remain as caretakers of the American underclass.

As the most immediate target for the resentments of the poor (while
creating an objective basis for many of their grievances), the caretakers
will be embroiled in local political controversy. At the same time, however, they may keep conflict local, deflecting it from the national centers
of economic and political power. The caretakers will serve as societal
lightning rods, often at considerable cost to some of their numbers — witness physical attacks on firemen and assassinations of policemen. The
greatest cost, however, will not be to the caretakers — who, after all, do
receive compensation for their work; nor to the entire society, for middle-
class America could go on without cities; but rather to the poor.

The relative — and maybe absolute — situation of the urban lower
class can deteriorate while most of the population has *less* stake in reversing the direction of change. If the public can do without cities, and can
physically protect itself from their populations, then the interests of the
public — the public interest if you will — may not be in redistributing
income to the urban poor, in investing in a massive program of public
housing, and in the other social policies necessary to the significant ame-
lioration of the conditions in which our deprived citizens live. Improvement of the situation of the poor may only take place if costs are incurred
by other segments of the society. Sympathetic political activists who want
to "save our cities" may have to make a moral commitment to the poor,
rather than to an illusory "public interest."

A cursory examination of this book will indicate that the editors have
made such a commitment. The readings include descriptions of the cultural and structural situation of the urban poor, of their relation to the
caretaker bureaucracies, and of governmental policy as it affects (or fails

to affect) their day-to-day lives. This descriptive analysis permits rational consideration of alternative strategies for advancing the interests of the urban poor. The authors discuss what political activity can do toward improving the social, economic, and political positions of inner-city residents. Quite naturally, they disagree on the viability and attractiveness of different strategies for change, but the arrangement of the articles in the form of a dialogue should clarify the central issues of analysis and value choice that characterize the literature. The emphasis is on urban politics as it affects the poor; the book does not include questions of importance to other groups, in or outside the city. This is our value choice, for we wish to examine urban politics "from the bottom" with the goal of changing political outcomes to the advantage of the lower class.

Urban Politics as Outcome

A poor person living in an American urban slum views city government primarily in terms of how its policies affect him. In other words, he has a strong, immediate stake in who gets what from municipal government; the quality of his life depends significantly on the nature and quantity of public services available. Although middle-class citizens also are concerned with urban services, they depend less on governmental activities in such areas as health and housing than do the poor, and they are much more able to seek out alternatives if they are dissatisfied with such services as schools or recreation. The middle-class person may never have to deal personally with any employee of the city government except his child's teacher and an occasional building inspector; the lower-class individual who must rely on city hall or the local emissaries of the federal government for his income, housing, medical care, job training opportunities, food stamp eligibility, recreational outlets, and addiction services can never escape from direct involvement with the local administration.

The salient aspect of urban politics for the middle class is primarily the arena of major policy decisions and traditional political competition. The politically involved middle-class citizen cares about urban renewal planning, the possibility of metropolitan government, and who is going to be mayor. These questions are less pertinent for a lower-class person than are decisions on eligibility for various programs, the number of public housing units to be constructed, the hours that the well-baby clinic will be open, and the candidates for local welfare administrator or municipal judge. He is concerned with the decisionmaking process, but more significantly, with the implementation of policy.

The concern of poor people and their representatives with the implementation of urban policy and with the characteristics of personnel in the urban public services has led to the politicization of a sphere of life that previously passed under the rubric of "administration." The legitimacy of urban government is being challenged by the poor on the grounds that the principal policymakers do not serve their lower-class constituencies. In addition, it is charged that lower-level personnel, chosen on the basis of "impersonal" criteria, are making political rather than administrative decisions, yet are not subject to the control of the people who are affected by their decisions. Thus, the principal and the policeman, the welfare worker and the doctor are suddenly thrust into the political arena and, in fact, frequently become targets for the hostility of ghetto inhabitants.

This rapid broadening of the political sphere has paralleled important qualitative changes in the study of urban politics. Before Robert Dahl wrote *Who Governs?*,[1] municipal politics was studied mainly as a specialized area in public administration. In this context, administration was viewed as nonpolitical and subject to general norms of efficiency. There was little empirical research to examine whether the precepts of good government set forth in the textbooks bore any resemblance to the real workings of the municipal government. Nor did anyone attempt to determine, given the divergence between actual practice and the standards of behavior prescribed in the textbooks, whether the differences resulted from political necessity.

Underlying most analyses was an unstated assumption that operation according to good government norms benefitted the *entire* public and that the municipal administration could, if appropriate institutional forms were established, automatically carry out the will of the people as expressed through elections. For example, many political scientists recommended the city-manager form of government, whereby councilmen elected at large would express the public will on general questions and the city manager, under the direction of the council, would perform the "business" of government. Most writers did not consider the possibility that a city government elected on an at-large basis would not respond to the different needs of minority groups, nor that an administration run according to business principles would be at odds with important segments of the population. They assumed that the public conformed to the ideals of equality and the melting pot rather than consisting of conflicting groups. Only such a view of the public could justify the expectation that everyone would benefit from a centralized government elected by a citywide majority. Only a refusal to see various group interests could lead to the wholesale endorsement of an administration operating under norms of efficiency and impersonality rather than responsiveness and the recognition of differing interests.

---

[1] Robert Dahl, *Who Governs?* (New Haven: Yale University Press, 1961).

Municipal Politics Found

In *Who Governs?* Robert Dahl analyzed empirically what one critic has called "the lost world of municipal government." [2] He asked who really governed cities, and examined closely the process by which important policy decisions were made. His analysis prompted the principal debate in American political science for the succeeding decade, as scholars sought to determine whether, as Dahl insisted, cities were run by people from diverse social strata and whether elected officials did possess real power rather than being only puppets of the upper class.

Dahl's major interest was in the decisionmaking process and reflected the middle-class concern, noted earlier, with major policy decisions and traditional political competition. Although he studied New Haven, later the scene of the earliest major poverty program and subsequent rioting in the black ghetto, his work barely touched on the role of blacks in the city and did not look at all at policy implementation. Thus, although Dahl succeeded in illuminating the urban political process, he avoided scrutinizing its outcomes. He asked who governed, but he did not inquire who benefitted.

Recent political events and a heightened awareness of poverty and racism as the major problems of the central city have led analysts to look at the distribution of benefits and to challenge the traditional distinction between politics and administration. Although the study of urban politics is still primarily the analysis of public decisionmaking, it has also become the examination of governmental outputs. As such, the scope of urban politics is defined by the population being studied rather than by the source of policy — it includes those political processes which significantly affect urban populations. The study of urban politics thus becomes the analysis of governmental outputs in two senses — it looks at the relationships between the purveyors of governmental services and their clients; and it considers the effects of federal, state, and local policies on city residents.

The Federal Government and Local Politics

If the study of urban politics focuses on the impact of public policy on the poor, it must include a discussion of federal programs even though they are largely out of the control of local political bodies. Indeed the principal authority over many of the programs that most affect the urban

---

[2] Lawrence J. R. Herson, "The Lost World of Municipal Government," *American Political Science Review*, 51 (June 1957), pp. 330–345.

poor resides in Washington. Because the resources required to meet the needs of poor people can only be raised nationally, local authorities are often incapable of responding to the demands of their constituencies. Since, however, the poor usually press their grievances on the unit of government closest to them, municipalities become the arenas for conflicts that cannot be solved within them. Moreover, municipally operated programs with support from federal grants-in-aid must conform to federal requirements which often specify the relationship between program administrators and clients, the eligibility standards for programs, and the use of funds. Thus, even programs nominally subject to the decisionmaking powers of local bodies are severely constrained by federal policy.

Local politics then reflects national political decisions and is limited by federal social policy. The two most significant aspects of federal policy as it applies to the urban poor are an avoidance of income redistribution as a solution to poverty and an emphasis on providing services aimed at enabling poor people to assist themselves and escape poverty through individual achievement.

Federal programs to aid the poor have largely eschewed direct transfer payments, such as a negative income tax or social insurance. The United States' principal social insurance scheme — social security — does not particularly assist the indigent and is not redistributive. In fact, because of the ceiling on yearly salary from which premiums are paid, social security taxes take proportionately more of the income of the working poor than of the wealthy. Most federal programs involve either services such as those offered by the United States Employment Service, or funds earmarked for special purposes such as education of the disadvantaged or mental health programs. Federal assistance, whether through the provision of direct services or indirectly, through special purpose grants to local agencies, usually requires large cadres of personnel for research, general administration, and client aid. The result has been the burgeoning of an officialdom that depends, for its own sustenance, on the continued existence of an impoverished lower class. The social service bureaucracies have become intermediaries between the poor and policy-making bodies: on the one hand translating lower-class demands for assistance into calls for increased services and thus more bureaucratic expansion; on the other hand integrating the poor into the system through requirements of appropriate behavior in return for aid.

Despite the increase in federally sponsored social programs that occurred in the 1960s, many policymakers and spokesmen for the poor perceive that these programs have largely failed to change the situation of the poor. This dissatisfaction has caused moderate critics to demand better programs; it has led radicals to challenge the legitimacy of the system.

The authors in this book evaluate the situation of the urban poor and the effect on it of governmental programs; in the latter part of the book they examine the possibilities for moderate and radical change of institutional structures and social policies. The remainder of this introductory section is a description of the general patterns which characterize urban reform movements and an examination of the relationship between urban politics and urban political analysis.

The Modes of Urban Reform

Looking back over the last century of urban history, and particularly the last fifty years, one can distinguish two basic types of reform. The first is reform of the Progressive mode. Progressive reform is usually identified with a number of early twentieth century middle- and upper-class movements. We believe, however, that more recent efforts at urban social and political change (e.g., the War on Poverty) should also be classified as Progressive. In fact, Progressivism is the dominant mode of reform within the American political tradition.

While Progressivism has been the more prevalent approach to reform, a second type has appeared from time to time. This is reform initiated from below, i.e., social movements with a lower-class basis. Recent efforts at reform from below are most clearly manifested in "client movements." These center on the relationship between urban bureaucracies — the caretakers — and their clients. Client movements have aimed at greater participation at the local level; their symbolic banner has been "community control."

Reform from below differs from Progressivism, both old and new, not only in its lower-class social basis, but also in its more radical ideology. At the extreme, it becomes revolutionary. Some groups appear to be revolutionary to the extent that they tie urban reform in with basic changes in the socio-economic fabric (e.g., eliminating capitalism) and are willing to employ extralegal methods to attain their ends. For several reasons, though, it would be unproductive to try to separate revolutionary from reformist movements. The ideology of a group may have little relationship to its actions. The use of nonlegal actions is so common among lower-class reformers as to tell us little about the character of a group. Most significantly, whether a group is revolutionary or reformist depends very much on how the larger social system reacts. Even terrorism may be employed by groups whose success makes them "reformist" — to which the history of the labor movement bears witness. The "revolutionaries" among urban groups working for change from the bottom may simply be those groups so defined by political authorities, especially by the police.

A group that is the victim of authoritative violence becomes labeled as revolutionary, for otherwise how could its oppression be legitimated? Thus, it becomes a moot point, for example, whether the Panthers are revolutionary or reformist.

Efforts at reform from the bottom differ considerably from those with roots in the middle and upper classes. The poor bring about change through direct illegal or quasi-illegal, sometimes violent, actions. Progressive reform is carried out through legal procedures by the left wing of the establishment. We first turn to an examination of Progressivism; then to a discussion of our second type of reform.

Progressive Reform: Old and New

From a historical viewpoint it is ironic that the sector of urban government presently under the most severe attack should be the civil service bureaucracies. These bureaucracies represent the triumph of an earlier reform movement directed at increasing the efficiency and responsiveness of municipal institutions. The Progressive movement of the early twentieth century aimed at making government operate in the public interest. One of its goals was opening municipal jobs to those best qualified. The result was a series of exams and credentials requirements for bureaucratic positions which presumably made jobs available on the basis of merit rather than influence, but excluded ethnic groups with low levels of educational attainment. Moreover, the Progressive intention of protecting jobholders from removal by the dispensers of political patronage led to the inviolability of tenure for many municipal employees. The unintended consequence was to make it nearly impossible to remove workers of mediocre performance.

Middle- and upper-class citizens, alarmed at the corruption and inefficiency of urban government, provided the basis for the Progressive movement. Their manifest goal was not the improvement of the cities for the benefit of their own class only but for the good of everyone. They tended, however, to interpret the public interest as requiring that people of their own class and outlook should occupy service positions within municipal government.

The Progressive effort to "clean up" and improve local administration can be identified by several unchanging characteristics. First, it was supported by the "best citizens." The composition of reform groups was entirely middle- and upper-class and inevitably reflected the interests and predispositions of the upper portion of the social hierarchy, even when the reformers' efforts were directed at what Jacob Riis called "the other half." Second, its operational goal was the separation of politics from administration. Those who argued that "there is no Democratic or Republican way to pave a street" overlooked the fact that the choice of which street to pave was a political decision. The attempt to separate politics from administration led to placing decisionmaking power over a broad range of issues — such as which street to pave, where to build a hospital or school, who should qualify for public assistance — with people who were insulated from the control of service recipients. This has led directly to present charges of "welfare colonialism"; service personnel are accused of being alien to the communities they supposedly assist. The alleged result is that they shape policy not on the basis of the needs of the community, but according to the logic of bureaucratic self-perpetuation, based on false perceptions of client groups and overresponsiveness to special interests.

The Progressive concern with social welfare led to the development of many institutions for bettering the lot of the poor. Settlement houses, parks, playgrounds, vocational education, and tenement codes were all part of the Progressive program. Underlying the various attempts to assist poor people was a faith that they could be incorporated into middle-class America without any loss to those already occupying middle- and upper-class positions. Advancement was to be achieved through individual mobility, and the Progressives greatly stressed the role of the public schools in preparing lower-class youth for their rise up the social ladder. The Progressive ideology denied the inevitability of conflict between rich and poor and supported policies aiding poor people as individuals rather than as a class. Progressivism reflected an optimistic belief that, through rational policymaking under the direction of disinterested persons, human misery could be eliminated.

Progressive reform arose in opposition to the political machine, and its content was largely shaped by the institution it sought to demolish. The political machine dispensed public office to individuals on the basis of their relationship to the political boss; in reaction the Progressives sought to ensure that office holders were disinterested and qualified on the basis of impersonal tests. Progressivism did succeed in lessening corruption and personal dealings within the municipal services, but it also led to a lack of responsiveness among municipal office holders toward the public.

The recognition of this lack of responsiveness has helped to initiate a new wave of reform in reaction to certain of the earlier programs but sharing a number of elements with Progressivism. We shall call this movement modern Progressivism. The main similarities between the old and new Progressivism are their source in middle- and upper-class segments of society, their emphasis on improving the quality of urban services through more efficient bureaucratic functioning, and their stress on education as a vehicle for mobility. They are less radical than movements emanating directly from the urban poor and aimed at the redistribution of income and power.

The reform program of the 1960s has resulted in federal legislation to aid education for the disadvantaged, improve job training programs, coordinate various local assistance programs, and involve poor people in community development projects. Although recent policy can be traced partly to pressures exerted by black leaders, its content was framed by college professors, foundation executives, and federal officials. As Daniel P. Moynihan acidly commented, when discussing the origins of the Economic Opportunity Act of 1964: "The war on poverty was not declared at the behest of the poor: it was declared in their interest by persons confident of their own judgment in such matters." [3]

Despite the many similarities between early and modern Progressivism, they have differed in a few important ways. First, the present programs attempt to make urban public services more flexible, more innovative, and more representative of the people they serve. One of their goals has been to establish new institutions, such as local poverty councils and decentralized school districts, functioning outside the regular civil service framework, and thus able to hire personnel without standard credentials. The hope is that such institutions will be less alien to their clients and also freer of traditional rivalries and patterns of behavior. This endeavor has led opponents to argue that the programs are bringing back patronage and corruption to the civil service.

The second major difference between modern and early Progressivism is the effort to involve the poor in the formulation of policy. The Economic Opportunity Act provided for "maximum feasible participation" of the program's target groups and set a precedent for other programs such as Model Cities. These new institutions have created bases from which spokesmen for previously unrepresented portions of the population have mounted attacks on the regular city government.

But, when Progressive reformers begin to create structures that can significantly affect the distribution of power and income, they tend to pull back. Liberal advocates of reform justify their programs by arguing that the stability of the entire system depends upon some changes being made. Once reform threatens overall stability, the social and economic roots of the Progressive reformers become salient. Thus, the advocates of maximum feasible participation of the poor began to retreat when it became apparent that boards of poor people, instead of making moderate demands, were attacking urban governments and becoming the basis for a new political force.

---

[3] Daniel P. Moynihan, *Maximum Feasible Misunderstanding* (N.Y.: Free Press, 1969), p. 25.

Despite their social basis in the upper classes and their interest in maintaining the extant socioeconomic system, Progressives have contributed much to urban social change in the United States. Although their social position and ideology limit the extent to which they can work for radical goals, their ties with social and political elites and their rhetoric of the "public interest" and social meliorism make them respectable and effective advocates of "reasonable" change.

Since Progressives tend to see the social fabric through the lenses of their own ideology, they avoid conflict analyses and overlook divisive group interests. The result is that they may unwittingly initiate programs with a radical potential.

It may be argued that had Progressive reformers understood the implications of Maximum Feasible Participation they would never have advocated the concept (see Lillian Rubin's article in this volume). But when Progressives pull back after seeing the consequences of the changes they have helped initiate, they may lose control over the process of change. Progressivism may therefore do more than advance its own end. It may also provide — as its conservative critics have charged — the stimulus for more radical movements from below. In short, Progressive programs (like the drive against racial segregation or for political participation by the poor) may raise the expectations of the poor, facilitate the development of alternative (radical) analyses of their condition, and provide the political mechanisms for independent collective action.

Reform Movements from Below

Until recently the radical thrust in American cities was associated with the labor movement and the Socialist and Communist parties. These today constitute the old left, and have receded in political significance. In their place are predominantly white and middle-class new-left groups and generally black lower-class groups. It is the activity of the latter which is directed toward local government and a redistribution of power within American cities.

Of the significant lower-class reform movements, many can be identified as client movements. Today the status of client in respect to an urban bureaucracy seems to offer the most effective foundation for group solidarity and large-scale collective political action. Common social class and race alone are not sufficient for mobilizing city residents. Similar client status on the other hand appears to increase significantly the likelihood of concerted political action.

The "we" feeling within client movements is based largely on differentiation from and opposition to the "they" of a particular urban bureaucracy.[4] The enemy of client movements is thus usually highly specific. "They" are the management of public housing, the educational bureaucracy, the police department, and so forth. Much less frequently is the enemy described in class or racial terms, and such generalized enemies are less effective in advancing group solidarity.

Many black and Spanish-speaking people have begun to associate their social condition with the action or nonaction of local government agencies. They evaluate negatively the performance of such institutions as schools, hospitals, and housing agencies, and the personnel of these institutions have suffered a loss of legitimacy. More and more it has been felt that the "governors" (broadly defined to include bureaucrats) have no right to govern; they have no legitimate basis for their power.

This loss of legitimacy resulting from what is perceived as inadequate performance is reinforced by two other major categories of grievance. The first is the accusation that local agencies are racist in their staff recruitment policies and in their attitude toward clients. The second is an attack against the basic powerlessness of the client role. The political position of the urban lower-class individual is defined primarily by the intersection of a number of client statuses. He is a client of the welfare department, of the public hospital, of the school system, of the housing authority, of the police department — the list is long. In each client role he is virtually powerless. The net result is relegation to the status of noncitizen. The aim of client movements has been to change the status of the bureaucratic client by altering the distribution of power between the client and the professional.

Client movements produce localized eruptions rather than a concerted attack on the seat of power in the national capital. They do not have a direct impact on the social policy of the federal government. Nor do they have the potential, as would a national political party, of winning or usurping control of power in Washington. Nonetheless, these movements from below can have positive functions for improving the lot of their adherents.

First, client movements educate the urban poor and train leaders and potential leaders. Although there is only limited evidence as to the effect of these movements on the consciousness of the larger urban population,

---

[4] Although most client movements have local targets, a few have now gained sufficient political resources to have a national impact. This is significant, because the power to change social policy outcomes is often located in Washington, rather than in city hall. Of the groups trying to be heard in Washington, the National Welfare Rights Organization is probably the most important. Nonetheless, the vast majority of lower-class black activists are working in "bureaucracy specific" local organizations.

they will probably further the changes initiated by the Community Action Program and other components of the War on Poverty. Some of these changes are an increase in the expectations of nonwhites, a heightening of their sense of relative deprivation, and the development of the political infrastructure of the ghettos.

Second, client movements by themselves can bring about some meaningful change in the behavior of city agencies and their employees. The presence of organized "watchdogs" and the "pressuring" of bureaucrats can elicit more responsive behavior on their part. This is especially true when the clients can stress the official norms of the bureaucracy, demanding only that officials live up to them.

However, poor clients have very limited resources themselves, and must frequently use political tactics which emphasize symbolic action — picketing, demonstrating, and sitting-in are examples. In doing so they are appealing to sympathetic "third parties" to intervene on their behalf. To the extent that clients can find "patrons" in the form of liberal groups, the media, foundations, organized labor, or universities, they can be much more successful in achieving their goals. But, as Michael Lipsky points out, the dependence on third parties is an inadequate substitute for power resources. Moreover, the gains, which are at best attainable at the local level, are limited. City bureaucrats may behave more responsively, but their budgets are still determined at the state and national capitals. And local bureaucracies have almost no control over the broad outlines of national social policy in regard to employment, housing, public welfare, and health care, areas that define the quality of life for poor city dwellers. Thus, one should not overemphasize the potential of locally based movements from below.

Even with this reservation in mind, it is possible to suggest a third function for client movements. Many localized attacks can add up to considerable pressure on city officials and a great deal of turmoil and possibly violence in our major population centers. Under certain circumstances, mass unrest and demands can be used by liberal reformers to buttress their calls for change. With major groups to their left, the Progressives become more and more defined as "moderates." With violence erupting and with a real potential for uprisings from below, Progressive arguments to the effect that only reform can stabilize the system look much more convincing to a broad segment of the political elite. Client movements may therefore create a political situation conducive to Progressive reform of national social policy.

In sum, then, client movements can achieve some goals of the poor directly. They may also contribute to the success of Progressive reform. The chances that collective action by the poor will help to improve their situation are thus significant and probably worth the risk of political reaction. But one should not be sanguine about the prospect of radical changes in the social order being effected by such movements from beneath as are present in America today.

The Uses of Political Analysis

Scholarly analysis of urban politics tends to reflect political controversy. When the focus of urban reform movements was on the elimination of the machine and the establishment of efficient and impartial urban administrations, political scientists concerned themselves with administrative norms and alternative governmental institutions designed to further these norms. During the politically quiet fifties and continuing into the more turbulent sixties, political science tried to show the virtues of "interest group liberalism," at both the national and the local level. The thrust of this analysis was that although the United States lacked widespread political participation and contained inequalities of wealth and position, nonetheless all levels of society had the potential for affecting public policy. In other words, during a time when there seemed to be a widespread public consensus on national goals and little political debate, academic political science tended to legitimize the system, discovering its virtues and showing the positive functions of even such seemingly undesirable features as voter apathy and the power of organized interest groups.

Within the most recent period, one of political controversy, racial self-consciousness, and demands for power and benefits by militant minorities, the emphasis of scholarship has shifted again. Increasingly there is an examination of the substance of public policy — not just in terms of its ideal content but also with reference to its differential effects on various social groups. Political science is no longer restricted to the study of institutional forms and decisionmaking processes but includes also an analysis of the outcome of policymaking. The writings in the first two sections of this volume epitomize the concern with substantive policy. The authors represent several academic disciplines, including sociology, economics, and city planning as well as political science, demonstrating the fact that the study of policy outcomes is perforce interdisciplinary.

Besides studying the effects of governmental policies, social scientists — and thinkers without the normal scholarly credentials — are seeking to discover the ways in which social change takes place and the effect of conscious human activity on the direction of change. Dissatisfaction with the outcomes of the American political system has led directly to a search for strategies aimed at changing the beneficiaries of policy. The more radical analysts represented in this book consider that change for the benefit of deprived groups will take place only through mobilizing such groups sufficiently to threaten present power holders.

There seem to be two possible roles for political analysts within the context of general political life. Social scientists may act either as legitimizers of the existing system or as proponents of social change. Few thinkers fall entirely into either category, and the scholar's commitment to intellectual honesty compels him to attempt reasoned analysis rather than impassioned exhortation. Nonetheless, we see that, despite ambiguous cases, scholars tend to line up along a political spectrum ranging from defense of the status quo to advocacy of extensive change.

Among those supporting change are two subgroups, paralleling Progressive and radical groupings within the political world. The emphasis of the Progressive scholars is on policymaking as a governmental function. These authors concentrate on specific policies concerning, for instance, health or housing; they try to improve the quality of these policies within the confines of the existing social reality.

Radical thinkers have tended to use policy analysis to attack the legitimacy of the political system and to seek not better policies but methods for the redistribution of power within that system. The research of the radical scholar seeks to discover strategies for change and to raise the consciousness of members of deprived groups. For the radical, public policy is largely an outcome of the distribution of wealth and income rather than an independent variable to be studied in isolation from the general social fabric. Thus, his main objective must be to seek ways to redistribute those resources on which, he believes, public policy ultimately depends.

As political analysis has oscillated between the two poles of legitimation and advocacy of change, it has also swung between two views of the functions of knowledge. Closely tied with the legitimizing role has been a view of research as value-free, as the scientific quest for explanation. This viewpoint has led to the search for knowledge for its own sake and has opened up social scientific research to the charge of irrelevance. Linked with the role of change-advocate has been a concept of the committed scholar who justifies knowledge in the name of action. He, in turn, has been vulnerable to the accusation of bias, of a failure to examine society with sufficient impartiality to permit an honest appraisal.

We respect objectivity but we also accept the value of scholarly commitment when openly expressed. This volume overrepresents those students of urban politics who espouse political change, partly because there are already a large number of readers presenting more conservative points of view. Nonetheless, several primarily descriptive or dispassionately analytic pieces, such as the Gordon article on income and welfare and Glazer's essay on health care, as well as articles by Banfield and Bell and

Held that are largely unsympathetic with the rebellious poor, are included. Among the articles on policy reform and strategies for change are pieces representing both the Progressive and radical tendencies. Prescriptions for change range from the moderate suggestions concerning housing policy made by George Sternlieb to the forceful demands for redistribution pressed by Bobby Seale.

We hope that this reader can be used within the classroom to raise the crucial issues of race and poverty within American cities and the promise of moderate and revolutionary reform. It is, we trust, still possible to discuss the issues within the confines of reasoned debate and we believe that the material presented herein will contribute to the formation of more intelligent arguments on both sides of the issues.

Poverty and Race

1

In order to analyze the causes of poverty in American cities one must understand who the poor are and how extensive poverty is. Only with this information can one decide whether poverty is a result of low wages or refusal to work; whether racial discrimination or promiscuous sexual behavior leading to unsupportably large families is the more important factor; whether the federal welfare program contributes to continued poverty through "welfare dependency" or not. Even complete factual knowledge of the incidence of poverty will probably not settle the claims of rival explanations, but it can at least place parameters on the discussion. Here David Gordon's article makes an important contribution.

Gordon shows that, in New York City, poverty, as defined by Bureau of Labor Statistics consumption standards, is widespread; 36 percent of the city's residents are classified as poor or low income. Fully 59.5 percent of New York's black and Puerto Rican families fall into these two categories, and while whites have been improving their economic position since 1960, minority group members — comprising 70 percent of poor families in 1968 as opposed to 25 percent in 1960 — have not. Gordon points out that although New York is atypical of all American central cities, it is not dissimilar to Chicago and Los Angeles in terms of the persistence of poverty.

In his analysis of the rapid increase in the welfare rolls during the 1960s, Gordon concludes that the largest source of growth could be traced to increases in the welfare grant level. In other words potential recipients chose to accept welfare benefits rather than work at jobs that paid less than they would receive on welfare. How one interprets this finding depends largely on one's predispositions toward the poor. It is possible to reach either of two conclusions: people electing welfare benefits over poverty wages are only acting rationally and should not be expected to choose to work until well-paying jobs are available to them; or, welfare recipients prefer to extract money that they do not deserve from the general public instead of earning their keep through honest labor.

The latter view is held by Edward Banfield, who contends that the lower class persists because of the "existence of an outlook and style of life which is radically present-oriented and which therefore attaches no value to work, sacrifice, self-improvement, or service. . . ." For Banfield, membership in the lower class results not only from an individual's lack of money, but from financial destitution combined with cultural values that preclude economic improvement. Thus, even if the poor were to be given large sums of money, lower-class individuals would maintain their undesirable modes of behavior and would squander their new resources.

Banfield's interpretation that stable cultural factors are a fundamental cause of the persistence of a lower class leads him to prescribe policies not directly aimed at destroying the *fact* of poverty itself. Rather, he suggests methods of removing poor children from the overwhelming influence of the *culture of poverty*. Where Gordon's view of poverty as the maldistribution of income leads him to recommend redistributive policies, Banfield's cultural interpretation causes him to propose service programs, with indoctrination of middle-class values as their ultimate aim.

Elliot Liebow attributes the negative work attitudes which he observes in black lower-class men to both objective factors (the nature and low wages of available jobs) and to subjective ones. He, however, considers that these subjective factors are not the irrational product of cultural history but the result of a realistic appraisal by the poor black man of his situation:

> What appears as a "present-time" orientation to the outside observer is, to the man experiencing it, as much a future orientation as that of his middle-class counterpart. The difference between the two men lies not so much in their different orientations to time as in their different orientations to future time or, more specifically, to their different futures.[1]

In other words, Liebow sees the culture of the poor not as an independent force making improvement in their situation impossible, but rather as the logical product of that situation. Whereas Banfield places the onus for poverty upon the poor themselves, Liebow argues that the black men he studied were forced by their situation into their "present-oriented" modes of behavior.

Herbert Gans equates the two views of poverty as resulting from culture or from situation to the ancient division over whether the poor are undeserving or deserving. He notes that those supporting the

---

[1] Elliot Liebow, *Tally's Corner* (Boston: Little, Brown, 1967), pp. 64–65.

cultural view have too facilely confused behavioral norms — that is, those norms that govern day-to-day life and are largely a response to situational factors — with aspirations, or life goals. He also argues that supporters of the cultural view take an overly rigid view of culture as unchanging and holistic. As a result, Gans thinks that there is too little recognition of cultural diversity, of the possibilities of cultural change, and of the greater propensity of some norms to change than others. Gans concludes by listing research questions that must be answered if public policy toward the poor is to take adequate account of both cultural and situational factors.

According to Lillian Rubin, the failure of governmental policy-makers to grasp the relationship between cultural and situational factors led to the clause requiring maximum feasible participation of representatives of the poor under the Economic Opportunity Act. Based on a stereotype of poor people as apathetic, the Poverty Act enabled them to participate in the formulation of programs. The result was controversy and an attempt by the previously apathetic to seize control of the programs. The mobilization of poor communities resulting from the participation clause of the Poverty Act seemed to indicate that changes in situational factors could indeed have an immediate impact on behavioral norms.

Lillian Rubin's article illuminates the debate over the primacy of cultural or situational factors and indicates the possibility that what we have called modern Progressivism will contribute to lower-class militance. She describes the poverty program as a catalyst for an awakened consciousness and heightened militance among ghetto inhabitants. Interestingly, the change in situational factors caused by the formation of the Community Action Program (CAP) boards did not result, as undoubtedly had been hoped by the formulators of the program, in individual advancement or the adoption of middle-class norms by community activists. Rather, it led to the espousal of radical, solidaristic concepts of community.

Indeed, an examination of the CAP alerts one to the potential of value systems other than those usually considered in the culture versus structure arguments. Such arguments tend to presume a choice between lower-class, selfish, present-oriented values and privatistic middle-class aspirations directed toward self-improvement. But there is a third alternative — common consciousness aimed at the progress of the lower class as a group and leading to the substitution of rebellion for apathy. Most social science literature about lower-class blacks concentrates on the development of present-time orientation and social disorganization within ghetto communities; little published material documents the growth of militant ideologies among the de-

prived despite the volumes devoted to presentations of these ideologies.

The five articles in this section reveal the extreme difficulty of de-
signing governmental policy to eliminate poverty in America. Increases in welfare payments alone would seem likely to increase
welfare dependency. Such increases combined with vast changes
in the structure of the job market, so that poor people could realistically strive toward occupational success, would require a degree of
governmental control over employment that is quite foreign to American economic practices and would be heavily resisted by both
unions and management. Direct intervention into the family situation of lower-class people, as suggested by Banfield, would obviously
intrude on the freedom of these people, would be contrary to generally held values concerning the rights of parents to control the raising of their children, and thus would be sure to evoke strong resentment. The history of such intervention, as caricatured in the image of
the prying welfare worker, does not lead one to think that it would
be very successful in changing the attitudes of the poor. The path of
community development, as initially envisioned in the poverty program, on the other hand, leads the government into contributing directly to the growth of ghetto militancy, precipitating threats to its
own legitimacy and to overall social stability. Although such a path
might arouse poor people to attempt to improve their life situation, it
is unlikely to be persevered in by government policymakers. For they
would eventually find their positions threatened and policies attacked
by their own protégés, while simultaneously having to defend themselves from accusations coming from their right that they are foment-
ing revolution.

These essays, then, tell us more about the nature of poverty in
America than what to do about it. Other sections of this book contain proposals for specific policies in areas such as health or housing,
and the last two parts describe strategies directed at improving the
political and social position of the urban poor. The later readings,
however, must be viewed within the overall context outlined in this
section, which indicates the serious constraints on attempts to change
the situation of the poor in America.

Income and Welfare in New York City

David M. Gordon

Until very recently Americans paid almost no attention to information about the distribution of income in this country. For one thing, we totally ignored available facts about the persistence of poverty. We also neglected important data about the shares of the pie consumed by different groups among the nonpoor — probably because the flush of postwar prosperity convinced us that everyone was doing equally well.

Only in the 1960's did we begin to organize and publicize bits of income distribution data. We suddenly recognized that millions of Americans continued to live in poverty, and arguments began to rage about the exact numbers of the poor. Some standard definitions of poverty emerged from the debates. At first, families with less than $3,000 income were considered poor. Then the perception that consumption needs varied by family size forced the adjustment of poverty incomes for the number of people in a family; those adjustments led to some widely accepted estimates of the number of poor Americans.

But the problem is really not the exact line at which one defines poverty, but the shares of income going to different groups in the society. Serious attention to the shape of the income distribution is overdue, for many recent debates about public policy have depended completely on our assumptions about changes in the dispersion of income. In New York City, examples abound. If we knew how many poor people live in the city and how those numbers had been changing during the 1960's, we could begin to choose sensibly among the welter of conflicting explanations for the rapid growth of welfare in New York. Equally, if public officials knew more about how many of the white middle class remain in the city, how many have moved to the suburbs, and how much the less affluent middle class must struggle to subsist in New York, they could be more responsive to the cries of neglect among lower middle class whites. And if they knew how many people were clustered in income brackets where the tax bite is most severe, perhaps policies addressed to the "taxpayers' revolt" could evolve less capriciously. . . .

The principal purpose of this article is to present some new estimates of the income distribution in New York City for the years since the 1960 census, and to relate them to some of the issues of current importance in the city. The information to be presented has not been available before.

Reprinted by permission of the author and publisher from *The Public Interest,* Summer 1969, pp. 64–88. Copyright © 1969 by National Affairs, Inc.

Based on an extremely detailed income distribution estimated for January 1968, I shall provide information about household income by race, age, sex of head of household, and family size. The underlying distribution was born more or less by Caesarean section — delivered by statistical surgery on various surveys and reports of local trends. A few reasonable assumptions and guesses were indispensable. The figures are in no sense official, in that they do not depend at any level on U.S. Bureau of the Census data. As estimates, they have been developed through an ad hoc process not normally acceptable by academic or statistical standards. Most analysts, presumably, would have been reluctant to endure the contortions necessary to produce some of the more recent figures.

Despite their unusual origins, however, the estimates can be presented with confidence that they do not seriously distort reality. In the course of their development, they were subjected to several independent tests of their reliability. In view of the necessarily tentative methods by which the distributions were calculated, the results of these tests offer surprisingly strong confirmation of the numbers' accuracy.

First, they were compared with a recent Census Bureau estimate of the number of white and nonwhite families living below the "poverty line" in New York City in March 1968. . . . Because poverty lines differ by type of family, the comparison required that we develop our own estimates of household income by race, sex of head of household, and family size. Our distribution produced totals within 5 per cent of the "official" figures, a statistically acceptable margin of error used by the census itself in discussing the reliability of its New York figures.[1]

Second, we used our estimates of the growth of the number and kinds of households *eligible* for welfare to "predict" retroactively the growth in the city welfare caseload from January 1968 to June 1968. Our predictions missed the real numbers by only 1 per cent, an error 12.5 times smaller than that obtained if we had simply projected past trends in the caseload itself.

Third, the numbers have provided a more reliable anticipation of the demand for Medicaid in New York City than any other sets of figures available. All other income distribution estimates apparently underestimate the number of people whose incomes fall in the range that would qualify them for Medicaid benefits.

With these tests as a basis for some confidence in the numbers, therefore, I feel relatively secure that the interest and usefulness of the estimates described below substantially outweigh their potential inaccura-

---

[1] Specifically, our estimate exceeded that of the Census Bureau by 4.8 per cent, an excess at least partially attributable to our attempt to compensate slightly for some of the "unfound" black males notoriously missing from census surveys.

cies. I want, first, to present a variety of information about the income distribution in New York City for 1968; second, to discuss changes since 1960; and third, carefully to relate that information to the welfare "crisis."

I hope to work toward answering the following central questions: How many New Yorkers share in the city's glittering mountains of corporate wealth? How authentic are the apocalyptic cries of the white lower middle class? Has the welfare "crisis" been caused by migration, by the burgeoning welfare rights movement, by plain poverty, or by more imponderable phenomena? The answers, however tentative, seem quite shocking.

The New York City Income Distribution

It is always difficult to organize information about income distributions in meaningful ways. Table 1 presents our estimate of the basic income distribution of New York City's total population in January 1968. By itself, the table reveals relatively little. Without information about family size, one cannot make sensible interpretations about poverty and differential standards of living. In Table 1, for instance, all those in large families could conceivably be concentrated near the bottom, middle, or top of the income scale, or scattered evenly throughout. In each case, the table would invite very different conclusions. A poor, large family is not

TABLE 1

Income Distribution of the New York City Population by Household Income, January 1968

INCOME CLASS ($1000)[a]	NUMBER OF PEOPLE	PERCENTAGE OF POPULATION
0–1	193,363	2.4
1–2	409,295	5.1
2–3	525,573	6.6
3–4	698,771	8.8
4–5	676,881	8.5
5–6	867,076	10.8
6–7.5	1,416,085	17.8
7.5–10	1,274,952	16.0
10–15	1,118,911	14.0
15 & over	795,093	10.0
Total	7,975,930	100.0

[a] Refers to total household income earned during 1967. Columns may not add to totals owing to rounding.

circumstantially identical with an equal number of poor, unrelated individuals. The federally defined poverty line moves upward with family size, as do "moderate" family budgets recently calculated by the Bureau of Labor Statistics. In view of those limitations, I have tried to massage the information into some more useful tabulations.

The first transfiguration comes easily. Table 2 presents the income distribution for families, rather than for total people within households. (A household is frequently more or less than a family.) It also separates families ethnically, affording comparisons of the relative affluence of white and minority families. It will be seen that the total distribution of *families* by income class does not differ very substantially from the total income distribution of *people*. The proportions of families within each income class with different numbers of children tend to remain fairly constant; families at the lower end of the income scale are larger, as one expects, but not by very much.

Table 2 suggests some other, much more startling conclusions, however. Apparently, the differences in the distributions of white and minority family incomes have remained extremely large, despite the contributions

TABLE 2

*Income Distribution of New York City Families by Ethnicity,
January 1968*

INCOME CLASS ($1000)[a]	WHITE FAMILIES		BLACK AND PUERTO RICAN		TOTAL	
	NO.	%	NO.	%	NO.	%
0–1	17,000	1.1	20,600	3.3	37,600	1.7
1–2	35,500	2.3	63,100	10.6	98,600	4.6
2–3	55,600	3.6	69,500	11.4	125,100	5.8
3–4	78,800	5.1	120,200	19.6	199,000	9.2
4–5	101,900	6.6	76,800	12.6	178,700	8.3
5–6	173,000	11.2	70,500	11.7	243,500	11.3
6–7	185,400	12.0	60,900	10.0	246,300	11.4
7–8	173,000	11.2	41,400	6.8	214,400	10.0
8–9	132,800	8.6	25,000	4.1	157,800	7.3
9–10	92,700	6.0	18,900	3.1	111,600	5.2
10–11	78,800	5.1	10,400	1.7	89,200	4.1
11–12	63,300	4.1	5,500	0.9	68,800	3.2
12–13	52,500	3.4	4,300	0.7	57,800	2.7
13–14	44,800	2.9	2,400	0.4	47,200	2.2
14–15	37,000	2.4	1,200	0.2	38,200	1.8
15 & over	222,500	14.4	17,600	2.9	240,100	11.1
Total	1,546,000	100.0	608,700	100.0	2,153,900	100.0

[a] Refers to total income earned during 1967. All numbers have been rounded to the nearest 100. Columns may not add to totals owing to rounding.

of welfare, poverty programs, and scattered minority gains in employment opportunity. The proportion of black and Puerto Rican families with household incomes below $4,000 is almost four times as great as the incidence of white families within that range. Conversely, the proportion of white families with incomes over $10,000 is almost five times as great as the percentage of minority families. Although the ratio of minority to white families overall is only two to five, the ratio of minority to white families with incomes below $4,000 is three to two.

Figure 1 illustrates the ethnic comparison strikingly. The unusual peak in the curve for minority families stems from two factors: the increasing reliance of minority families on welfare income during the 1960's has concentrated many with average family sizes into a small range of the distribution; and an extremely high portion of Puerto Rican families fall within the $3,000 to $4,000 class — roughly one quarter of Puerto Rican families. The latter phenomenon, in turn, probably stems from the heavy reliance of Puerto Rican men with poor English and little education on jobs paying near the minimum wage.

Unfortunately, even Table 2 and Figure 1 do not illumine the shape of New Yorkers' well-being very clearly. Within any given income class, some families with few or no children could be living very comfortably, whereas other families with three, four, or more children could be struggling to fill their mouths.

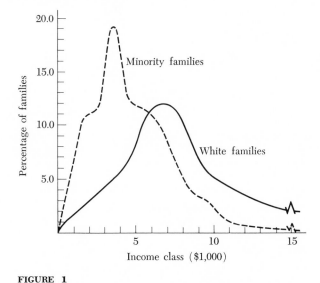

FIGURE 1

Family Income Distribution for White and Minority Families, New York City, January 1968

For example, about 304,000 households — including single individuals — received between $10,000 and $15,000 income during 1967. Of these households, there were roughly 45,000 singles, 65,000 couples, and 81,000 families with one child. All were living quite comfortably, generally above what the Bureau of Labor Statistics calls a "higher than moderate" standard of living for their respective family sizes. On the other hand, 68,000 families of four in this income bracket did only fairly well, falling roughly between the "modest but adequate" budget level and the "higher than moderate" standard. Nearly half of the 45,000 families with five or more members enjoyed even less than the "modest but adequate" level of consumption, scrambling to stretch their incomes.

Clearly, then, one needs to standardize family income by family size in order best to appreciate the relative poverty or affluence of different groups of New York City residents. Some studies already count the numbers of people living below "poverty lines" as these vary by family size, but no one has ever divided the nonpoor into such standardized income classes. Because the increasingly noisy clatter about the costs of New York city hinge not on income but on how adequately income provides for family members at all levels, I have made some special calculations to evaluate these kinds of complaints. The results are very interesting. Briefly, they suggest that a clear majority of New Yorkers have every reason to complain loudly.

The Classes of New York

To begin with, I have defined five standardized income classes, relying on four official budget standards as boundaries. Each budget standard defines a certain quality of standard of living and then calculates the income required by different family sizes to achieve that standard of living.

The first level is the Social Security Administration's family-adjusted "poverty line." All families living below the poverty line for their family size are considered poor. For average families of four living in New York City in 1967, $3,500 annual income was required to reach the poverty line.

The next three boundary standards come from a very recent study by the Bureau of Labor Statistics. In that study, BLS defined the quantities and qualities of goods required for a "modest but adequate" standard of living, and then calculated the costs of achieving that standard for different metropolitan areas in 1967. In New York City, an average family of four required $9,400 during 1967 to maintain that standard. The study also calculated the costs of a "lower than moderate" standard and a "higher than moderate" standard for different family sizes. The annual cost of the former for a family of four in New York was $6,000, whereas the cost of the latter was $14,500.

The study described the differences among the three standards quite simply. The middle, moderate, "modest but adequate" standard centers around an inflection point at which "families stop buying 'more and more' of a category of goods and services and begin buying other goods or items of higher quality." At the "lower than moderate" level "this goal has not yet been reached"; at the "higher than moderate" level, "it has been exceeded." [2]

Calculating these four budget levels and standardizing them by family size finally permits the definition of some relatively meaningful "constant consumption" income classes for New York City. The five classes, with their respective qualitative and quantitative descriptions, follow:

CLASS I "poor" families; $0 to $3,500 annual income for a family of four.

CLASS II "low income" families earning between the poverty line and the "lower than moderate" budget level; $3,500 to $6,000 for a family of four.

CLASS III "modest income" families receiving between the "lower than moderate" and "modest but adequate" standards; $6,000 to $9,400 for a family of four.

CLASS IV "moderate income" families receiving between the "modest but adequate" and the "higher than moderate" standards; $9,400 to $14,500 for a family of four.

CLASS V "affluent families" receiving above the "higher than moderate" budget level; above $14,500 for a family of four.

Having defined those five standardized income classes, I distributed everyone in New York City among the five classes according to their household income and family size. The data immediately provoke an endless stream of observations. The following seem most important.

1. Most people in New York live sparely. Table 3 presents the distribution of people and families among the five classes. As the first column shows, 15.3 per cent of New York City residents live in poor families. Nearly half live in "low income" and "modest income" families. Almost two thirds of New Yorkers live in families receiving less than a "modest but adequate" income for their family sizes. Barely more than a third live

---

[2] U.S. Department of Labor, Bureau of Labor Statistics, "Three Standards of Living," *Bureau of Labor Statistics Bulletin*, No. 1570–5 (1969), p. 4.

TABLE 3

*Distribution of New York Residents and Families among
"Constant Consumption" Income Classes, January 1968*

	CLASS	PERCENTAGE OF PEOPLE	PERCENTAGE OF FAMILIES[a]
I	Poor families	15.3	10.7
II	Low income families	21.2	18.6
III	Modest income families	27.0	27.9
IV	Moderate income families	19.5	23.4
V	Affluent families	17.0	19.4
		100.0	100.0

[a] Excluding families with heads sixty-five years or older.

in families with incomes above that, and only 17 per cent live in "affluent" families, despite the concentration of corporate wealth in the city.

The second column suggests a somewhat similar picture. In tabulating the distribution of families or households throughout, I have excluded single individuals sixty-five years old and above, and families of two with heads of sixty-five or over, on the premise that the elderly have such an entirely different relationship to income than all other families that including them in general distributions would uselessly bias the results. Thus, the second column of Table 3 distributes families (excluding single individuals) headed by a resident under sixty-five years. In Classes IV and V, the proportion of families is slightly higher than that of people, and conversely for Classes I and II. This simply confirms a recurrent trend in central cities: the poorer families are larger, and the more affluent large families move outside the central city into the suburbs.

2. Table 4 distributes families separated by ethnicity, presenting distributions among the five classes for white and minority families (with heads under sixty-five). The differences are staggering.

Although minority families represent only 28.6 per cent of all families in the city, they comprise a full 75.6 per cent of "poor" families, almost half (47.9 per cent) of "low income" families, and only 6.3 per cent of "affluent" families.

Organizing the numbers in a different way, a full 59.5 per cent of minority families fall into Classes I and II, compared with only 17.3 per cent of white families. Almost exactly conversely, 53.1 per cent of white families are in Classes IV and V, compared with only 17.2 per cent of minority families.

3. Even more meaningful comparisons emerge from distinguishing between those households with children and those without. The latter include single individuals and couples, whereas the former include fam-

TABLE 4

Distribution of Families ᵃ *in New York among "Constant Consumption" Income Classes, January 1968, by Ethnicity*

INCOME CLASS	PERCENTAGE OF WHITE FAMILIES[a]	PERCENTAGE OF BLACK AND PUERTO RICAN FAMILIES[a]
I Poor families	3.7	28.4
II Low income families	13.6	31.1
III Modest income families	29.6	23.3
IV Moderate income families	27.5	13.0
V Affluent families	25.6	4.2
	100.0	100.0

[a] Excluding families with heads of sixty-five and over.

ilies of two with one child (primarily female-headed families) and all families of three or more. (Again, families headed by the elderly are excluded.) Among households without the responsibilities of supporting children, exactly two thirds are "moderate income" and "affluent" households, and the remaining one third are spread evenly between Classes I and II on the one hand, and Class III on the other. In short, households without children live very comfortably in New York.

On the other hand, less than one third of families with children live in Classes IV and V, a full 36.2 per cent are "poor" and "low income," and another 31.8 per cent receive "modest" incomes. Families with children have more difficulty, and quite dramatically so.

4. More dramatically still, the differences between households with and without children by ethnicity seem extraordinary. Among white singles and couples, nearly half (47.2 per cent) live in Class V alone, and more than three quarters (76.3 per cent) receive more than a "modest but adequate" income.

In extraordinarily sharp contrast, only 9.5 per cent of black and Puerto Rican families with children live in Classes IV and V combined, more than one third (33.8 per cent) are "poor" alone, another 34.8 per cent receive "low" incomes, and the remaining 22.0 per cent live "modestly."

The other two groups, white families with children and minority households without, are distributed among the classes in much more similar proportions. Of white families with children, 42.6 per cent live in Classes IV and V, whereas 41.8 per cent of minority singles and couples live at the same levels. Only 21.1 per cent of white families with children live in Classes I and II, whereas 31.5 per cent of black and Puerto Rican households without receive "poor" or "low" incomes. The remainder —

36.5 per cent of the whites and 26.8 per cent of the black and Puerto Ricans — live "modestly."

5. At an even more specific level, the different distributions for different family size groups further confirm the relative poverty of larger families. Among white families with children, the distributions of families with two, three, or four members and those with five, six, or more members differ sharply. Within the former group, nearly half (48 per cent) of the families live in Classes IV and V, and only 15.2 per cent live in Classes I and II. In contrast, only 23.3 per cent of white families with five, six, or more members live in Classes IV and V, whereas 42.4 per cent of those families live in Classes I and II.

The same kind of differences appear for minority families with children. Of those with five, six, or more members, over half (51.4 per cent) are poor, 32.9 per cent receive "low" incomes, and the remaining 15.7 per cent live in Class III or above. On the other hand, only 24.8 per cent of black and Puerto Rican families with two, three, or four members live in poverty, whereas 39.4 per cent receive "modest," "moderate," or "affluent" incomes.

6. Those comparisons can be sliced in another way. One of the impressions suggested by reams of cross-tabulations is that *the distribution of minority households simply lags one class behind that for white households.* Thus, the family size distributions within "constant consumption" classes for the ethnic groups match almost perfectly *if* minority households within one class are compared with white households in the class directly above. For instance, as Table 5 shows, the family size distribution of minority families in Classes III–IV matches the family distribution of white families in Classes IV–V; similarly, minority families in Classes I–II match white families in Classes II–III.

TABLE 5

Percentages in Family Size Groups [a]

		SINGLES AND COUPLES	ONE CHILD	4, 5, 6, OR MORE MEMBERS	TOTAL
1	White households in Classes IV–V	57.8	25.9	16.3	100.0
	Minority households in Classes III–IV	57.0	26.4	16.6	100.0
2	White households in Classes II–III	19.7	29.7	50.6	100.0
	Minority households in Classes I–II	23.2	26.4	50.4	100.0

[a] Excluding families headed by the elderly.

The Few Crucial Categories

Though perhaps a bit bewildering, all the observations in points one to six above seem to lead in one direction. Using the five "constant consumption" income classes as bench marks, one can begin to see how heavily the city's population is concentrated in just a few crucial socioeconomic categories. Most meaningfully, one can consider the distribution of the population (excluding those in families headed by the elderly) among twenty ethnic family-consumption cells: the five standard income classes for white and minority families with and without children. If everyone were distributed equally among all those cells, each cell would contain 5 per cent of the 7.335 million people in families headed by citizens under sixty-five. To a striking degree, however, the population clusters in eight of the twenty cells. Those eight cells seem to represent four distinct groups: first, white families with children living on "low" or "modest" incomes (Classes II–III), a group one could choose to characterize as the white working and lower middle class; second, white families with children living very comfortably (in Classes IV–V); third, black and Puerto Rican families with children living in or near poverty (Classes I–II); and fourth, whites without children living very comfortably (Classes IV–V). Together, those four groups include 81.8 per cent of the 7.335 million. Every other cell includes less than 5 per cent of that total. Table 6 details the concentration within those four groups.

Table 6 needs to be considered carefully. It suggests that the pool of people who must struggle to subsist in New York remains extremely large. Although minority families must endure acute poverty, many white families live only relatively more comfortably. The largest identifiable group of city residents — the white working and lower middle class — lives modestly at best, in near poverty at worst. However the city's politics evolve, the two groups of struggling families — whites in Classes II–III and minority families in Classes I–II — will continue to dominate the life style of the city's economy. Now they comprise almost exactly half the population in families with heads under sixty-five. In the future, their share may even exceed 50 per cent as more affluent whites continue to leave the city.

At the same time, it may become increasingly true that the city's more affluent citizens live in childless families. Before very long, a full quarter of the households represented in Table 6 may be clustered among relatively affluent white singles and couples, with no children around to share the goods.

Above all, the table crystallizes the difference between looking at income alone, and looking at the standard of living that income can afford.

TABLE 6

Distribution of Residents and Households ᵃ *among Socioeconomic Groups*

	NUMBER OF PEOPLE	PER-CENTAGE OF TOTAL PEOPLE	PER-CENTAGE OF HOUSEHOLDS
1. Four major groups			
a. White families with children (Classes II-III)	2,161,936	29.4	21.2
b. White families with children (Classes IV-V)	1,466,042	20.0	16.8
c. Minority families with children (Classes I–II)	1,454,009	19.8	12.6
d. White households without children (Classes IV–V)	923,684	12.6	22.9
2. Six minor groups			
a. Minority families with children (Class III)	356,835	4.9	4.1
b. White households without children (Classes I–III)	271,336	3.7	7.1
c. Minority households without children (Classes I–III)	230,364	3.2	7.0
d. Minority households without children (Classes IV–V)	190,361	2.6	5.0
e. White families with children (Class I)	148,900	1.8	1.5
f. Minority families with children (Classes IV–V)	132,100	2.0	1.8
	7,335,567	100.0	100.0

ᵃ Excluding families headed by the elderly.

Thousands of jobs in New York pay extremely high salaries. Particularly if one lives on the Upper East Side in Manhattan, one is sometimes convinced that everyone in the city has cash to burn. Unfortunately, many residents of the city who most need all that money are not getting it. If anyone needed reminding, Marx's dictum — "from each according to his ability, to each according to his needs" — hardly applies in New York.

Poverty Persists

We assume that the situation described above represents a change since 1960. But how? Have the affluent with children only recently begun to leave for the suburbs? Have prices outstripped earnings among low and modest income families? Has the incidence of poverty increased in the city since 1960?

Unfortunately, relatively few of these kinds of questions can be answered. The Bureau of Labor Statistics did not begin estimating its three budget standards until well after 1960, precluding comparison of the distribution of families among Classes II through V for 1960 and 1968. No other sources allow similar definitions of "constant consumption" income classes for use with the 1960 census.

Two kinds of comparisons can be made. First, the basic distribution of families among less meaningful *unstandardized* income classes can be compared for 1960 and 1968. Table 7 presents the same information for 1959 incomes (in 1967 prices) as did Table 2 for 1967 incomes (in current prices). Comparison of the two tables affords a rough feeling for the trends of income among white and minority families. Figures 2 and 3 present those comparisons graphically.

As both the tables and figures show, *whites have improved their economic position since 1960, whereas minority groups have not.* During the

TABLE 7

Income Distribution of New York City Families by Ethnicity, 1960 [a]

INCOME CLASS	WHITE NO.	%	BLACK AND PUERTO RICAN NO.	%	TOTAL NO.	%
0–1	38,800	2.3	23,600	6.0	62,400	3.0
1–2	65,800	3.9	30,500	7.8	96,300	4.6
2–3	92,800	5.5	43,400	11.1	136,200	6.6
3–4	131,600	7.8	59,000	15.1	190,600	9.2
4–5	167,100	9.9	60,600	15.5	227,700	11.0
5–6	214,400	12.7	56,700	14.5	271,100	13.0
6–7	200,800	11.9	43,000	11.0	243,800	11.7
7–8	155,300	9.2	22,700	5.8	178,000	8.6
8–9	119,800	7.1	14,100	3.6	133,900	6.4
9–10	94,500	5.6	8,200	2.1	102,700	4.9
10–11	76,000	4.5	6,300	1.6	82,300	4.0
11–12	59,100	3.5	4,300	1.1	63,400	3.0
12–13	49,000	2.9	2,900	.9	51,900	2.5
13–14	38,900	2.3	2,300	.6	41,200	2.0
14–15	32,100	1.9	2,100	.5	34,200	1.6
15 plus	151,900	9.0	11,100	2.8	163,000	7.8
Total	1,687,800	100.0	390,800	100.0	2,078,600	100.0

[a] Income refers to total income received in 1959. Figures for $1,000 classes from $10,000 to $15,000 have been interpolated. All numbers have been rounded to the nearest hundred. Columns may not add to totals owing to rounding.

34

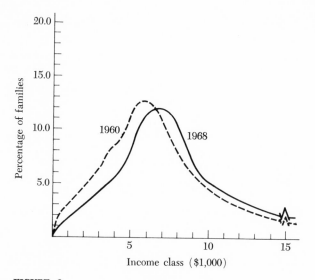

FIGURE 2

*Family Income Distribution for Whites, New York City,
1960 and 1968 Compared (in Constant 1968 Dollars)*

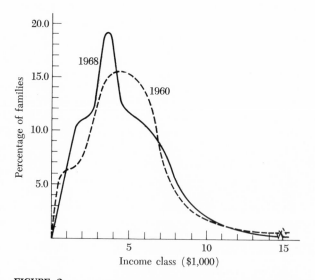

FIGURE 3

*Family Income Distribution for Blacks and Puerto Ricans,
New York City, 1960 and 1968 Compared
(in Constant 1968 Dollars)*

period between 1960 and 1968, the number of white families (excluding Puerto Ricans, who are counted as whites in the census) in New York City declined from about 1.688 million to about 1.546 million. Many families who left the city presumably came out of the middle income ranges. The fact that white families moved up in income so uniformly over the entire income distribution, despite the loss of many middle income families to the suburbs, gives strong evidence of the extent to which whites were able to take advantage of prosperity during that period.

For minority groups, the graphs depict much starker developments. The number of minority families increased from about 391,000 to about 609,000, reflecting substantial in-migration of both black and Puerto Rican families and the steady high rates of family formation among young black and Puerto Rican adults. It is impossible to determine from our information how the income of in-migrants compared with that of continuing minority residents. Whatever the case, the combined effect of in-migration and the failure of many low wage jobs to keep pace with rising prices created an extremely large concentration in the income class from $3,000 to $4,000.

A second, more meaningful kind of comparison can be made. Although defined and calculated in 1964, the Social Security Administration's family-adjusted poverty levels were also calculated for 1960. With these levels in hand, one can, with minimal statistical exertion, compare the changes in size and composition of the poor in New York City. Indeed, the U.S. Bureau of the Census recently released that set of calculations. Although my own estimates differ slightly from theirs, we come to the same conclusion. No matter what the source of estimates, poverty has declined only slightly in New York since 1960.

The Census Bureau estimated in February 1969 that about 10 per cent of the families (or 208,000 families) in New York in early 1968 had had incomes below their respective poverty lines in 1967. Including single individuals, this amounted to a little more than 1 million people, so that this 10 per cent of New York's families amounted to about 13 per cent of the city's total population. By official standards, this represented a slight decrease since 1960 in the numbers of families living in poverty; then — again according to the census — 266,000 families, or 13 per cent of the city's families, had lived below the poverty line in 1960 prices.

Unfortunately, those official estimates understate the extent of poverty in New York City in 1968 in two ways. First, the poverty lines used are measured in 1966 prices, ignoring the increase in prices from 1966 through 1967 (about 2.6 percent for New York City). Second, they neglect the extent to which prices in New York City are higher than the average for all cities in the United States (by about 3 per cent for families at the "lower than moderate" income level). Taking those two factors into ac-

count, one gets a considerably higher estimate of the city's poverty population — largely because so many people are concentrated in the narrow
ranges of the income distribution affected by the margin of those price
adjustments.

Having incorporated those adjustments in the official poverty criteria,
our estimates suggest the following conclusions about changes in poverty
in New York City during the 1960's:

1. *There has been very little decline since 1960 in the number of
New York families living in poverty.* In January 1968, about 11.5 per
cent of the families in New York — or 245,000 families — had 1967 incomes below their respective poverty lines. This represented a decrease
of only 21,000 poor families since 1960 and a 1.5 per cent decline in the
percentage of total families living in poverty. Further, the total number
of people living in poor families (including single individuals) increased
from slightly more than 1 million in 1960 to 1.22 million in 1968, and
from 13 per cent to 15 per cent of the total population. The increase in
total people in poor families stems both from a larger family size among
poor families and from a slight increase in the number of poor single individuals.[3]

2. *Though slight, the decrease in poor families in New York reflected
greater improvement than in the other two large American cities for
which similar comparisons can be made.* Census estimates of poverty in
Chicago and Los Angeles adjusted for the same price factors as the New
York numbers portray poverty more tenacious than in New York. From
1960 to 1968, the percentage of families in poverty actually increased in
Chicago, from 13 per cent to 15.4 per cent. In Los Angeles, the percentage
of families in poverty decreased, but even less than in New York — from
12 per cent to 10.8 per cent.

3. *The composition of poor families in New York has changed radically since 1960.* In 1960, about 25 per cent of the poor families in New
York were nonwhite, about 18 per cent were Puerto Rican, and about 57
per cent were white. By 1968, nonwhites comprised 39 per cent of the
poor families, Puerto Ricans 29 per cent, and whites only 32 per cent. In
short, minority families represented 43 per cent of poor families in 1960,
a bare minority; by 1968, their total share had increased to just under 70
per cent, a clear majority. Further, their share of poor families with heads
under sixty-five years had reached about 76 per cent.

---

[3] The differences in trends for people and families exist nationally too. From
1959 to 1966, the ratio of nonwhite to white family units in poverty nationally remained constant at 2.52 to 1. For individuals, however, the ratio of nonwhites to
whites in poverty rose from 3.03 to 1 in 1959 to 3.41 to 1 in 1966.

4. *The absolute numbers of poor minority families increased very rapidly as well.* In 1960, there were about 114,000 poor black and Puerto Rican families. By 1968, the number of poor minority families had grown to about 166,000, an increase over 1960 of roughly 40 per cent. Conversely, the numbers of poor white families decreased significantly from about 142,000 in 1960 to about 79,000 in 1968.

5. *Both relatively and absolutely, the trends in minority group poverty traced a very different path in New York from that in other central cities.* The absolute number of nonwhite families living in poverty in all American central cities declined, in the years 1960 to 1968, from 783,000 to 665,000, according to the same Census Bureau estimates (which do not give separate data for Spanish-speaking minority groups). As noted above, the absolute number of poor minority families increased in New York City. In addition, the proportion of nonwhite families living in poverty declined by even larger degrees in all central cities after 1960, dropping from 37 to 26 per cent, the incidence of poverty among minority families in New York remained nearly constant, dropping from 29 to 28 per cent.

The City's Welfare Burden

Despite the indications of all those trends, the persistence of poverty in New York City does not by itself go very far toward explaining its enormous welfare burden, as some simple comparisons with other cities can show. In early 1968, according to the same adjusted Census Bureau estimates, New York City had a total of 245,000 families living in poverty. Chicago had about 130,000 families in poverty, and Los Angeles-Long Beach had about 89,000. Yet in February 1968, about 780,000 people received welfare in New York City (excluding the aged) compared with about 271,000 in Chicago and 200,000 in Los Angeles-Long Beach (also excluding the aged). Thus, although the ratio of New York's poor families to the total of poor families in the other two central cities combined was only 1.12 to 1, the ratio of welfare populations was 1.67 to 1. New York had about twice as many poor families as Chicago, but almost three times as many welfare clients. It had around three times as many poor families as Los Angeles-Long Beach, but almost four times as many people on welfare.

A variety of explanations can be offered for the relatively heavier burden of public assistance in New York than in Chicago and Los Angeles. One that seems most direct centers around the level of welfare benefits in the three cities. In February 1968, recipients of Aid to Families of Dependent Children received an average of $60.60 a month in New York, $44.70

in Illinois, and $44.75 a month in California. The ratio of AFDC recipi-
ents to numbers of poor families is greater in New York City than in the
other two cities by roughly the same degree as the average grants per
AFDC recipients in New York are higher.

If that slightly obscure relationship has any meaning, it must be that
high welfare grant levels automatically create large numbers of welfare
eligibles because of the grants' relation to the income distribution. New
York State, almost alone in the country, has finally offered welfare grants
that match or exceed the federally defined poverty level. During the recent years in which grants were raised to those levels, thousands of poor
families in New York City suddenly became "eligible" for welfare in the
simple sense that their total disposable incomes now fell below what they
were eligible to receive through welfare benefits or supplementary grants.
Many of these families naturally decided to claim what the state had decided to offer.

Once that decision was made, a choice of welfare options — whether
the husband should desert and the wife should apply for AFDC or the
husband should remain and the entire family should apply for Home
Relief — was relatively secondary. Under the AFDC option the family
could receive a higher total income if the husband received more than
about $1,400 earnings per year from employment and shared them with
his family. Under the Home Relief option, the family would receive more
if the husband earned less than that. In either case, the latter option presumably has some psychic advantages. The two programs have grown
rapidly over the past few years, with Home Relief increasing a bit more
quickly than AFDC.

An obvious initial clue to the causes of recent growth in the welfare
caseload, therefore, can be provided by the shape of the income distribution in the range through which welfare grant levels have been rising.
If families are packed with high frequency into small ranges affected by
grant increases, then large increases in eligibles — and in recipients as a
consequence — could easily be expected.

From our estimates, it was in fact possible to calculate for January
1968 the numbers of people in families whose incomes fell below the
average welfare grants for their family sizes. We labeled those people
the "eligible" population. We estimated that 1.32 million people lived in
families eligible for welfare in January 1968, excluding the aged, or about
18 per cent of the city's total population under sixty-five. Of those in eligible families, about 1 million, or 77 per cent, were black or Puerto Rican.
Only 6.5 per cent of the white population under sixty-five lived in eligible
families, whereas 41.7 per cent of the minority population under sixty-five
lived in eligible families. *Because there were only 760,000 people receiving welfare in January 1968* (excluding Old Age Assistance), the pool of
"eligibles" was by no means close to exhaustion.

Then, in August 1968, welfare grant levels were increased again by an average of about 7 per cent for AFDC cases, or about $250 per year for a family of four. That slight dollar increase immediately caused an increase of 300,000 in the numbers of eligibles, bringing the total to 1.621 million. After the August increases, close to half the city's minority population lived in eligible families — nearly 1.2 million blacks and Puerto Ricans. Even without further analysis, one would be tempted to ascribe a large bulk of the welfare crisis to the effects of such grant increases. One additional piece of information can serve to strengthen this point.

Between January 1964 and January 1968, average welfare grant levels increased by about 45 per cent in New York State. *If one had known in 1964 what the income distribution in the city looked like, and if one had known further the extent to which welfare grant levels were going to rise over the next four years, one would automatically have expected an enormous increase in welfare.* Because we have this information in hindsight, we have made the calculations we only wish we could have made in 1964. Specifically, we calculated the number of blacks and Puerto Ricans in families whose incomes in 1964 were above 1964 grant levels but below 1968 grant levels. They represented those minority people in the city who would become eligible for welfare during the next four years, in the simple sense that their low incomes would be overtaken by rising welfare grant levels. Because of the extraordinarily dense concentration of minority families in those particular ranges of the income distribution, we estimated that about 400,000 people (excluding the aged), or over 5 per cent of the total city population, fell into that particular category. If we had included whites as well, obviously the numbers would have been much higher. Over 16 per cent of blacks and fully one quarter of Puerto Ricans (excluding the aged) living in New York in 1964 were compressed into those potentially eligible bands of the income distribution. It should be no surprise that many of them later appeared on the welfare rolls.

The Rise in the Caseload

Table 8 presents the size of the New York City public assistance caseload as it grew during the 1960's. Sometime in March 1969, the total number receiving welfare assistance in New York City passed the 1 million mark. By the time of this article's publication, the level will probably have reached about 1.050 million.

Treating welfare principally as an economic phenomenon — as a source of income for the poor — one can isolate three principal hypotheses as to why New York City's caseload grew so rapidly, particularly after about 1966.

First, the number receiving welfare could have grown because an in-

TABLE 8

Number of Public Assistance Recipients in New York City

DATE	NUMBER (TO NEAREST 1,000)
January 1964	411,000
January 1966	533,000
January 1968	807,000
June 1968	872,000
November 1968	961,000
January 1969	995,000

creasing percentage of those eligible for welfare actually chose to receive it (or because the rules permitting eligibles to receive it had become more liberal).

Second, even if the benefits available under welfare had not increased at all, the number of people on welfare could have increased because the number of eligibles increased. This could have occurred because of a downward shift in the income distribution due to inmigration or to the lag of wages behind prices in certain kinds of jobs.

Third, even if the income distribution (measured in constant prices) did not change at all as a result of migration or wage-price effects, the number of people eligible for welfare could have increased because the welfare grant levels (measured in constant prices) increased over time, effectively blanketing into eligibility large numbers of the population.

Needless to say, it is impossible rigorously to separate the actual or potential weight of those three factors. A reasonable guess would have been that all three were operative, and that perhaps the first factor — the increasing propensity of eligibles to claim their benefits — was responsible for the largest share of the increase.

However tentative, our estimates of the income distribution allow a first attempt at an answer that is more than a guess. Using our distributions, we attempted to separate these three factors principally for the period between January 1964 and November 1968. We concluded that *the largest source of the increase in welfare stemmed from the increase in real grant levels, that changes in the income distribution accounted for a smaller share, and that those eligible for welfare showed no greater propensity to join the rolls.*

The basis for these conclusions can be summarized quite quickly.

To begin with, the number of people in eligible families (excluding the aged) was calculated for four different points in time. The calculations were made by the kind of straightforward definitions of eligibility described above. Of these eligibles, a given number were receiving welfare (excluding those receiving Old Age Assistance). Dividing the latter by the former allowed an estimate of the percentage of eligibles actually receiving public assistance. With the help of the 1960 census, we were able to make such calculations for March 1960, January 1964, January 1968, and November 1968.[4]

Table 9 presents the results of those comparisons. As the table clearly shows, the percentage of eligibles actually receiving welfare has been *declining* slightly over the period since 1964, when the welfare caseload began rapidly to increase. Thus, it appears that those eligible for welfare are no more likely to be receiving assistance than before. As a corollary, it does not appear that more liberal administrative practices have contributed very much to the increase either.

It further follows that the increase in welfare in recent years must necessarily have stemmed from *large* increases in the numbers eligible for welfare. Indeed, as Table 9 shows, between January 1964 and November 1968 the number of people in families eligible for welfare increased by about 170 per cent, whereas the number receiving welfare increased by 140 per cent.

To try to account for the large increase in the numbers of eligibles, we tried to separate this vast increase into two trends. Between January 1964 and November 1968, the number of eligibles (again excluding the aged) grew from about 605,000 to 1.621 million, an increase of almost exactly 1 million. Two factors were central to that increase: first, the changes in the income distribution which produced absolutely larger numbers of people within given income classes, and second, the increases in real welfare benefits that blanketed in large numbers of people with incomes which would not have qualified them for welfare in 1964.

To estimate the relative magnitude of those two trends, we began by calculating the number of people who would have been eligible for welfare in November 1968 *if there had been no increases in the real level of*

---

[4] To allow comparability, it was important to compare January 1968 with November 1968 and not, for instance, September 1968. Now that welfare grant levels are so high, thousands of additional families become eligible for welfare each time the grant levels are raised (in constant prices). As soon as the benefits are raised, some of those newly eligible families will begin joining the rolls each month. The first month after the increase in grant levels, the percentage of eligibles on welfare will be much lower than in the fourth month after the increase. So in the recent period, it was important to compare months that came the same length of time after a real benefit increase. The two most recent increases occurred in October 1967 and August 1968. Thus, we compared January 1968 with November 1968, each point coming three months after the benefit increase. For the earlier years, benefits were increased by so little that the month chosen for comparison did not make very much difference.

TABLE 9

People Receiving and Eligible for Public Assistance,
New York City, 1960–1968

DATE	PUBLIC ASSISTANCE RECIPIENTS (EXCLUDING OLD AGE ASSISTANCE)	NUMBER IN FAMILIES ELIGIBLE FOR PUBLIC ASSISTANCE (EXCLUDING THE AGED)	% OF ELIGIBLES ON PUBLIC ASSISTANCE
March 1960	315,000	530,000	59.3
January 1964	379,000	605,000	62.6
January 1968	760,000	1,324,000	57.4
November 1968	906,000	1,621,000	55.9

welfare grants over the intervening fifty-eight months. To do this, we calculated the number of people in the November 1968 income distribution who had incomes below the average grant levels provided in January 1964, adjusting those grant levels for the general increase in the price level between the two periods. According to our calculations, only 777,000 people would have lived in families eligible for welfare if 1964 real grants had applied in November 1968 — an increase of only 172,000 in the number of eligibles from January 1964. By definition, the remaining increase of 844,000 in the number of eligibles occurred because real grant levels increased over the period by between 44 and 47 per cent. (Because grant levels are defined by average benefits received, the measured increase varies somewhat by family size.)

During this period, returning to Table 9, the total number of people receiving welfare (excluding the aged) increased from 379,000 to 906,000, an absolute increase of 527,000. Assuming that a conservative 52 per cent of those blanketed in by grant level increases between 1964 and 1968 actually joined the rolls, one can conclude that 438,000 of the increase in welfare population resulted from the increase in welfare grant levels. That amounts to about 83 per cent of the total increase.

We made one final and important calculation from the same set of figures. As noted, the increase in real grant levels between 1964 and 1968 "caused" an increase of 844,000 in the number of people living in families eligible for welfare. Of that number, some lived in New York in 1964, whereas some arrived between 1964 and 1968, receiving incomes once they arrived which fell into the range over which real grant levels increased. The relative magnitudes of these two groups could also be estimated. By calculating the number of people living in the city in 1964 who would have been eligible if November 1968 grant levels had been in effect in January 1964 (in constant dollars), we get some rough idea of how many people fell into the first group, i.e., the group of new eligibles who were already in the city when the grant increases began. The remainder of the 844,000 presumably arrived in that range of income distribution — either as a result of in-migration or income-slippage — after 1964.

Performing these calculations, we found that roughly 55 per cent of the total 844,000 belonged to the first group, the new eligibles already in that range of the distribution in 1964. The remaining 45 per cent arrived in that range of the distribution after 1964.

These results are all summarized in Table 10, which presents our estimates of the statistical components of the increase in eligibles between 1964 and 1968. The implications of the table are quite clear. If New York

Statistical Components of Increase of People in Families Eligible for Public Assistance (Excluding Those Sixty-five and Over), New York City, January 1964 to November 1968

		NUMBER	ABSOLUTE INCREASE FROM JANUARY 1964	NET INCREASE	% OF TOTAL INCREASE
1	Number of eligibles in January 1964	605,000	—	—	—
2	Number who would have been eligible in November 1968 if 1964 grant levels were in effect in November 1968	777,000	172,000	172,000	16.8
3	Number who would have been eligible in November 1968 if November 1968 grant levels were in effect and if the January 1964 income distribution had described the situation in November 1968	1,242,000	637,000	465,000	45.8
4	Actual number of eligibles in November 1968, given November 1968 grant levels and November 1968 income distribution	1,621,000	1,016,000	379,000	37.3
				1,016,000	100.0

State had not decided to offer people an income at least equal to what the federal government calls the poverty line, there would be no welfare crisis at all. We would, in its place, have a far greater amount of poverty.

Conclusions

The implications of such extended statistical calisthenics seem difficult to sort out. One gratuitous observation can be tossed into the mixing bowl quickly. If nothing else, the tortuous rounds of calculations ought to have shown that we can make much more meaningful use of income distribution information than we have in the past. Beyond that, the numbers induce considerable pessimism. In answer to the questions posed too floridly at the beginning:

1. Relatively few New York residents share in the city's mountains of wealth and income. Those in the city who need the money most are getting inadequate shares.

2. In particular, hundreds of thousands of blacks and Puerto Ricans live in or near poverty, and even greater numbers of whites live on tight budgets, on what I have called "low" or "modest" incomes. The complaints of working and lower middle class whites about their standards of living seem justified.

3. Concomitantly, one can easily argue that the cause of the welfare "crisis" is simply the widespread poverty in the city — not chiseling or welfare rights organizations or liberal administrative practices.

Do rainbows shine across the horizon, including more optimistic expectations for the future? Not particularly.

In the first place, inequalities in the distribution of American income have not been declining for over twenty years. One of the verities about income shares that has applied throughout the postwar period in the United States is that the top 5 per cent of the people receive 20 per cent of the income, whereas the bottom 20 per cent of the people receive 5 per cent of the income.

Second, the tax system does nothing to help those who must stretch their budgets most tightly. Every study of the incidence of taxes at all levels of government reports that those receiving between $3,000 and $15,000 annual income pay almost exactly the same proportions of their income in taxes. My own quick calculations for taxes paid by New York residents suggest exactly the same results. Despite talk of tax reform, that will remain true until absolutely massive federal aid to states and cities permits declines in the level of unprogressive sales and property taxes.

Third, there is little reason to believe that the movement to the suburbs of more affluent families with children will begin to decelerate.

Fourth, the structure of employment earnings — itself an initial cause of inequality of income — will probably not change much either. By the best calculations one can make from available data, about 21 per cent of the jobs available in New York City in 1968 paid less than $80 a week, and another 11 per cent paid between $80 and $90 a week. Roughly one third of the city's job's therefore, or about 1.3 million jobs, paid less than $4,600 a year if they were filled continuously. Because a male-headed family of five needs $4,400 a year to stay at the "poverty line," it seems clear that tens of thousands of families will continue to live in poverty — unless wages increase radically or many more females can become dual earners. The former eventuality seems unlikely at the moment. Some very rough calculations suggest that 27 per cent of annual job openings in the city over the next five years will pay less than $90 a week — only barely below the one third of total jobs paying less than that now. Although high-paying technical and clerical jobs are opening up rapidly in the city's supply of jobs, so are menial, low-paying service jobs as well.

Perhaps the only pleasant conclusion one can draw concerns the city's fisc. Now that New York State welfare grant levels have reached the poverty lines stipulated by the federal government, it seems likely that they will not rise very much in the future (and, indeed, were even cut by the state this spring). The in-migration of blacks and Puerto Ricans is apparently slowing down. The federal government seems ready to consider greater support of state and local welfare costs. All three factors suggest that the welfare caseload and the city's share of its costs will grow much more slowly in the future.

We can perhaps find solace in a final observation. To the extent that the basic source of discontent in New York is the inadequate dispersion of income, the city's problems do not differ from those of the nation as a whole. The uniqueness of New York is merely that those who suffer — "poor," "low," and "modest income" families alike — seem to complain about it much more vociferously.

46

The Future of the Lower Class

Edward C. Banfield

So long as the city contains a sizable lower class, nothing basic can be done about its most serious problems. Good jobs may be offered to all, but some will remain chronically unemployed. Slums may be demolished, but if the housing that replaces them is occupied by the lower class it will shortly be turned into new slums. Welfare payments may be doubled or tripled and a negative income tax instituted, but some persons will continue to live in squalor and misery. New schools may be built, new curricula devised, and the teacher-pupil ratio cut in half, but if the children who attend these schools come from lower-class homes, they will be turned into blackboard jungles, and those who graduate or drop out from them will, in most cases, be functionally illiterate. The streets may be filled with armies of policemen, but violent crime and civil disorder will decrease very little. If, however, the lower class were to disappear — if, say, its members were overnight to acquire the attitudes, motivations, and habits of the working class — the most serious and intractable problems of the city would all disappear with it.

. . . The serious problems of the city all exist in two forms — a normal-class and a lower-class form — which are fundamentally different from each other. In its normal-class form, the employment problem, for example, consists mainly of young people who are just entering the labor market and who must make a certain number of trials and errors before finding suitable jobs; in its lower-class form, it consists of people who prefer the "action" of the street to any steady job. The poverty problem in its normal-class form consists of people (especially the aged, the physically handicapped, and mothers with dependent children) whose only need in order to live decently is money; in its lower-class form it consists of people who would live in squalor and misery even if their incomes were doubled or tripled. The same is true with the other problems — slum housing, schools, crime, rioting; each is really two quite different problems.

The lower-class forms of all problems are at bottom a single problem: the existence of an outlook and style of life which is radically present-oriented and which therefore attaches no value to work, sacrifice, self-improvement, or service to family, friends, or community. Social workers, teachers, and law-enforcement officials — all those whom Gans calls "care-takers" — cannot achieve their goals because they can neither change nor circumvent this cultural obstacle. . . .

It cannot be taken for granted that eventually the process of middle-class-ification will eliminate the lower class. That many millions of the poor, the unschooled, and the low-status have risen dramatically on the class-cultural scale from one generation to another does not necessarily mean that the lower class has risen. It may be that those who rose were all at least somewhat future-oriented; on *a priori* grounds, a present-oriented person could not be expected to take even a first step toward self-improvement. On empirical grounds, too, this proposition is somewhat plausible. With the exception of the autobiographical accounts of a few very gifted individuals — Frederick Douglas, Malcolm X, and Claude Brown, for example — there is no direct evidence of there ever having been any upward mobility from the lower class.

There is, perhaps, some *indirect* evidence of such mobility in the past. Most lower-class persons in the city now are not descendants of the lower-class persons who lived in them fifty or one-hundred years ago. This is evident from the fact that the present lower class is mostly black, whereas the former one was mostly white. It may be that the descendants of the old lower class have been assimilated into the other classes.

It is possible, however, that the old lower class produced very few descendants. It may even have died off without reproducing itself. Since it probably had a high birthrate, the number of its descendants could have been small — and thus the amount of assimilation small — only if its deathrate was phenomenal. . . .

Fifty or more years ago, the Malthusian checks of poverty and vice may have been operating so strongly on the lower class of the largest cities as to cause it nearly to die out every generation or two. There is no "hard" evidence to support this proposition, however. Moreover, even if the lower class did fall far short of replenishing itself, *some* of those born into it probably entered the higher classes.

Whatever was the case half a century or more ago, the lower class is probably growing now. Poverty is no longer a major cause of death in the cities. Improvements in public sanitation and in medical and hospital care for the indigent, together with the development of antibiotics and other miracle drugs, keep many lower-class people alive, often in spite of themselves, as it were. Since 1940 infant mortality among the poor has dropped sharply. For instance, in that year the mortality among Negro males under one year of age was 101.2 per 1,000, which was about what it had been among slum dwellers in general for several decades. By 1950 it was down to 59.9 and by 1963 to 44.8. This rate was still twice that of the population as a whole, but the decrease meant (to quote a writer who neglected to point out the class basis of Negro crime) "that fifty more Negro infants of every 1,000 now born can reach an age where they have a chance of contributing to statistics on crime and delinquency." [1] . . .

If the lower-class birthrate falls far enough, the decline in the death-rate may be offset, so that the lower class will again fail to replenish itself. There is reason to believe that, in general, the poor *want* to limit the size of their families and also that they have the necessary information about contraceptive techniques. A study of mothers on welfare in New York City found that among those under thirty years of age and with fewer than three children, 60 percent did not want more children, and a large majority knew about "the pill." [2] It by no means follows that there will be a dramatic decline in the birthrate, however; as Lee Rainwater points out in his book *Family Design*, among lower-class women, in particular, knowledge about birth-control techniques is often "not integrated into either their own sense of available technology or their world's." [3] (It is interesting that although 60 percent of the welfare mothers in the study cited did not want more children, 63 percent expected to have more.) In most sizable cities public clinics have recently been established to make birth-control information and devices available to all women who request them, and in some cities volunteer workers are energetically trying to persuade the poor to have fewer children. Whether because of these efforts or for other reasons, the birthrate of the poor in the cities has been dropping; probably it would drop a good deal faster if the clinics were in a position to give more intensive care and supervision, but probably, too, a substantial proportion of the *lower class* could not or would not limit the size of their families no matter what the clinics did. These conclusions are suggested by the results of an experimental effort in Britain to provide contraceptive care on an intensive basis to 150 casual laborers and their wives. In the course of five years it reduced the number of pregnancies to one-fifth of what might have been expected. Since "failure" was found to be correlated with "personal and social grade," a considerable proportion of those in the lowest grade must have been impervious even to intensive care. [4]

---

[1] Albert D. Biderman, in Raymond A. Bauer (ed.), *Social Indicators* (Cambridge, Mass.: M.I.T. Press, 1966), p. 123.

[2] Lawrence Podell, *Families on Welfare in New York City*, Preliminary Report No. 6, "Fertility, Illegitimacy, and Birth Control," Center for Social Research, City University of New York, January 31, 1968.

[3] Lee Rainwater, *Family Design: Marital Sexuality, Family Size, and Contraception* (Chicago: Aldine, 1965), p. 212.

[4] Mary Perbedy, "Fertility Control for Problem Parents: A Five-Year Experiment in Newcastle Upon Tyne," in J. E. Meade and A. S. Parkes (eds.), *Biological Aspects of Social Problems* (New York: Plenum, 1965), pp. 191–198.

Two things appear to be necessary before a substantial reduction in the lower-class birthrate can take place. One is the development of a technique of contraception that even the most present-oriented can use without difficulty. The other is the discovery of a way to motivate lower-class people to begin birth control before unwanted children have arrived and to use it regularly. The first of these problems will very likely be solved in the laboratory before long. The other will be hard to solve, however — it may even turn out to be insoluble. Failure to make early and regular use of birth-control methods may reflect features of lower-class culture that cannot be changed short of changing — that is, eliminating — lower-class culture itself. Rainwater mentions three such features: lack of communication between husband and wife, knowledge on their part that the cooperation required for family limitation is not possible within their kind of marital relationship, and lack of sexual interest on the wife's part.[5] The present-orientedness of lower-class culture is also of importance in this connection. Rainwater does not discuss this explicitly, but he presents some data that may be pertinent. The accompanying table is reproduced from *Family Design*.[6] . . .

Attitude Toward Likelihood of Success in Limiting
Family to Desired Size (in percent)

	PLANFUL AND SELF-ASSURED	HOPEFUL BUT UNSURE	PASSIVE AND FATALISTIC
Middle-class Protestants (60)[a]	63	37	—
Middle-class Catholics (51)	23	63	14
Upper-lower class (whites and Negroes) (126)	18	58	24
Lower-lower class (whites and Negroes) (152)	5	32	63

[a] Numbers in parentheses represent number interviewed.

Evidently, it cannot be taken for granted that the lower-class birthrate will fall very much. Despite its high deathrate, the lower class may more than maintain itself in the future even if it gains no recruits from immigration from rural America or from abroad. In fact, some immigration — perhaps a considerable amount of it — is to be expected. There-

[5] Rainwater, *op. cit.*, pp. 231, 239, 248.
[6] *Ibid.*, p. 201.

fore, unless lower-class persons, display an unprecedented amount of upward mobility, the lower-class population of the city may grow, perhaps rather rapidly. The question of what, if anything, may be done to hasten the assimilation of the lower class into normal culture is for this reason of added importance.

It will be convenient to enter upon this question by making some conceptual distinctions that have not been needed until now. Three analytical types of present-orientedness will be described. An individual of one type acts very much like one of another: all are improvident, irresponsible, without strong attachments to family, friends, or community, and unable or unwilling either to control impulses or to put forth any effort at self-improvement. The types differ according to the *cause* of the individual's present-orientedness.

TYPE 1: COGNITIVE. An individual of this type is *psychologically incapable* either of taking account of the future or of controlling impulses — that is, of what will here be called "investing": exchanging present for future satisfaction. The future simply does not enter into the world as the cognitively present-oriented individual perceives it. In the case of small children, whose inability to take the future into account or to control impulses is notorious, such present-orientedness presumably has a physiological basis. Adults who were brought up in a group or society whose culture does not provide concepts by which to think about the future are cognitively present-oriented by virtue of their culture. Other adults may be cognitively present-oriented despite having been socialized into a culture that is not present-oriented; with them, present-orientedness is a personality disturbance.

TYPE 2: SITUATIONAL. A representative of this type is psychologically capable both of taking the future into account and of controlling his impulses. He lives from moment to moment because he believes his *situation* to be such that investment in the future is either impossible or unprofitable. For example, an individual whose resources barely suffice to keep body and soul together would be foolish to give much thought to the future — especially to a future the essential features of which he knows he cannot change. . . . Since his present-orientedness is a rational adaptation to reality as he perceives it, an individual of this type becomes future-oriented whenever he perceives changes in the situation that make providing for the future profitable.

TYPE 3: VOLITIONAL. This type of individual, despite being psychologically capable of providing for the future and despite being in a situation which (as he perceives it) may afford excellent opportunities for investing, nevertheless lives from moment to moment simply because he *prefers* that style of life. It may be that for him the "good things in life" are "good" precisely because they require no planning, or he may strongly prefer present over future satisfaction merely because it is present. In either case he is present-oriented by choice. ("One suspects," writes economist Kenneth Boulding, "that a certain amount of the poverty of the hillbilly or the subsistence farmer, and even perhaps of the urban slumdweller and of the bum, involves the rejection of the whole middle-class way of life rather than the inability to find opportunities.") [7]

The three types being analytical, there is no reason why the "real-life" individual's present-orientedness should not be a mixture of types. For example, the individual might (as the quotation from Boulding suggests) be at once volitionally and situationally present-oriented. . . .

Perhaps from fear of saying things that might be used politically against efforts at reform, social scientists tend to stress the situational causes of present-orientedness and to ignore or play down the others. Miller, Riessman, and Seagul, for example, "feel that many lower-income people have a shorter time perspective than do many middle-income persons," but they caution against theories that explain behavior on psychodynamic rather than on situational grounds, because emphasis on the former "leads to social policies which emphasize 'rehabilitation' rather than expanding opportunity." [8] It is not surprising that economists view the individual's time horizon as a function of his opportunities; most economic theory assumes that the individual is rational in the sense that he acts so as to maximize utility. The economist, therefore, naturally assumes that an individual will invest more (that is, in the terms used here, become more future-oriented) when his situation changes so as to make doing so more profitable. It *is* surprising, however, that sociologists and anthropologists, who for the most part consider the economist's model of *homo economicus* to be ludicrously unreal, are equally willing to assume that one who lives from moment to moment will change his ways once he is given good incentives to provide for the future. For example, anthropologist Elliot Liebow (from whom, incidentally, the terms *cognitive* and *situational* were borrowed) in his book about Negro streetcorner men, *Tally's Corner*, claims that the men live from moment to moment not because a present-oriented style of life has been culturally transmitted to them, but because each has discovered, from his own experience, that

---

[7] Kenneth Boulding, "Reflections on Poverty," *Social Welfare Forum, 1961* (New York: Columbia University Press, for the National Conference on Social Work, 1961), p. 51.

[8] S. M. Miller, Frank Riessman, and Arthur A. Seagul, "Poverty and Self-Indulgence: A Critique of the Non-Deferred Gratification Pattern," in Louis A. Ferman *et al.* (eds.), *Poverty in America: A Book of Readings* (Ann Arbor, Mich.: University of Michigan Press, 1965), p. 301.

trying to provide for the future is futile and hopeless.[9] When, and only when (Liebow says), the men's experience of life convinces them that they have a real chance of gaining something important by providing for the future will they do so. Because they have the same goals in life as other people, he says, they will respond much as others would to improvements in their job, educational, and other opportunities.

The assumption that individuals, and for that matter cultures, adapt rationally to the incentives and disincentives offered to them is highly congenial to the present writer. Although it is metaphorical to speak of a culture's "rationality," much empirical evidence suggests that people *by and large* tend to act rationally in the sense of making choices that promise to give them more rather than less of whatever it is that they want, even without engaging in conscious calculation and indeed even when they are intellectually incapable of making the required calculations. Consider, for example, a sociologist's finding that a reformatory inmate's sense of control over his environment affects the amount of attention and effort he devotes to acquiring information relevant to his prison career.[10] This finding is consistent with the proposition that even a present-oriented individual (it can probably be assumed that most prison inmates are more than normally present-oriented) will take account of the future *when he has reason to think that it will "pay" him to do so.*

Some general implications for policy follow from this analysis. One is that present-oriented people ought to be given genuine opportunities to make large gains in both material and nonmaterial income, and ought also to be persuaded of the reality of these opportunities. A related implication is that the present-oriented person should be helped to see the world as a less chaotic, risky, and unpredictable place than it now appears to him to be: a rational person does not exchange present for future satisfaction if the world appears so full of uncertainty as to make a return on the investment most unlikely. A third implication, related to the others, is that the present-oriented individual should be helped to acquire confidence in his ability to influence the future in matters of importance to him; being able to make things happen does, after all, reduce uncertainty. Of course, the individual's confidence in his ability to influence the future cannot be increased except as his actual ability to influence it is increased.

It is, however, much easier to formulate these very general guides to policy than it is to specify particular measures that will prove effective in particular circumstances. How, for example, is it possible to give a "really good job" to someone who has no skills and perhaps cannot or will not

---

[9] Elliot Liebow, *Tally's Corner* (Boston: Little, Brown, 1967), pp. 63–66.

[10] Cited by James S. Coleman in "Seeman's 'Alienation and Social Learning in a Reformatory,'" *American Journal of Sociology*, 70 (July 1964), p. 78.

acquire any? Even if he is capable of learning skills, a vicious circle may have to be broken somewhere; perhaps only giving him a "really good job" will convince him that it is worthwhile to prepare himself for one. Similarly how is one to make rewards "contingent upon the individual's own behavior" (a recommendation that James S. Coleman bases upon the finding that reformatory inmates acquire information when they think they can use it to their advantage)? [11] This principle implies that the individual should be allowed to suffer penalties (loss of the reward at the very least) if he does not behave as he should. Herbert Spencer was prepared to follow this principle to its logical conclusion, allowing those who failed to provide for the future to starve in their old age in order that others might see from their example the advantage of saving. Few people today, however, would consider the issue settled by the principle that a cruel deterrent may in the long run be less cruel than the consequences of not deterring. Indeed, few people recognize that there sometimes *is* a problem of choice between these alternatives. The almost universal opinion today is that, both for his own sake and for that of his society, an individual must not be left to suffer the consequences of his actions. If, for example, he has chosen a life of improvidence, he cannot for that reason be allowed to remain below the poverty line. To give him money, however, is to give him an incentive to persist in his ways. Indeed, there is perhaps no better way to make converts to present-orientedness than to give a generous welfare check to everyone. Between giving "the poor" strong material incentives to exchange present for future satisfactions and giving them equally strong ones to do the opposite, it may as a practical matter be possible to draw only a very faint and fine line.

Moreover, the assumption that individuals tend to respond rationally to incentives and disincentives does not imply that *all* individuals respond to the *same* incentives or that they respond to any *particular* incentives with equal sensitivity. It is to be expected that the situationally present-oriented individual will adapt more readily to improvements in his opportunities than will other present-oriented persons, but even he may adapt slowly and incompletely. He may think it not worth his while to change his style of life even slightly if the advantage of doing so would be small and transitory (as an economist might put it, he may place a "reservation price" on adapting). It is also possible that over a long period of time he may have become habituated to a style of life; the more deeply rooted his habits, the larger (it may be conjectured) the incentives necessary to bring about a change in his behavior. One whose present-orientedness is volitional may be expected to be about as resistant to incentives as

---

[11] *Ibid.*

the habitually present-oriented individual; indeed, incentives are not evaluated as such by him (and therefore, strictly speaking, are not incentives at all) except as they are compatible with his value system. It is possible, too, that an individual may more or less deliberately choose a present-oriented style of life even when he recognizes that there exists for him an alternative that *measured by another set of values* is very good. Pondering why welfare workers have not had more success in luring men "away from a life of irresponsibility, sensuality, and free-wheeling aggression," Alvin Gouldner, a sociologist, concludes that many men may simply judge that the bargain offered them – " 'give up promiscuous sex, give up freely expressed aggression and wild spontaneity . . . and you, or your children, may be admitted to the world of three square meals a day, to a high school or perhaps even a college education, to the world of charge accounts, of secure jobs and respectability' " – is not a very attractive one.[12] In short, it is not enough that the "market basket" of incentives be well filled: if it does not contain things that the individual wants, he will not "buy" it even though it is filled to overflowing.

Cognitive present-orientedness (it would seem) must be the slowest of the three types to respond to incentives to change. Over the short run, it may be that the best that can be done is to insure that cognitive present-orientedness is not reinforced by situational or volitional constraints. If an individual's cognitive incapacity is culturally given, as it is in the case of the lower class, his adaptation to new opportunities may be extremely slow – slower, probably, than that of an individual whose present-orientedness is habitual (or "overlearned"). The crucial difference between culture and deeply rooted habit is that the former consists of traits that are mutually supportive and hence harder to change piecemeal. It is not at all unlikely that cultures (as opposed to individuals) change their time horizons so as to adapt to changes in environment, but any such change must occur very slowly: a certain stability over time is a defining characteristic of culture.

.   .   .

It is reasonable to suppose . . . that no matter how successful improvement of opportunity proves to be as a general method of dealing with present-orientedness, there will be some persons, if only a few, whose present-orientedness will remain almost unaffected. Also, even if provision of good opportunities were sure to eliminate all present-orientedness within two or three generations, there would be good reason to look

---

[12] Alvin W. Gouldner, "The Secrets of Organizations," in *The Social Welfare Forum,* Proceedings of the National Conference on Social Welfare (New York: Columbia University Press, 1963), p. 175.

for ways by which this outcome might be secured more quickly. Without prejudice to the idea that making it in some sense profitable for people to take account of the future is in general a necessary and possibly a sufficient condition of getting them to do so, the remainder of this chapter will discuss the uses and limitations of some quite different approaches.

Psychotherapy holds almost no promise as a means of changing the lower class. It possesses no techniques for changing personality; even if it did, there would be obstacles — perhaps insuperable ones — in the way of wholesale application of them to the lower class. One problem is that the nature of lower-class culture makes its bearers bad subjects. Lower-class people, write Hollingshead and Redlich,

> are not able to understand how thinking and talking can help them. They have not learned to verbalize and symbolize in the same way higher class persons have. Neither have they learned to sublimate present needs for the realization of future goals.[13]

In any case, there are not nearly enough therapists to treat the insane, let alone the present-oriented.

Two different lines of experiment and analysis in the field of child development are of special interest. Adherents of neither approach expect to be able to derive a formula for turning present-oriented children into future-oriented adults, but both approaches have clear implications, albeit perhaps mainly negative ones, for policy.

Language and Class Culture

In the last half-century, philosophers, anthropologists, and psychologists have all become increasingly interested in the way language shapes thoughts and feelings. A psychologist at the University of London, Basil Bernstein, has taken the lead in applying this line of analysis to problems of child development.[14] His thesis is that linguistic codes ("fashions of speaking") are shaped by social structure (by the nature of family, work,

[13] A. B. Hollingshead and F. C. Redlich, *Social Class and Mental Illness* (New York: Wiley, 1958), p. 348. See also J. Myers and L. Schaffer, "Social Stratification and Psychiatric Practice: A Study of an Out-Patient Clinic," *American Sociological Review*, 19 (June 1954), p. 310.

[14] For a critical review of work in this field, and of that of Bernstein in particular, see Denis Lawton, *Social Class, Language, and Education* (New York: Schocken Books, 1968). The writings of Bernstein on which the account in the text is based are the following: "Some Sociological Determinants of Perception," *British Journal of Sociology*, 9 (1958); "The Role of Speech in the Development and Transmission of Culture," in Gordon J. Klopf and William A. Holman (eds.), *Perspectives on Learning* (New York: Mental Health Materials Center, Inc., 1967); and "Social Structure, Language and Learning" in Joan I. Roberts (ed.), *School Children in the Urban Slum* (New York: The Free Press, 1967).

and community groups, for example) and in turn shape class culture. The lower classes (that is, semiskilled and unskilled), for example, are oriented toward the communal rather than the individual, toward the concrete rather than the abstract, and toward the here and now rather than the future. Linguistic codes thus set certain limits on what a child learns and on how it will learn it. The lower classes use only a "restricted" code, which is a language of largely implicit meanings; the speaker relies heavily upon gestures, intonation, and other nonverbal cues; his meaning is never abstract or complicated. He calls attention to features of the situation that his listener will perceive and evaluate as he does. The middle and upper classes, by contrast, use "elaborated" as well as restricted codes. Communication by means of an elaborated code employs more varied and complicated syntactic elements; the message is relatively individualized rather than conventionalized, explicit rather than implicit, and abstract rather than concrete. Bernstein illustrates these codes with two imaginary conversations, each between a mother and a child who sits on her lap in a bus.

MOTHER: Hold on tight.
CHILD: Why?
MOTHER: Hold on tight.
CHILD: Why?
MOTHER: You'll fall.
CHILD: Why?
MOTHER: I told you to hold on tight, didn't I?

MOTHER: Hold on tightly, darling.
CHILD: Why?
MOTHER: If you don't you will be thrown forward and then you'll fall.
CHILD: Why?
MOTHER: Because if the bus suddenly stops you'll jerk forward onto the seat in front.
CHILD: Why?
MOTHER: Now hold on tightly darling and don't make such a fuss.[15]

The low level of conceptualization in the lower-class mother's communication code influences, Bernstein thinks, the child's basic model of thinking and feeling as well as his desire and ability to learn. This low level of conceptualization constrains, among other things, the intensity and extent of his curiosity, his attitude toward authority (as opposed to power), and his ability to identify with the aims and principles of a society (as opposed to a local group), to verbalize feelings and to express

---

[15] Bernstein, "Social Structure," p. 145.

them in socially approved ways, and to take an instrumental (which is to say a future-oriented) attitude toward people and things.

It seems likely that linguistic limitations are a cause, although not necessarily the only one, of present-orientedness. Without language one could have no sense of a future — one could not hope, much less plan. The more limited one's linguistic (and, therefore, conceptual) equipment, it seems reasonable to suggest, the less able one will be either to take account of the future or to control impulses. . . .

Relation to a Mother-Figure in Childhood

Another line of theory and experiment that appears to be particularly relevant in this context stresses the importance for normal personality development of a close and satisfying relation in the early years of life with a mother or mother substitute. The infant and young child, Bruno Bettelheim writes, "must have a star to steer by." [16] Erik H. Erikson explains that a "regular and mutual affirmation and certification" between the infant and one who cares for it will in later life reassert itself in strong emotional ties to others — family, friends, and political leaders. Failure to form such bonds "can harm an infant radically, by diminishing or extinguishing his search for impressions." [17]

The supportive function need not necessarily be performed by a single person, however. As Bettelheim puts it: "a constellation can replace the individual star provided what is lost in intensity is made up for in the definiteness of the direction by which to navigate."

Typically, the lower-class child does not get from its mother or from anyone else the support and stimulation that it needs. This is not to say that lower-class mothers do not love their children. It may be, as Rainwater asserts, that they find fulfillment in motherhood in a way that middle-class mothers, who are taught the value of outside interests for establishing their validity as persons, do not.[18] However this may be, the lower-class mother or mother substitute is not ordinarily a "star to steer by," especially after the child has passed babyhood. Consider the following report on child-rearing among 250 urban (Negro) women "who all belong to the lowest social class":

> [The child] was permitted to grow at his own speed. If he was unable to perform, he did not meet with criticism and pressure to do better.

---

[16] Bruno Bettelheim, *The Empty Fortress* (New York: The Free Press, 1968), p. 48.
[17] Erik H. Erikson, "The Development of Ritualization," in Donald R. Cutler (ed.), *The Religious Situation, 1968* (Boston: Beacon Press, 1968), p. 714.
[18] Lee Rainwater, *And the Poor Get Children* (Chicago: Quadrangle Books, 1960), pp. 82–83.

He learned how to work. He was encouraged to fight for his rights. On the other hand, there was confusion as to who had authority over him and what behavior was acceptable, since many persons with different expectations had a parental role. He was accustomed to extremes of adult authority, being very controlled at times, and not at all controlled in others. He early became used to corporal punishment. He was treated with relative coldness and he was not praised for achievement. The stimuli which are supplied by books, toys, and cultural experiences were often missing. There was little opportunity for a boy to identify with a male figure. There was lack of interest in the personality characteristics which differentiate one individual from the other and which contribute to a strong feeling of self-identification.[19]

.   .   .

While either of the factors just discussed — namely, language patterns and the support of a mother or mother-substitute — may by itself profoundly influence the child's development, the *interaction* of the two factors would seem likely to produce the most marked effects. In the lower class, language deficiencies and lack of support, stimulation, and direction from a mother or mother-substitute are found together. So, at the upper end of the class-cultural scale, are the opposites — verbal facility and a close relation to mother. It is noteworthy that in one of the most upwardly mobile and presumably future-oriented of all ethnic groups, the Jewish, the pattern of child-rearing in the last generation emphasized both of these elements to an extraordinary degree. The Jewish mother, as described by Zena Smith Blau, was in this respect the exact opposite of the lower-class Negro mother, as described earlier. The Jewish mother held her son in bonds of love and mutual dependence beyond his childhood and even his youth, all the while subjecting him to intense and constant verbal stimulation.

> Whatever Yiddishe Mamehs did for their children . . . was accompanied by a flow of language, consisting of rich, colorful, expressive words and phrases. Their vocabulary of endearments alone can fill a modest-sized paperback, but they also had a superb store of admonishments, curses, imprecations, explanations, songs, and folksayings that they effortlessly invoked as they went about ministering to the needs of their children and their husbands. The freedom that they exhibited with the spoken word invited a similar response from their children and it carried over into school. . . .[20]

---

[19] H. Wortis *et. al.*, "Child-Rearing Practices in a Low Socio-Economic Group," in Joan I. Roberts (ed.), *School Children in the Urban Slum* (New York: The Free Press, 1967), p. 469.

[20] Zena Smith Blau, "In Defense of the Jewish Mother," *Midstream* (February 1967), p. 47.

It would seem that the problems posed by the lower class can be solved fundamentally only if the children of that class are removed from their parents' culture. As a matter of policy, the implication is that efforts to change the culture of the lower-class child should concentrate, whenever possible, on the early, formative years — when the child most needs "a star to steer by." Anecdotal evidence suggests that damage done to the child's personality may occasionally be repaired as late as adolescence. However, it is probably safe to say that the earliest possible exposure of the child to the culture of the larger society will increase the chance of successful adaptation while lowering costs, both emotional and material, to all concerned.

A second implication is that in many cases helping the mother or mother-substitute will be a prerequisite to helping the child. How the father relates to the child apparently matters less.[21] His effect on the child's development in its early years is indirect for the most part, making itself felt through the mother's attitudes. Although there seems to be no clinical or experimental evidence on the subject, one suspects that it is better for a child not to have a father present at all than to have one who keeps the mother upset and distracted.

A third implication may seem to be that the child should be taken from its lower-class parents at a very early age and brought up by people whose culture is normal. It will do little good to explain to a lower-class mother wherein her child-rearing practices are wrong: she is not really interested in improving her practices, perhaps because she cannot see anything wrong with them. In this and in other areas as well, her class culture sets sharp limits on what it is possible for her to do. It may seem, therefore, that the only thing to do is to take the child from her and put it in the care of a substitute who will bring it up properly.

However, the case is not as clear as it may at first appear. It is not certain that taking the child from its mother may not cause even greater injury to it than would leaving it with her. . . . After a comprehensive review of the scientific literature, psychologist Leon J. Yarrow concludes that keeping a child with "grossly inadequate parents in a depriving and hostile environment" does not seem warranted by what is known of the dangers in separating a child from its mother; he stresses, however, that before a child is removed, strong efforts should be made to improve family conditions.[22]

---

[21] Very little research has been done on the effects of father-separation on the child. Although such research as exists is inconclusive, it is possible that father-separation may create problems for the child with respect to sex-role identification and superego formation. Leon J. Yarrow, "Separation from Parents During Early Childhood," in M. L. Hoffman and L. W. Hoffman (eds.), *Review of Child Development Research* (New York: Russell Sage Foundation, 1964), I: 117–121.

[22] *Ibid.*, p. 128.

Presumably, the danger to the child in taking it from its mother is a function not only of the mother's incompetence but also of the ability of the mother-substitute to give it the support and stimulation that it needs. Even supposing (as it seems plausible to do) that at present the average substitute provides a much better environment for the child than does the average mother from whom children are taken, one still cannot conclude that *all* lower-class children should be taken from their mothers. For as the number of such removals increased, the quality of the average substitute would surely fall and that of the average mother would probably increase. It is one thing to provide proper adoptive homes and institutions for a few thousand children a year and an altogether different one to provide them for several hundred thousand. With respect to institutions, at least, it is likely that "depersonalized and affectionless but otherwise adequate" care is the best that can be expected on a large scale.

Finally, it is questionable whether the state has a right to take a child from its parents in order to prevent an injury as impalpable and contingent as its socialization into lower-class culture. Even if it were certain (and of course it is not) that a child brought up in the lower class would turn out to be a "social problem" of some sort, it would not automatically follow that society has a right to interfere so drastically in people's lives. If failure to provide a child with adequate linguistic equipment is considered sufficient grounds for removing a child from its parents, so in consistency ought failure to provide it with "a star to steer by." This latter criterion would probably find almost as much application in the upper classes as in the lower. As a practical matter there is, of course, not the slightest possibility of a rule being adopted that might be applied to the rich as well as to the poor; this appears from the practice of the courts at the present time. "Neglect" and "abuse," the grounds for child removal in the law of most states, are everywhere interpreted narrowly to mean abandonment of the child, failing to supply it with food, clothing, shelter, and medical care, grossly mistreating it (as, for example, beating it or locking it in a closet for a long time), or outrageously endangering its moral welfare (as, for example, by carrying on the trade of prostitution in its presence). "Emotional neglect seems the most obvious type to social workers," one of them writes, "but it is the most obscure to the courts in our experience." [23] The inability of psychiatrists to specify precisely what "emotional neglect" consists of is one reason why the courts do not take note of it.[24] One suspects, however, that if the condition were found

---

[23] Personal communication.
[24] K. B. Cheney, "Safeguarding Legal Rights in Providing Protective Service," *Children*, 13 (May–June 1966), pp. 86–92.

only among the poor, it would prove no more difficult to define for legal purposes than, say, loitering.

In fact, even laws with respect to gross physical neglect and abuse are not enforced stringently or uniformly. Most cases of neglect and abuse never come to the attention of the authorities. Neighbors are reluctant to "interfere," teachers rarely report it when a pupil comes to school with cuts and bruises, and physicians frequently either fail to recognize the "child abuse syndrome" or decline to take the risk of being sued for damages if the parents are acquitted. Even when a case is reported and the facts are beyond dispute, the court may be unwilling to take custody of the child.[25] . . .

[One] possibility would be to offer "scholarships" to lower-class infants in amounts sufficient to induce their parents to place them in approved schools on a year-round basis. These schools could be located in or near the children's neighborhoods and could be staffed by working-class women and girls from those neighborhoods. These arrangements would enable parents to see their children without having any responsibility for their care. This, of course, is the basic principle of *kibbutzim* in Israel. The teaching of the children could not be done entirely on a classroom basis, however. In the early stages of the acquisition of a new subject matter like reading or arithmetic, a tutorial arrangement (which is what the middle-class child gets from his parents at home) may be necessary; in effect, substitute mothers would have to be provided at least part of the time.

If it is not feasible to establish boarding schools, day nurseries may be the next thing. They are, however, a poor substitute. Even under the best of circumstances, they are not likely to succeed in bring children out of lower-class culture. In an experimental project in Boston, twenty-one children, aged two and one half to six, from disorganized, lower-class families spent two to three mornings a week in a nursery school generously staffed with highly trained personnel. The school was intended to help the child "gain a sense of mastery over his immediate surroundings." . . .

After attendance of from one to three years, there was noticeable improvement in the children's appearance, body use, and self-esteem, and many had "learned to express their thoughts, feelings, and experiences with accuracy sufficient for communication." These gains certainly justified all the effort that was put forth, but the lives of the children did not change drastically. Language problems, for example, continued to ham-

25 Cf. Larry B. Silver, "Child Abuse Syndrome: A Review," *Medical Times Magazine,* 96 (August 1968), pp. 803–820.

per the children's ability to learn even after three years, and the experimenters doubted that these problems would ever be overcome. Reports that filtered back to them after the experiment had ended were not at all encouraging.

> Many of the children were placed in situations where more demands were made on them than they were mature enough to fulfill. At least five of them repeated one of the early grades.
>
> It is our impression that as failures began to follow one another, the inevitable regression to more discouraged, impatient, frightened, passive behavior occurred.[26]

Lower-class children could probably benefit a great deal more than they do from day nurseries were it not for the fact that they are at once confused and stultified by what they are (and are not) exposed to at home. When the influence of the nursery has made conditions for changing the child's outlook and life style feasible, even small improvements in home life might have large effects. As a rule, it is on the mother, or mother-substitute, that efforts to improve the home environment should concentrate. She is best able to give the child the support and stimulation it needs, and, fortunately, she is likely to be less — perhaps much less — improvident, irresponsible, and violent than her mate. . . . It is the male, especially the young one, to whom lower-class culture comes most "naturally." For some reason — perhaps because extreme present-orientedness is incompatible with the childbearing function, perhaps because lower-class sex is sometimes too much like rape to be enjoyable to women, or perhaps because "toughness" (one of Walter B. Miller's foci of lower-class culture) is usually regarded as a male attribute — women born and brought up in the lower class very often behave in ways that are not characteristic of that class. The lower-class mother — but not the father — is often very much concerned about the children's welfare: she may try to keep them in school and out of trouble; sometimes she struggles to buy a house. Usually, her efforts are futile. Her mate and, as soon as they are old enough, her sons are at best noncontributors to any "family" project and at worst active opponents. If she manages to save anything, they soon lay hands on it and squander it. "Getting ahead" is her idea, not theirs.

It would seem, then, that the aim of policy should be to encourage the mother's aspirations and to strengthen her hand as much as possible. This is easier said than done, however. One suggested innovation is the "peace bond," an arrangement by which a man incurs an agreed-upon penalty, usually the forfeiture of a small sum, if he does what he has agreed not to do. It is unlikely that the lower-class male will be deterred

---

[26] Eleanor Pavenstedt (ed.), *The Drifters* (Boston: Little, Brown, 1967), p. 218.

by such a penalty, nor even perhaps by the prospect of jail. Another proposal is that police powers be redefined to allow arrests for misdemeanors on probable cause (in most states a police officer who did not see a misdemeanor committed cannot make an arrest without a signed complaint). This suggestion is open to several objections. One is that such a redefinition of police powers might lead to greater embarrassment and inconvenience for those persons who (because of color, low income, or whatever) are taken to be lower class when in fact they are not. Moreover, the lower-class woman may be just as unwilling to offer the police a verbal complaint as she is to offer them a signed one. There is still another reason why workable ways of protecting the woman from her mate are unlikely to be found: the lower-class woman will often tolerate considerable abuse rather than lose the companionship of a man. Rather than risk being abandoned, she may deny that she and her children were beaten, that the welfare money was spent on a drunken spree, and all the rest. (In Illinois, the police *can* arrest for probable cause on many misdemeanors but they almost never do, partly for these reasons, partly because they do not want to create additional frictions within families, and partly because they want to avoid assaults by angry mates.) Against her own unwisdom (if this is what it really is) the police, the courts, and the whole power of government cannot protect her. And so it appears that it will be very difficult if not impossible to realize even the minimum goal of policy — namely, to protect the lower-class woman and her children against the violence of her mate.

The conclusion is unavoidable that for at least several decades there will be a lower class which, while small both in absolute numbers and as a percentage of the whole population, will nevertheless be large enough to constitute a serious problem — or, rather, a set of serious problems — in the city. The question arises, therefore, as to what policies might minimize the difficulties that must inevitably exist when a lower-class minority lives in the midst of an increasingly middle- and upper-class society.

When the lower class lived on farms and in small cities . . . its members were to some extent both held in check and protected by being physically isolated from each other. Also, there were few, if any, opportunities for easy money, and without money the lower-class person was effectively tied down. An even greater constraint on him, perhaps, was his visibility. In the slums of a big city, it is easy to drop out of sight. In a town or small city, on the other hand, there is no place to hide. The individual is known personally by the landlord, corner merchant, and policeman; he cannot escape into anonymity. In the big city he need never see the same merchant, landlord, or policeman twice. As an economist might put it, one who wants to lead a lower-class style of life has the advantage of numerous "economies of scale" in the big city.

Therefore, from the standpoint of a society that wants at once to protect lower-class people from each other and to protect itself from them, there are advantages in having lower-class people live in the town or small city, or, if they must live in the large one, in having them scattered in a way such that they will not constitute a "critical mass" anywhere.[27] These considerations suggest that government programs (subsidies to large farmers, for example) that tend to push unskilled people off the land and out of rural areas ought to be stopped, that welfare programs should aim at making life in towns and small cities much more advantageous to the chronically poor than it is now (thereby reducing one of their incentives to come to the city), and that, within the large cities, there should be an end to that kind of urban renewal (almost the only kind, in fact) the tendency of which is to dislodge lower-class families who live in or near neighborhoods that are largely middle class.

It might be argued that the hardest cases among the lower class ought to be treated as semicompetent (incompetents being those — for example, children, the insane, the feeble-minded — who are incapable of knowing where their own interest, not to mention the social interest, lies). Such persons could be cared for in what may be called semi-institutions, which would consist of small enclaves of lower-class people who, either because they wanted help in "staying out of trouble" or because they desired certain material benefits (extragenerous allowances for housing, food, clothing and health care) would agree to accept certain limitations on their freedom. For example, they might agree to receive most of their income in kind rather than in cash, to forego ownership of automobiles, to have no more than two or three children, and to accept a certain amount of surveillance and supervision from a semi-social worker–semi-policeman.

Several considerations, however, argue against semi-institutional care for the lower class. As a practical matter, it is unlikely that many of the hardest cases — those from whom society most needs protection — would choose semiaffluence in a semi-institution in preference to the life of the slum. If these hardest cases are to be controlled at all, they must be controlled totally — that is, put into prison. This approach is obviously out of the question, since "being lower class" is not a crime or commitable condition and is not at all likely to be made one. The tendency, in fact, is in the opposite direction: to confine fewer and fewer of those who have been convicted of crimes or have been judged to be mentally incompetent.

A very important danger in such efforts to restrain the lower class is that they might be applied also to people who are *not* lower class, thus

---

[27] Cf. Jack Lessinger, "The Case for Scatteration," *Journal of the American Institute of Planners,* 28 (August 1962), pp. 159–169.

abridging the freedom of these others without justification. This danger exists in part because euphemisms — e.g., "the poor" — have collapsed necessary distinctions between the competent and the semicompetent. (The blind, for example, are often lumped together in welfare programs with the lower-class poor.) It exists also because prejudice or convenience sometimes causes caretakers to treat externals — skin color, speech ways, and so forth — as indicators of lower-class culture.

Another objection arises from the fact that at the present time (fifty or more years ago it was otherwise) most lower-class people in the large cities are black. Putting them in semi-institutions would inevitably appear to be a reflection of racial inferiority or an expression of racial prejudice. What is even more important, perhaps, is that taking the lower-class black out of the slum of the great city would tend to cut him off psychologically from the black community. It is by no means inconceivable that the "black pride" movement may engender morale in the mass of black people — morale that the lower class may in some degree share if it is in close physical contact with the main body of blacks. To be sure, one could argue this the other way, contending, first, that nothing would do more for the morale of the black community than to have the worst of the lower class removed from its midst and, second, that lower-class people are by the nature of their culture immune to any moral influence from the surrounding society.

Finally, there is clearly a tension if not an out-and-out incompatibility between the goal of restraining the lower-class individual and that of stimulating him. The first calls for reducing his freedom, the second for enlarging it. If it were possible to identify persons who are irremediably lower class and to place them and them alone under restraints, this objection would not apply. In fact, there is no way of knowing which individuals would respond significantly to incentives and which would not. The danger of perpetuating and increasing present-orientedness while endeavoring to restrain it makes the whole enterprise of restraint suspect. Despite the high costs to society and to the lower-class individual himself that follow from increasing his freedom, doing so may well be the best course of action in the long run.

Men and Jobs

Elliot Liebow

A pickup truck drives slowly down the street. The truck stops as it comes abreast of a man sitting on a cast-iron porch and the white driver calls out, asking if the man wants a day's work. The man shakes his head and the truck moves on up the block, stopping again whenever idling men come within calling distance of the driver. At the Carry-out [a "take-home" food shop] corner, five men debate the question briefly and shake their heads no to the truck. The truck turns the corner and repeats the same performance up the next street. In the distance, one can see one man, then another, climb into the back of the truck and sit down. In starts and stops, the truck finally disappears.

What is it we have witnessed here? A labor scavenger rebuffed by his would-be prey? Lazy, irresponsible men turning down an honest day's pay for an honest day's work? Or a more complex phenomenon marking the intersection of economic forces, social values and individual states of mind and body?

Let us look again at the driver of the truck. He has been able to recruit only two or three men from each twenty or fifty he contacts. To him, it is clear that the others simply do not choose to work. Singly or in groups, belly-empty or belly-full, sullen or gregarious, drunk or sober, they confirm what he has read, heard and knows from his own experience: these men wouldn't take a job if it were handed to them on a platter.[1]

Quite apart from the question of whether or not this is true of some of the men he sees on the street, it is clearly not true of all of them. If it were, he would not have come here in the first place; or having come, he would have left with an empty truck. It is not even true of most of them, for most of the men he sees on the street this weekday morning do, in fact, have jobs. But since, at the moment, they are neither working nor sleeping, and since they hate the depressing room or apartment they live in, or because there is nothing to do there, or because they want to get

---

Reprinted from *Tally's Corner* by Elliot Liebow by permission. Copyright © 1967 by Little, Brown and Company (Inc.).

[1] By different methods, perhaps, some social scientists have also located the problem in the men themselves, in their unwillingness or lack of desire to work: "To improve the underprivileged worker's performance, one must help him to learn *to want* . . . higher social goals for himself and his children. . . . The problem of changing the work habits and motivation of [lower class] people . . . is a problem of changing the goals, the ambitions, and the level of cultural and occupational aspiration of the underprivileged worker." (Emphasis in original.) Allison Davis, "The Motivation of the Underprivileged Worker," p. 90.

away from their wives or anyone else living there, they are out on the street, indistinguishable from those who do not have jobs or do not want them. Some, like Boley, a member of a trash-collection crew in a suburban housing development, work Saturdays and are off on this weekday. Some, like Sweets, work nights cleaning up middle-class trash, dirt, dishes and garbage, and mopping the floors of the office buildings, hotels, restaurants, toilets and other public places dirtied during the day. Some men work for retail businesses such as liquor stores which do not begin the day until ten o'clock. Some laborers, like Tally, have already come back from the job because the ground was too wet for pick and shovel or because the weather was too cold for pouring concrete. Other employed men stayed off the job today for personal reasons: Clarence to go to a funeral at eleven this morning and Sea Cat to answer a subpoena as a witness in a criminal proceeding.

Also on the street, unwitting contributors to the impression taken away by the truck driver, are the halt and the lame. The man on the cast-iron steps strokes one gnarled arthritic hand with the other and says he doesn't know whether or not he'll live long enough to be eligible for Social Security. He pauses, then adds matter-of-factly, "Most times, I don't care whether I do or don't." Stoopy's left leg was polio-withered in childhood. Raymond, who looks as if he could tear out a fire hydrant, coughs up blood if he bends or moves suddenly. The quiet man who hangs out in front of the Saratoga apartments has a steel hook strapped onto his left elbow. And had the man in the truck been able to look into the wine-clouded eyes of the man in the green cap, he would have realized that the man did not even understand he was being offered a day's work.

Others, having had jobs and been laid off, are drawing unemployment compensation (up to $44 per week) and have nothing to gain by accepting work which pays little more than this and frequently less.

Still others, like Bumdoodle the numbers man, are working hard at illegal ways of making money, hustlers who are on the street to turn a dollar any way they can: buying and selling sex, liquor, narcotics, stolen goods, or anything else that turns up.

Only a handful remains unaccounted for. There is Tonk, who cannot bring himself to take a job away from the corner, because, according to the other men, he suspects his wife will be unfaithful if given the opportunity. There is Stanton, who has not reported to work for four days now, not since Bernice disappeared. He bought a brand new knife against her return. She had done this twice before, he said, but not for so long and not without warning, and he had forgiven her. But this time, "I ain't got it in me to forgive her again." His rage and shame are there for all to see as he paces the Carry-out and the corner, day and night, hoping to catch a glimpse of her.

And finally, there are those like Arthur, able-bodied men who have no visible means of support, legal or illegal, who neither have jobs nor want them. The truck driver, among others, believes the Arthurs to be representative of all the men he sees idling on the street during his own working hours. They are not, but they cannot be dismissed simply because they are a small minority. It is not enough to explain them away as being lazy or irresponsible or both because an able-bodied man with responsibilities who refuses work is, by the truck driver's definition, lazy and irresponsible. Such an answer begs the question. It is descriptive of the facts; it does not explain them.

Moreover, despite their small numbers, the don't-work-and-don't-want-to-work minority is especially significant because they represent the strongest and clearest expression of those values and attitudes associated with making a living which, to varying degrees, are found throughout the streetcorner world. These men differ from the others in degree rather than in kind, the principal difference being that they are carrying out the implications of their values and experiences to their logical, inevitable conclusions. In this sense, the others have yet to come to terms with themselves and the world they live in.

Putting aside, for the moment, what the men say and feel, and looking at what they actually do and the choices they make, getting a job, keeping a job, and doing well at it is clearly of low priority. Arthur will not take a job at all. Leroy is supposed to be on his job at 4:00 P.M. but it is already 4:10 and he still cannot bring himself to leave the free games he has accumulated on the pinball machine in the Carry-out. Tonk started a construction job on Wednesday, worked Thursday and Friday, then didn't go back again. On the same kind of job, Sea Cat quit in the second week. Sweets had been working three months as a busboy in a restaurant, then quit without notice, not sure himself why he did so. A real estate agent, saying he was more interested in getting the job done than in the cost, asked Richard to give him an estimate on repairing and painting the inside of a house, but Richard, after looking over the job, somehow never got around to submitting an estimate. During one period, Tonk would not leave the corner to take a job because his wife might prove unfaithful; Stanton would not take a job because his woman had been unfaithful.

Thus, the man-job relationship is a tenuous one. At any given moment, a job may occupy a relatively low position on the streetcorner scale of real values. Getting a job may be subordinated to relations with women or to other non-job considerations; the commitment to a job one already has is frequently shallow and tentative.

The reasons are many. Some are objective and reside principally in the job; some are subjective and reside principally in the man. The line between them, however, is not a clear one. Behind the man's refusal to take a job or his decision to quit one is not a simple impulse or value choice but a complex combination of assessments of objective reality on the one hand, and values, attitudes and beliefs drawn from different levels of his experience on the other.

Objective economic considerations are frequently a controlling factor in a man's refusal to take a job. How much the job pays is a crucial question but seldom asked. He knows how much it pays. Working as a stock clerk, a delivery boy, or even behind the counter of liquor stores, drug stores and other retail businesses pays one dollar an hour. So, too, do most busboy, car-wash, janitorial and other jobs available to him. Some jobs, such as dishwasher, may dip as low as eighty cents an hour and others, such as elevator operator or work in a junk yard, may offer $1.15 or $1.25. Take-home pay for jobs such as these ranges from $35 to $50 a week, but a take-home pay of over $45 for a five-day week is the exception rather than the rule.

One of the principal advantages of these kinds of jobs is that they offer fairly regular work. Most of them involve essential services and are therefore somewhat less responsive to business conditions than are some higher paying, less menial jobs. Most of them are also inside jobs not dependent on the weather, as are construction jobs and other higher-paying outside work. . . .

. . . The objective fact [however] is that menial jobs in retailing or in the service trades simply do not pay enough to support a man and his family. This is not to say that the worker is underpaid; this may or may not be true. Whether he is or not, the plain fact is that, in such a job, he cannot make a living. Nor can he take much comfort in the fact that these jobs tend to offer more regular, steadier work. If he cannot live on the $45 or $50 he makes in one week, the longer he works the longer he cannot live on what he makes.

Construction work, even for unskilled laborers, usually pays better, with the hourly rate ranging from $1.50 to $2.60 an hour. Importantly, too, good references, a good driving record, a tenth grade (or any high school) education, previous experience, the ability to "bring police clearance with you" are not normally required of laborers as they frequently are for some of the jobs in retailing or in the service trades.

Construction work, however, has its own objective disadvantages. It is, first of all, seasonal work for the great bulk of the laborers, beginning early in the spring and tapering off as winter weather sets in. And even during the season the work is frequently irregular. Early or late in the season, snow or temperatures too low for concrete frequently sends the laborers back home, and during late spring or summer, a heavy rain on Tuesday or Wednesday, leaving a lot of water and mud behind it, can

mean a two or three day work-week for the pick-and-shovel men and
other unskilled laborers.[2]

The elements are not the only hazard. As the project moves from one
construction stage to another, laborers — usually without warning — are
laid off, sometimes permanently or sometimes for weeks at a time. The
more fortunate or the better workers are told periodically to "take a walk
for two, three days."

Both getting the construction job and getting to it are also relatively
more difficult than is the case for the menial jobs in retailing and the
service trades. Job competition is always fierce. In the city, the large construction projects are unionized. One has to have ready cash to get into
the union to become eligible to work on these projects and, being eligible,
one has to find an opening. Unless one "knows somebody," say a foreman
or a laborer who knows the day before that they are going to take on
new men in the morning, this can be a difficult and disheartening search.

Many of the nonunion jobs are in suburban Maryland or Virginia.
The newspaper ads say, "Report ready to work to the trailer at the intersection of Rte. 11 and Old Bridge Rd., Bunston, Virginia (or Maryland),"
but this location may be ten, fifteen, or even twenty-five miles from the
Carry-out. Public transportation would require two or more hours to get
there, if it services the area at all. Without access to a car or to a car-pool
arrangement, it is not worthwhile reading the ad. So the men do not. Jobs
such as these are usually filled by word of mouth information, beginning
with someone who knows someone or who is himself working there and
looking for a paying rider. Furthermore, nonunion jobs in outlying areas
tend to be smaller projects of relatively short duration and to pay somewhat less than scale.

Still another objective factor is the work itself. For some men,
whether the job be digging, mixing mortar, pushing a wheelbarrow, un-
loading materials, carrying and placing steel rods for reinforcing concrete, or building or laying concrete forms, the work is simply too hard.
Men such as Tally and Wee Tom can make such work look like child's
play; some of the older work-hardened men, such as Budder and Stanton,

---

[2] In a recent year, the crime rate in Washington for the month of August jumped
18 percent over the preceding month. A veteran police officer explained the increase
to David L. Bazelon, Chief Judge, U.S. Court of Appeals for the District of Columbia.
"It's quite simple. . . . You see, August was a very wet month. . . . These people
wait on the street corner each morning around 6:00 or 6:30 for a truck to pick them
up and take them to a construction site. If it's raining, that truck doesn't come, and
the men are going to be idle that day. If the bad weather keeps up for three days
. . . we know we are going to have trouble on our hands — and sure enough, there
invariably follows a rash of purse-snatchings, house-breakings and the like. . . .
These people have to eat like the rest of us, you know." David L. Bazelon, Address to
the Federal Bar Association, p. 3.

can do it too, although not without showing unmistakable signs of strain and weariness at the end of the workday. But those who lack the robustness of a Tally or the time-inured immunity of a Budder must either forego jobs such as these or pay a heavy toll to keep them. For Leroy, in his early twenties, almost six feet tall but weighing under 140 pounds, it would be as difficult to push a loaded wheelbarrow, or to unload and stack 96-pound bags of cement all day long, as it would be for Stoopy with his withered leg.

Heavy, backbreaking labor of the kind that used to be regularly associated with bull gangs or concrete gangs is no longer characteristic of laboring jobs, especially those with the larger, well-equipped construction companies. Brute strength is still required from time to time, as on smaller jobs where it is not economical to bring in heavy equipment or where the small, undercapitalized contractor has none to bring in. In many cases, however, the conveyor belt has replaced the wheelbarrow or the Georgia buggy, mechanized forklifts have eliminated heavy, manual lifting, and a variety of digging machines have replaced the pick and shovel. The result is fewer jobs for unskilled laborers and, in many cases, a work speed-up for those who do have jobs. . . .

Men who have been running an elevator, washing dishes, or "pulling trash" cannot easily move into laboring jobs. They lack the basic skills for "unskilled" construction labor, familiarity with tools and materials, and tricks of the trade without which hard jobs are made harder. Previously unused or untrained muscles rebel in pain against the new and insistent demands made upon them, seriously compromising the man's performance and testing his willingness to see the job through.

A healthy, sturdy, active man of good intelligence requires from two to four weeks to break in on a construction job. Even if he is willing somehow to bull his way through the first few weeks, it frequently happens that his foreman or the craftsman he services with materials and general assistance is not willing to wait that long for him to get into condition or to learn at a glance the difference in size between a rough 2″ x 8″ and a finished 2″ x 10″. The foreman and the craftsman are themselves "under the gun" and cannot "carry" the man when other men, who are already used to the work and who know the tools and materials, are lined up to take the job.

Sea Cat was "healthy, sturdy, active and of good intelligence." When a judge gave him six weeks in which to pay his wife $200 in back child-support payments, he left his grocery-store job in order to take a higher-paying job as a laborer, arranged for him by a foreman friend. During the first week the weather was bad and he worked only Wednesday and Friday, cursing the elements all the while for cheating him out of the money he could have made. The second week, the weather was fair but he quit at the end of the fourth day, saying frankly that the work was too hard for him. He went back to his job at the grocery store and took a second job working nights as a dishwasher in a restaurant,[3] earning little if any more at the two jobs than he would have earned as a laborer, and keeping at both of them until he had paid off his debts.

Tonk did not last as long as Sea Cat. No one made any predictions when he got a job in a parking lot, but when the men on the corner learned he was to start on a road construction job, estimates of how long he would last ranged from one to three weeks. Wednesday was his first day. He spent that evening and night at home. He did the same on Thursday. He worked Friday and spent Friday evening and part of Saturday draped over the mailbox on the corner. Sunday afternoon, Tonk decided he was not going to report on the job the next morning. He explained that after working three days, he knew enough about the job to know that it was too hard for him. He knew he wouldn't be able to keep up and he'd just as soon quit now as get fired later. . . .

Sometimes, the strain and effort is greater than the man is willing to admit, even to himself. In the early summer of 1963, Richard was rooming at Nancy's place. His wife and children were "in the country" (his grandmother's home in Carolina), waiting for him to save up enough money so that he could bring them back to Washington and start over again after a disastrous attempt to "make it" in Philadelphia. Richard had gotten a job with a fence company in Virginia. It paid $1.60 an hour. The first few evenings, when he came home from work, he looked ill from exhaustion and the heat. Stanton said Richard would have to quit, "he's too small [thin] for that kind of work." Richard said he was doing O.K. and would stick with the job.

At Nancy's one night, when Richard had been working about two weeks, Nancy and three or four others were sitting around talking, drinking, and listening to music. Someone asked Nancy when was Richard going to bring his wife and children up from the country. Nancy said she didn't know, but it probably depended on how long it would take him to save up enough money. She said she didn't think he could stay with the fence job much longer. This morning, she said, the man Richard rode to work with knocked on the door and Richard didn't answer. She looked in his room. Richard was still asleep. Nancy tried to shake him awake. "No more digging!" Richard cried out. "No more digging! I can't do no more God-damn digging!" When Nancy finally managed to wake him, he dressed quickly and went to work.

Richard stayed on the job two more weeks, then suddenly quit, osten-

---

[3] Not a sinecure, even by streetcorner standards.

sibly because his pay check was three dollars less than what he thought it should have been.

In summary of objective job considerations, then, the most important fact is that a man who is able and willing to work cannot earn enough money to support himself, his wife, and one or more children. A man's chances for working regularly are good only if he is willing to work for less than he can live on, and sometimes not even then. On some jobs, the wage rate is deceptively higher than on others, but the higher the wage rate, the more difficult it is to get the job, and the less the job security. Higher-paying construction work tends to be seasonal and, during the season, the amount of work available is highly sensitive to business and weather conditions and to the changing requirements of individual projects. Moreover, high-paying construction jobs are frequently beyond the physical capacity of some of the men, and some of the low-paying jobs are scaled down even lower in accordance with the self-fulfilling assumption that the man will steal part of his wages on the job.

Bernard assesses the objective job situation dispassionately over a cup of coffee, sometimes poking at the coffee with his spoon, sometimes staring at it as if, like a crystal ball, it holds tomorrow's secrets. He is twenty-seven years old. He and the woman with whom he lives have a baby son, and she has another child by another man. Bernard does odd jobs — mostly painting — but here it is the end of January, and his last job was with the Post Office during the Christmas mail rush. He would like postal work as a steady job, he says. It pays well (about $2.00 an hour) but he has twice failed the Post Office examination (he graduated from a Washington high school) and has given up the idea as an impractical one. He is supposed to see a man tonight about a job as a parking attendant for a large apartment house. The man told him to bring his birth certificate and driver's license, but his license was suspended because of a backlog of unpaid traffic fines. A friend promised to lend him some money this evening. If he gets it, he will pay the fines tomorrow morning and have his license reinstated. He hopes the man with the job will wait till tomorrow night.

A "security job" is what he really wants, he said. He would like to save up money for a taxicab. (But having twice failed the postal examination and having a bad driving record as well, it is highly doubtful that he could meet the qualifications or pass the written test.) That would be "a good life." He can always get a job in a restaurant or as a clerk in a drugstore but they don't pay enough, he said. He needs to take home at least $50 to $55 a week. He thinks he can get that much driving a truck somewhere. . . . Sometimes he wishes he had stayed in the army. . . . A security job, that's what he wants most of all, a real security job. . . .

When we look at what the men bring to the job rather than at what

the job offers the men, it is essential to keep in mind that we are not looking at men who come to the job fresh, just out of school perhaps, and
newly prepared to undertake the task of making a living, or from another
job where they earned a living and are prepared to do the same on this
job. Each man comes to the job with a long job history characterized by
his not being able to support himself and his family. Each man carries
this knowledge, born of his experience, with him. He comes to the job
flat and stale, wearied by the sameness of it all, convinced of his own incompetence, terrified of responsibility — of being tested still again and
found wanting. Possible exceptions are the younger men not yet, or just,
married. They suspect all this but have yet to have it confirmed by repeated personal experience over time. But those who are or have been
married know it well. It is the experience of the individual and the group;
of their fathers and probably their sons. Convinced of their inadequacies,
not only do they not seek out those few better-paying jobs which test
their resources, but they actively avoid them, gravitating in a mass to the
menial, routine jobs which offer no challenge — and therefore pose no
threat — to the already diminished images they have of themselves. . . .

Lethargy, disinterest and general apathy on the job, so often reported
by employers, has its streetcorner counterpart. The men do not ordinarily
talk about their jobs or ask one another about them. Although most of the
men know who is or is not working at any given time, they may or may
not know what particular job an individual man has. There is no overt
interest in job specifics as they relate to this or that person, in large part
perhaps because the specifics are not especially relevant. To know that
a man is working is to know approximately how much he makes and
to know as much as one needs or wants to know about how he
makes it. After all, how much difference does it make to know whether
a man is pushing a mop and pulling trash in an apartment house, a
restaurant, or an office building, or delivering groceries, drugs, or liquor,
or, if he's a laborer, whether he's pushing a wheelbarrow, mixing mortar, or digging a hole. So much does one job look like every other that
there is little to choose between them. In large part, the job market consists of a narrow range of nondescript chores calling for nondistinctive,
undifferentiated, unskilled labor. "A job is a job."

A crucial factor in the streetcorner man's lack of job commitment is
the overall value he places on the job. *For his part, the streetcorner man
puts no lower value on the job than does the larger society around him.*
He knows the social value of the job by the amount of money the employer is willing to pay him for doing it. In a real sense, every pay day,
he counts in dollars and cents the value placed on the job by society at
large. He is no more (and frequently less) ready to quit and look for another job than his employer is ready to fire him and look for another man.

Neither the streetcorner man who performs these jobs nor the society which requires him to perform them assesses the job as one "worth doing and worth doing well." Both employee and employer are contemptuous of the job. The employee shows his contempt by his reluctance to accept it or keep it, the employer by paying less than is required to support a family. Nor does the low-wage job offer prestige, respect, interesting work, opportunity for learning or advancement, or any other compensation. With few exceptions, jobs filled by the streetcorner men are at the bottom of the employment ladder in every respect, from wage level to prestige. Typically, they are hard, dirty, uninteresting and underpaid. The rest of society (whatever its ideal values regarding the dignity of labor) holds the job of the dishwasher or janitor or unskilled laborer in low esteem if not outright contempt. So does the streetcorner man. He cannot do otherwise. He cannot draw from a job those social values which other people do not put into it.

Only occasionally does spontaneous conversation touch on these matters directly. Talk about jobs is usually limited to isolated statements of intention, such as "I think I'll get me another gig [job]," "I'm going to look for a construction job when the weather breaks," or "I'm going to quit. I can't take no more of his shit." Job assessments typically consist of nothing more than a noncommittal shrug and "It's O. K." or "It's a job."

One reason for the relative absence of talk about one's job is, as suggested earlier, that the sameness of job experiences does not bear reiteration. Another and more important reason is the emptiness of the job experience itself. The man sees middle-class occupations as a primary source of prestige, pride and self-respect; his own job affords him none of these. To think about his job is to see himself as others see him, to remind him of just where he stands in this society. And because society's criteria for placement are generally the same as his own, to talk about his job can trigger a flush of shame and a deep, almost physical ache to change places with someone, almost anyone, else. The desire to be a person in his own right, to be noticed by the world he lives in, is shared by each of the men on the streetcorner. Whether they articulate this desire (as Tally does below) or not, one can see them position themselves to catch the attention of their fellows in much the same way as plants bend or stretch to catch the sunlight.[4]

Tally and I were in the Carry-out. It was summer, Tally's peak earning season as a cement finisher, a semiskilled job a cut or so above that of

---

[4] Sea Cat cuts his pants legs off at the calf and puts a fringe on the raggedy edges. Tonk breaks his "shades" and continues to wear the horn-rimmed frames minus the lenses. Richard cultivates a distinctive manner of speech. Lonny gives himself a birthday party. And so on.

the unskilled laborer. His take-home pay during these weeks was well over a hundred dollars — "a lot of bread." But for Tally, who no longer had a family to support, bread was not enough.

"You know that boy came in last night? That Black Moozlem? That's what I ought to be doing. I ought to be in his place."

"What do you mean?"

"Dressed nice, going to [night] school, got a good job."

"He's no better off than you, Tally. You make more than he does."

"It's not the money. [Pause] It's position, I guess. He's got position. When he finish school he gonna be a supervisor. People respect him. . . . Thinking about people with position and education gives me a feeling right here [pressing his fingers into the pit of his stomach]."

"You're educated, too. You have a skill, a trade. You're a cement finisher. You can make a building, pour a sidewalk."

"That's different. Look, can anybody do what you're doing? Can anybody just come up and do your job? Well, in one week I can teach you cement finishing. You won't be as good as me 'cause you won't have the experience but you'll be a cement finisher. That's what I mean. Anybody can do what I'm doing and that's what gives me this feeling. [Long pause] Suppose I like this girl. I go over to her house and I meet her father. He starts talking about what he done today. He talks about operating on somebody and sewing them up and about surgery. I know he's a doctor 'cause of the way he talks. Then she starts talking about what she did. Maybe she's a boss or a supervisor. Maybe she's a lawyer and her father says to me, 'And what do you do, Mr. Jackson?' [Pause] You remember at the court-house, Lonny's trial? You and the lawyer was talking in the hall? You remember? I just stood there listening. I didn't say a word. You know why? 'Cause I didn't even know what you was talking about. That's happened to me a lot."

"Hell, you're nothing special. That happens to everybody. Nobody knows everything. One man is a doctor, so he talks about surgery. Another man is a teacher, so he talks about books. But doctors and teachers don't know anything about concrete. You're a cement finisher and that's your specialty."

"Maybe so, but when was the last time you saw anybody standing around talking about concrete?"

The streetcorner man wants to be a person in his own right, to be noticed, to be taken account of, but in this respect, as well as in meeting his money needs, his job fails him. The job and the man are even. The job fails the man and the man fails the job.

Furthermore, the man does not have any reasonable expectation that, however bad it is, his job will lead to better things. Menial jobs are not, by and large, the starting point of a track system which leads to even better jobs for those who are able and willing to do them. The busboy or dishwasher in a restaurant is not on a job track which, if negotiated skillfully, leads to chef or manager of the restaurant. The busboy or dishwasher who works hard becomes, simply, a hard-working busboy or dishwasher. Neither hard work nor perseverance can conceivably carry the janitor to a sit-down job in the office building he cleans up. And it is the apprentice who becomes the journeyman electrician, plumber, steam fitter or bricklayer, not the common unskilled Negro laborer.

Thus, the job is not a stepping stone to something better. It is a dead end. It promises to deliver no more tomorrow, next month or next year than it does today.

Delivering little, and promising no more, the job is "no big thing." The man appears to treat the job in a cavalier fashion, working and not working as the spirit moves him, as if all that matters is the immediate satisfaction of his present appetites, the surrender to present moods, and the indulgence of whims with no thought for the cost, the consequences, the future. To the middle-class observer, this behavior reflects a "present-time orientation" — an "inability to defer gratification." It is this "present-time" orientation — as against the "future orientation" of the middle-class person — that "explains" to the outsider why Leroy chooses to spend the day at the Carry-out rather than report to work; why Richard, who was paid Friday, was drunk Saturday and Sunday and penniless Monday; why Sweets quit his job today because the boss looked at him "funny" yesterday.

But from the inside looking out, what appears as a "present-time" orientation to the outside observer is, to the man experiencing it, as much a future orientation as that of his middle-class counterpart. The difference between the two men lies not so much in their different orientations to time as in their different orientations to future time or, more specifically, to their different futures.[5]

The future orientation of the middle-class person presumes, among other things, a surplus of resources to be invested in the future and a belief that the future will be sufficiently stable both to justify his investment (money in a bank, time and effort in a job, investment of himself in marriage and family, etc.) and to permit the consumption of his investment at a time, place and manner of his own choosing and to his greater satisfaction. But the streetcorner man lives in a sea of want. He does not, as a rule, have a surplus of resources, either economic or psychological. Gratification of hunger and the desire for simple creature comforts cannot be long deferred. Neither can support for one's flagging self-esteem.

---

[5] This sentence is a paraphrase of a statement made by Marvin Cline at a 1965 colloquium at the Mental Health Study Center, National Institute of Mental Health.

Living on the edge of both economic and psychological subsistence, the streetcorner man is obliged to expend all his resources on maintaining himself from moment to moment.

As for the future, the young streetcorner man has a fairly good picture of it. In Richard or Sea Cat or Arthur he can see himself in his middle twenties; he can look at Tally to see himself at thirty, at Wee Tom to see himself in his middle thirties, and at Budder and Stanton to see himself in his forties. It is a future in which everything is uncertain except the ultimate destruction of his hopes and the eventual realization of his fears. The most he can reasonably look forward to is that these things do not come too soon. Thus, when Richard squanders a week's pay in two days it is not because, like an animal or a child, he is "present-time oriented," unaware of or unconcerned with his future. He does so precisely because he is aware of the future and the hopelessness of it all.

Sometimes this kind of response appears as a conscious, explicit choice. Richard had had a violent argument with his wife. He said he was going to leave her and the children, that he had had enough of everything and could not take any more, and he chased her out of the house. His chest still heaving, he leaned back against the wall in the hallway of his basement apartment.

> "I've been scuffling for five years," he said. "I've been scuffling for five years from morning till night. And my kids still don't have anything, my wife don't have anything, and I don't have anything.
>
> "There," he said, gesturing down the hall to a bed, a sofa, a couple of chairs and a television set, all shabby, some broken. "There's everything I have and I'm having trouble holding onto that."
>
> Leroy came in, presumably to petition Richard on behalf of Richard's wife, who was sitting outside on the steps, afraid to come in. Leroy started to say something but Richard cut him short.
>
> "Look, Leroy, don't give me any of that action. You and me are entirely different people. Maybe I look like a boy and maybe I act like a boy sometimes but I got a man's mind. You and me don't want the same things out of life. Maybe some of the same, but you don't care how long you have to wait for yours and I — want — mine — right — now." [6]

---

[6] This was no simple rationalization for irresponsibility. Richard had indeed "been scuffling for five years" trying to keep his family going. Until shortly after this episode, Richard was known and respected as one of the hardest-working men on the street. Richard had said, only a couple of months earlier, "I figure you got to get out there and try. You got to try before you can get anything." His wife Shirley confirmed that he had always tried. "If things get tough, with me I'll get all worried. But Richard get worried, he don't want me to see him worried. . . . He *will* get out there. He's shoveled snow, picked beans, and he's done some of everything. . . .

Thus, apparent present-time concerns with consumption and indulgences — material and emotional — reflect a future-time orientation. "I want mine right now" is ultimately a cry of despair, a direct response to the future as he sees it.[7]

In many instances, it is precisely the streetcorner man's orientation to the future — but to a future loaded with "trouble" — which not only leads to a greater emphasis on present concerns ("I want mine right now") but also contributes importantly to the instability of employment, family and friend relationships, and to the general transient quality of daily life.

Let me give some concrete examples. One day, after Tally had gotten paid, he gave me four twenty-dollar bills and asked me to keep them for him. Three days later he asked me for the money. I returned it and asked why he did not put his money in a bank. He said that the banks close at two o'clock. I argued that there were four or more banks within a two-block radius of where he was working at the time and that he could easily get to any one of them on his lunch hour. "No, man," he said, "You don't understand. They close at two o'clock and they closed Saturday and Sunday. Suppose I get into trouble and I got to make it [leave]. Me get out of town, and everything I got in the world layin' up in that bank? No good! No good!"

In another instance, Leroy and his girl friend were discussing "trouble." Leroy was trying to decide how best to go about getting his hands on some "long green" (a lot of money), and his girl friend cautioned him about "trouble." Leroy sneered at this, saying he had had "trouble" all his life and wasn't afraid of a little more. "Anyway," he said, "I'm famous for leaving town."

He's not ashamed to get out there and get us something to eat." At the time of the episode reported above, Leroy was just starting marriage and raising a family. He and Richard were not, as Richard thought, "entirely different people." Leroy had just not learned, by personal experience over time, what Richard had learned. But within two years Leroy's marriage had broken up and he was talking and acting like Richard. "He just let go completely," said one of the men on the street.

[7] There is no mystically intrinsic connection between "present-time" orientation and lower-class persons. Whenever people of whatever class have been uncertain, skeptical or downright pessimistic about the future, "I want mine right now" has been one of the characteristic responses, although it is usually couched in more delicate terms: e.g., Omar Khayyam's "Take the cash and let the credit go," or Horace's *"Carpe diem."* In wartime, especially, all classes tend to slough off conventional restraints on sexual and other behavior (i.e., become less able or less willing to defer gratification). And when inflation threatens, darkening the fiscal future, persons who formerly husbanded their resources with commendable restraint almost stampede one another rushing to spend their money. Similarly, it seems that future-time orientation tends to collapse toward the present when persons are in pain or under stress. The point here is that, the label notwithstanding (what passes for) present-time orientation appears to be a situation-specific phenomenon rather than a part of the standard psychic equipment of Cognitive Lower Class Man.

Thus, the constant awareness of a future loaded with "trouble" results in a constant readiness to leave, "make it," to "get out of town,"
and discourages the man from sinking roots into the world he lives in.
Just as it discourages him from putting money in the bank, so it discourages him from committing himself to a job, especially one whose
payoff lies in the promise of future rewards rather than in the present.
In the same way, it discourages him from deep and lasting commitments to family and friends or to any other persons, places or things,
since such commitments could hold him hostage, limiting his freedom of
movement and thereby compromising his security which lies in that
freedom.

What lies behind the response to the driver of the pickup truck, then,
is a complex combination of attitudes and assessments. The streetcorner
man is under continuous assault by his job experiences and job fears. His
experiences and fears feed on one another. The kind of job he can get —
and frequently only after fighting for it, if then — steadily confirms his
fears, depresses his self-confidence and self-esteem until finally, terrified
of an opportunity even if one presents itself, he stands defeated by his
experiences, his belief in his own self-worth destroyed and his fears a
confirmed reality.

Poverty and Culture

Herbert J. Gans

The argument between those who think that poverty can best be
eliminated by providing jobs and other resources and those who feel that
cultural obstacles and psychological deficiencies must be overcome as
well is ultimately an argument about social change, about the psychological readiness of people to respond to change, and about the role of culture in change. The advocates of resources are not concerned explicitly
with culture, but they do make a cultural assumption: whatever the culture of the poor, it will not interfere in people's adaptation to better opportunities for obtaining economic resources. They take a *situational*
view of social change and of personality: that people respond to the situ-

Edited version of chapter 8 from *On Understanding Poverty* edited by Daniel P.
Moynihan, with the assistance of Corinne S. Schelling, © 1968, 1969 by the American Academy of Arts and Sciences, Basic Books, Inc., Publishers, New York.

ations — and opportunities — available to them and change their behavior accordingly. Those who call attention to cultural (and psychological) obstacles, however, are taking a *cultural* view of social change, which suggests that people react to change in terms of prior values and behavior patterns and adopt only those changes which are congruent with their culture.[1]

Since academicians have been caught up in the debate over the deservingness and undeservingness of the poor as much as the rest of American society, the situational and cultural views of change have frequently been described as polar opposites, and theorists have battled over the data to find support for one pole or the other. Clearly, the truth lies somewhere between, but at present, neither the data nor the conceptual framework to find that truth is as yet available.

The situational view is obviously too simple; people are not automatons who respond either in the same way or with the same speed to a common stimulus. Despite a middle-class inclination on the part of researchers to view the poor as homogeneous, all available studies indicate that there is as much variety among them as among the affluent. Some have been poor for generations; others are poor only periodically. Some are downwardly mobile; others are upwardly mobile. Many share middle-class values, others embrace working-class values; some have become so used to the defense mechanisms they have learned for coping with deprivation that they have difficulty in adapting to new opportunities, and some are beset by physical or emotional illness, poverty having created pathologies that now block the ability to adapt to nonpathological situations.[2] Sad to say, there is as yet no research to show quantitatively what proportion of poor people fit into such categories.

The Shortcomings of the Cultural View of Change

The cultural view of social and personal change is also deficient. First, it uses an overly behavioral definition of culture which ignores the existence of values that conflict with behavior; and second, it sees culture as a holistic system whose parts are intricately related, so that any individual element of a culture cannot be changed without system-wide reverberations.

The behavioral definition identifies culture in terms of how people act; it views values as *behavioral norms* which are metaphysical and

---

[1] See, for example, Louis Kriesberg, "The Relationship between Socio-Economic Rank and Behavior," *Social Problems*, X (Spring 1963), pp. 334–353.

[2] Hylan Lewis, "Culture, Class, and the Behavior of Low Income Families," *Culture, Class, and Poverty* (Washington: Cross-Tell, 1967).

moral guidelines to behavior and are deduced from behavior. For example, Walter Miller sees values as "focal concerns" which stem from, express, and ultimately maintain behavior. As he puts it, "The concept 'focal concern' . . . reflects actual behavior, whereas 'value' tends to wash out intracultural differences since it is colored by notions of the 'official' ideal." [3] This definition, useful as it is, pays little or no attention to *aspirations*, values which express the desire for alternative forms of behavior.

The behavioral conception of culture can be traced to anthropological traditions and to the latent political agenda of anthropological researchers. The field worker who studied a strange culture began by gathering artifacts, and as anthropology matured, he also collected behavior patterns. The cultural relativist, who wanted to defend these cultures against involuntary change, sought to show that the behavior patterns were functional to the survival of the group. How people felt about their behavior did not interest him unduly. He noted that infanticide was functional for the survival of a hunting tribe, but he did not devote much attention to how people felt about the desirability of infanticide — or about less deadly patterns of culture.

His approach may have been valid at its time; it was in part a reaction against nineteenth-century idealism which identified culture solely with aspirations and was not interested in how people really behaved. The behavioral view of culture was also a useful tool to fight the advocates of colonialism, who viewed all cultures in terms of the aspirations of their own Western society and were ready to alter any culture they encountered to achieve their own goals. Moreover, the approach was perhaps empirically valid; it may have fitted the preliterate group whose culture had developed around a limited and homogeneous economy and ecology. Tribes who devoted themselves exclusively to agriculture or hunting developed cultures which fitted such single-minded economies. Such cultures gave their people little if any choice; they bred fatalists who did not know that alternative ways of behaving were possible, usually because they were not possible, and this left no room for diverging aspirations.

But such a definition of culture is not applicable to contemporary Western society. Many poor people in our society are also fatalists, not because they are unable to conceive of alternative conditions, but because they have been frustrated in the realization of alternatives. Unlike preliterate people — or at least the classic version of the ideal type preliterate — they are unhappy with their state; they have aspirations which

---

[3] Walter Miller, "Lower Class Culture as a Generating Milieu of Gang Delinquency," *Journal of Social Issues*, XIV (1958), pp. 5–19.

diverge from the focal concerns underlying their behavior. Of course, they can justify, to themselves and to others, the behavioral choices they make and must make, and Walter Miller's insightful analysis of focal concerns indicates clearly how they "support and maintain the basic features of the lower class way of life." [4] Even so, people who are forced to create values and justifications for what they must do may also be well aware of alternatives which they would prefer under different conditions.

For generations, researchers made no distinction between norms and aspirations, and most research emphasis was placed on the former. Lay observers and practitioners were only willing to judge; they saw the behavioral norms among the poor which diverged from their own and bade the poor behave like middle-class people. In reaction, social scientists who had done empirical work among the poor defended their behavioral norms as adaptations to their existential situation or as an independent culture, but paid little attention to aspirations diverging from these norms. Walter Miller has taken perhaps the most extreme position; he implies that lower-class aspirations as well as norms are different from those of the rest of society, and if poor people express middle-class values, they do so only because they are expected to endorse the "official ideals." [5] Their real aspirations, he seems to suggest, are those of their own lower-class culture.

Recent research has begun, however, to distinguish between aspirations and behavioral norms. Starting with a debate among anthropologists over whether Caribbean lower-class couples in "living" or consensual relationships preferred formal marriage, several studies have shown that poor people share many of the aspirations of the affluent society, but also develop norms which justify their actual behavior. Rodman conceptualizes the divergence between aspirations and norms as lower-class value stretch; Rainwater argues that poor people share the aspirations of the larger society, which he calls conventional norms, but knowing that they cannot live up to them, develop other norms which fit the existential conditions to which they must adapt. [6]

At present, there are only enough data to affirm the existence of a divergence between aspirations and behavioral norms and to insist on more research, particularly in areas of life other than marriage. In a heterogeneous or pluralistic society, such divergence is almost built in; where a variety of cultures or subculture coexist, aspirations diffuse

---

[4] *Ibid.*, p. 19
[5] *Ibid.*, p. 7.
[6] Hyman Rodman, "The Lower Class Value Stretch," *Social Forces*, XLII (December 1963), pp. 205–215; Lee Rainwater, *Neutralizing the Disinherited: Some Psychological Aspects of Understanding the Poor*, Pruitt-Igoe Occasional Paper No. 30, mimeographed (St. Louis: Washington University, June 1967).

freely. Among affluent people, the gap between aspirations and behavioral norms is probably narrower than among poor people; the former
can more often achieve what they want. Even if they cannot satisfy occupational aspirations, they are able to satisfy other aspirations; for instance, for family life. The poor have fewer options. Lacking the income
and the economic security to achieve their aspirations, they must develop
diverging behavioral norms in almost all areas of life. Nevertheless, they
still retain aspirations, and many are those of the affluent society.

Consequently, research on the culture of the poor must include both
behavioral norms and aspirations. The norms must be studied because
they indicate how people react to their present existence, but limiting the
analysis to them can lead to the assumption that behavior would remain
the same under different conditions, when there is no reliable evidence,
pro or con, to justify such an assumption today. As Hylan Lewis puts it,
"It is important not to confuse basic life chances and actual behavior
with basic cultural values and preferences." [7] Cultural analysis must also
look at aspirations, determining their content, the intensity with which
they are held, and, above all, whether they would be translated into behavioral norms if economic conditions made it possible.

The second deficiency of the cultural view of change is the conception of culture as holistic and systemic. When a behavior pattern is identified as part of a larger and interrelated cultural system, and when the
causes of that pattern are ascribed to "the culture," there is a tendency to
see the behavior pattern and its supporting norms as resistant to change
and as persisting simply because they are cultural, although there is no
real evidence that culture is as unchanging as assumed. This conception
of culture is also ahistorical, for it ignores the origin of behavior patterns
and norms. As a result, too little attention is paid to the conditions that
bring a behavior pattern into being or to the conditions that may alter it.
Culture becomes its own cause, and change is possible only if the culture
as a whole is somehow changed. . . .

The systemic concept of culture is however inappropriate. Modern
societies are pluralist; whether developed or developing, they consist of a
diverse set of cultures living side by side, and researchers studying them
have had to develop such terms as subculture, class culture, and contra-
culture to describe the diversity. Holistic functionalism is irrelevant too;
no culture is sufficiently integrated so that its parts can be described as
elements in a system. In modern sociology and anthropology, functionalism can survive only by identifying dysfunctions as well as functions and
by showing that cultural patterns which are functional for one group may
well be dysfunctional for another.

---

[7] Lewis, *op. cit.*, pp. 38–39.

An ahistorical conception of culture is equally inapplicable to modern societies. In such societies, some behavior patterns are persistent, but others are not; they change when economic and other conditions change, although we do not yet know which patterns are persistent, and for how long, and which are not. More important, culture is a response to economic and other conditions; it is itself situational in origin and changes as situations change. Behavior patterns, norms, and aspirations develop as responses to situations to which people must adapt, and culture originates out of such responses. Changes in economic and social opportunities give rise to new behavioral solutions, which then become recurring patterns, are later complemented by norms which justify them, and are eventually overthrown by new existential conditions. Some behavioral norms are more persistent than others, but over the long run, all the norms and aspirations by which people live are nonpersistent; they rise and fall with changes in situations.

These observations are not intended to question the validity of the concept of culture, for not all behavior is a response to a present situation, and not all — and perhaps not even most — behavior patterns change immediately with a change in situation. A new situation will initially be met with available norms; only when these norms turn out to be inapplicable or damaging will people change: first their behavior, and then the norms upholding that behavior. Nevertheless, the lag between a change in existential conditions and the change of norms does not make the norms immutable.

An Alternative Conception of Culture

People's behavior is thus a mixture of situational responses and cultural patterns, that is, behavioral norms and aspirations. Some situational responses are strictly *ad hoc* reactions to a current situation; they exist because of that situation and will disappear if it changes or disappears. Other situational responses are internalized and become behavior norms which are an intrinsic part of the person and of the groups in which he moves and are thus less subject to change with changes in situation. The intensity of internalization varies; at one extreme, there are norms which are not much deeper than lip service; at the other, there are norms which are built into the basic personality structure, and a generation or more of living in a new situation may not dislodge them. They become culture, and people may adhere to them even if they are no longer appropriate, paying all kinds of economic and emotional costs to maintain them.

The southern white reaction to racial integration offers many examples of such intensely internalized norms, although it also offers examples of norms which were thought to be persistent, but crumbled as soon as the civil-rights movement or the federal government applied pressure to eliminate them. Indeed, there are probably many norms which can be toppled by a threat to exert power or to withdraw rewards; the many cultural compromises which first- and second-generation ethnics make to retain the affection of their children is a good example. Conversely, some norms are maintained simply because they have become political symbols, and people are unwilling to give them up because this would be interpreted as a loss of power. Thus, acculturated ethnic groups often preserve ethnic cultural traits for public display to maintain their ethnically based political influence. The role of power in culture, culture change, and acculturation deserves much more attention than it has so far received.

Not all behavioral norms are necessarily conservative; some may make people especially adaptable to change and may even encourage change. Despite what has been written about the ravages of slavery on the southern Negro, he went to work readily during World War II when jobs were plentiful. Similarly, the southern businessman operates with behavioral norms that make him readier to accept racial change than others; he cannot adhere with intensity to any beliefs that will cut into profit.

To sum up: I have argued that behavior results initially from an adaptation to the existential situation. Much of that behavior is no more than a situational response which exists only because of the situation, and it changes with a change in situation. Other behavior patterns become behavioral norms which are internalized and are then held in varying degrees of intensity and persistence. If they persist with a change in situation, they may then be considered patterns of *behavioral culture*, and such norms may become causes of behavior. Other norms can encourage change. In addition, adaptation to a situation is affected by aspirations, which also exist in various degrees of intensity and persistence and forms an *aspirational culture*. Culture, then, is that mix of behavioral norms and aspirations that causes behavior, or maintains present behavior, or encourages future behavior independently of situational incentives and restraints.

Culture and Poverty

This view of culture has important implications for studying the poor. It rejects a concept that emphasizes tradition and obstacles to change and sees norms and aspirations within a milieu of situations against which the norms and aspirations are constantly tested. Moreover, it enables the researcher to analyze, or at least to estimate, what happens to norms under alternative situations and thus to guess at how poor people would adapt to new opportunities.

With such a perspective, one can — and must — ask constantly: to what situation, to what set of opportunities and restraints, do the present behavioral norms and aspirations respond and how intensely are they held; how much are they internalized, if at all, and to what extent would they persist or change if the significant opportunities and restraints underwent change? To put it another way, if culture is learned, one must ask how quickly and easily various behavioral norms could be unlearned, once the existential situation from which they sprang had changed.

Moreover, supposing this change took place, and opportunities — for decent jobs and incomes, for example — were made available to poor people, what behavioral norms, if any, are so deeply internalized that they interfere, say with taking a good job? Answers to this question lead directly to policy considerations. One alternative is to seek a change in norms; another, to design the job in such a fashion that it can be accepted without requiring an immediate change in strongly persisting norms. Since such norms are not easily changed, it may be more desirable to tailor the opportunity to fit the norm, rather than the other way around. For example, if the inability to plan, often ascribed to the poor, is actually a persisting behavioral norm that will interfere in their being employable, rather than just an *ad hoc* response to an uncertain future, it would be wrong to expect people to learn to plan at once, just because jobs are now available. The better solution would be to fit the jobs to this inability and to make sure that the adults, once having some degree of economic security, will learn to plan or will be able to teach their children how to do so.

The prime issue in the area of culture and poverty, then, is to discover how soon poor people will change their behavior, given new opportunities, and what restraints or obstacles, good or bad, come from that reaction to past situations we call culture. To put it another way, the primary problem is to determine what opportunities have to be created to eliminate poverty, how poor people can be encouraged to adapt to those opportunities that conflict with persistent cultural patterns, and how they can retain the persisting patterns which do not conflict with other aspirations.

Because of the considerable divergence between behavioral norms and aspirations, it is clearly impossible to think of a holistic lower-class culture. It is perhaps possible to describe a *behavioral lower-class culture,* consisting of the behavioral norms with which people adapt to being poor and lower-class. There is, however, no *aspirational lower-class culture,* for much evidence suggests that poor people's aspirations are similar to those of more affluent Americans. My hypothesis is that many and perhaps most poor people share the aspirations of the working class; others, those of the white-collar lower-middle class; and yet others, those of the

professional and managerial upper-middle class, although most poor people probably aspire to the behavioral norms of these groups — to the ways
they are living now — rather than to their aspirations.

Under present conditions the aspirations which poor people hold may
not be fulfilled, but this does not invalidate them, for their existence, and
the intensity with which they are held, can be tested only when economic
and other conditions are favorable to their realization. If and when poor
people obtain the resources for which they are clamoring, much of the
behavioral lower-class culture will disappear. Only those poor people
who cannot accept alternative opportunities because they cannot give up
their present behavioral norms can be considered adherents to a lower-
class culture.

In short, such conceptions of lower-class culture as Walter Miller's
describe only part of the total reality. If Miller's lower-class culture were
really an independent culture with its own set of aspirations, its practitioners would presumably be satisfied with their way of life. If they are
not satisfied, however, if they only adapt to necessity but want something different, then ascribing their adaptation to a lower-class culture is
inaccurate. It is also politically undesirable, for the judgment that behavior is cultural lends itself to an argument against change. But if data
are not available for that judgment, the researcher indulges in conceptual
conservatism.

Miller does not indicate specifically whether the adolescents he
studied adhered to both a behavioral and an aspirational lower-class culture. He suggests that "the motivation of 'delinquent' behavior engaged
in by members of lower-class corner groups involves a *positive* effort to
achieve states, conditions or qualities valued within the actor's most significant cultural milieu," [8] that is, that the adolescents valued the behavior norms for which they were rewarded by their reference groups.

Perhaps the Roxbury adolescents [whom Miller studied] did not
share the aspirations of the larger society; they were, after all, delin-
quents, youngsters who had been caught in an illegal act and might be
cynical about such aspirations. Moreover, the hippies and other "youth
cultures" should remind us that adolescents do not always endorse the
aspirations of an adult society. The crucial question, then, is how did
lower-class adults in Roxbury feel? I would suspect that they were less
positive about their youngsters' delinquent activities, partly because they
are more sensitive to what Miller calls "official ideals," but partly because
they do adhere to a nonlower-class aspirational culture.

My definition of culture also suggests a somewhat different interpretation of a culture of poverty than Oscar Lewis' concept. If culture is
viewed as a causal factor, and particularly as those norms and aspirations

---

[8] Miller, *op. cit.*, p. 18 (italics added).

which resist change, then a culture of poverty would consist of those specifically cultural or nonsituational factors which help to keep people poor, especially when alternative opportunities beckon.

Lewis' concept of the culture of poverty puts more emphasis on the behavior patterns and feelings that result from lack of opportunity and the inability to achieve aspirations. According to Lewis, "The culture of poverty is both an adaptation and a reaction of the poor to their marginal position in a class-stratified, highly individuated society. It represents an effort to cope with feelings of hopelessness and despair which develop from the realization of the improbability of achieving success in terms of the values and goals of the larger society." [9] His conception thus stresses the defense mechanisms by which people cope with deprivation, frustration, and alienation, rather than with poverty alone; it is closer to a culture of alienation than to a culture of poverty. In fact, Lewis distinguishes between poor people with and without a culture of poverty, and in indicating that people can be poor without feeling hopeless, he seems to suggest that the culture of poverty is partly responsible for feelings of hopelessness. Moreover, if poor people can overcome their malaise and resort to political action — or if they live in a socialist society like Cuba, in which they are presumably considered part of the society — they give up the culture of poverty. "When the poor become class-conscious or active members of trade-union organizations, or when they adopt an internationalist outlook on the world, they are no longer part of the culture of poverty although they may still be desperately poor." [10]

Lewis' distinction between poverty and the culture of poverty is important, for it aims to separate different kinds of poverty and adaptations to poverty. Lewis' emphasis on alienation suggests, however, that his concept pertains more to belonging to an underclass than to being poor, while his identification of the culture of poverty with class-stratified, highly individuated societies suggests that for him the culture is an effect rather than a cause of membership in an underclass. The various traits of the culture of poverty which he describes are partly social psychological consequences, partly situational responses, and partly behavioral norms associated with underclass membership, but the major causal factor is the class-stratified, highly individuated society. From a causal perspective, Lewis' concept is thus less concerned with culture than with the situational factors that bring about culture; it is less a culture of poverty than a sociology of the underclass.

Whether or not the families who tell their life histories in Lewis' books adhere to a culture which is a direct or indirect cause of their remaining in poverty is hard to say, for one would have to know how they

---

[9] Oscar Lewis, *La Vida* (New York: Random House, 1966), p. xliv.
[10] *Ibid.*, p. xlviii.

would react under better economic conditions. Such data are almost impossible to gather, so that it is difficult to tell how the Sanchez and Rios families might respond, for example, if Mexico and Puerto Rico offered the men a steady supply of decent and secure jobs. Since almost all the members of the families aspire to something better, my hunch is that their behavioral and aspirational cultures would change under improved circumstances; their culture is probably not a cause of their poverty.

As I use the term *culture of poverty*, then, it would apply to people who have internalized behavioral norms that cause or perpetuate poverty and who lack aspirations for a better way of life; particularly people whose societies have not let them know change is possible: the peasants and urbanites who have so far been left out of the revolution of rising expectations. The only virtue of this definition is its emphasis on culture as a causal factor, thus enabling the policy-oriented researcher to separate the situational and cultural processes responsible for poverty.

If the culture of poverty is defined as those cultural patterns which keep people poor, it would be necessary to include in the term also the persisting cultural patterns among the affluent which, deliberately or not, keep their fellow citizens poor. When the concept of a culture of poverty is applied only to the poor, the onus for change falls too much on them, when, in reality, the prime obstacles to the elimination of poverty lie in an economic, political, and social structure that operates to protect and increase the wealth of the already affluent.

Culture and Class

My definition of culture also has implications for the cultural aspects of social stratification. Class may be defined sociologically to describe how people stand in the socioeconomic hierarchy with respect to occupation, income, education, and other variables having to do with the resources they have obtained, but it is often also defined culturally, in terms of their class-bound ways of life, that is, as class culture. Generally speaking, descriptions of class cultures pay little attention to the distinction between behavioral and aspirational culture, on the one hand, and situational responses, on the other hand. Descriptions which determine people's class position on the basis of situational responses, but ascribe them to culture, make *ad hoc* behavior seem permanent and may assign people to class positions on a long-term basis by data which describe their short-run response to a situation. For example, if poor people's inability to plan is a situational response, rather than a behavioral norm, it could not be used as a criterion of lower-class culture, although it might be considered a pattern associated with lower-class position. Class, like culture, should be determined on the basis of norms which restrain or encourage people in adapting to new conditions.

Class-cultural descriptions must therefore focus on behavioral norms, on the intensity with which they are held, and on people's ability to adapt to new situations. Moreover, if culture is defined to include aspirations, assignments of class position would have to take people's aspirations into account. Since these aspirations may be for working-class, lower-middle-class, or upper-middle-class ways of life, it becomes difficult to assign poor people to a single lower-class culture. In addition, if the previous criterion of ability to adapt is also included, those who can adapt to change would have to be classified further on the basis of whether their aspirations are for one or another of the "higher" classes. The resulting classification would be quite complex and would indicate more accurately the diversity within the poverty-stricken population than current concepts of lower-class culture. More important, the number who are, culturally speaking, permanently and inevitably lower-class is much smaller than sometimes imagined, for that number would include only those whose aspirations are lower-class and whose behavioral culture prevents easy adaptation to change.

This approach would, of course, limit the use of current typologies of class. Dichotomies such as working class and lower class, or upper-lower and lower-lower class, can be used to describe the existential condition in which people find themselves and the situational responses they make, that is, as *sociological* typologies of class, but they cannot be used as *cultural* typologies, for people who share the same existential situation may respond with different behavioral norms and aspirations. Combining sociological and cultural criteria into a single holistic category not only underestimates the diversity of people but also implies that they are satisfied with or resigned to being lower-class, so that class culture is used to explain why poor people remain lower-class when in reality their being poor and members of an underclass is responsible. No doubt cultural patterns do play a causal role in class culture, but they must be determined empirically. Any other approach would reify the concept of class culture and give it a conservative political bias which suggests the poor are happy with or resigned to their lot.

Moreover, dichotomies such as working and lower class are in many ways only a sociological version of the distinction between the deserving and undeserving poor, even if their formulators had no such invidious distinction in mind. These labels are also too formalistic; they only chart the social and economic distances between people on a hierarchical scale. The terms lower and middle class are positional; they do not describe people's behavioral or aspirational culture. In fact, they really refer only to the economic, behavioral, and status deviation of poor people from the middle classes, for most current models of the class system are based on the amount of deviation from middle-class norms and aspirations.

Ideally, definitions and labels of class should include substantive ele-

ments which refer to the major themes of each class culture and indicate the real differences of culture, if any, between the classes. If the data
for a thematic cultural analysis were available, we might discover that
there is no distinctive lower-class culture; there are only tendencies
toward distinctiveness, many of which are but functions of the situations
with which people must cope and might disappear altogether once situations were changed.

Sociologists cannot ignore present situations, however, even if they
are undesirable, and despite my reservations about the concepts of class
and culture, ultimately I would agree with Lee Rainwater when he
writes: "If, then, we take subculture to refer to a distinctive pattern of
existential and evaluative elements, a pattern distinctive to a particular
group in a larger collectivity and consequential for the way their behavior
differs from that of others in the collectivity, it seems to me that there is
no doubt that the concept of lower class subculture is useful." [11] I would
add only that I am skeptical of the existence of lower-class evaluative
elements, or what I have called aspirational culture.

An Outline of Basic Research and Policy Questions

The remainder of this paper attempts to apply the frame of reference
I have outlined by suggesting some of the questions that ought to be
asked by researchers and by indicating the methodological implications
of the approach.

Studies of the poor should give up the notion of culture as largely
behavioral, with little concern about divergent aspirations; as holistic;
and as persistent causal factor in behavior. Instead, insofar as poverty
research should focus on the poor at all — a point I shall consider below
— it should deal with behavior patterns, norms, and aspirations on an
individual basis, relate them to their situational origin, and determine
how much the behavioral norms related to poverty would persist under
changing situations. Whether or not there is a persisting and holistic
culture (or a set of subcultures) among the poor should be an empirical
question.

In studying behavioral norms and aspirations among the poor, the
following questions are most important: Does a given behavioral pattern
block a potential escape from poverty, and if so, how? Conversely, are
there aspirations related to this behavioral pattern, and do they diverge?

---

[11] Lee Rainwater, "The Problem of Lower-Class Culture and Poverty-War Strategy," in Daniel P. Moynihan (ed.), *On Understanding Poverty* (New York: Basic
Books, 1969), p. 241.

If so, are they held intensively enough to provide the motivation for an escape from poverty when economic and other opportunities are available? Are there behavioral norms which encourage this escape?

In analyzing the behavior patterns that do block the escape from poverty, one must look for the social and cultural sources of that behavior. Is the behavior a situational response that would change readily with a change in situation, or is it internalized? If it is internalized, how does it become internalized (and at what age), what agents and institutions encourage the internalization, and how intensive is it? How long would a given behavioral norm persist if opportunities changed, and what are the forces that encourage its persistence?

Similar questions must be asked about aspirations: What are their sources, how are they internalized, and how intensely are they held? How responsive are they to changes in situation, and can they enable people to give up poverty-related behavior once economic opportunities are available? And what kinds of noneconomic helping agents and institutions are needed to aid poor people in implementing their aspirations?

Equally important questions must be addressed to the affluent members of society. Indeed, if the prime purpose of research is the elimination of poverty, studies of the poor are not the first order of business; they are much less important than studies of the economy which relegate many people to underemployment and unemployment and nonmembers of the labor force to welfare dependency. They are also less important than studies of the political, social, and cultural factors that enable and encourage the affluent population to permit the existence of a poverty-stricken underclass. In the final analysis, poverty exists because it has many positive functions for the affluent society; for example, by providing a labor force to do the "dirty" work of that society.

Consequently, assuming that lower-class culture is less pervasive than has been thought and that poor people are able and willing to change their behavior if economic opportunities are made available to them, one must ask what kinds of changes have to take place in the economic system, the power structure, the status order, and the behavioral norms and aspirations of the affluent members of society for them to permit the incorporation of the poor into that society? Which of the functions of poverty for the affluent population can be eliminated, which can be translated into functional alternatives that do not require the existence of poverty, and which functions absolutely require the existence of either a deprived or a despised class, or both?

In addition, one must ask questions about the affluent society's attitudes toward behavior associated with poverty. Many behavior patterns may be the result of poverty, but they do not necessarily block the escape from poverty. They do, however, violate working- and middle-class values

and thus irritate and even threaten working- and middle-class people. For
example, the drinking bouts and extramarital sexual adventures which
have been found prevalent among lower-class people may be correlated
with poverty, but they do not cause it and probably do not block the
escape from poverty.

They might persist if people had secure jobs and higher incomes, or
they might not, or they might take place in more private surroundings,
as they do in the middle class. But since they shock the middle class, one
must also ask which behavior patterns must be given up or hidden as
the price of being allowed to enter the affluent society. This question
must be asked of affluent people, but one would also have to determine
the impact on poor people of changing or hiding the behavior. In short,
one must ask: What changes are *really* required of the lower class, which
ones are absolutely essential to the escape from poverty and the move
into the larger society, and which are less important?

These rather abstract questions can perhaps be made more concrete by
applying them to a specific case: the set of behavioral norms around the
female-based or "broken" family. The first question, of course, is: Does
this family structure block the escape from poverty? Assuming that the
answer could be "Yes," how does it happen? Is it because a mother
with several children and without a husband or a permanently available
man cannot work? Or is the female-based family per se at fault? Does
it create boys who do poorly in school and on the job and girls who
perpetuate the family type when they reach adulthood? If so, is the
matriarchal dominance to blame (perhaps by "emasculating" boys) or is
it the absence of a father? Or just the absence of a male role-model?
If so, could surrogate models be provided through schools, settlement
houses, and other institutions? Or are there deeper, dynamic forces at
work which require the presence of a stable father figure? Or is the failure of the boys due to the mother's lack of income, that is, a result of
her being poor and lower-class? Or does their failure stem from the
feelings of dependency and apathy associated with being on welfare? Or
is their failure a result of lack of education among the mothers, which
makes it difficult for them to implement their aspirations for raising their
children to a better life? (But lack of income and education are not restricted to the female-based family.)

Next, what are the social, economic, political — and cultural — sources
and causes of the female-based family, and to what situations, past and
present, does this institutional array of behavioral norms respond? Moreover, how persistent are the norms that uphold this family type, and what
aspirations exist that would alter or eliminate it if conditions changed?
If the female-based family is an adaptive response to frequent and continuing male unemployment or underemployment, as I suspect it is, one
must then ask whether the family structure is a situational response which

would disappear once jobs were available. But if the norms that underlie this family have been internalized and would persist even with full employment, one would then need to ask: Where, when, and how are these norms internalized? Do the men themselves begin to lose hope and become so used to economic insecurity that they are unable to hold a good job if it becomes available? Do the women develop norms and even aspirations for independence, so that, doubting that men can function as husbands and breadwinners, they become unable to accept these men if they are employed?

Are such attitudes transmitted to the children of female-based families, and if so, by whom, with what intensity, and at what age? Do the boys learn from their mothers that men are unreliable, or do they conclude this from the male adults they see around them? At what age does such learning take place, and how deeply is it internalized? If children learn the norm of male unreliability during the first six years of their life, would they have difficulty in shedding their beliefs under more favorable economic conditions? If they learn it when they are somewhat older, perhaps six to nine, would they be less likely to internalize it? If they learn this norm from their mothers, is it more persistent than if they learn it later from their peers and the male adults they see on the street? And at what age does the boy begin to model himself on these male adults?

It may be that the entire set of norms underlying the female-based family are much less persistent than the questions in the previous paragraph assume. Whether or not they are persistent, however, one would have to go on to ask: Under what conditions is it possible for people, adults and children, to give up the norms of the female-based family? Would it follow quickly after full employment, or would adults who have become accustomed to economic insecurity and female-based families pass on these norms to their children even if they achieved economic security at some time in their lives? If so, the female-based family might persist for another generation. Or are there helping institutions which could aid parents and children to give up irrelevant norms and speed up the transition to the two-parent family? And if it were impossible to help adults to change, how about eighteen-year-olds, or thirteen-year-olds, or six-year-olds?

Moreover, what aspirations exist among the poor for a two-parent family? Do lower-class Negro women really "want" a two-parent family, and are their aspirations intense enough to overcome the behavioral norms that have developed to make them matriarchs?

In addition, one must also ask what functions the female-based family performs for the affluent members of society and what obstacles the latter might put in the way of eliminating this family type. How quickly could they overcome their belief that Negro family life is often characterized by instability, illegitimacy, and matriarchy? Would they permit public policies to eliminate male unemployment and to provide higher and more dignified income grants to those who cannot work? And most important, would they permit the changes in the structure of rewards and in the distribution of income, status, and power that such policies entail?

If such questions were asked about every phase of life among the poor, it would be possible to begin to determine which of the behavioral norms of poor people are causally associated with poverty. I suspect that the answers to such questions would show what Hylan Lewis found among the people he studied: "The behaviors of the bulk of the low income families appear as pragmatic adjustments to external and internal stresses and deprivations experienced in the quest for essentially common values." [12]

Structuring New Opportunities

If the major aim of research is to eliminate poverty, one would also have to ask questions about how to structure new economic and non-economic opportunities to enable poor people to accept them, so that the incentives created by these opportunities will overcome the restraints of persisting behavioral norms. Current experiments with providing job training and even jobs to the unemployed have encountered enough re-fusals to indicate quite clearly that giving unemployed men any kind of job training or any kind of job is not enough. Since unemployed youth do not have lower-class aspirations, but want the kinds of jobs that are considered decent, dignified, and status-bearing by working- and middle-class cultures, the new opportunities must be designed accordingly.

The first policy question is: What kinds of opportunities have highest priority, economic or noneconomic opportunities? Assuming that the first priority is for economic opportunity, what is most important for whom, a job or an income grant? And what types of jobs and income grants are most desirable? What type of job would actually be considered an opportunity by poor people, both unemployed and underemployed, and what type would be inferior to present methods of earning and income; for example, welfare payments, illicit employment provided by the num-bers racket, or various forms of male and female hustling?

This would require an analysis both of job aspirations and of persis-tent behavioral norms that interfere with holding a job. What elements of a decent job are most important to poor people: the wage or salary, the security of the job, physical working conditions, the social characteristics of the work situation, the relationship to the boss, the skills required, the opportunities for self-improvement and promotion, or the status of the job — and in what order of priority?

---

[12] Hylan Lewis, *op. cit.*, p. 38.

What behavioral norms function as incentives to holding a job? And what are the obstacles? Is it the lack of skills; the unwillingness to work every day, or an eight-hour day; the pressures to associate with the peer group; or the inability or unwillingness to adapt to the nonwork requirements of the job; for instance, in terms of dress, decorum, or submission to impersonal authority? What kinds of incentives, monetary and otherwise, can overcome these obstacles, and what kinds of training programs, job guarantees, and social groupings on the job would be necessary to "acculturate" people who have never or rarely held a full-time job in the society of workers?

Similarly, for those who cannot work, what kinds of income grants would provide the best means for a permanent escape from poverty for them and particularly their children? Is the amount of income alone important? If not, how important is the release from stigmatization and identification as poor that would be provided by a family allowance, rather than by welfare payments or a negative income-tax grant? What forms of payment will provide the least discouragement and the most encouragement to go to work among people who want to be in the labor force? Would across-the-board grants be more desirable than a set of categorical grants, such as family allowances, rent supplements, and Medicaid?

Also, what kinds of noneconomic opportunities are necessary or desirable? Would jobs and income grants replace the need for social case work, or would people be more likely to ask for help from social workers once they did not depend on them for welfare payments? And what helping milieu is most effective? Should services be provided in special institutions for the poor, or should the poor be given grants so that they can buy the same services purchased by affluent people? Would poor people go more often to a private physician whom they pay like everyone else, or would they be readier to visit a superior clinic or group practice which is set up specially for them? Which alternative would be most compatible with the behavioral norms and aspirations of different kinds of poor people — and what are the benefits and costs of grants to use private medical and other services, as compared to expenditures that would offer improved services expressly for the poor?

Finally, how long must special opportunities be made available before poor people can truly be on their own? How much security, economic and other, must be provided for how long in order for people to take the risk of grasping at new opportunities and to be able to give up present behavioral norms and associations?

Other questions must be asked of the affluent society; for example, of employers and employees who will be working alongside the newly employed poor. Yet other questions arise because many of the poor are non-white, and their poverty is a result of segregation. Eventually, questions

must also be asked of the voters, to estimate the political feasibility of
instituting the needed programs and to determine what program designs
have the greatest chance of political acceptance. In the last analysis, the
shape of an effective antipoverty program probably depends more on the
willingness of affluent voters to accept such a program than on the economic and cultural needs of the poor. . . .

Maximum Feasible Participation:
The Origins and Implications

Lillian B. Rubin

Recognizing the corrosive effects of poverty, men in all times have
sought to assess the causes, fix the blame, and mitigate the consequences.
The Economic Opportunity Act of 1964 (EOA) is part of recent American attempts to deal with this age-old problem. Since the passage of the
act, the section that calls for the development of Community Action Programs (CAP's) and requires that these programs be "developed, conducted, and administered with the *maximum feasible participation* of
residents of the areas and members of the groups served"[1] has burst
upon the public consciousness. Right-wing critics, both in and out of
Congress, have branded community action programs as nothing less than
a "blueprint for revolution." Mayors across the nation charged the federal
government with financing an attack on city hall and undermining local
influence and authority. Welfare agencies, responding to a threat to their
jurisdiction and claim to professional expertise, simply asserted that involving the poor is not feasible. In city after city, attempts to implement
community action programs met with a struggle over both the meaning
of the clause and the extent and character of "participation" by the poor.

Despite the tumult and the shouting, no one seemed to know the
origins, the legislative history, or the intent of the "maximum feasible
participation" clause. What streams of thought were then current in
American life that would have suggested such an approach? Was it the
result of a changed view of the poor and their capabilities? Was there an

Reprinted from *The Annals*, September 1969, pp. 14–29 by permission of the author
and the American Academy of Political and Social Science. Copyright © 1969 by
the American Academy of Political and Social Science.
[1] 78 *Statutes at Large*, vol. 508, sec. 202 (a); emphasis added.

awareness of the revolutionary implications to both the welfare and the political establishments in local communities, and ultimately to the nation as a whole? How was the notion of participation by the poor interpreted and implemented? These are some of the questions that guided this inquiry.

"Maximum Feasible Participation"

The Origins

From the President's "Message on Poverty" on March 16, 1964, wherein he commended the bill to the Congress, to its passage five months later, there was no public discussion of the participation clause. Although a great deal of debate centered on the general provisions of Title II, congressional committee hearings reveal that, with the exception of the statement by then Attorney General Robert F. Kennedy, there is no mention of the clause by any other government official in several thousand pages of testimony. Even after Kennedy's testimony stressing the importance of participation in treating a community's ailments, not one congressman questioned his meaning or intent. The congressional debates are equally devoid of discussion about "maximum feasible participation."

In retrospect, it is indeed curious that this most controversial aspect of the bill was so little heeded. In the years to follow congressional hearings and debate on EOA were preoccupied largely with the controversy that had erupted over the mandate that the poor must participate in Community Action Programs.

Immediately after his declaration of war on poverty, President Johnson asked Sargent Shriver to direct a task force to draft the legislation to be submitted to Congress. Many people gathered in the little antipoverty office, representing interests both in and out of government — representatives of the Departments of Health, Education, and Welfare, Defense, Labor, Agriculture, and Commerce; of the President's Committee on Juvenile Delinquency and Youth Crime; and legal, community relations, poverty, and welfare experts.[2] Among them there is little consensus about the origins of the command that the poor must participate in CAP.

The clause . . . relating to participation of the poor was inserted with virtually no discussion in the task force and none at all on

---

[2] Interestingly enough, according to Moynihan, there was not one Negro "involved in any significant way at any significant stage in planning the Economic Opportunity Act of 1964." See "The Professors and the Poor," 46 *Commentary* (August 1968), p. 23.

Capitol Hill. . . . I cannot say that I was aware of the implications
of the clause. It just seemed to me like an idea that nobody could
quarrel with.[3]

Its language was the result of countless hours of discussion among
a dozen or so key people.[4]

It emerged from an evening drafting session which included Daniel
P. Moynihan . . . , Harold Horowitz . . . , John Steadman . . . , and
myself. None of us is quite sure who first thought of the phrase.[5] The
phrase "maximum feasible participation" entered into our discussions
largely at the insistence of Dick Boone. . . . At one point after he
had used it several times, I said, "You've used that phrase four or
five times now." "Yes, I know," he replied. "How many more times
do I have to use it before it becomes part of the program?" "Oh, a
couple of times more," I told him. So he did, and it did become part
of the program.[6]

OEO officials even disagree on what would seem to be matters of
fact.

Our General Counsel assures me that, although *there is a positive
legislative history of the phrase and its related intentions,* the section
of the Act was adopted in its present form within the House and
Senate Labor Committees while in Executive Session. No written
record of their session was kept.[7]

There is no explicit legislative history covering this particular phrase
in the Economic Opportunity Act. The legislation as introduced in
1964 contained this phrase. It was never challenged. Its full meaning
and implementation was developed following the enactment and
continues to be defined and implemented to this date.[8]

Clearly, it is neither of great interest nor of great importance to know
who thought of the words "maximum feasible participation" in that particular sequence. The story concerns us only insofar as it illustrates the
degree of confusion and obscurity that surrounds the formulation and the
meaning of the concept.

Perhaps it is true, as one observer suggests, that "the idea was in the
air." If so, we can be sure that certain social forces put it there.

---

[3] Personal communication, James L. Sundquist, December 14, 1966.
[4] Personal communication, Hyman Bookbinder, December 6, 1966.
[5] Personal communication, Frank Mankiewicz, January 9, 1967.
[6] Adam Yarmolinsky, "The Origin of Maximum Feasible Participation," *Social
Sciences Forum* (Fall–Winter, 1966–1967), p. 19.
[7] Personal communication, Theodore M. Berry, December 9, 1966; emphasis
added.
[8] Bookbinder, *loc. cit.;* emphasis added.

The History of an Idea

Although, obviously, the idea of "maximum feasible participation" had a social history before it became a legal reality, information is difficult or impossible to get. This analysis, therefore, is necessarily speculative.

By 1964 many ideas about how to combat poverty and its consequences had been tested. As early as the 1930's the area projects of Chicago, whose watchwords were self-help, local autonomy, and local responsibility, were mobilizing community resources to combat juvenile delinquency. Yet, one idea stands out as dominant in its influence — the concept of "community development," which, under the sponsorship of the United States government in the early 1950's, had been translated into successful action programs abroad.

The realignment of forces after World War II, the onset of the Cold War, and the restive demands of colonial nations for freedom and self-expression turned the attention of American foreign policy planners overseas. In his inaugural address of 1949, President Truman proposed the Point Four Program to sponsor and support community development programs in underdeveloped nations throughout the world. These programs rested on the canons that indigenous leadership and resources could be discovered and developed in each community, and that such leaders would be able to articulate the needs, desires, and aspirations of the community.

Community organization specialists and others concerned with these problems have long found these ideas intriguing. The theme of the Seventh International Conference of Social Work in 1954 was self-help in a community action context. The American report to that Conference showed great sensitivity to the same questions which are now being debated with such heat. How can indigenous leadership and resources be discovered and developed? How can external leadership and resources contribute to the development of self-help programs? How can people participate significantly in the development and execution of such programs? Nevertheless, the report noted, there were few such domestic programs, none with government sponsorship. Subsequent conferences continued to articulate interest in community development and to discuss the problems and feasibility "of involving the active participation of the people themselves at the local level." [9]

---

[9] "Rural and Urban Community Development," 2 *International Social Work* (April 1959), p. 15, and "Mobilizing Resources for Social Needs," Statement by the Pre-Conference Working Party to the Ninth International Conference of Social Work, *ibid.*, pp. 1–9.

The lessons of our foreign aid programs in Africa and Asia were not lost on the American Negro. The new African nations, freed from their colonial bonds, turned energetically to solving community problems, demonstrating their latent capabilities and resources. Their visibility on the world scene was high; they soon became the model for the American civil rights movement founded on the same demands of antipaternalism and individual dignity — on the insistence that a person has the right to help decide his own fate. Long before the passage of the antipoverty act, local groups in many places were operating their own pre-school, tutoring, adult education, and retraining programs. It was precisely because the civil rights movement had already built organizations and mobilized community resources that "maximum feasible participation" was translated so quickly from abstraction to reality. When the law was passed, the black leaders of the ghettoes were ready to participate; indeed, they threw the full weight of their organized power into the demand that they be permitted to do so fully.

With the election of . . . President Kennedy, Moynihan writes, American commitments to the developing nations

> attained an extraordinary personification in the Peace Corps volunteer. . . . [T]he program was and is a great popular success, and the idea of doing something of the sort through Community Action Programs with the "underdeveloped peoples of the United States" came as a direct and obvious carry-over.[10]

Providing the added impulse was the growing recognition among many thoughtful observers that just as the paternalism of colonial powers had been a disabling factor in the development of colonial people, so the paternalism of existing welfare programs enfeebled and sapped the strength of the poor. For those who shared this view, participation was thought of as sociotherapy, a notion that says: Involve a man in successful and significant social action, give him a hand in decisions and institutions that affect his life, and he will soon develop psychological and social competence that will enable him to climb out of poverty.

This, then, is the developmental background of the concept that community action is a vehicle for community development. The civil rights movement and its demands, and the disillusion with the existing welfare programs in eliminating the poverty syndrome, furnished the thrust for translating the idea into action.

Some Precursors of CAP

THE CHICAGO EXPERIMENTS. The 1930's saw some of the earliest successful efforts in community action organization. Emphasizing the need

---

[10] Daniel P. Moynihan, "What Is Community Action?," *The Public Interest* (Fall 1966), p. 6.

for indigenous leadership, the Chicago Area Project of Clifford Shaw and associates helped neighborhoods to organize into effective working units to combat delinquency. At the same time, Saul Alinsky helped to organize Chicago's Back of the Yards Neighborhood Council, which turned the stockyards area into one of the most desirable working class neighborhoods in Chicago. Alinsky has since established the Industrial Areas Foundation, a non-profit institution dedicated to community development and community action. One of its most striking successes is The Woodlawn Organization (TWO) founded in 1960 — a large, broadly representative organization in the black ghetto to the south of the University of Chicago campus. Unlike other community organizing efforts, Alinsky rejects the search for consensus and the alliance with the white liberals, seeking instead to organize ghetto residents into an effective power bloc. In training community leaders to use the politics of conflict and confrontation, the task, he says, is "to rub raw the sores of discontent" — a job he does with obvious relish. With the advent of the civil rights movement and the ferment in urban black communities, his methods have gained national attention, and his services have been widely sought.

Although the debate and controversy over Alinsky and his methods is heated, and consensus about his effectiveness is lacking, there is little argument about his impact on those whose job it is to deal with the problems of poverty. The very existence of the controversy gives testimony to that. Abrasive, forceful, impolite, and irreverent, he has forced the professionals to continue to re-evaluate their doctrines and their dogma. Moynihan goes so far as to lump the rest of the programs to be discussed below under the rubric "The Alinsky Concept." [11]

THE FORD FOUNDATION. Throughout the 1950's the Ford Foundation was showing increasing concern for the problems of American cities. Beginning in 1960, the Foundation instituted the Great Cities School Improvement Program in ten cities. Grants totalling $3.2 million were made for a series of educational experiments focused on the needs of culturally disadvantaged children. These exploratory programs led the Foundation to a conviction that a more coordinated attack on all aspects of deprivation was necessary. By late 1961, the Community Development Program (more commonly known as the Gray Areas Projects) was born with a three-year $2 million grant to the city of Oakland to mount an integrated effort to ameliorate slum conditions and to bring slum residents into the mainstream of American life. Soon after, New Haven, Boston, Philadelphia, and North Carolina received grants.

Two articles of faith of the Foundation's philosophy were that effective community action needed participation of the groups involved and

---

[11] Moynihan, "What Is Community Action?," p. 5.

that indigenous leadership was necessary to provide communication between the planners and the community. Both were considered essential to
ensure that projects met the felt needs of the community, and to facilitate
the continuity of any programs undertaken. The manner in which affected groups would participate, however, was never clarified; each program developed its own definitions locally. Sometimes participation meant
that some members of the target area sat on the agency's policy board;
more often, it meant that a few indigenous leaders were hired by the
community organization agency.

New Haven was soon displayed as the model of how an antipoverty
program can work. The city organized Community Progress, Inc., a nonprofit corporation with a small board, which was highly ballyhooed as
broadly representative of the community. Three of its members were to
be appointed by the Mayor, and one each by the Redevelopment Agency,
the Board of Education, the Community Council, the United Fund, The
Citizens' Action Commission, and Yale University — a board representative of everyone but the residents of the target areas.

In Philadelphia, the Council for Community Advancement, set up
by the Ford grant, had scarcely begun organizing when it was met with a
wave of protest from black militants demanding recognition. The planning staff, wrote its executive director some time later, "had to learn to
plan *with* the community and not *for* the community." [12] Therefore, its
prospectus recommended the expansion of a center in North Philadelphia
(that city's black ghetto) so that "if the citizenry should want to 'Go
Fight City Hall,' *they should have an effective mechanism to speak for them
at a local level.*" [13] In telling this story, Charles Silberman comments with
some acerbity: "The notion that the citizens conceivably might want to
speak for themselves obviously never occurred to the academicians, government officials, and civic leaders who drew up the document." [14]

PRESIDENT'S COMMITTEE ON JUVENILE DELINQUENCY AND YOUTH CRIME.
Finally, with the appointment of the President's Committee on Juvenile
Delinquency and Youth Crime on May 11, 1961, . . . President Kennedy took a major step toward moving the federal government into domestic community development and action programs. The supporting
legislation, known as the Juvenile Delinquency and Youth Offenses Control Act of 1961, authorized $10 million for each of three fiscal years
through June 30, 1964, for demonstration and training projects in the most

---

[12] *American Community Development: Preliminary Reports by Directors of Projects Assisted by the Ford Foundation in Four Cities and a State,* Twenty-Ninth
Annual National Conference, National Association of Housing and Redevelopment
Officials, Denver, October 1, 1963. (New York: Office of Reports, Ford Foundation,
1964), p. 26.
[13] Quoted in Silberman, p. 353; emphasis added.
[14] *Ibid.,* p. 353.

effective ways of using total resources to combat juvenile delinquency in local communities. Grants were made to sixteen cities to develop delinquency prevention programs and to carry them out within limited target areas.

Leonard Cottrell, chairman of the Grant Review Panel of the Committee, had long been concerned with the issue of "competence." By 1961 his thinking had enlarged to encompass the concept of "community competence." Accordingly, he laid great stress on programs that encouraged the development of competence — on the "necessity for upgrading the capabilities of the inarticulate and disadvantaged to become more articulate and more capable of participating effectively in the setting of goals and implementing those goals in the life of the community." [15]

The most widely heralded and the most controversial of these programs were Harlem Youth Opportunities Unlimited (HARYOU) and Mobilization for Youth (MFY), both in New York City. Describing the activities and dimensions of HARYOU to a congressional committee, Robert Kennedy said:

> In central Harlem, youth of the area were involved throughout the development of the program. This project will employ, to work with other people, 2,000 young people who live in central Harlem. It will employ mothers, who are receiving welfare payments, as teachers and assistants in preschool nurseries. Youth and adults who live in Harlem will sit on the five neighborhood governing boards.[16]

MFY also spurned the traditional rehabilitation and support programs. Its goal: to uproot poverty by engaging the total local community in self-help, assisting residents to teach and to help one another instead of relying on professional social workers. Although the agency itself took no position, MFY workers counseled and advised on issues of concern to the area, stimulating community awareness of available remedies. Lawyers and community action workers helped to organize a rent strike; supported the civil rights boycott of the New York City schools in February 1964; and acted to protect citizens from capricious police and welfare decisions. Militant social action was to be the vehicle through which the community would learn to help itself — a policy that soon put the organization into direct conflict with the political and welfare establishments of the city who moved quickly to decimate it.

Responding to a question about the relationship of these ideas and

---

[15] Personal communication, January 10, 1967. See also Leonard S. Cottrell, Jr., "Social Planning, the Competent Community, and Mental Health," November 1964, Xeroxed.

[16] U.S. House Committee on Education and Labor, *Hearings on Economic Opportunity Act of 1964*, p. 305.

programs to the participation clause in the antipoverty act, Mr. Cottrell
writes:

> When the Economic Opportunities Act was formulated, the section
> on Community Development was formulated by people who worked
> on the President's Committee staff, and who carried some of my ideas
> into the wording of the Act.

Most observers agree.[17]

The Intent

From the preceding analysis, it is clear that by the time the task force
on poverty began to work, several blueprints for action were in existence.
Furthermore, many of the people had drawn those blueprints were now
called upon to bring their experience to bear on the broader problems of
poverty. What their intentions were when they called for maximum feasible participation is still unsettled; indeed, it probably will remain so
forever.

Daniel Moynihan and Nathan Glazer have variously described CAP
as "an effort to change the poor who are produced by the system," [18] and
"the art of using government funds for . . . controlled revolution." [19]
There is some truth in both views. Some of the drafters may have understood and advocated its revolutionary implications; most would probably
agree with the observer who writes: "None of us in the CAP program
really predicted that the concept would become such a controversial
issue." [20] Had their intention been to foment "controlled revolution,"
surely the controversy would have been foreseeable.

In fact, it is this very lack of foresight about the implications of
"maximum feasible participation" — the apparent inability to foretell
the nature of the response — that is so puzzling. By 1964, the profound
relationship between poverty and race was widely recognized and understood. The civil rights movement had developed organization and leadership in urban ghettos; an ethos of rising expectation and militant

---

[17] Personal communications from Sanford L. Kravitz, December 7, 1966; Robert
Morris, November 21, 1966; James N. Adler, December 5, 1966; and Bookbinder, loc.
cit. Also, Boone, "The Poor and the War on Poverty" and Daniel P. Moynihan,
"Three Problems in Combating Poverty," in Poverty in America, ed. Margaret S. Gordon (San Francisco: Chandler, 1965), pp. 41–53; and Yarmolinsky, "The Origin of
Maximum Feasible Participation."
[18] Moynihan, ibid., p. 47.
[19] Nathan Glazer, "A Sociologist's View of Poverty," in Gordon, ed., Poverty in
America, p. 24.
[20] Kravitz, loc. cit.

demands had replaced the passivity of earlier times. Yet, the men who framed the act seem to have missed the point.

One can only speculate that despite their disaffection with the welfare system, despite their sympathetic concern for civil rights, these men were themselves bound by the power of American preconceptions. Still powerful are notions that the poor are really lazy, irresponsible, apathetic, satisfied with their lot; that the Negro — that special case of poverty — is poor because black men know less, need less, are less. A lifetime spent in an atmosphere dominated by racism and the casework emphasis of modern rehabilitation philosophy infects even the most sophisticated and sympathetic. It is difficult indeed to penetrate the stereotype fully — to envision and comprehend a poor man grasping abstract concepts of participation, a black man asserting his manhood. The comments of one task force member are illustrative.

> I had never really conceived that it [participation] would mean control by the poor of the community action organization itself. . . . I expected that the poor would be represented on the community action organization but that such representation would be something in the order of 15 to 25% of the board. . . . *Moreover, I don't think it ever occurred to me, or to many others, that the representatives of the poor must necessarily be poor themselves.*[21]

Many men with diverse backgrounds and commitments came together to draft the antipoverty bill. There were, no doubt, some shared understandings, orientations, and experiences, and a common goal — to alleviate the distress of poverty. One can reasonably suggest that they were responding to the demands of the civil rights movement and to their own convictions about the failure of welfare colonialism. But what, if anything, they as a body actually intended when they insisted on participation by the poor remains unclear.

The Problem of Definition and Implementation

Almost immediately after the passage of the act, the problem of defining participation emerged. With no legislative history to serve as a guide, the debate rose quickly to a deafening roar. Did participation mean that poor people would work in the programs, or that they would share the policy-making role? Some opted for the former as the central meaning of participation; others for the latter. Those who spoke for the poor wanted both. Four years later, after several congressional attempts at clarification, the debate continues.

HIRING THE POOR TO WORK WITH THE POOR. Most clearly articulated

---

[21] Adler, *loc. cit.;* emphasis added.

by Frank Riessman and his associates,[22] the idea of employing the poor in subprofessional jobs calls for aggressive recruitment of those whose main qualification is that they are part of the "culture of poverty" — people who might serve their communities in a variety of ways, as mental-health aides, mothers' aides, recreation aides, research aides, parent education aides, and many more.

The essential value of the indigenous nonprofessional is his capability for acting as a bridge between the middle-class professional and his client. "This ability . . . is not based on things they have been taught, but on what they *are*." [23] Ideally, the nonprofessional aide is able to interpret community life and values to the professionals, helping them to establish better rapport with their clientele, and to serve as interpreter of the professionals to the community. By communicating the needs and values of the community to the agency, it is hoped that he will be instrumental in reshaping agency programs, procedures, and values.

The logic of this argument would not seem to lend itself readily to controversy. Yet, professionals in welfare agencies see a threat to their professionalism in these concepts and have offered stubborn resistance. An OEO sponsored program evaluation revealed in 1966 that "while the personal relationships between the professionals and their aides was reported as good, there is no evidence of significant change in policies or values of the institutions or of the professionals employing them." [24] Complicating the picture is the fact, pointed out by Riessman, that one of the greatest problems of the nonprofessional is "role ambiguity or lack of role identity: he doesn't know who he is or who he is becoming. . . . He is a highly marginal person." [25] Thus, although the evidence is not conclusive

---

[22] Frank Riessman, "Anti-Poverty Programs and the Role of the Poor," in Gordon, ed., *Poverty in America*, pp. 403–412; Frank Riessman, "The New Anti-Poverty Ideology and the Negro," prepared for the White House Conference on Civil Rights, November 17–18, 1965, mimeographed; Frank Riessman, "Suggestions for Community Action Programs," June 1966, mimeographed; Arthur Pearl and Frank Riessman, *New Careers for the Poor* (New York: Free Press, 1965); Robert Reiff and Frank Riessman, *The Indigenous Nonprofessional: A Strategy of Change in Community Action and Community Mental Health Programs*, National Institute of Labor Education, Mental Health Program Reports, no. 3, November 1964; Frank Riessman and Emanuel Hallowitz, "The Role of the Indigenous Nonprofessional in a Community Mental Health Neighborhood Service Center Program," prepared for the American Orthopsychiatry Association Meeting, San Francisco, California, April 1966, mimeographed; Martin Rein and Frank Riessman, "A Strategy for Antipoverty Community Action Programs," 11 *Social Work* (April 1966), pp. 3–12; Frank Riessman, "Issues in Training the New Nonprofessional," 2 *Poverty and Human Resources Abstracts* (September–October 1967), pp. 5–17.

[23] Reiff and Riessman, *ibid.*, p. 8.

[24] Oscar Ornati, "Program Evaluation and the Definition of Poverty," Paper prepared for the Industrial Relations Research Association Meetings, San Francisco, December 27–29, 1966, p. 10.

[25] Riessman, "Issues in Training . . . ," p. 8.

and the reasons are not clearly understood, the failure of the subprofessionals to constitute a force for change seems to be related both to the attitude of their professional superiors and to the fact that these nonprofessional workers often are distant from and do not identify with the troubled members of the poor community whom they must represent.

The program has been only slightly more successful in providing employment opportunities. By the end of fiscal 1967 only 41,000 poor people were working in CAP programs [26] — a pitifully small number when measured against the millions of unemployed and underemployed poor.[27]

Current information about the sociodemographic characteristics of these nonprofessional workers is unavailable from OEO; but the 1966 study already cited showed that while the total employed labor force in nine cities sampled was 89 percent white, nonprofessional aides were 79 percent black. Further findings indicate that the majority of the nonprofessional aides were not hardcore poor; only 47 percent were actually unemployed at the time of accepting a job with CAP. Except for race, they were not significantly different from the bulk of the employed work force.[28] These data suggest that there is a considerable amount of "creaming" — selection of those who are the most acceptable and offer the most likelihood of success. We observe here one of the universal attributes of the welfare bureaucracy — the tendency to concentrate efforts on those who are most likely to assure the institution a favorable image and an impressive record. Harold Wilensky notes this principle in operation:

> There are strong resistances built into the antipoverty agencies and programs themselves. Just as vocational training until 1963 reached only the already literate, the already work-oriented youngster, so the Job Corps program avoids seriously delinquent or disturbed youth. . . . Especially in new programs and in areas of controversy, welfare administrators, afraid of recalcitrant clientele and anxious to minimize risk of failure, concentrate on salvaging the almost saved.[29]

Yet, if the program is to be more than a vehicle that facilitates the upward movement of those already most mobile, we must face these and other tough questions. How do we recruit more effectively to attract the indigent unemployed? What shall be the selection process? Clearly, ordinary tests and measures that aid personnel selections are inadequate to a

[26] U.S. Office of Economic Opportunity, *Third Annual Report*, p. 13. These figures represent only those employed by CAP. It should be noted that Riessman estimates the total number of indigenous subprofessionals employed in various antipoverty efforts to be well over 100,000. Riessman, "Issues in Training . . . ," p. 5.

[27] Perhaps it ought to be said that this is due not so much to any inadequacy in the program as to the tragic funding limitations of the antipoverty skirmish.

[28] Ornati, "Program Evaluation and the Definition of Poverty," pp. 10, 15.

[29] Harold L. Wilensky and Charles N. Lebeaux, *Industrial Society and Social Welfare* (New York: Free Press, 1965), p. xxxvii.

population with low educational levels and verbal skills. What training procedures can we devise to ensure that we tap the capabilities of the worker adequately? What placement procedures must we use to assure that workers and jobs are matched for compatibility with capabilities and temperament? Do the jobs in community action programs offer "new careers," providing opportunity for learning and holding out the promise of advancement? Or, are they both the beginning and the end of the line? As we confront these questions and attempt their solution, we must be prepared to risk an initial reduction in efficiency, increased costs, and the political pressures of the attendant unfavorable publicity.

PLANNING AND POLICY-MAKING. The notion that the poor should be actively and effectively involved in policy-making led to even more serious controversy and raised critical questions. How many poor people must serve on a Community Action Agency (CAA) board to guarantee effective representation? How shall they be selected? Who shall select them? The controversy quickly organized around "how many." At stake was a fundamental problem: Is it possible for the poor — inarticulate, uneducated, suffering from feelings of low esteem, unaccustomed to the rules and procedures of organization — to make an effective contribution on councils heavily weighted with representatives of powerful organizational interests?

For two years OEO's *post hoc* interpretations offered little clarity. Sargent Shriver made public statements insisting that flexibility was the keystone of CAP programs, that each community would decide how many poor people on the board were "feasible." Privately, however, he sent memoranda to OEO regional directors proposing that representatives of the poor should number approximately one-third of the CAP governing body.

In cities like San Francisco, Los Angeles, Rochester, and Syracuse the issue was settled only after long, bitter, and costly struggles. Most often the poor neighborhoods had to settle for one-third. In San Francisco, however, the target areas won a majority of the seats on the Economic Opportunity Council, the city-wide CAA, as well as a majority on the area boards. But the victory has carried a price. The boards have been rent by seemingly endless quarrels, born, in part, from a basic lack of understanding of the difference between policy-making and administrative functions and from a fear that to give up any part of decision-making is to let slip the reins of control. Consequently, critics insist that until poor people gain the requisite skills and experience, experts must run the programs. But if we adopt that stance, how will the poor ever acquire the experience? Perhaps we must endure this period of transition while poor communities develop leadership and create community resources with which to help themselves.

The issue in the numbers game was clear — power. With billions of dollars to be spent, he who controls the purse strings may also control the votes, and will surely influence the programs — a serious threat to both the political establishment and the welfare bureaucracy. Experience with militant social action programs like MFY and HARYOU had already frightened these groups who have so much to lose from an organization of the poor dedicated to social and institutional change. If the representation mandate were implemented with vigor and poor people controlled the policy councils, they would acquire experience in community affairs. There might emerge from such experience a political consciousness and political organizations not beholden to incumbent officeholders and party leaders — a new and coherent force in the cities. Out of the most elementary instincts of self-preservation, this is the last thing which incumbents wish to see in their jurisdictions.

Meanwhile, the strident charges and countercharges escalated. The Republicans feared (not entirely without justification) that CAP was a national Democratic party plot to replace its fading urban, ethnic political base with the organized, urban poor equally beholden to Democratic politicians. The Democrats, they charged, were making a political pork barrel of CAP. On the other hand, local Democratic officials, fearing a challenge to their control of city hall and the county courthouse, complained vociferously that CAP was disruptive of the urban status quo — that the federal government was financing an attack on city hall. All the critics agreed in their insistence that the poor were being used and duped by political troublemakers. From whatever the source, and whatever the reason, the result seemed to be one vast, shrill cry demanding the end of CAP.

With the Economic Opportunity Amendments of 1966 Congress tried to end the arguments about the number of the poor to be included on CAA boards by stipulating that the poor must comprise at least one-third of the board membership. Still the wrangling continued. Finally, the 1967 amendments further specified the composition of a CAA board. It can have no more than fifty-one members — a minimum of one-third poverty area representatives; a maximum of one-third public officials or their appointed representatives; and the remainder representatives of business, industry, labor, welfare, education, or other major groups and interests in the community. Although this provision has often been interpreted ominously by participation advocates, in effect, Congress has simply articulated publicly the rule of thumb for CAA participation with which the OEO had been working privately. And by providing a maximum of one-third from the public sector and a *minimum* of one-third from the poor community, the law *need* have no effect on existing relations. For example, the San Francisco Economic Opportunity Council now has a fifty-one member board, twenty-six of whom are representatives of the five target areas in the city.

As this is being written, however, the Mayor appointed seventeen city officials to the board, including himself and three members of the city's Board of Supervisors — an action that brings questions about effective participation sharply to mind. Even on councils where they are *not* greatly outnumbered, will an alliance between public officials and the representatives of the other major community interests still the voices of the poor and block their will? Can poor people compete successfully against the organizational skills of politicians, businessmen, and bureaucrats?

The 1966 amendments also tried to deal with the problems and controversies that had, by then, developed around the selection of representatives of the poor. The new law requires that these representatives are to be selected democratically by the residents in the poverty areas, that representatives of the poor must live in the geographic area which they represent, and that special emphasis is to be given to the participation of those who are poor. These provisions have helped to eliminate the spectacle of programs that technically meet the numerical requirements, but in which the representatives of the poor are, in Alinsky's apt phrase, "poverty specimens hand-picked by the prevailing political powers."[30]

The preoccupation with numbers and the process of selection, however, has diverted attention from equally important questions about the *quality* of representation. Not only must we ask how many representatives and how they will be chosen, but also to what extent they will be responsible to a constituency. Is the choice made from among those who have demonstrated some qualities of leadership and are, therefore, already somewhat removed from the mainstream of community problems? Once having been selected as representatives or leaders of the poor, how can cooptation into the established power structures be avoided? Given a taste of success, can a representative of the poor remain unseduced by the offerings of the world to which he has just been admitted?

In the final analysis, the pressure against CAP was too strong to be resisted. While Congress was clarifying and specifying the meaning of participation, it was at the same time earmarking ever larger proportions of CAP funds to what are called in the trade "canned" programs — those, like Head Start, Follow Through, Upward Bound, Legal Services, and Comprehensive Health Services, which are initiated and controlled by Washington — and cutting back on the politically troublesome activities of the local agencies. Thus, in fiscal 1967, the OEO had $66 million less for versatile and flexible community action activities than in fiscal 1966.[31]

---

[30] Saul D. Alinsky, "The War on Poverty — Political Pornography," 21 *Journal of Social Issues* (January 1965), pp. 41–47.

[31] *The 23rd Annual Congressional Quarterly Almanac*, 90th Cong., 1st sess., 1967. (Washington: Congressional Quarterly Service, 1968), p. 1077.

And, although the 1967 amendments have eliminated congressional ear-marking of funds, Congress carefully specified the kind of programs that would qualify for assistance and enumerated eight (all national in scope) that must take precedence in funding.[32] The guide for funding priorities distributed by national OEO to regional and local offices clearly reflects congressional sentiments. OEO officials advise that while the total CAP appropriation increased from $864 million in 1968 to $931 million in 1969, each year has seen a decrease in funds for versatile, locally initiated pro-grams.

Further circumscribing the creative potential of CAP, the 1967 amendments provide that no more than 15 percent of community-action appropriations may be allocated to research and pilot programs, and that one-third of that amount must be devoted to a program to stem the rural to urban migration.

Finally, to the anguished cries of the Republican minority — their worst fears that CAP is a Democratic party plot to retain control of the urban areas about to be realized — the administration-backed Green Amendment was included in the 1967 EOA. This requires that com-munity action agencies must become instrumentalities of state or local governments. As of June 30, 1968, the private, nonprofit agency can exist as the CAA only if it is so designated by the state or local government, or when appointed by the OEO director, in the event that the state or local government fails to establish a CAA. Representative Charles Goodell (R-NY) promptly dubbed it "the bosses and boll weevil amendment," charging that hence forth CAP's would be dominated by a northern city hall or a southern county court-house. The sudden surge of support for CAP from local Democratic politicians who had earlier been hostile sug-gests that Mr. Goodell's fears may not be unfounded.

At this writing, however, it is still too early to determine the effect of the Green Amendment on CAP.[33] Much will depend on the political complexion and persuasion of the various local and state officials, and on what the nature of the struggle has been between the existing CAA and the politicians. Just as in the past, the picture will probably be mixed, and the range and freedom of local agencies will vary. In those communities

---

[32] These eight programs are: Head Start, Upward Bound, Legal Services, Com-prehensive Health Services, Follow Through, Emergency Food and Medical Services, Family-Planning, and Senior Opportunities and Services.

[33] An OEO survey of the effects of the Green Amendment shows that of 790 local governments reporting, as of August 30, 1968 (of 1,018 CAA's across the na-tion), about 97 percent, or 768, plan to continue to operate with existing CAA's. It is important to notice, however, that the survey does not report how many of those 768 responses came from communities where the CAA is already under the control of the local government. — U.S. Office of Economic Opportunity, *A News Summary of the War on Poverty*, September 23, 1968.

where CAA's have established a strong constituency and can count on support, it is unlikely that local politicians will infringe on their jurisdictions.[34] On the other hand, where political hostilities are intense, placing the CAA's under the control of local officials may lead to their demise through a spinning off of programs at the local level, with different agencies picking up the various programs.

Regardless of which path local politicians may choose, the heat of the controversy has long since made OEO officials less than enthusiastic about this troublesome problem-child. And the very existence of the amendment may well be enough to make CAA's move ever more cautiously. In any case, the Republican victory in November may pose the greatest threat yet to CAP since it could portend some fundamental changes in the administration of antipoverty programs. A major objective of Republican critics has been to disassemble the OEO and to disperse its programs throughout the appropriate federal departments — a goal that may be more readily attainable with a sympathetic President. CAP could easily fail to survive such a reorganization in any viable form.

Summary and Conclusions

To summarize, this analysis argues that the idea of maximum feasible participation by the poor has its roots in the community development programs sponsored by the United States in underdeveloped nations; that the burgeoning, militant civil rights movement gave impetus to translating these conceptions to the domestic scene; and that there was disquietude with existing welfare policy and patterns of paternalism that debilitate rather than rehabilitate. Together these forces resulted in several precursors of CAP — demonstration projects emphasizing the need for citizen participation. The notions of participation that these programs were exploring were incorporated into the antipoverty act by much the same people who had designed the programs already in existence. This, then, is the confluence of ideas and forces in American life which suggested such an approach to the problem of poverty.

Although it is also argued that there was no unitary intention in the task force, it can be said with some certainty that many of its members were motivated by a concern about what Richard Boone calls

> the increasing constrictions imposed by professionalism in social work and public education [and a] dehumanizing helping system which demanded that the individual adjust to community institutions rather

---

[34] Yet even in San Francisco, where the CAA has developed a sizable constituency, the Mayor recently exercised his control option by designating the City Controller as the financial officer of the Economic Opportunity Council, in effect ousting the agency appointed financial director.

than trying to change those institutions to meet the needs of the poor. It was a concern about a system of referral from nowhere to nowhere.[35]

While these considerations were not explicitly articulated in relation to a changed view of the poor and their capabilities, they did call the whole welfare system into question, and offered a program of community action as a substitute or a supplement. This suggests that these men believed that, given the tools and the chance, poor people would use them well — a judgment about the capabilities of the poor which, it turns out, seems to be well ahead of its time.[36]

Yet, the revolutionary implications of what they were proposing escaped the framers of the act. Richard Boone writes:

> The full ramification of the idea dictating the involvement of the poor was probably not considered at the time. . . . Even now the implications seem staggering. The government was preparing to let those at the bottom of the society have a say in the administration of a major piece of antipoverty legislation designed to coordinate federal antipoverty efforts.[37]

It seems never to have occurred to them that the poor would take it so seriously. Considering the time — 1964; considering the men: sophisticated, urbane intellectuals who were keenly attuned to the civil rights movement; considering the militancy of that movement — the extent to which ghetto communities in northern cities had already demonstrated a capacity for action; this is indeed anomalous. The answer, I suggest, lies in the preconceptions about poverty, race, and welfare that grip American thought and distort our vision.

Finally, the dimensions of the struggle over defining and implementing the participation clause are highlighted, the discussion focusing on the two major aspects — policy-making and jobs. While both threatened some already existing interests, the most profound controversy settled around the policy-making component. Although their motives may have differed, welfare agencies and politicians made massive efforts to retain their doctrine, dogma, and power, while the leaders of the poor did, indeed, use federal funds to try to force institutional change.

In conclusion, I would suggest that the idea has had a profound im-

---

[35] Boone, "The Poor and the War on Poverty," pp. 5–6.

[36] The "welfare backlash" implicit in the recent presidential elections, which saw about 9.9 million votes cast for George Wallace, suggested that general attitudes towards the poor are still influenced by the individualist ethic of America, by the myth that every boy can grow up to be President. Much sentiment still views the poor man as a victim of his own deficiencies. Complicating the matter is the fact that, in the cities, the poor are usually black. Insistence that their condition is due to their own failings comports with prevailing racist attitudes and obviates the need to reappraise those beliefs.

[37] Boone, "The Poor and the War on Poverty," p. 7.

pact on the society in general, and on communities of the poor in particular. Although fearful politicians may ultimately emasculate CAP. I
must agree with Leonard Cottrell who says: "The seed has been planted,
and the idea will not die out." [38]

Despite its limitations in practice, the concept of "new careers" for
the poor has taken root; tens of thousands of people are now working in
city and neighborhood organizations in self-respecting jobs in which one
major asset is their background of poverty and their knowledge of their
communities' problems. With the Scheuer-Nelson Amendment, Congress
gave further encouragement and legitimacy to the notion.

Most significant: for the first time, poor people have been told by
legislative mandate that they are capable of taking a hand in their affairs.
They have been called upon to speak in their own behalf, to assess their
needs, and to join in the design and implementation of programs to meet
those needs. The response has been overwhelming at times. In communities all over America militant groups have organized independently
to alleviate their distress. Small victories are won — a tenants' council in
San Francisco's Hunters Point forces the Housing Authority to paint the
buildings; a rent strike in New York wins some rodent control; another
compels landlords to supply more adequate heating; a coalition of organizations defeats a San Francisco urban renewal plan that threatens homes
and community without offering satisfactory alternatives. And each victory generates confidence in self — a necessary precondition to action —
and confidence in the efficacy of organization to correct the gnawing grievances that plague their lives. Finally, four years after maximum feasible
participation was written into law, we witness the Ocean Hill-Brownsville struggle in New York City, where demands for local determination
and control so terrified the city's educational bureaucracy; and we see
the rise of black militant groups like the Black Panthers, whose goals include local autonomy and control of all ghetto institutions including
police functions.

As the struggle has grown, the dilemmas inherent in notions about
participation become increasingly apparent. For the bureaucracy, participation has often served to ensure that its programs will function smoothly
and meet with minimal resistance. For the poor, however, who have few
effective political resources, participation is steadily being reinterpreted
to mean control. "Maximum feasible participation" has, indeed, captured
the imagination of the leaders of the poor with the force of an idea whose
time has come. It has helped to validate and legitimate the aspirations of
the poor and the minorities in America for self-determination. The problem is no longer whether, nor even when, it should be implemented;
rather, it is how.

---

[38] Cottrell, "Social Planning, the Competent Community, and Mental Health."

Urban Services and
Social Welfare

2

There are two interlocking strands of analysis which help to explain the relationship of the urban poor to the providers of education, housing, health care, policing, and consumer goods.

The first examines the relationship of the poor to the governmental bureaucracies which are supposed to secure their welfare. Here the focus is on the most salient political status of the poor person, that of client. The unequal distribution of power between the client and the caretaker bureaucracy, the alienation of clients from the local institutions of the larger society, and the meaning of a dependent status to the individual's social and personal identity all help to explain the quality of life in poor communities. In addition, study of the interface between the poor and the caretaker bureaucracies contributes to our understanding both of urban political phenomena (such as sit-ins and rent strikes) and of the more general forces associated with race, class, and bureaucracy in American society.

The second strand of analysis emphasizes the economic situation of the poor, who are disadvantaged in an economy where the allocation of many goods and services is left largely to the market. The poor depend upon government for things that others can buy privately. At the same time, poor neighborhoods require more expenditure per capita for those items usually provided by government (e.g., education, policing) if the same level of service is to be maintained. The aggregate effect is that the need — and often the demand — for governmental services is much greater than the amount government has been supplying. This relative failure of urban social services has been identified as contributing to "black rage," organized political movements, and the social pathology represented by crime and riots.

Each of the articles in this section emphasizes — in varying degrees — one or both of these analytical perspectives. David Boesel et al. provide data on how representatives of white institutions in the ghetto understand their own roles and their clients' behavior. The authors have obtained their evidence from a survey conducted during

the late 1960s in fifteen Northern cities at the behest of the National
Advisory Commission on Civil Disorders. The data indicate that most
whites do not empathize with the black man's sense of social deprivation and that they tend to blame the poor for their own poverty. The
attitudes of the white groups interviewed ranged from the "optimistic denial" of major employers (57 percent of whom felt that blacks
are treated at least as well as whites at the same income level) to the
more overt racism of the police. Whites in such ghetto roles as merchant, employer, and policeman feel threatened by blacks, and this
perception involves a subtle combination of racial and political attitudes and a real basis in fact. Blacks, in contrast, tend to believe
they are the victims of racial discrimination, of the unavailability of
jobs, and of other factors beyond their personal control. The effect
of client status upon blacks is often a rage against white institutions
which in turn exacerbates the threat the whites feel, thereby aggra-
vating a condition of enmity and making the provision of adequate
services to the poor increasingly difficult.

No local institution is more devoted to the mission of helping the
black poor than the school. Indeed, within the context of our national
belief system, education is seen as the prime vehicle for moving the
poor out of poverty. Yet, as Gerald Levy shows, the ghetto child as
client of the urban school is a political subject who is both a victim
of the school and a contributor to the institutional breakdown helping to assure his own failure.

"Ghetto School" permits us to see how the relationship between
the white caretaker and the poor black client, as structured by the
institutional order of the social service bureaucracy, contributes
both to mutual hostility and the inability of the caretaker to accomplish his helping mission. In particular, Levy dispels the naive view
that bureaucrats — in this case teachers — are ill-willed or corrupt.
Rather, he shows how the constraints of the "system" force individuals into role behaviors which have the *effect* of victimizing children; how, for example, the principal of Midway School engages in
ritual acts to assure his immediate superiors that all looks well, because he knows that appearance determines how he will be evaluated.

The constraints present at Midway are generalizable to many
ghetto bureaucratic situations. First, client and caretaker are recruited from different cultural systems and often misinterpret each
other's behavior. Because the caretaker is in a more powerful position
than the client, his interpretation defines the relationship, and the
client suffers as a result. This is especially true when the caretaker
views the client's cultural behavior according to racial or class-based

stereotypes. The "different" behavior of the client (whether of the child wearing a hat in school or the young men sitting on a stoop) then becomes socially unacceptable or even dangerous and must be suppressed.

Second, the distribution of power in caretaker bureaucracies means that clients are not a significant reference group for bureaucrats. What the clients think does not have much bearing on the bureaucrat's self-esteem or on his career success. The teacher or welfare worker or policeman who wants to change organizational structure and practice is little helped by the fact that the institution's clients would support such a move; the clients are usually powerless. What matters are the opinions of his peers and superiors. But other members of the system are concerned about their careers and about not rocking the boat. The result is stasis.

Finally, we see at Midway that the bureaucrat's resources are inadequate for his mission. Even those teachers who try very hard have, at best, a small impact on the educational development of a few children. They are worn down by the psychological and sometimes physical cost of trying to do a good job. Moreover, when parents rise in ire against the school they may not differentiate between these teachers and the others. Society tells the caretaker to educate people or to guarantee their health or safety; yet, at best it provides him with only enough resources to keep his clientele from erupting. The caretaker becomes cynical and feels threatened. He devotes his attention to protecting himself from perceived threat. Yet this diversion of energy (e.g., to keeping order in the classroom) guarantees that he will not accomplish his ostensible goal of providing adequate help, while his defensive behavior frequently elicits the very attack he fears.

The articles on health care and housing direct our attention to the level of social services available to the poor, and to the issues associated with creating social policies that will guarantee equitable outcomes. The Health Policy Advisory Center (Health PAC) charges that the medical establishment has taken on the characteristics of a guild, using political power to establish, protect, and expand a "health empire" that monopolizes health services to benefit primarily its own members. While great hospitals are enlarging themselves at the cost of low-income residents living on their peripheries, the health care provided the poor is inadequate. The outcome is that, according to a large number of indicators — such as infant mortality rate, life expectancy, and so forth — America lags behind most of the other advanced industrial societies, with our lower strata even more disadvantaged.

Nathan Glazer's data raise some interesting and perplexing questions about appropriate policy for improving the health of all Americans, especially the poor. Although Glazer accepts the facts (asserted by Health PAC) which show the relative weakness of American public health, he argues that one should not jump to quick conclusions as to the causes of the situation. He shows, for example, that countries with fewer doctors and hospitals per capita have healthier populations than does the United States; so we cannot be sure that greater input necessarily improves output. In addition, Glazer finds significant differences in the health of different ethnic groups *at the same level of income*. He concludes that general environmental and cultural factors may become very important in affecting the health of a population once some level has been attained — i.e., that the amount of medical care makes a big difference up to some point, and then other things become salient in determining how healthy a group will be.

Glazer's evidence does not, however, refute the Health PAC analysis. Doctors may still be growing rich at the expense of other groups in the population, and the poor are undoubtedly disadvantaged in terms of the amount and quality of medical attention they receive. Moreover, Glazer's hypothesis concerning the importance of group culture may be countered by the argument that nonwhites have higher infant mortality, etc. than whites at the same income level because they suffer from discrimination in terms of their medical treatment, because they live in neighborhoods where adequate facilities are unavailable, and because their level of housing, type of occupation and the like are poorer than that of whites. In other words, controlling for level of income in a racist society does not create groups who live under similar objective conditions. Nonetheless, even if we question some of Glazer's conclusions, the significance of his analysis should not be lost. For he shows how little we know about the relationship between input and output in health care. Without further knowledge, the would-be reformer, although recognizing the interests that resist change, may not be able to delineate rational policy goals.

George Sternlieb's research on Newark provides some of the answers upon which formulation of rational housing policy depends. From an extensive survey of housing in a sample of neighborhoods, and from intensive interviews with property owners, Sternlieb concludes that economic interest alone is insufficient to encourage the improvement of rundown housing. As the author puts it, the market game is one of "heads, you win, tails we lose," at least from the perspective of poor tenants: "When the apartment market is very strong the landlord need not improve; when the apartment market is very weak the landlord fears for his investment and does not improve." Resident ownership, however, is the single best guarantor of well-kept property. Sternlieb thus finds that the man who lives in the house he owns has a stake in property maintenance and improvement which makes him a better landlord than the man whose interest is only economic. From this, Sternlieb concludes that the best social policy would encourage resident ownership (through tax incentives, loans, and rent subsidies).

Michael Stegman questions whether Sternlieb's market solution is realistic. Even if blacks, like most Americans, have a strong desire to be property owners, it may be that too few have enough money to purchase houses in the slums. Obviously Sternlieb recognizes this problem in suggesting various subsidies. However, the subsidies might have to be so large as to amount to income redistribution, in which case the housing problem would presumably solve itself if our society could deal with the more fundamental problem of economic inequality. Furthermore, as Stegman points out in attacking the "myths" of housing analysis, realty institutions have been loath to provide mortgage money for blacks. In fact, the American realty industry may be unmatched in racial bias. Could we expect that industry to reverse its past performance and permit blacks equal access to ownership opportunities, even if they had the money?

Perhaps, however, the market solution is the one most likely to be effected in the United States. Stegman discusses the power of the private housing industry and shows the government's unwillingness to embark on a meaningful program of public housing. Even at the peak of the reformist wave of the Kennedy and Johnson years, the federal housing programs like 221 (d) (3) failed to have much impact on the ghettos. If the interest groups that support the status quo cannot be defeated, then Sternlieb's answer may, indeed, be the most realistic. In that case, one cannot be sanguine about radical change in the level of housing available to the urban poor. In housing, as in health care and other social services, more affluent Americans have been unwilling to close the gap at the bottom of the social hierarchy, while the poor have not mobilized sufficient political power to force the concessions necessary for significant improvement in their relative condition.

White Institutions and Black Rage

David Boesel, Richard Berk, W. Eugene Groves, Bettye Eidson, and Peter H. Rossi

Five summers of black rebellion have made it clear that the United States is facing a crisis of proportions not seen since the Great Depression. And one of the root causes of this crisis, it has also become clear, is the performance of white institutions, especially those institutions in the ghetto. Some of these institutions — police and retail stores, for example — have done much to antagonize Negroes; others, such as welfare departments and black political organizations, have tried to help and have failed.

Why have these white institutions helped engender black rage? One way to find out might be to study the attitudes of the men working for them — to discover what their personnel think about the racial crisis itself, about their own responsibilities, about the work they are doing. Therefore, at the request of the National Advisory Commission on Civil Disorders (the riot commission), we at Johns Hopkins University visited 15 Northern cities and questioned men and women working for six different institutional groups: major employers, retail merchants, teachers, welfare workers, political workers (all Negro), and policemen. All of the people we questioned, except the employers, work right in the ghetto, and are rank-and-file employees — the cop on the beat, the social caseworker, and so on.

Employers' Social Responsibility

The "employers" we questioned were the managers or personnel officers of the ten institutions in each city that employed the most people, as well as an additional 20 managers or personnel officers of the next 100 institutions. As such, they represented the most economically progressive institutions in America. And in their employment policies we could see how some of America's dominant corporate institutions impinge on the everyday lives of urban Negroes.

Businessmen are in business to make a profit. Seldom do they run their enterprises for social objectives. But since it is fashioned these days, most of the managers and personnel officers we interviewed (86 percent, in fact) accepted the proposition that they "have a social responsibility to make strong efforts to provide employment for Negroes and other minority groups." This assertion, however, is contradicted by unemployment in the Negro community today, as well as by the hiring policies of the firms themselves.

Businessmen, as a whole, do not exhibit openly racist attitudes. Their position might best be described as one of "optimistic denial" — the gentlemanly white racism evident in a tacit, but often unwitting, acceptance of institutional practices that subordinate or exclude Negroes. One aspect of this optimistic denial is a nonrecognition of the seriousness of the problems that face black people. Only 21 percent of our sample thought that unemployment was a very serious problem in the nations' cities, yet 26 percent considered air pollution very serious and 31 percent considered traffic very serious. The employers' perspective is based upon their limited experience with blacks, and that experience does not give them a realistic picture of the plight of Negroes in this country. Employers don't even think that racial discrimination has much to do with the Negroes' plight; a majority (57 percent) felt that Negroes are treated at least as well as other people of the same income, and an additional 6 percent felt that Negroes are treated *better* than any other part of the population.

This optimistic denial on the part of employers ("things really aren't that bad for Negroes") is often combined with a negative image of Negroes as employees. Half of those employers interviewed (51 percent) said that Negroes are likely to have higher rates of absenteeism than whites, so that hiring many of them would probably upset production schedules. Almost a third thought that, because Negro crime rates are generally higher than white crime rates, hiring many Negroes could lead to increased theft and vandalism in their companies. About a fifth (22 percent) thought that hiring Negroes might bring "agitators and troublemakers" into their companies, and another one-fifth feared that production costs might rise because Negroes supposedly do not take orders well.

The employer's views may reflect not only traditional white prejudices, but also some occasional experience he himself has had with Negroes. Such experiences, however, may stem as much from the employer's own practices and misconceptions as from imputed cultural habits of Negroes. As Elliot Liebow observed in his study of Negro street-corner men (*Tally's Corner*), blacks have learned to cope with life by treating menial, low-status, degrading jobs in the same way that the jobs treat them — with benign nonconcern.

Most of the employers believe that Negroes lack the preparation for anything but menial jobs. A full 83 percent said that few Negroes are qualified for professional jobs, and 69 percent thought that few are qualified for skilled positions. When it comes to unskilled jobs, of course, only

23 percent of the employers held this view. The employers seem to share a widespread assumption — one frequently used as a cover for racism — that for historical and environmental reasons Negroes have been disabled to such an extent as to make them uncompetitive in a highly competitive society. And while it is certainly true that black people have suffered from a lack of educational and other opportunities, this line of thinking — especially among whites — has a tendency to blame the past and the ghetto environment for what is perceived as Negro incompetence, thus diverting attention from *present* institutional practices. So, many employers have developed a rhetoric of concern about upgrading the so-called "hardcore unemployed" in lieu of changing their employment policies.

To a considerable extent our respondents' assessment of Negro job qualifications reflects company policy, for the criteria used in hiring skilled and professional workers tend to exclude Negroes. The criteria are (1) previous experience and (2) recommendations. It is evident that because Negroes are unlikely to have *had* previous experience in positions from which they have long been excluded, and because they are unlikely to have had much contact with people in the best position to recommend them, the criteria for "qualification" make it probable that employers will consider most Negroes unqualified.

Negroes Get the Worst Jobs

In short, the employers' aversion to taking risks (at least with people), reinforced by the pressure of labor unions and more general discriminatory patterns in society, means that Negroes usually get the worst jobs.

Thus, although Negroes make up 20 percent of the unskilled workers in these large corporations, they fill only a median of one percent of the professional positions and only 2 percent of the skilled positions. Moreover, the few Negroes in the higher positions are unevenly distributed among the corporations. Thirty-two percent of the companies don't report Negroes in professional positions, and 24 percent do not report any in skilled positions. If these companies are set aside, in the remaining companies the median percentage of Negroes in the two positions rises to 3 percent and 6 percent respectively. Further, in these remaining companies an even larger percentage (8 percent in both cases) of *current* positions are being filled by Negroes — which indicates, among other things, that a breakthrough has been accomplished in some companies, while in others Negro employment in the upper levels remains minimal or nonexistent.

Even among those companies that hire blacks for skilled jobs, a Negro applicant's chances of getting the job are only one-fourth as good as those of his white counterpart. For professional positions, the chances are more nearly equal: Negro applicants are about three-fourths as likely to get these jobs as are white applicants. It seems that Negroes have come closest to breaking in at the top (though across all firms only about 4 percent of the applicants for professional positions are Negro). The real stumbling-block to equal employment opportunities seems to be at the skilled level, and here it may be that union policies — and especially those of the craft unions — augment the employers' resistance to hiring Negroes for and promoting Negroes to skilled positions.

What do urban Negroes themselves think of employers' hiring practices? A survey of the same 15 cities by Angus Campbell and Howard Schuman, for the riot commission, indicates that one-third (34 percent) of the Negro men interviewed reported having been refused jobs because of racial discrimination, and 72 percent believed that some or many other black applicants are turned down for the same reason. Almost as many (68 percent) think that some or many black people miss out on promotions because of prejudice. And even when companies do hire Negroes (presumably in professional positions), this is interpreted as tokenism: 77 percent of the black respondents thought that Negroes are hired by big companies for show purposes.

The companies we studied, which have little contact with the ghetto, are very different from the other institutions in our survey, whose contact with the ghetto is direct and immediate. The corporations are also up-to-date, well-financed, and innovative, while the white institutions inside the ghetto are outdated, underfinanced, and overloaded. In historical terms, the institutions in the ghetto represent another era of thought and organization.

Ghetto Merchants

The slum merchants illustrate the tendency of ghetto institutions to hark back to earlier forms. While large corporations cooperate with one another and with the government to exert substantial control over their market, the ghetto merchant still functions in the realm of traditional laissez-faire. He is likely to be a small operator, economically marginal and with almost no ability to control his market. His main advantage over the more efficient, modern retailer is his restricted competition, for the ghetto provides a captive market. The difficulty that many blacks have in getting transportation out of the ghetto, combined with a lack of experience in comparative shopping, seems to give the local merchant a competitive aid he sorely needs to survive against the lower prices and better goods sold in other areas of the city.

The merchants in our study also illustrate the free-enterprise character of ghetto merchandising. They run very small operations — grocery stores, restaurants, clothing and liquor stores, and so on, averaging a little over three employees per business. Almost half of them (45 percent) find it difficult to "keep up with their competition" (competition mainly *within* the ghetto). Since there are almost no requirements for becoming a merchant, this group is the most heterogeneous of all those studied. They have the widest age range (from 17 through 80), the highest percentage of immigrants (15 percent), and the lowest educational levels (only 16 percent finished college).

Again in contrast to the large corporations, the ghetto merchant must live with the harsh day-to-day realities of violence and poverty. His attitudes toward Negroes, different in degree from those of the employers, are at least partly a function of his objective evaluations of his customers.

Running a business in a ghetto means facing special kinds of "overhead." Theft is an especially worrisome problem for the merchants; respondents mentioned it more frequently than any other problem. There is, of course, some basis in fact for their concern. According to the riot commission, inventory losses — ordinarily under 2 percent of sales — may be twice as great in high-crime areas (most of which are in ghettos). And for these small businesses such losses may cut substantially into a slender margin of profit.

Thus it is not surprising that, of all the occupational groups interviewed in this study, the retail merchants were among the most likely to consider Negroes violent and criminal. For example, 61 percent said that Negroes are more likely to steal than whites, and 50 percent believed that Negroes are more likely to pass bad checks. No wonder, then, that black customers may encounter unusual surveillance and suspicion when they shop.

Less understandable is the ghetto merchant's apparent ignorance of the plight of ghetto blacks. Thus, 75 percent believe that blacks get medical treatment that is equal to or better than what whites get. A majority think that Negroes are not discriminated against with regard to treatment by the police, recreation facilities and so forth. Logically enough, 51 percent of the merchants feel that Negroes are making too many demands. This percentage is the second-highest measured (the police were the least sympathetic). So the merchants (like all other groups in the survey except the black politicians) are inclined to emphasize perceived defects in the black community as a major problem in their dealings with Negroes.

The shaky economic position of the merchants, their suspicion of their Negro customers, and the high "overhead" of doing business in the ghetto (because of theft, vandalism, bad credit risks) lead many merchants to sell inferior merchandise at higher prices — and to resort to other strategems for getting money out of their customers. To elicit responses from the merchants on such delicate matters, we drew up a series of very indirect questions. The responses we obtained, though they no doubt understate the extent to which ghetto merchants provide a poor dollar value per unit of goods, are nevertheless revealing. For example, we asked the merchants to recommend various ways of "keeping up with business competition." Some 44 percent said that you should offer extra services; over a third (36 percent) said you should raise prices to cover unusually high overhead; and the same number (36 percent) said that you should buy "bargain" goods at lower prices, then sell them at regular prices. (To a small merchant, "bargain goods" ordinarily means "seconds," or slightly spoiled merchandise, because he doesn't do enough volume to gain real discounts from a wholesaler.) A smaller but still significant segment (12 percent) said that one should "bargain the selling price with each customer and take whatever breaks you can get."

The Campbell-Schuman study indicates that 56 percent of the Negroes interviewed felt that they had been overcharged in neighborhood stores (24 percent said often); 42 percent felt that they had been sold spoiled or inferior goods (13 percent said often). Given the number of ghetto stores a customer may visit every week, these data are entirely compatible with ours. Since one-third of the merchants indicated that they were not averse to buying "bargain" goods for sale in their stores, it is understandable that 42 percent of the Negroes in these areas should say that at one time or another they have been sold inferior merchandise.

It is also understandable that during the recent civil disorders many Negroes, unable to affect merchants by routine methods, struck directly at the stores, looting and burning them.

Teachers in the Ghetto

Just as ghetto merchants are in a backwater of the economy, ghetto schools are in a backwater of the educational system, experimental efforts in some cities notwithstanding.

Negroes, of course, are most likely to be served by outmoded and inadequate schools, a fact that the Coleman Report has documented in considerable detail. In metropolitan regions of the Northeast, for example, 40 percent of the Negro pupils at the secondary level attended schools in buildings over 40 years old, but only 15 percent of the whites did; the average number of pupils per room was 35 for Negroes but 28 for whites.

The teachers covered in our survey (half of whom were Negro) taught in ghetto schools at all levels. Surprisingly, 88 percent said that they were satisfied with their jobs. Their rate of leaving, however, was not consistent with this. Half of the teachers had been in their present schools for no more than four years. Breaking the figures down year by year, we find that the largest percentage (17 percent) had been there only one year. In addition, the teachers' rate of leaving increased dramatically after they had taught for five years.

While the teachers thought that education was a major problem for the cities and especially for the ghettos, they did not think that ghetto schools were a source of the difficulty. A solid majority, comparing their own schools with others in the city, thought that theirs were average, above average, or superior in seven out of eight categories. The high quality of the teaching staff, so rated by 84 percent of the respondents, was rivaled only by the high quality of the textbooks (again 84 percent). The one doubtful area, according to the teachers, was the physical plant, which seemed to them to be just barely competitive; in this respect, 44 percent considered their own schools below average or inferior.

The teachers have less confidence in their students than in themselves or their schools. On the one hand, they strongly reject the view that in ghetto schools education is sacrificed to the sheer need for order: 85 percent said it was not true that pupils in their schools were uneducable, and that teachers could do little more than maintain discipline. On the other hand, the teachers as a group could not agree that their students were as educable as they might be. There was little consensus on whether their pupils were "about average" in interest and ability: 28 percent thought that their pupils were; 41 percent thought it was partially true that they were; and 31 percent thought it was not true. But the teachers had less difficulty agreeing that their students were *not* "above average in ability and . . . generally co-operative with teachers." Agreeing on this were 59 percent of the teachers, with another 33 percent in the middle.

The real problem with education in the ghetto, as the teachers see it, is the ghetto itself. The teachers have their own version of the "Negro disability" thesis: the "cultural deprivation" theory holds that the reason for bad education in the ghetto is the student's environment rather than the schools. Asked to name the major problems facing their schools, the teachers most frequently mentioned community apathy; the second most-mentioned problem, a derivation of the first, was an alleged lack of preparation and motivation in the students. Fifty-nine percent of the teachers agreed to some extent that "many communities provide such a terrible environment for the pupils that education doesn't do much good in the end."

Such views are no doubt detrimental to education in the ghetto, for they imply a decided fatalism as far as teaching is concerned. If the students are deficient — improperly motivated, distracted, and so on — and if the cause of this deficiency lies in the ghetto rather than in the schools themselves, then there is little reason for a teacher to exert herself to set high standards for her students.

There is considerable question, however, whether the students in ghetto schools are as distracted as the teachers think. Events in the last few years indicate that the schools, especially the high schools and the junior high schools, are one of the strongest focuses of the current black rebellion. The student strike at Detroit's Northern High School in 1966, for example, was cohesive and well-organized. A boycott by some 2,300 students, directed against a repressive school administration, lasted over two weeks and resulted in the dismissal of the principal and the formation of a committee, including students, to investigate school conditions. The ferment in the ghetto schools across the country is also leading to the formation of permanent and independent black students' groups, such as the Modern Strivers in Washington, D.C.'s Eastern High, intent on promoting black solidarity and bringing about changes in the educational system. In light of such developments, there is reason to think that the teachers in the survey have overestimated the corrosive effects of the ghetto environment on students — and underestimated the schools' responsibility for the state of education in the ghetto.

Social Workers and the Welfare Establishment

Public welfare is another area in which old ideas have been perpetuated beyond their time. The roots of the present welfare-department structure lies in the New Deal legislation of the 1930s. The public assistance provisions of the Social Security Act were designed to give aid to the helpless and the noncompetitive: the aged, the blind, the "permanently and totally" disabled, and dependent children. The assumption was that the recipient, because of personal disabilities or inadequacies, could not make his way in life without outside help.

The New Deal also provided work (e.g., the W.P.A.) for the able-bodied who were assumed to be unemployed only temporarily. But as the Depression gave way to the war years and to the return of prosperity, the massive work programs for the able-bodied poor were discontinued, leaving only those programs that were premised on the notion of personal disability. To a considerable extent today's Negro poor have had to rely on the latter. Chief among these programs, of course, is Aid for Dependent Children, which has become a mainstay of welfare. And because of racial discrimination, especially in education and employment, a large part of the Negro population also experiences poverty as a permanent state.

While most of the social workers in our survey showed considerable sympathy with the Negro cause, they too felt that the root of the problem lay in weaknesses in the Negro community; and they saw their primary task as making up the supposed deficiency. A hefty majority of the respondents (78 percent) thought that a large part of their responsibility was to "teach the poor how to live" — rather than to provide the means for them to live as they like. Assuming disability, welfare has fostered dependency.

The social workers, however, are unique among the groups surveyed in that they are quite critical of their own institution. The average welfare worker is not entirely at one with the establishment for which she works. She is likely to be a college graduate who regards her job as transitional. And her lack of expertise has its advantages as well as its disadvantages, for it means that she can take a more straightforward view of the situations she is confronted with. She is not committed to bureaucracy as a way of life.

The disparity between the welfare establishment and the average welfare worker is evident in the latter's complaints about her job. The complaints she voices the most deal *not* with her clients, but with the welfare department itself and the problems of working within its present structure — the difficulty of getting things done, the red tape, the lack of adequate funds, and so on. Of the five most-mentioned difficulties of welfare work, three dealt with such intra-agency problems; the other two dealt with the living conditions of the poor.

There is a good deal of evidence to support the social worker's complaints. She complains, for example, that welfare agencies are understaffed. The survey indicates that an average caseload is 177 people, each client being visited about once a month for about 50 minutes. Even the most conscientious of caseworkers must be overwhelmed by such client-to-worker ratios.

As in the case of the schools, welfare has engendered a countervailing force among the very people it is supposed to serve. Welfare clients have become increasingly hostile to the traditional structure and philosophy of welfare departments and have formed themselves into an outspoken movement. The welfare-rights movement at this stage has aims: to obtain a more nearly adequate living base for the clients, and to overload the system with demands, thus either forcing significant changes or clearing the way for new and more appropriate institutions.

Black Political Party Workers

Usually when segments of major social institutions become incapable of functioning adequately, the people whom the institutions are supposed to serve have recourse to politics. In the ghetto, however, the political machinery is no better off than the other institutions. Around the turn of the century Negroes began to carve out small niches for themselves in the politics of such cities as Chicago and New York. Had Negro political organizations developed along the same lines as those of white ethnic groups, they might today provide valuable leverage for the ghetto population. But this has not happened. For one thing, the decline of the big-city machine, and its replacement in many cities by "nonpolitical" reform governments supported by a growing middle class, began to close off a route traditionally open to minority groups. Second, black politicians have never been regarded as fullfledged political brokers by racist whites, and consequently the possibility of a Negro's becoming a powerful politician in a predominantly white city has been foreclosed (the recent election of Carl Stokes as Mayor of Cleveland and Richard D. Hatcher, Mayor of Gary, Indiana, would be exceptions). Whites have tended to put aside their differences when confronting Negro political efforts; to regard Negro demands, no matter how routine, as racial issues; and hence to severely limit the concessions made to black people.

Today the sphere of Negro politics is cramped and closely circumscribed. As Kenneth B. Clark has observed, most of the Negroes who have reached high public office have done so *not* within the context of Negro politics, but through competition in the larger society. In most cities Negro political organizations are outmoded and inadequate. Even if, as seems probable, more and more Negro mayors are elected, they will have to work within the antiquated structure of urban government, with sharply limited resources. . . . The first Negro mayor of Newark, for example, presides over a bankrupt city.

Our survey of Negro political workers in the 15 cities documents the inadequacy of Negro politics — and the inadequacy of the larger system of urban politics. The political workers, understandably, strongly sympathize with the aspirations of other black people. As ghetto politicians, they deal with the demands and frustrations of other blacks day after day. Of all the groups surveyed, they were the most closely in touch with life in the ghetto. Most of them work in the middle and lower levels of municipal politics; they talk with about 75 voters each week. These political workers are, of course, acutely aware of the precipitous rise in the demands made by the black community. Most (93 percent) agreed that in the last few years people in their districts have become more determined to get what they want. The strongest impetus of this new determination comes from the younger blacks: 92 percent of the political workers agreed that "young people have become more militant." Only a slight majority, however (56 percent), said the same of middle-aged people.

Against the pressure of rising Negro demands, urban political organizations formed in other times and on other assumptions, attentive to other interests, and constrained by severely limited resources, find themselves unable to respond satisfactorily. A majority of the political workers, in evaluating a variety of services available to people in their districts, thought that all except two — telephone service and the fire department — were either poor or fair. Worst of the lot, according to the political workers, were recreation, police protection, and building inspection.

In view of these respondents, the black community has no illusions about the ability of routine politics to meet its needs. While only 38 percent of the political workers thought that the people in their districts regarded their councilmen as friends fighting for them, 51 percent said that the people considered their councilmen "part of the city government which must be asked continually and repeatedly in order to get things done." (Since the political workers were probably talking about their fellow party members, their responses may have been more favorable than frank. A relatively high percentage of "don't know" responses supports this point.)

Almost all the Negro politicians said that they received various requests from the voters for help. Asked whether they could respond to these requests "almost always, usually, or just sometimes," the largest percentage (36 percent) chose "sometimes" — which, in context, is a way of saying "seldom." Another 31 percent said they "usually" could respond to such requests, and 19 percent said "almost always." Logically enough, 60 percent of the political workers agreed that in the last few years "people have become more fed up with the system and are becoming unwilling to work with politicians." In effect, this is an admission that they as political workers, and the system of urban politics to which they devote themselves, are failing.

When economic and social institutions fail to provide the life-chances that a substantial part of a population wants, and when political institutions fail to provide a remedy, the aspirations of the people begin to spill over into forms of activity that the dominant society regards either as unacceptable or illegitimate — crime, vandalism, noncooperation, and various forms of political protest.

Robert M. Fogelson and Robert D. Hill, in the *Supplemental Studies* for the riot commission, have reported that 50 percent to 90 percent of the Negro males in ten cities studied had arrest records. Clearly, when the majority of men in a given population are defined as criminals — at least by the police — something more than "deviant" behavior is involved. In effect, ghetto residents — and especially the youth — and the police are in a state of subdued warfare. On the one hand, the cities are experiencing a massive and as yet inchoate social rising of the Negro population. On the other hand, the police — devoted to the racial status quo and inclined to overlook the niceties of mere law in their quest for law and order — have found a variety of means, both conventional and otherwise, for countering the aims of Negroes. In doing so, they are not only adhering to the norms of their institution, but also furthering their personal goals as well. The average policeman, recruited from a lower- or middle-class white background, frequently of "ethnic" origins, comes from a group whose social position is marginal and who feel most threatened by Negro advances.

The high arrest rate in the Negro community thus mirrors both the push of Negroes and the determined resistance of the police. As the conflict intensifies, the police are more and more losing authority in the eyes of black people; the young Negroes are especially defiant. Any type of contact between police and black people can quickly lead to a situation in which the policeman gives an order and the Negro either defies it or fails to show sufficient respect in obeying it. This in turn can lead to the Negro's arrest on a disorderly conduct charge or on a variety of other charges. (Disorderly conduct accounted for about 17 percent of the arrests in the Fogelson-Hill study.)

Police Harassment Techniques

The police often resort to harassment as a means of keeping the Negro community off-balance. The riot commission noted that:

> Because youths commit a large and increasing proportion of crime, police are under growing pressure from their supervisors — and from the community — to deal with them forcefully. "Harassment of youths" may therefore be viewed by some police departments — and members even of the Negro community — as a proper crime prevention technique.

The Commission added that "many departments have adopted patrol practices which, in the words of one commentator, have 'replaced harassment by individual patrolmen with harassment by entire departments.'"

Among the most common of the cops' harassment techniques are breaking up street-corner groups and stop-and-frisk tactics. Our study found that 63 percent of the ghetto police reported that they "frequently" were called upon to disperse loitering groups. About a third say they "frequently" stop and frisk people. Obviously then, the law enforcer sometimes interferes with individuals and groups who consider their activities quite legitimate and necessary. Black people in the ghetto — in the absence of adequate parks, playgrounds, jobs, and recreation facilities, and unwilling to sit in sweltering and overcrowded houses with rats and bugs — are likely to make the streets their front yards. But this territory is often made uninhabited by the police.

Nearly a third of the white policemen in our study thought that most of the residents of their precinct (largely Negro) were not industrious. Even more striking about the attitudes of the white police working in these neighborhoods is that many of them deny the fact of Negro inequality: 20 percent say the Negro is treated better than any other part of the population, and 14 percent say he is treated equally. As for their own treatment of Negroes, the Campbell-Schuman survey reported that 43 percent of the black men, who are on the streets more than the women, thought that police use insulting language in their neighborhoods. Only 17 percent of the white males held this belief. Of the Negro men, 20 percent reported that the police insulted them personally and 28 percent said they knew someone to whom this had happened; only 9 percent and 12 percent, respectively, of the whites reported the same. Similarly, many more blacks than whites thought that the police frisked and searched people without good reason (42 percent compared to 12 percent), and that the police roughed up people unnecessarily (37 percent as compared to 10 percent). Such reports of police misconduct were most frequent among the younger Negroes, who, after all, are on the receiving end most often.

The policeman's isolation in the ghetto is evident in a number of findings. We asked the police how many people — of various types — they knew well enough in the ghetto to greet when they saw them. Eighty-nine percent of the police said they knew six or more shopowners, managers, and clerks well enough to speak with, but only 38 percent said they knew this many teenage or youth leaders. At the same time, 39 percent said that most young adults, and 51 percent said that most adolescents, regarded the police as enemies. And only 16 percent of the white policemen (37 percent of the blacks) either "often" or "sometimes" attended meetings in the neighborhood.

The police have wound up face to face with the social consequences of the problems in the ghetto created by the failure of other white institutions — though, as has been observed, they themselves have contributed to those problems in no small degree. The distant and gentlemanly white racism of employers, the discrimination of white parents who object to having their children go to school with Negroes, the disgruntlement of white taxpayers who deride the present welfare system as a sinkhole of public funds but are unwilling to see it replaced by anything more effective — the consequences of these and other forms of white racism have confronted the police with a massive control problem of the kind most evident in the riots.

In our survey, we found that the police were inclined to see the riots as the long range result of faults in the Negro community — disrespect for law, crime, broken families, etc. — rather than as responses to the stance of the white community. Indeed, nearly one-third of the white police saw the riots as the result of what they considered the basic violence and disrespect of Negroes in general, while only one-fourth attributed the riots to the failure of white institutions. More than three-fourths also regarded the riots as the immediate result of agitators and criminals — a suggestion contradicted by all the evidence accumulated by the riot commission. The police, then, share with the other groups — excepting the black politicians — a tendency to emphasize perceived defects in the black community as an explanation for the difficulties that they encounter in the ghetto.

The state of siege evident in many police departments is but an exaggerated version of a trend in the larger white society. It is the understandable, but unfortunate, response of people who are angry and confused about the widespread disruption of traditional racial patterns and who feel threatened by these changes. There is, of course, some basis for this feeling, because the Negro movement poses challenges of power and interest to many groups. To the extent that the movement is successful, the merchants, for example, will either have to reform their practices or go out of business — and for many it may be too late for reform. White suburbanites will have to cough up funds for the city, which provides most of them with employment. Police departments will have to be thoroughly restructured.

The broad social rising of Negroes is beginning to have a substantial effect upon all white institutions in the ghetto, as the situation of the merchants, the schools, and the welfare establishment illustrates. Ten years ago, these institutions (and the police, who have been affected differently) could operate pretty much unchecked by any countervailing power in the ghetto. Today, both their excesses and their inadequacies have run up against an increasingly militant black population, many of whom support violence as a means of redress. The evidence suggests that unless these institutions are transformed, the black community will make it increasingly difficult for them to function at all.

Ghetto School

Gerald Levy

Upon first arriving at Midway School, new teachers are overwhelmed with the rhetoric of control. All the orientation conferences with administrators and bull-sessions with older teachers stress the overriding priority of classroom discipline and order in the halls. The central theme of these orientation conferences is that if a teacher is "firm" and "knows what he is doing" control will take care of itself. Even in the bull-sessions with chronic teachers there is much talk about the consequences of losing control but not much said about the specific techniques for its maintenance. Listening to Dobson, the Principal, and Morton, the Assistant Principal, describe the process of achieving control in terms of "thorough planning," "interesting lessons," "being consistent," "establishing rapport," "taking anecdotal records," and "being professional," the new teacher is somewhat mystified and unsure of what is expected of him.

However, after being in Midway for only a short time and observing how older teachers and administrators treat the children, the new teacher realizes that most of the effective methods for control are publicly defined as immoral if not illegal and thus cannot be discussed at Midway's staff meetings. Likewise, old teachers are at first hesitant to discuss their methods with those new recruits who, in their idealistic statements about how they plan to treat the children, imply a criticism of traditional methods and appear to take a morally superior attitude toward traditional teachers. Thus the new teacher's initial self-righteousness and the "illegal" and "immoral" nature of those activities he is self-righteous about prevent him from learning the real strategies of control.

When describing to colleagues their proven skills and any combination of useful disciplinary options, teachers refer to these skills and options as "the system." Teachers refer to using these options directly with children as "playing the system." In effect, establishing control means "playing the system."

Once the new teacher realizes that he cannot survive in Midway unless he controls his class and that survival is preferred to moral purity, he suppresses his moral scruples and begins to play the system. Through the experience of being destroyed, the absorption of advice from old teachers, the sharing of experience with other new teachers, and trial and error, most new teachers acquire those skills necessary to intermittently maintain a minimal degree of control. While it is possible that few if any teachers are aware of or utilize all the possibilities and dimensions of "the system," it is our concern here to describe the entire system that Midway's teachers play.

"Not Taking It Personally"

Confronted with the children's irreverence and disobedience the new teacher responds with anger and deep feelings of personal inadequacy and unworthiness. He takes it personally. In not being able to fulfill his image of an educator and becoming instead an object of ridicule and a source of entertainment for the children, he experiences his humiliation directly and intimately. In the act of failing he reacts as if the failure were happening *to* him.

Previous to and during this period of destruction, the new teacher is warned by old teachers and administrators that when he "takes it personally," "gets involved," and allows the children to "get to him," the children will intensify the very behavior that got him "involved" in the first place. The experienced advisors add that when children exploit a teacher's "weak spot," the exploitation is not directed against him as a person but only as a teacher. Since the teacher is only a symbol anyway, and since personal responses to the children make teaching unbearable, the teacher is encouraged not to respond as a person. Midway encourages the new recruit to show as little emotion as possible, detach himself from his own destruction and act as if it were not happening to him. This is what Midway's teachers mean by "not taking it personally."

Eventually, new teachers realize the impracticality of their emotional responses. They learn to ignore all attempts of children to elicit a personal response. Children are often disappointed when viewing a teacher who is in the process of becoming impersonal. When all efforts at eliciting the rants and raves fail, they may beg the teacher to "get mad." By disengaging himself and hence becoming able to respond to the children's baiting in bland and unrewarding ways, the teacher sours the children's sense of victory. Once having achieved this coolness under fire, the new teacher can begin to choose appropriate responses and apply them more effectively. Self-control and impersonality are necessary prerequisites for establishing control.

"Setting up Routines"

The object of routines is to fill time safely. The more the enterprising teacher can involve his children in routines, the less likely they are to threaten his control. For the nature of the routines themselves prevents all sorts of activity that might otherwise take place.

In many classes the typical day is filled up with a succession of marches to the classrooms, hanging-up of coats, pledges to the flag, watering of plants, checking of homework, handing out paper, collecting papers, trips to the bathroom, getting drinks of water. The succession of activities is governed by rules which specify when and how they are to be done. The detailed specifications of what *can* be done have the effect of defining what *cannot* be done.

Many teachers become involved in the aesthetics of their routines. One teacher disliked her children coming straight forward from their seats to her desk. She claimed it blocked her vision and upset her concentration. She now has her children walk to the back of the room, around all the desks, and approach her desk from the side. Another teacher spends much of her time perfecting already established routines. Her children are controlled enough not to get out of their seats or talk without permission. So now, her major concern is *how* they sit (straight back), stand in line (at attention), and pledge to the flag (right hand over the *heart*, not the belly). She maintains that her class "almost runs by itself."

By refining routines and thus "tightening up" their classes, teachers protect themselves from the loss of control, present themselves as experienced professionals, and establish their superiority over other teachers.

Economy of Force

The effective use of routines presumes the teacher has the power to enforce them. When children challenge the teacher's power, it is crucial that they be defeated. So, on the first day of school a teacher picks out the potential rebel leader, and, at the first sign of disobedience, makes an example of him. He grabs the disobedient child and threatens to beat him up if he doesn't stop what he is doing. In many instances he smacks the child in front of the class. If the leader is decisively defeated, other children are less likely to rebel.

Many teachers are proud of the technique of example-making. They say that they are using minimum force to establish control. They stress the importance of establishing "who's boss" on the first day. "A little muscle" guarantees that they "won't have to be knocking heads all year." They compare themselves favorably with those teachers who "start off wrong" and end up "hitting the children ten times as much as I do." Many conclude that by defeating the children early and decisively they are actually doing them a favor.

One teacher can hit a child so rapidly on the back of the head or ear that the act is barely observable. He can teach a lesson in front of the class, swiftly walk to the back of the room, and hit the child without breaking the rhythm of the lesson. Other teachers discuss with each other the finer points of striking children by using pressure points and the ways of causing a child considerable pain without appearing to do so. Like those who stress routines, there are teachers who make an aesthetic of force.

The more a teacher convinces himself that skillful violence brings control, the less inhibited he becomes in its use. The opportunity for the prolonged use of force usually occurs when the initial battle is not as decisive as hoped. It often drags on for weeks. The teachers, having used their ultimate weapons, find that they must use it repeatedly to maintain control. Some teachers come to expect a prolonged engagement in which they must be prepared to administer a continuous barrage of "slaps on the face," "pinches on the neck," "whacks on the behind," and "knocked heads." Some teachers claim they will hit a child in the beginning "even if he looks like he is about to do something wrong." Even teachers who expect an extended battle with the children justify violence by pointing to its long-term results. As one teacher concluded, "They finally learned that I meant business."

Force is so crucial to Midway's stability and its staff's security that many teachers become fixated on the technologies of violence and literally prevent chaos in the classroom by the effective use of terror.

.   .   .

Regardless of the historical period in which they are trained and the political values and moral scruples they bring to the school, control eventually becomes the major task of Midway's teachers. At different points after varying degrees of resistance, Midway's teachers approach their task with a determination and attention to detail which suggests the quality of a foot soldier, his rifle, and his terrain. While some teachers justify their military preparedness with the notion that control is a prerequisite for education, and that the enemy will be made free through combat, others merely express their concern with survival and leave the question of military purpose to the generals and the politicians. A few teachers maintain that their survival does not depend on educating the children but on "containing them." No matter what educational views they hold, Midway's teachers know that their general well-being, sense of personal adequacy, and self-worth, confidence of masculinity, and knowledge of professional competence rapidly decline when they lose control. The personal anxieties aroused in a teacher by the prospect of loss of control is a much more salient source of motivation than is the realization that the children's education may be inadequate.

Midway provides its teachers with a system of disciplinary techniques and administrative options for survival on the job. While most of these techniques are publicly immoral and formally illegal, teachers justify their use by declaring that "it's part of the job." When they say this, they mean that regardless of the public definition of their activity and their personal views toward what they do, anyone who calls himself a teacher engages in these activities if he expects to remain in the school. Teachers further admonish parents and administrators for their hypocrisy in demanding law and order in the school and then looking askance at the means by which it is achieved.

·   ·   ·

Most teachers are unaware of Midway's significance in the lives of its students. Teachers know that the children live in a "ghetto" and are failing. But most have never ventured beyond the delicatessen two blocks from the school. For them it is nine-to-three, a quick drive out of Randolph Park, or a quick walk to the nearby subway. When inside Midway, they concern themselves with survival. In all their reflections on the state of the school, the difficulty of their jobs, and the failure of the children, Midway's teachers may not realize that the children are learning something that is crucial.

For the children, life in Midway takes on greater significance than whether they are controlled or fail in the narrow sense. Throughout their seven-year career in the school, Midway's Black and Puerto Rican children have extensive contact with white teachers who live outside of Randolph Park. As representatives of the larger society these middle-class commuting teachers, in their contact with Midway's lower-class children, communicate to them the terms of success and failure in white society, and how they are meeting those terms. Through contact with Midway's teachers and administrators, the children learn what the larger society thinks of them and what types of social and economic claims they can make on the larger society. Through Midway School, American society communicates to Randolph Park children what can be expected out of life.

·   ·   ·

Regardless of the intensity of the warfare, children are still addressed as if education were happening. The children are not told that they have already failed, only that they are now failing. The cumulative nature of a child's failure is never stated. He is passed to the next grade even though the objective tests given each year show that he is farther and farther behind.

DOBSON: Now I know what is going on in this class. You are not learning anything, and it does not matter how good a teacher you have. If you don't want to learn, no teacher, no matter how hard he tries, can teach you. Now, you're lucky to have a teacher at all. Many classes in the school system are left uncovered because there are not enough teachers; and if we were not on a triple session, you would not have a teacher. But you have a teacher and you are wasting his time and yours, because you spend all your time getting him to bawl you out for not cooperating, rather than let him spend his time teaching you something. Everytime you (he points) and you and you cause him to yell at you and go over to you to correct something disruptive that you are doing, you are wasting your precious time and your classmate's as well as the teacher's time. There are some children who are trying to learn in this class, and everytime you take away the energy of the teacher and use it for correction, that means he can't teach the ones who want to learn. Now, there is no one in this class who is reading up to grade level. In fact, there is not one person in this class who is less than two years behind grade level. Now, if you don't catch up, it will mean that you will never get through high school. You will never get the education you need, and you will never be able to get a good job when you grow up. Now, if you want to catch up, only you can do it. You should be using every precious moment in class doing your work so you can learn to read. You should be reading books outside of class, practicing reading all you can, learning to read not just by reading words, but by trying to understand the meaning of what you read.

The communication of failure increases as control breaks down. In the midst of classroom chaos a teacher may shout, "You can have your fun now, but you'll be sorry in a few years!" A teacher in the process of being destroyed reminds the children that *they* are the ones who are failing.

Many children soon come to habitually negate their own work. The teachers' preoccupation with routines and control leads inevitably to evaluating children's work almost exclusively on its form. Children are rarely rewarded for content. The emphasis is always on neatness in handwriting and arithmetic calculation, clearness in speech, and formulaic answers in social studies and science. Children come to judge their work almost totally in terms of whether or not they have "messed up." A child may spend an entire forty-five minute period doing nothing but heading and reheading his paper, declaring with each reheading, "I messed up." Rejecting everything that isn't perfectly neat "like the book," they succeed in doing nothing. In art class, this preoccupation with tidyness is sadly compulsive. Some children will not allow themselves to finish a drawing because they always "mess up." By adopting these aseptic standards with a vengeance, the children fail themselves more irrevocably than do their teachers.

At the same time the children are being convinced that they are failures, they are urged not to give up. Built into each communication of failure is a corresponding invitation to success. Teachers know that a child who has given up is totally uncontrollable. So, the hope for success must be sustained. The child is always given another chance to succeed on the condition that he conform to the values of the school.

Some teachers succeed temporarily in getting a "disruptive" child interested in some academic activity. They even make vast claims to him about possible future occupational success. Each day they discover budding writers, artists, musicians, mathematicians, and scientists. But these exhortations to perform and invitations to conform have little or no relationship to any possible future success. Children are indiscriminately urged to reform whether they are in the second grade or graduating in a few weeks, whether they are one year below grade level in reading or four years below. By trying to keep alive the children's hope for success *even when they have none,* the teachers hope to avoid the children's rebellion.

Gradually, the children begin to catch on. Graduates of Midway, who attend Porter Junior High School across the park, enter the school late in the day, run wild in the halls, bait the teachers, and innervate the children's rebellion. They are visible evidence of Midway's failure. The children also see their older brothers and sisters dropping out of Porter. Some older brothers and sisters, because they were placed in Midway's high-level classes, have been admitted to better high schools outside Randolph Park where white children also attend. However, in these high schools they are placed in the low-level classes with other Black and Puerto Rican children from other ghettos. The children are subjected to a barrage of evidence that contradicts whatever illusions they might harbor about the worth of their education and the possibility of their future success.

Some perceptive children catch on to the teachers' trick of dangling "success" before their eyes to control them. These children see that, in fact, their failure is cumulative and irreversible; frequently their bitterness shows. In tears, one boy screamed, "You don't care about me! You never taught me nothin'!" The myth that they are being educated is always breaking down.

Midway has a complicated relationship to its children. Under the guise of liberal education calculated to insure the children's upward mobility, Midway assumes the task of both communicating the failure and sustaining the myth of mobility. Thus the school has to maintain a delicate balance between preparing its children for failure and sustaining their hope for success. When the balance is not maintained and the reality of failure overrides the hope for success, the children lose faith in the myth. When the children become aware of the *pointlessness* of their study, they are forced to reassess the whole school, the teachers, the routines, the bribes, the punishment, and the control. They look for opportunities open to them that may be more profitable than those offered in the educational world.

.   .   .

Midway School is a world of harassed teachers, angry parents and disillusioned children. It is a chaotic, often brutal world in which teachers and children destroy each other. The chief characteristic of the administration is that it lacks the ability to control the situation. In the face of this chaos it attempts at best to impose a countervailing administrative reality. So that for everything that occurs in Midway, there are two co-existing interpretive and descriptive languages — the emotional outbursts of parents, teachers, and children and the bland professional language of administration. . . .

The Principal and the Higher Administrative Echelons

To his administrative superiors in the central office of the Board of Education and the district office, Mr. Dobson has to comply with a complex network of legalistic and bureaucratic directives. The directives cover everything: what curriculum should be taught and in what manner; when, and in what way teachers and children should be dealt with in cases of infractions; how parents should be treated and how teachers and children should feel. Often Dobson reads or paraphrases directives from the higher offices to children over the loud speaker in each classroom. He also does this to teachers in staff conferences and training sessions. However, most of the directives are communicated through the hundreds of circulars distributed to the teachers each year. The circulars describe the techniques and procedures for everything: minutes allotted per week per curriculum area, how to teach lessons, write lesson plans, decorate the classrooms and hall bulletin boards, set up routines and control classes, send children through the halls, conduct fire and air raid drills, order supplies, use "audio-visual aids," refer "problem children" to reading and hearing specialists and "disruptive" children to the guidance counselor for "guidance" or "suspension." In their total effect, the circulars attempt to delineate how teachers should act in all possible situations.

All these rules, procedures, techniques, and priorities comprise a system which, if it operated ideally, would leave nothing that occurred in the school to chance. Midway would operate like a machine.

Of course, Midway does not operate according to the model described in the circulars; and Dobson's crucial problem with the higher administrators is that he has to appear as if he and the school were responding to their directives. One way of appearing to do so is to pass the directives down to the teachers. While Dobson is aware that most of the directives are not followed and many are not even read, at least he can claim that he has passed them down and thus cover himself with his superiors.

But the higher administrative echelons also want evidence that the directives are being applied. Dobson satisfies this demand by presenting statistical data that so many children are being taught so many subjects on such and such a level by a qualified specialist in accordance with rules and procedures described in the circulars. At the same time he attempts to keep any information about what is actually going on in Midway from filtering up to his superiors. They do not want to learn what is going on, because direct knowledge of the school involves them on a personal level. This is distasteful to them. Thus Dobson's central task is to maintain distance between Midway and higher administrative echelons.

The major task of the higher offices is to compile statistical evidence that Midway and other schools in District 7 are complying with the directives. So that when politicians, civil rights groups, community-control advocates, and journalists attempt to expose Midway, the higher offices will have a mass of evidence showing that "the school has done its best," that a "rational educational process has been going on," that "directives against corporal punishment" have been issued, and that "new and innovative programs are being tried in depth."

The statistical evidence is also used to justify claims on the federal and state budgets. Among the highest priorities in Midway is the taking of attendance. Careful attendance records have to be kept, not only to cover the school with the courts but to document the legitimacy of the dollar-and-a-half the Board of Education receives from the state per child per day. Inexperienced teachers are continually reminded, "If you do nothing else, take attendance properly." Those secretaries responsible for pooling attendance records and other information behave toward teachers as if collecting data were the school's only task and the teacher's only duty.

It is expected by his superiors that Dobson will insulate them from any situations in Midway which could be used as a basis for attacking the district and central office. Whenever an administrative superior is made vulnerable to attack by a situation in Midway, he attempts to redirect the responsibility for the situation back to Dobson. . . .

Only when he informs the higher echelons of the smooth running of Midway and keeps other communications to a minimum can Dobson feel that he is doing an acceptable job in the eyes of his superiors. But when Dobson is unable to prevent information that tarnishes Midway's public image from getting out of the school, these superiors view it as evidence that Dobson is not controlling his school. Also, when his superiors make an unpopular decision over which he has no control, they pass the buck back to him. Thus, the more routine and normalized his communication with his superiors becomes, the more he can feel that he is doing his job.

The Administration and the Teachers

As a public figure in Midway, Dobson is seen by teachers as a caricature of the very directives he is supposed to implement. Most of his public pronouncements reflect the style and line of his administrative superiors to such an extent that it is difficult to tell whether he is reading a handed-down directive or one he has written himself. Once, the teachers returned to Midway from summer vacation the Friday before the onset of a teachers' strike. Dobson, knowing that no one would show up for work the following Monday, welcomed back the staff in all seriousness and expressed the hope that when school opened the following Monday it would be the beginning of a very successful teaching year for all of them.

At the beginning of each school year Dobson addresses the new teachers and tells them that their first year at Midway School will be "the hardest job they have ever or will ever have," that if they "make it through the first year, no matter how impossible it seems, the next year will be easier." Throughout the year, whenever a newly destroyed tearful teacher comes into the principal's office, he repeats what he said at the beginning of the year. When emergencies occur that are not covered by the rules or that do not seem applicable to any of the known options, he picks out a stock response that seems to him to fit the situation.

This formulaic approach also characterizes the relationships of assistant principals to teachers. For example, whenever an inexperienced teacher is having difficulty controlling a child, the assistant principal tells the teacher to "take an anecdotal record," "send a letter home to his parents," "call his mother in," or "threaten to have him suspended." There is a variety of recipes that the administration has for the solution of the teachers' problems.

There is a prescribed series of steps to be taken by a teacher before any problem can be legitimately referred elsewhere, so an administrator can put off a teacher indefinitely by holding him to the letter of the protocol. An administrator who uses protocol as a way of protecting himself from Midway's problems need not anger the teachers. Though aware that they are being simply put off in a socially acceptable way, most teachers prefer "Have you been keeping an anecdotal record?" or, "Did you send a letter home?" to a "Don't bother me. I have enough problems," or "Go away. I'm not here." Thus, a tactful administrator who knows his options well enough and uses them skillfully can protect himself from the teachers problems without appearing to do so.

.   .   .

While the teachers see Dobson as a patsy and a doubledealer, he sees them as incompetent. Their incompetence springs from their combined lack of experience, professionalism, and dedication. They do not read and follow the circulars. Many have not yet learned how to control their classes. Many are thought not to care. They do not take their jobs seriously, refuse to carry out administrative assignments such as decorating bulletin boards and handing in clerical work on time, are often late, and are absent as much as possible. They do not plan their lessons. In effect they do not work for the children. With so many inexperienced, uncommitted teachers it is impossible to raise reading scores and complete other tasks crucial to academic success.

.   .   .

Midway's administrators give up the educational vision and lapse into a garrison mentality. The school is viewed as a fortress in which each area is vulnerable to attack by uncontrolled children. The administrators come to see their job as securing the fortress, and their immediate task is to see that all classes are covered and other areas of the school such as the halls, the lunchrooms, and the assembly hall are secured. Securing the school involves the judicious placing and use of available teachers, aides,[1] and volunteers. Their task is complicated by the average daily absence of seven teachers. There are seldom enough teachers to secure the school.

.   .   .

Breakdown in control increases in proportion to the number of teachers who are absent on a given day and the lack of substitutes. Since Midway is considered a "rough" school, substitutes are difficult to obtain. Even with all the calculation in the placement of teachers and bargaining for preferred assignments, the administration only rarely secures the school completely.

The administration is then faced with the problem of avoiding uncontrolled children. Harassed teachers put pressure on administrators by

-----

[1] Persons hired from the community to help out with control and administrative jobs.

sending "disruptive" children to their offices. The administrators retaliate by sending the child back to the classroom and reminding the teacher that it is his responsibility to maintain discipline. The teacher sends the child back to the office and reminds the administrator that if a "disruptive" child is making it impossible for him to teach, he can demand that the child be removed from class. In Midway, children are often shuffled back and forth between the office and the classroom in a war of nerves between administrators and teachers.

But when the pressure from children is too intense or teachers are too aggressive in asserting their rights to relief, the administrators retaliate through their channels of reprimand. If a teacher fails to hand in clerical work or complete other administrative tasks on time, is late for work, or takes five minutes extra for lunch, the administrator can send him a letter of reprimand, have him sign it, and put it in his permanent file. As teachers' pressure on administration increases, so do the letters of reprimand.

At one point, a committee of five was chosen to represent the teachers in meetings with administration to discuss grievances and "ways of improving the school." During two meetings administrators and teachers blamed each other for the state of the school. After the second one, letters about lateness and incomplete clerical work appeared in the committee members' mailboxes. In many instances those teachers who received letters were generally acknowledged to be among the most effective and dedicated in the school. The barrage of letters had the immediate effect of silencing the attack on administration. Only one more sparsely attended meeting was held.

However, the use of mass reprisals is an extreme tactic that administration would like to avoid. As long as teachers appear to have a certain amount of understanding of the administrations' problems and empathy with their difficulties, do not attempt to hold them to all their formal responsibilities as administrators, and do not blame them for the state of the school, administrators overlook a certain number of infractions. In exchange for exemption from moral responsibility for the school, the administrators exempt teachers from a few legalistics and clerical chores.

Though administrators and teachers would like to publicly expose one anothers' irresponsibility, mutual security dictates a more conciliatory relationship. When things are going smoothly between teachers and administrators, they affirm each other by criticizing children and parents, acknowledging their common difficulties with them. Through the repeated denigration of children and parents, the teachers and administrators attempt to convince each other that they are friends rather than enemies. But this compulsive and ritualistic denigration of the enemy only thinly masks their mutual ambivalence and distrust. . . .

The Administration and the Parents

As Midway's principal, Dobson is the most accountable to the parents. He is the most visible and available symbol on whom parents can focus their frustrations and hostility when they feel that the school is failing their children. Parents are permanently dissatisfied with Midway, for they accept the school's terms of success for their children. They take the objective scores on reading tests at face value. They also accept the notion that before the children can learn they must be controlled. When they learn of their children's low reading and math scores and see them running around in the halls and taking over the classrooms, the parents conclude that the school is not doing its job.

The parents affirm a caricature of middle-class education. They would like to see their children controlled to the point where challenging the authority of the school would be unthinkable. The school would operate like a well-oiled machine engaged in the production of marketably educated children.

The parents want basic reading, writing, and arithmetic skills stressed and music and art deemphasized. They are aware that their children are behind in basic skills and that the reading test scores are the major indications of future academic success or failure. Every minute in the classroom should be used to further the chances of their children getting through the educational system with its accrued occupational rewards at the end. Anything which cannot be seen as directly furthering this end is viewed as a waste of time.

The nature of parental expectations exacerbates their relations with administration. The parents want immediate results and the administration has failed them. The parents charge Dobson with this failure; for, from the standpoint of parents, it is not the "nature of the community" or the "state of the home" which is responsible for the lack of results, but the policies of the school and the quality of its teachers and administrators.

Parents are somewhat aware of the real difficulty in educating their children. And they might be willing to overlook some of Midway's shortcomings if its principal would only communicate with them. Lacking immediate satisfaction they might settle for an honest statement of the problem from Dobson. Because of his chronically passive relationship to his superiors, Dobson is incapable of the type of diagnosis that would be acceptable to parents.

He tries to handle all complaints from parents rationally. A parent tells him the books are inadequate and the teachers incompetent. To a complaint about books, Dobson asks which books and which classes they are used for. The parent specifies the books, and says that they are no good because her children can't understand them. Dobson replies with the formula, "These books are being used throughout the school system." If this is not feasible, he admits that the books are inadequate but that the school doesn't have sufficient funds to order new books. To a complaint about the incompetence of a teacher, Dobson asks the parent where she got her information. If she got it from her child, he discredits the child's complaint with the statement, "Children sometimes make up stories about their teachers." If this does not satisfy the parent, and the teacher is new, Dobson maintains that he is an "inexperienced teacher" and that the school will soon be offering him an in-service training course so that he can become more effective. While Dobson demands maximum specificity in parents' complaints, he is as evasive as possible in his replies.

Teachers usually ask children to write a composition about "what I did this summer" on their first day back to school. Parents are suspicious of the educational value of this practice. Children groan when this is asked of them year after year. When an angry parent questioned this policy, Dobson got up and gave a long speech explaining how the writing of the paragraph involved "oral communication," "writing and composition," "sentence structure," "phonics," "spelling and grammar." He further stated that writing the paragraph about the summer vacation interrelated and combined all of the skills needed in "language arts." "It's not what happened during the summer that's important, but all the activities involved in *communicating* what was done during the summer." Dobson redefines the parent's complaint and answers as if he had been asked about pedagogic ideology.

By rationalizing and redefining all complaints in ways that no longer indict the school and its staff, the complaints lose their critical relevance. By redefining the nature of the complaint and the basis upon which it can be legitimately rectified, Dobson has a self-exonerating answer for anything that occurs in the school. He need not come to terms with parents' feelings about Midway.

The parents are not satisfied. They are convinced that Dobson is devious and evasive, that he is concerned with his own survival, and that he doesn't care about the children. The more Dobson tries to talk his way out of responsibility for the state of the school, the more the parents hold him responsible for its state.

Dobson's problems with parents comes to focus in his relationship with the P.T.A. The P.T.A. has about fifteen active members and for the past two years has been dominated by its president, Mrs. Jackson. Jackson is extremely critical toward teachers and administrators. She says that many teachers are not interested in the children but are just in the school to "collect a paycheck" and "avoid the draft."

I know why there are so many white men here. They aren't interested in teaching . . . Vietnam!"

Mrs. Jackson's attack is best illustrated in the monthly P.T.A. meeting. She begins the meeting by asking everyone to stand and recite the twenty-third Psalm. After the prayer, she speaks:

> I want to welcome you all to this Parent-Teachers' Association. Now it's very important that we all of us parents unite and work together so we can get the education that we want for our children. We know our children are behind. They're getting dumber and dumber every day. We know that their education is at stake and without education — it comes out in the paycheck, and without the education you can't get a decent job. (Applause and shouts of approval from the audience.) Now we were united last year and we fought hard and I think, I hope, we got something done. I think, I hope, all our children got the books. Now I say we fought hard last year and this year we got to stay united, and if we do — if we stick together — we can get anything we want for our children. It's up to us. It does my heart a good turn to see all these other schools with parents getting together for things they want, and we can do it, too. So spread the word and let's get to work. What we got to have is a parent checking on the teachers in each class and reporting to me. When they don't teach right, I can take it up with Mr. Dobson.

Mrs. Jackson then responds to questions and statements from other parents.

> PARENT: Well, what's the use of the children bringing home the book if, well, they bring them home every night but don't read them. The teachers don't make homework assignments in them.

> ANOTHER PARENT: Not only that, but we know how far behind our children are in reading — usually two years, and so what good is it if you have a fifth-grade book in social studies and the child can only read in the third grade. My son said to me he didn't even like the book.

> JACKSON: Well, I'm glad you brought that up because it shows what kind of teachers we got, some of them, and what we got to do; and give me the class of your child. I'm going to bring this up to Mr. Dobson. I'll face him first thing tomorrow and he better get his teachers on the ball. Now he says half of them are very young. They are inexperienced and we can't expect them to teach so good, so the books will have to do it. They just have to assign homework in the books. Well, he better, or they shouldn't be teaching — getting paid for doing nothing. Now, I don't expect the teachers to love our children, but they better teach and we're going to have parents and the children checking on every teacher to see she does her job if she is going to be paid and go on strike and our children miss three weeks of school and all those holidays. I tell you the only way we are gonna get anything is if we fight for it. So now let me write that down

and I'll face Mr. Dobson tomorrow and Mr. Morton and Miss Ryley
better get down on those young teachers. There's other things I know.
I know the teachers aren't teaching and I'm not going to bring it
up here but when I face Mr. Dobson and if I don't get satisfaction
from him I go to Mr. Stratton. The teachers they got the TV on from
9 to 10:30 in the morning. I find out these things and I'm going to
face him with it.

Dobson's public response to Jackson's attacks varies with his audience. In direct encounters with Jackson he is typically formal, but his
logical explanations infuriate her even more. Her verbal attacks on Dobson intensify in relation to the "reasonableness" of his response.

With new teachers just assigned to Midway, Dobson understates the
problem:

> About our P.T.A., we have a very inactive P.T.A. One woman who
> is president of the P.T.A. is articulate. She is not really articulate
> because I can't always understand her. Well, she makes her demands
> fairly well known. Her ideas don't always go along with ours. P.T.A.
> meets the second Wednesday of every month. There is an average
> of fifteen to thirty parents. What happens is that this woman does
> most of the talking and the rest of the parents listen. There may be
> more activity this year because we have gotten a few parents who
> really seem interested in doing something and just don't want to sit
> and listen.

In his joint appearances with Stratton [the Superintendent], he talks
to the teachers about the need to "absorb" or "neutralize" Mrs. Jackson.
They hope to do this by "better communication" and by· eventually bringing parents into the P.T.A. who are more compatible with the ideas of
administration.

But with the more experienced teachers. Dobson is more candid in
his image of Jackson. He has remarked that he feels that Jackson should
be "discredited" and "told off by the community." He senses that Jackson
is more feared and respected than he is. Furthermore, he is aware that
the teachers are convinced that "Jackson runs the school." In private he
has admitted to certain teachers that the "parents are becoming the
supervisors."

Dobson's inability to respond to the parents on their terms com-
pounds his difficulties with them. His inability to protect the teachers
from Jackson aggravates his relations with the teachers. When he attempts to protect the school and the teachers from the parents, he infuriates the parents. When he gives any credence to the complaints of
the parents he infuriates his teachers. When he attempts to deflect some
of the responsibility for the state of the school onto the district office and
the Board of Education, he meets with disapproval from Stratton. Caught

between contradictory demands of the parents, teachers, and his superiors, Dobson is in an impossible dilemma.

When he tries to moderate between conflicting parties or subtly change his line to favor those to whom he is talking, he is thought to be a two-timer and a phony. When he approaches all groups with the higher administrative rhetoric, he is considered an impersonal machine. Thus, whatever action Dobson takes, he further discredits himself in the eyes of his constituents.

Dobson would prefer to withdraw from all parties in the school by whom he is discredited. But he cannot, for he is daily faced with the responsibility of making and communicating decisions that vitally affect everyone. When forced to communicate a decision unfavorable to a person or group, he says he is sorry about what he has to do, that he would rather not do it, but that he has been forced to by other parties. When he fires a teacher, he maintains that he is acting on orders from Stratton or pressure from parents. When he suspends a child he tells the parent that this is the province of the guidance counselor and he could do nothing to stop it. When he tells a teacher that a child is *not* being suspended, he cites pressure from the parents and the district office. When he blocks an innovation in the school that parents are demanding, he cites a rule from central headquarters. In almost any instance Dobson can appear as if he has no power, but is only an extension of other pressure groups and outside agencies. Through him and upon him, all the contradictions of Midway are played out. As head of his school, he symbolizes and expresses the failure of administrative bureaucracy in education.

Midway's administrators are caught in a crossfire of parental anger, supervisory dissatisfaction, teacher disrespect, and child rebellion. All their activity is directed toward ducking the crossfire. But in doing so they unintentionally administrate and sustain those policies which undermine the interests of parents and children. It is ironic but not illogical, given society's relationship to its lower-class youth, that the very activities which enable administrators to survive in the school insure the children's failure.

The American Health Empire

Health PAC

The sixties took medicine out of the doctor's black bag and transformed it into a growth industry. Empires sprang up where before there had been only scattered fortresses, and engorged doctors, hospitals, health centers, and their dependent populations of human "material." Public spending on health grew from an irregular trickle into the geyser of Medicaid and Medicare, creating vast new areas of expansion for the empires and for the health products industry. The federal government brought forth potentially sweeping reorganizational programs to rationalize and harness the dynamism of this newer, bigger health system.

The empires, the medical-industrial complex, and the money which spawned them, are still big. But the "Health New Deal" — the mid-sixties' gesture towards a more rational and egalitarian health system — lies in wreckage across the land. Medicare is a disappointment; Medicaid is a scandal. Regional Medical Programs and Comprehensive Health Planning are two new overlays of irrationality on top of the system they were meant to restructure. Even the brave new federally financed neighborhood health and mental health centers have settled down as imperial fiefdoms or closed up shop on account of community problems.

Consumers, even the ones who don't read the glowing descriptions of the health industry in *The Wall Street Journal*, are aware that there's a new bigness to the health system: the bills are bigger; and the lines of people waiting for care are longer. The consumer's over-all impression is one of increased scarcity, not of growth. The proportion of general practitioners to the total population falls year after year, with no help in sight from any new kinds of supplementary medical personnel. Medical responsibility to the patient as a whole person declines with the emergence of each new hair-splitting medical subspecialty. There are more and more life-giving or beautifying drugs and devices to consume, but there is less and less chance of assessing their worth, or paying the price.

1970, like 1965, is bringing more and more talk of restructuring the health system. So far, the strategy advanced by the medical insiders and concerned outside interests seems to consist of redoubling the mistakes of the past: Medicaid, Medicare and Blue Cross taught that open-handed public subsidy of an unregulated health system is not only wasteful in the

From *The American Health Empire: Power, Profits and Politics,* prepared by Barbara and John Ehrenreich. Copyright © 1970 by Health Policy Advisory Center, Inc. Reprinted by permission of Random House, Inc.

short-run, but leaves permanent distortions on the pattern of health services delivery. So the medical "reformers" plan to consolidate Medicaid, Medicare and all other insurance schemes into one giant package, to sanction it with public authority, and to dignify it with the name "National Health Insurance." Empires have proved their inability to deliver, whether the task is something as limited as operating a community hospital or health center or as open-ended as creating a regional medical program. So the medical reformers propose that a "national" health system is one in which *all* the nation's health services would be arranged into imperial domains, or regional health authorities, under the trusteeship of medical schools and major teaching hospitals. The philosophy guiding the medical reform effort is like the philosophy guiding the American effort in Vietnam: if something was a mistake in the past, it deserves another try, but on a much bigger scale.

Not everyone is ready to go along with this. Just as the American soldier in Vietnam doesn't care whether he is participating in something called pacification, Vietnamization, or annihilation, the factory worker doesn't care whether the money taken out of his paycheck for health goes to something called Blue Cross, Metropolitan Life Insurance Company, or National Health Insurance. And the big city clinic-user couldn't care less that his neighborhood hospital is part of an integrated, modern, medical empire. In fact, more and more people, veterans of Medicaid and Medicare, are not even interested in seeing new money appropriated for health. It's harder and harder to find a place to spend it, and sometimes it doesn't even seem to be worth the trouble of trying.

What's come over people is not, as one New York medical emperor claimed, "the traditional public apathy about health," but a new understanding of the depth of the changes necessary to create a humane and effective health system. Brilliant new technical fixes, no matter how well-promoted, just don't sell anymore. Fewer and fewer people really believe that new arrangements like national health insurance, prepaid group practices, or regionalization, will be the wonder drugs which will save the health system. Like hearth transplants, all these miraculous new techniques for rationalizing and vitalizing the system have begun to look like last-ditch efforts to advertise a failing system to a jaded public. No one is interested in reshufflings and repackagings of the same old fragments. No one is interested in renovating a building which ought to be condemned.

The alternatives are just barely beginning to be heard. They do not have the appeal of technological gimmickry, or the dignity conferred by powerful and respected spokesmen, but they are simple: according to a growing movement of health workers, students and consumers, meaningful change must begin with a reordering of the priorities of the health system. Patient care must be put first; otherwise no amount of new reform — stable financing, new manpower, more efficient patterns of delivery of care — can mean anything to the patient. Research and training are important, but they must be financed and organized so that they are not parasitical on the care of the poor. Profits must be phased out, for they have no place in an enterprise in which human life is at stake. A publicly accountable system must replace private enterprise in providing all health care and health products. When the priorities of the health system have been reversed, then it will make sense to discuss the niceties of hospital planning, or clinic administration, or group practice design.

More and more consumers are beginning to think that this approach makes sense. The only trouble is that they haven't found anyone willing to do it for them. Traditionally, health care is something that the public entrusts to hospital trustees, scientists, medical school deans, drug company executives, government health officials, and the like, and none of these is about to sacrifice, profits, prestige, or personal empire in the cause of public service. The movement which is demanding change has begun to understand that only it can provide the leadership for change. The obstacles are almost paralyzingly huge — the almost impenetrable technological mystique of health care and health professionals, the increasing consolidation and monopolization of the health industry, and the political authority of the imperial and industrial trustees of the health system. But what is at stake is worth the struggle and the new responsibility.

The movement for revolutionary restructuring of the health system is in direct continuity with the larger American movement for a more democratic, egalitarian society. One stream comes out of the medical and nursing schools, which, starting in the late sixties, began to see students who bore no resemblance to the straight-laced, conservative classes of previous decades. The late-sixties' student entered professional school in the wake of four years' exposure of campus Vietnam, civil rights, and student power protests. By 1968, the student movement was busy "bringing the war home," to issues of university complicity in imperialism and racism; campus R.O.T.C. programs, limited admissions for blacks, university defense research, etc. A sizeable minority of the new crop of medical and nursing students started out with the suspicion that their professional schools were no more likely than the university to be innocent of racist and imperialist functions. At the same time, a new majority of medical and nursing students — certainly not radicals — came with idealistic expectations of learning how to serve, not how to make money or do research or be bureaucrats. The medical and nursing schools did the rest — thwarting the expectations of the liberals and confirming the suspicions of the radicals. The medical student movement became large enough to support its own national organization, the Student Health Organization.

Other medical and nursing students, along with recently graduated health professionals, poured into the Medical Committee for Human Rights. By 1970 the growing movement [was] large enough to support several publications around the country and has been strong enough to carry off militant actions around health issues in a number of cities.

A newer but fast-growing element of the health movement is the women's liberation movement. Starting in the mid-sixties, more and more young women, veterans of peace and civil rights activities, began to look into their own oppression as women in a male-dominated society. For a year or so the movement was barely visible, as it busied itself with one-to-one organizing around the issues of women's sexual exploitation in the home, the workplace and in the media. In 1968, the movement surfaced with organized attacks on the institutional sources of male domination, such as women's magazines and cosmetics companies. Women's groups in Boston, New York, and Washington took on the health system as a prime target. As health workers, women occupy subservient and underpaid slots: seventy percent of the nation's health workers are women, but only seven percent of the nation's physicians are women. As health consumers, women use more medical care than men (mainly because of childbirth and childrearing) and are subjected to specifically "sexist" (the analog of "racist") indignities in the course of getting that care. Women's liberation groups are increasingly taking action around specifically feminist demands — dignified obstetrical and gynecological care and legal abortions, for example — as well as more general demands for low-cost, high-quality health care.

The medical students' and women's branches of the health movement are largely white. But by far the largest element of the health movement is black and brown, including both health workers and health consumers. Blacks, Puerto Ricans and Mexican-Americans have always been at the very bottom of the health system — exploited as workers to support the hospitals financially, and exploited as patients to support hospitals' research and teaching activities. The idea of doing anything about it goes back to the civil rights sit-ins in the early sixties. The energy of the civil rights movement quickly spilled over into other areas: demands on schools for the right to education, demands on welfare agencies for the right to an adequate income, and, more recently, demands on health institutions for the newly perceived right to health care. In the mid-sixties, as the civil rights movement grew into the black liberation movement, the demands began to shift from equal rights in a white-run society to all-out self-determination for black communities. The demands put on health institutions were no longer just for more and better services, but for community participation in the planning and priority-setting of health centers, hospitals and even medical schools. As of 1970, New York had more than a dozen black and Puerto Rican neighborhood organizations concerned solely with health. Even in smaller cities, like Fresno and El Paso, and in Southern rural areas, there are the beginnings of black and brown movements for community control of local health institutions.

The message of [the] civil rights movement was not lost on black health workers either. Starting in the early and mid-sixties, unions such as New York's Local 1199, Drug and Hospital Workers, and the American Federation of State, County, and Municipal Employees, began a massive hospital organizing drive, borrowing the techniques and even the personnel of the larger civil rights movement. People like the Southern Christian Leadership Conference's Reverend Ralph Abernathy and Coretta Scott King (Mrs. Martin Luther King, Jr.) joined in the organizing drives, linking the issues of civil rights and the right to a decent living. Despite these promising associations, the unions representing hospital workers — from the Teamsters to 1199 — have shown little interest in health issues beyond the bread-and-butter concerns of their membership. But this in itself has been an important contribution. Workers who make a decent living and have some degree of job security have at least the possibility of struggling for career advancement or for better community health programs. In New York, where some two-thirds of the hospital workers are union members, workers in a number of institutions have joined with community groups in demands for better services and greater community involvement. In other health institutions, workers have formed black caucuses or radical caucuses to struggle for better services and greater democracy within their health facilities.

Only in the last couple of years have these separate streams — the medical and nursing students', women's, and black and brown communities' and workers' movements — begun to come together as a single health movement. White, middle-class, medical students realized that they would be imitating the patronizing style of their medical school mentors if they worked for, rather than with, the low-income community served by the medical school-hospital complex. Students in New York University, Columbia, and Einstein Medical Schools in New York, have gone off-campus to find leadership from neighborhood health organizations. In some cases, neighborhood consumer groups have sought out the radical medical students, and enlisted them in community struggles. Women's groups have joined forces with black women consumers, as in Washington, D.C., or linked up with black women hospital workers, as in Chicago. Health workers' groups are making contact with medical students and young doctors' organizations within the same institution, and with community groups outside.

What is emerging is a sense of common struggle, and the outlines of a common program. Health workers, including medical students, and health consumers obviously have different and even potentially conflict-ing interests. The basis for consensus is that health workers cannot really do their job, if their job is health care, in a system structured around profits, research, and education. At the same time health consumers can-not get good care, on a dignified basis, from a system that is internally hierarchical and oppressive to its workers. The kind of joint program which has been taking shape in New York and other cities calls for re-organizing and redirecting of the health system: health care should be free at the point of delivery (i.e., the costs should be borne by the entire society, through the tax system). Hospitals should move beyond their present "first aid" emphasis and focus on preventive health services. In-ternally, health institutions should be run democratically, with decision-making shared by health professionals, nonprofessionals and community people. Outside forces, such as trustees and philanthropic organizations, should be deposed, since they contribute little to the health service proc-ess (not even money any more). Doctors should be salaried employees, not free entrepreneurs. Medical schools and other schools of health ser-vices should open their doors to all black, brown, and white women appli-cants and white working-class youths, and should provide opportunities for professional training, up to the M.D. level, for all interested health workers — nurses to orderlies. In short, the health system should be re-created as a democratic enterprise, in which patients are participants (not customers or objects) and health workers, from physicians to aides, are all colleagues in a common undertaking.

An ambitious program for a movement which is still so young and small? Maybe, but the chances are that both the movement and its pro-gram will grow explosively in the next few years. Medical students, young women, and blacks as a whole are not the only groups that are op-pressed by the American health system. More and more ordinary, white, middle-class Americans are finding themselves up against a health system which promises far more than it delivers, and costs far more than it is worth. The first stirrings of discontent have been heard, and noted, by unions, management and government, but the chances of a meaningful response from them are slight. As the health system gets bigger, more industrialized, and more centralized, the differences between poor and middle-class, or black and white consumers begin to blur. No one is mak-ing it, and everyone has a stake in the creation of a revolutionary, people-oriented health system.

Paradoxes of Health Care

Nathan Glazer

Some intriguing questions — indeed, mysteries — seem to arise when one examines the field of health care. I intend to present some data — the best available, to my knowledge — bearing on three assumptions which most people accept as unquestionably valid: (1) that we need more health personnel, particularly doctors; (2) that the poor get less health care than the non-poor; (3) that the approaches to health to be found in England and Sweden are clearly superior to our own and should serve as a model for us. I then propose to raise a more general question about the cultural differences among groups as a neglected problem in the assessment of health care.

I

One reads everywhere about shortages of doctors, nurses, hospital personnel, technicians of all kinds. One knows of endless waits in hospitals, clinics, doctors' offices. The diligent reader of Congressional hearings will find experts in every field reporting that there is a need for more training, more training facilities, for more specialists and personnel of every kind. Thus, one Congressional committee in 1966 points out:

> The Public Health Service reports that we have approximately 10,000 trained home health aides as compared to 200,000 that are needed. . . .

Or,

> As long ago as 1953, it was concluded that adequate sanitation program staffing called for at least one sanitary engineer or sanitarian for each 15,000 persons. . . . A host of new areas of responsibility have been added since, but some local communities, counties and states do not meet the standards for environmental control set thirteen years ago. Over 13,000 sanitary engineers and sanitarians would be needed to meet those 1953 minimum staffing requirements. . . . Of this number, a 1962 survey concluded that between one-third and one-half are actually employed. . . .

Reprinted with permission from *The Public Interest,* Winter 1971, pp. 62–77. Copyright © 1971 by National Affairs Inc.

Or,

> The public spends 2.4 billion a year to maintain a standard of dental health in which only 40 per cent of the people visit a dentist even once a year.

And thus, logically, we would need at least a doubling of the 106,000 dentists and dental hygienists and technicians.

Dr. Howard Rusk makes a similar point:

> President Johnson in his health message pointed out that last year we broke the record and rehabilitated 120,000 disabled persons. . . . It was 40,000 in 1945. The President's 1966 budget called for funds to rehabilitate an additional 25,000. But when you realize there is a backlog of 2,000,000 and when we get 250,000 new cases a year. . . .

Once again we have a *prima facie* case for doubling expenses and personnel, and this in one of the most rapidly growing programs of the government.

If we look at needs from another perspective, the shortages are even greater. Thus, if we consider those areas of the country that are best served with personnel, and those that are worst served, the differences are of the order of magnitude of two or three to one.

In 1957, three states in the northeast averaged 176 doctors per 100,000 population; three states in the southeast averaged 71 per 100,000. In metropolitan counties, the ratio was 173 per 100,000; in counties neither metropolitan nor adjacent to metropolitan counties, the ratio was 74 per 100,000. In isolated rural parts of these counties, the ratio was 50 per 100,000. There has been no substantial change in this pattern in recent years, though it has been pointed to regularly for at least forty years. In 1965, New York State had 133 physicians per 100,000 population in private practice, Georgia 70, Mississippi 60. Isolated rural counties had less than half as many physicians as their share of the population (3.2 per cent of the population, 1.5 per cent of the doctors). Low-income sections of cities did even worse. In Watts before the start of the OEO-funded community health center, there were eight physicians for 35,000 people. The newspapers often report the plight of towns that are ready to provide doctors a house, a car, and a clinic — and get no takers. In New York State, with the best doctor-patient ratio in the country, 56 municipalities with populations of more than 2,000 have no doctor.

As for doctors, so for nurses; in 1957, Connecticut had 599 professional nurses per 100,000 population; Arkansas only 123. The northeast states, as a group, had 416 per 100,000; the east south central had 144 per 100,000. In 1963, it was estimated by the Surgeon General Consultant

Group on Nursing that 850,000 more nurses would be needed by 1970 — which was 100,000 more than were being used in all hospitals in 1963. And, in order to indicate that these estimates were not simple professional hyperbole, it could be pointed out that, in 1961, one-half of the positions for professional nurses in public hospitals in New York City were vacant; in hospitals in general throughout the country, the figure was 20 per cent. In 1967, three-quarters of the positions for professional nurses in New York City's municipal hospitals were vacant.

And Yet —

The case is overwhelming. Between 1955 and 1965, while population increased 17 per cent, medical auxiliary personnel increased 63 per cent. That should have made a difference — but, as we have seen, by the later date there was no let-up in projected shortages for the present and the future. If we estimate shortage by some standard established by a professional group as to how much of some kind of personnel is needed, there is indeed a shortage.

If we estimate shortages on the basis of health in well-served and poorly-served areas, the matter becomes more obscure. For example, William N. Hubbard has pointed out:

> In the United States the ratio of physicians to population varies from 188/100,000 in New York to 93/100,000 in Wisconsin, *with little difference in the general health status of the two states.* . . . During World War II there was a massive exodus of physicians from [civilian practice] in 1942, and a sudden return at the end of the war. *These shifts did not affect statistical measures of trends in general health.* [My italics]

And now let us observe the interesting experiment conducted by one expert health planner, Robert M. Sigmond, the director of a leading health planning council:

> During the past year I have been conducting an informal, unscientific, unstructured, confidential survey. I have presented dozens and dozens of practicing physicians with the following hypothetical suppositions and questions:
> *Suppose this country faced a national emergency like a long world war that required your region to contribute as many physicians, nurses and other health workers as possible. Suppose further that you were placed in charge of the health services in your region and were assured of the complete trust and cooperation of everyone. Would you be able to contribute any of the region's physicians, surgeons, nurses and other health workers for national emergency service, without impairing the quality of the health service provided in your region?*

Every single individual whom I questioned believed that if he could achieve complete cooperation and commitment, health manpower in the region could be substantially reduced without impairing quality of care and without adverse effect on the people's health. The unanimity of response was striking.

Even more striking were these physicians' responses with respect to the amount of reduction in health manpower that could be achieved without reducing the quality of effectiveness of service. When asked to estimate the proportion of the region's health manpower that could be released for national emergency service, the answers varied from about 10 to 40 per cent, with an average of about 20 per cent.

Equally as striking was the conviction of most of these doctors that the greatest proportion of health manpower could be spared among the most highly trained health personnel — physicians and nurses, for example, as contrasted with aides, orderlies, and kitchen workers.

How would manpower reductions be achieved? . . . There was a surprising consistency of basic themes.

1. grouping physicians (and other practitioners) in organized settings and centralized locations so that they can make full use of lesser skilled but specially trained workers in their "office practices" and thus provide more service per physician;

2. locating more physicians offices at hospitals and removing the distinction between "office" and "clinic" to reduce physician travel time and permit full use of the hospitals' manpower and technical resources without having to admit patients as bed patients;

3. redefining many health service tasks so that lesser trained personnel can take them on . . . ;

4. permitting nurses to make house calls in medically supervised home health programs;

5. creating closer linkages between related hospitals to permit grouping of maternity, open heart surgery, and other specialized low use services at fewer larger hospitals;

6. encouraging all families to develop more efficient medical care habits by identifying with one nearby physician group for provision and supervision of all needed health services.

Other ideas were mentioned less frequently: automation and computation, self-help units in hospitals, intensified health education, multiphasic screening, etc. No one in the group suggested any lengthening of the work week. . . .

Interestingly enough, many of the doctors whom I asked felt that the process of reorganizing to reduce manpower could produce improved quality with fewer health personnel. . . .

I . . . asked one last question: *suppose the great national crisis was not a long world war, but the spiralling cost of medical and hospital services and the many unmet health needs right in your own region, the deaths and suffering that could be avoided by expanded and im-*

proved health service. . . . Could you deliver? I wish I didn't have to report that most of my group doubted that it would be possible, under present circumstances, to achieve the degree of commitment and co-operation that would produce results. At least, as a number said, "not in my lifetime." [1]

What Are "Reasonable" Goals?

It is clear that Mr. Sigmond and his friends are not about to rush into combat to try to restrict the flow of federal funds into the medical schools, nursing schools, and other institutions which try to increase the quantity of personnel. Quite the contrary; when new legislation and new funding are proposed, they will come forward to support it, by pointing to the shortages of personnel. And they would have a reasonable argument. The reorganization of health services that might justify a reduction of personnel is not forthcoming, and in its absence we do face the reality of concrete shortages.

But in the light of such awkward evidence, one is entitled to ask: what "goals" for health personnel are "reasonable?" A few years ago, one health specialist went back many years to examine the regularly pre-dicted shortage of doctors that was to overwhelm us in this country. He concluded that, even though we never seemed to undertake action on the scale that each study said was absolutely necessary, the shortage never-theless did *not* overwhelm us. Indeed, one could argue that the extraordi-nary increase in doctors' fees in the last few years has not occurred because the doctor shortage finally caught up with us but because the government, through Medicare and Medicaid, guaranteed the payment of "customary" fees. As a result of these guarantees, those doctors who charged less to the aged and the poor no longer found it necessary to do so. If there had been 10 or 20 per cent more doctors, one wonders — I have no evidence for this point — whether the increase would have been moderated in any marked way. Perhaps, just as research shows that peo-ple may be found to fill whatever number of hospital beds are provided, people will be found, if there is a guarantee of payment, to patronize whatever doctors there are.

Whenever the health specialists regularly demand more personnel (as they demand more beds), skeptical economists will point out that, for example, there are enough trained nurses not working to overcome or mitigate the calculated shortages, and that salary increases would bring them back into the nursing profession. Interestingly enough, in this case,

---

[1] *Report of the National Conference on Medical Costs,* June 27–28, 1967 (Wash-ington, D.C.: U.S. Government Printing Office, 1967), pp. 190–192.

owing to the recent organization of nurses in many areas, and the resulting increase in wages, it was possible to test the analysis. The National Advisory Commission on Health Manpower of 1967 was the first of a whole series of postwar government reports to find that the projected number of nurses would not fall too short of need or demand in 1975. It was also rather moderate on the need for an increase in the number of physicians. In short, it seems clear that the "shortage" of doctors and nurses is not simply a matter of numbers but of efficiently utilizing the numbers that now exist.

II

There is no question that the poor are sicker. Unfortunately, there are no nationwide mortality statistics by income. One of the best studies has been a recent comparison of poverty and nonpoverty areas in Chicago. (This does not permit really fine analysis, because of the limitations of area comparisons.) Crude mortality in poverty areas was only three per cent higher than in nonpoverty areas; but the people in poverty areas are younger, and if it had been possible to compute age-specific rates, the differences would be much greater. Differentials in infant mortality were very large — 75 per cent higher in poverty than in nonpoverty areas. In both cases, the differences between white and nonwhite were even more substantial than between poverty and nonpoverty areas.

The clearest and best evidence of poorer health among the poor is to be found in studies of days of disability per person per year, where differences of the order of two-to-one are found. Those in families with income of under $2,000 a year have 29 restricted activity days a year, while those with family income over $4,000 a year have less than half that, 13 restricted activity days a year.

But while the poor are sicker, the differences in the utilization of health care are not as marked as one might expect. The same study which reported twice as many disability days for those under $2,000 a year as for those over $4,000 a year showed lesser differences with respect to the use of physicians. Fifty-nine per cent of the poorer group have consulted a physician in the previous year, 13 per cent a specialist, compared with 73 per cent and 28 per cent of the better-off income groups. These differences in health care utilization by poor and nonpoor, which were once extreme, are now declining. Indeed, in some settings they are now reversed. In 1928–31, families with an income of more than $5,000 spent *11 times as much* on medical care as families with incomes under $1,200. In 1962, families with incomes of more than $7,000 spent only 37 per cent more on medical care than families with incomes under $2,000. (Between

1928 and 1962, the proportion of the population in families with more than $7,000 in income rose from six to 31 per cent; the proportion in families with under $2,000 fell from 55 to 12 per cent.) The cut-off points for income in the two years are quite different, but they clearly record a great equalization of expenditure.

The correlation between income and hospital admission has also fallen. In the 1928 study, the admission rate for those over $10,000 a year was more than twice that for those in families between $1,200 and $2,000. A 1952–53 study showed almost no association between income and hospital admissions. This result came about because, in the insured portion of the population, there is *a negative* association between income and hospital admission (210 admissions per 1,000 for those in families with incomes under $2,000, 120 for those in families with incomes over $7,500). The National Health Survey of 1957–63 shows again almost no association, with a slight bulge for middle-income groups between $3,000 and $6,000. But, when one makes an adjustment for the fact that the poorer families are older, there is a slight association between income and hospital admission — 117 for those below $2,000, 128.5 for those above $7,000. The association is nothing as large as it was in 1928–31.

New York City, which in respect to social policy often seems to project the course that the rest of the country will follow in a few years, gives striking evidence of the increasing equalization of health resources among different income groups, owing to the elimination of income barriers to the use of health resources among the poor (that is, those on welfare, who number one-eighth of the population of the city, and an even larger number who are eligible for a substantial range of free medical services under Medicare). Indeed, economic barriers are now either nonexistent or minor for the poor, who thus may face fewer economic barriers to health care than most of the nonpoor, whose insurance generally only covers part of their health needs. Two recent studies demonstrate the substantial use of health care services by the poor. Thus, a 1966 study of a sample of New York women and children on welfare shows the mean number of physician contacts (visit to physicians, home visits, emergency clinic and other clinic visits) is 5.0 per year for the mothers, 7.7 for the children, which the authors of the study point out is comparable to national norms. The authors compare their sample with an National Opinion Research Center survey in 1955, which shows the following number of physician visits by women, by income:

under $2,000	5.0
$2,000–$3,999	4.3
$4,000–$6,999	4.5
$7,000 and over	4.9
all incomes	4.5

A 1964 study shows an average of 4.8 physician visits for the civilian, non-institutional population of New York City. Differences by income were reported only for those with family incomes under and over $4,000. Those under $4,000 had 6.6 physician visits per year, those over $4,000, 4.2. The comparable figures for the northeastern United States in 1963–64 still ran the other way: 4.3 for those under $4,000, 4.7 for those over $4,000. The differences by income in New York — with the poorer showing more visits — showed up for each of the major groups in the population (white, nonwhite, and Puerto Rican). The poorer remained sicker — the number of acute conditions was greater for those under $4,000.

Nationally, the statistics collected by the National Center for Health Statistics shows increasing convergence in utilization of health services — measured quantitatively — between 1958 and 1966. Income differences in utilization still exist, but they are declining. One analyst concludes: "Income level of family seems to play little part in the utilization of physician services when race, sex, age and education are considered." Similarly, "Less and less difference continued to be the case among educational groups and whites and nonwhites, although the differences remain quite significant in both instances."

Better, Worse — or Different?

But more significant than the scale of remaining differences in utilization between income and racial groups are two other elements. One is the quality of medical care. We pointed earlier to the fact that the poor see specialists less often than the better-off. Another difference is found in the *reasons* for which care is sought. The better-off have more preventive and diagnostic visits: the poorer have visits for acute conditions. These are clear differences, to be found in the data.

Other differences are harder to quantify but are certainly equally important. We know the poor go more often to clinics and emergency wards — but is the care better or worse than for those who go to private physicians? Whether better or worse, it has certainly been different. Perhaps one way of suggesting the difference is to reprint Oscar Lewis's description of a visit by a poor Puerto Rican mother to a New York clinic:

> Finally Soledad's turn came. A tall Negro woman in a navy-blue uniform handed her paper jackets, saying, "Here, put these on the children." Then she began to fill out a form for Soledad, beginning with her name and address.
> "And how many children have you?"
> "Four."
> "Names?"
> Soledad gave the children's names, explaining that her son, Quiquo, was in Puerto Rico with his father.

"How come this little girl's name is Alvarado?"

"Because she isn't my own daughter, I adopted her," Soledad answered.

"Well, I'd better put them all down as Rios," the woman said. "What is your husband's name?"

"My husband is dead."

"What did he die of?"

"In an accident." Soledad answered the woman's questions rather sullenly. "What busybodies these people are!" she said in an aside to Rosa. "You'd think I was being jailed for murder."

The attendant asked if Soledad was getting welfare aid. Soledad replied that she was not. "Don't you know you qualify for it?"

"Forget it," Soledad said shortly. "As long as I can work to support my children, I don't want welfare. Not the way they treat you."

"Have the children been in contact with anyone who had tuberculosis?" the woman asked.

"Well, yes, with a cousin of mine in Puerto Rico a long time ago. But it was the school doctor who told me to bring the children here." The attendant went out and a doctor came to give the children the tuberculin test. He then sent them to an adjoining room for chest X-rays, telling them to come back for the results a week later, on Friday.

Before they left the Health Bureau, Soledad spoke to the attendant who had filled out their forms. "Could you take care of my nephew? All he needs is to have these stitches cut."

"No, not here," the woman answered. "You'll have to take him to a hospital for that."

"But we can pay," Soledad said.

"No, we can't do it here," the woman repeated impatiently, waving them out.

"What sons of the great whore they are, all of them! They should have a bomb dropped on them," Soledad exclaimed. "Look," she said when they were outside, "I'm going to cut Gabi's stitches myself. I know they won't do it at the hospital either. They don't want to take care of him." [2]

This is not a particularly horrendous example of the treatment of the poor, but suggests its disjointed and often indifferent character. A hypothetical description by Lester Breslow is even more vivid:

Consider the case of a young woman whose family is receiving Aid to Families with Dependent Children. The most likely medical event in the life of such a woman is pregnancy. Assuming that she is a highly intelligent and well-motivated woman, she will seek prenatal care as soon as she finds that she may be pregnant. She seeks this

---

[2] From *La Vida* by Oscar Lewis. Copyright © 1965, 1966 by Oscar Lewis. Reprinted by permission of Random House, Inc.

care from her local health department clinic. When the time comes for her to deliver the baby, she is transferred (theoretically with her records but in actuality most likely not) to a public hospital. There she encounters a new set of documents and personnel for delivery of the baby. Before discharge, the baby will be examined by a pediatrician who will never see the child again. Now this highly intelligent, well-motivated young woman will take her baby to a well-child clinic operated again by her health department but at a different place from where she received her prenatal care and at a different time. After several such visits to the well-child clinic, the baby may become ill. When the mother takes the baby to the clinic where the doctors and the nurses have been providing care, she is informed that she cannot obtain care there any longer because the child is sick. She is advised to take the child to a physician near her home who is paid by the welfare department. This new physician establishes still another record for the baby and provides care in his office. If the child becomes sick enough to require hospitalization, the physician tells the mother that he is not able to admit her child to the hospital where he practices because she is on welfare and she must take the baby back to the public hospital. She turns again to the public hospital care for her sick child, but after a few days is informed that the child has a special condition making the baby eligible for crippled children's services, which must be provided in still another resource. . . .[3]

It is a depressing picture, and suggests the need for better *organization* of medical care for the poor, rather than simply a greater quantity of health resources. But when we speculate just what that organization should be, there is no clear answer, as we may see by considering the health care systems of other countries.

Our concern with the health care systems of other advanced countries has stemmed from three sources. First, they provide care at far lower costs than we do. Second, there is much less discontent with the health care system. And third, they not only provide cheaper care, and more satisfying care; the consumers of this health care also show up as healthier than Americans on the major indices.

The most important such index for international comparisons has been infant mortality. And all through the 1960's there has been considerable concern at the poor American performance in this respect. In 1963, against a United States infant mortality rate of 26.0, Sweden showed a rate of only 16.6, and Australia, Denmark, England, and Wales, Finland, the Netherlands, New Zealand, Norway, and Switzerland, all showed

---

[3] Lester Breslow, "Changing Patterns of Medical Care and Support," *Journal of Medical Education* 41:4 (April 1966), pp. 318–324.

lower rates. Later in the decade, the United States stood 24th in international comparisons — most of the industrially-developed nations of the world now did better than this nation. Nor did we do better with adult mortality. In 1959–61, every nation in the OECD but one showed a lower death-rate for males in the ages 45–54 than the United States, all but three showed a lower death rate for females, seven showed lower infant mortality rates, ten showed lower mortality rates over-all.

But, let us now consider Sweden and England more closely.[4] We will note, first, that, even if the AMA is now convinced along with almost everyone else, that we need more doctors, the fact is that we already have considerably more than England, and far more than Sweden. The United States, in 1958, had 140 doctors per 100,000 population, England and Wales 111, Sweden only 83. Perhaps the Swedish doctor works very hard and gets to see many patients? Not so if we estimate work-load by number of patients seen. In Sweden, the average number of visits to the doctor per person per year is 2.5, compared to 4.7 in England and Wales and 5.3 in the United States. On the other hand, the Swede goes to the hospital much more often than the Englishman, slightly more often than the American. The range in hospital use in the three countries is given in the following table:

TABLE 1

Hospital Admission Rates Per 100 Population

	BEDS PER 100 POPULATION	ALL	SHORT-STAY HOSPITALS	SHORT-STAY HOSPITALS, EXCLUDING DELIVERIES
England and Wales	10.5	86	77	68
Sweden	15.0	136	126	113
United States	9.1	134	125	105

If we think that the Swede is going to the hospital more often for minor ailments, and getting better care for them, this assumption is challenged by the fact that his hospital stay is much longer than the American's — 15 days (as is also true in England), compared to eight here. It's doubtful that many Swedes spend 15 days in a hospital for a minor ailment — hospitals are still just hospitals, not country clubs.

---

[4] This section is based on important comparative work by Osler Peterson and Odin Anderson.

So the Swedes see doctors less, use hospitals more. There are also remarkable differences in the use of hospital personnel. Odin Anderson estimates that, while Sweden has one employee per hospital bed, the United States has two and one-half.

We all know we shall have to spend more for medical care — every study so assures us. Yet, in comparisons made 10 years ago Sweden spent 3.5 per cent of GNP, compared with 5.3 per cent in the United States; yet its infant mortality rate was 63 per cent of that of the United States, and its mortality rate for males aged 45–54 was only 52 per cent of that of the United States. (England spent a higher proportion of GNP — 4.5 per cent — than Sweden, though still less than the United States, and did better than the United States, though not as well as Sweden; its infant mortality rate was 87 per cent of ours, its male mortality rate — 45 to 54 — 76 per cent of ours.) What does one conclude from such a comparison? That we need fewer doctors, fewer nurses, and more hospitals? Certainly, that would be one cheap way of making the United States, in some respects, more like Sweden.

Of course, the more reasonable conclusion is that the critical issue is not the *quantity* of health facilities or of health manpower, but the *system of organization* of health care. Yet having said that, we still have some problems. It is interesting that no one in this country, whether on the left or the right in issues of health care, proposes following what seems to be one of the most striking features of the system of health care in England and Sweden — the sharp separation between the general practitioner and the hospital physician. The hospital physician works full-time in a hospital; when patients are referred, the general practitioner gives up all claim to care, and the patient is now in the hands of the hospital staff. This means a sharp differentiation in status, and it means too that those opportunities for education and control of the physician treating his patient in a hospital under hospital rules that our system at least makes possible do not exist in those countries. The change most widely proposed in American health care — comprehensive care by a team of physicians and other professionals — is not at all common in England and Sweden, where the doctor is still the primary source of health care for people.

III

The elements of the English and Swedish system that we can most easily follow are those of universality of access to a common system and better provision of care in distant and rural areas. While simple decency requires that we move in that direction, we should not oversell the results in advance. One cannot help feeling, reviewing the amazing pattern of hospital understaffing — by our standards — in Sweden, that a good deal must be based on the fact that there are Swedes in the hospital, and Swedes serving them. In other words, there are aspects of culture that affect health and care, and these aspects may be quite independent of the health care system.

There is a good deal of evidence along these lines. Even in this country, there are substantial differences in health which seem quite independent of differences in health care systems. Consider the differences between states of the United States, all with about the same kind of health care system:

> The most important differential [in mortality] is race, but even considering the rates for whites only, the age-adjusted death rate (average 1959–61) in the highest state is 33 per cent greater than in the lowest; and the highest infant mortality rate is 55 per cent above the lowest; and the death rate for males 45–54 in the worst state is 60 per cent higher than in the state with the lowest rate.

And the variation between the states is not to be explained only by the resources they devote to medical care. In 1954–57, Utah and Iowa had the lowest infant mortality rates in the country, and they had by no means the largest input of resources. (Indeed, if one wants to push this further, it may well be the states with the highest proportion of Scandinavians who seem to do best in health.)

We can point to two major factors which help explain why the provision of health care, even when well organized, may be only indifferently related to the improvement of health. The first is the role of still poorly understood cultural factors in affecting health, independently of available health resources and the health care system. Thus, there are remarkable differences between different ethnic and racial groups in health, even when we hold constant the amount of health care available to these groups.

This is easy to illustrate. If we consider Negroes and Puerto Ricans in New York City, for example, and we hold constant the socio-economic

TABLE 2

Perinatal Mortality Rates for New York City, 1961–63

FATHER'S OCCUPATION	WHITE	NEGRO	PUERTO RICAN
Professional, managerial, and technical	16.7	24.2	22.5
Clerical and sales	20.8	31.5	24.4
Craftsmen and operatives	20.9	32.9	24.3
Laborers and service workers	25.9	36.6	27.8

background of parents, we find startling differences in infant mortality, as Alonzo Yerby has indicated in the table above.

Lester Breslow has pointed to the surprisingly better health records for Japanese and Chinese in California where the infant mortality rates for 1964 were: 33.9 for Negroes, 20.8 for Caucasians, 13.6 for other non-whites. And, in the case of the five-year relative survival rate from local-ized cancer of the breast: 73.4 for Negroes, 81.5 for Caucasians, 90.8 for Japanese.

Minako Kurokawa has studied the remarkably low childhood acci-dent rates of Japanese in California. Odin Anderson has pointed to the evidence that immigrant Jews, despite extreme poverty and overcrowd-ing, showed a remarkably low rate of infant mortality. Comparisons in eight cities in the period of 1911–16 showed that while the white rate averaged 108, the native born white 94, and the foreign-born white 127, the foreign-born Jewish rate was an incredibly low 54.

Culture, operating through socio-psychological factors, is thus clearly one element determining the health of a population. To unravel its influ-ence is enormously difficult; and to then go on from that to health care policies that will take these influences into account is even more difficult. Again, in countries of homogeneous population, these effects of culture on health are constant, or near constant — the health system takes them into account automatically, so to speak. In a country with a population of varied origins and distinct subcultures, the problem is not so simple.

One of the reasons these subtle socio-psychological differences be-tween subcultural groups continue to have consequences for health is that, as some major traditional causes of disease and death are conquered, personal and psychological factors become important in determining an individual's capacity to maintain health. Thus, Odin Anderson points out in connection with infant mortality:

> Once the [infant mortality] rate drops down to 30, the broad eco-nomic and social factors operate with lessening effect, and personal behavior factors of the families in the high impact mortality groups involved, particularly the mothers, begin to exercise an increasingly dominant influence.

And, Dr. Alfred Yankauer writes, in connection with child health care services:

> One must recognize, however, that not all countries seem convinced of the values of integrated services. The Netherlands and Sweden, which boast the lowest infant mortality rates in the world, seem con-tent with the current separation of their preventive and curative ser-vices. One wonders whether this is a reflection of their small popula-tions, homogeneous nation cultures, common values and traditions.

These might serve to promote an informal communication and basic understanding which in a large, complex, heterogeneous, mobile society such as the United States must be formalized through administrative and institutional channels.

There is a second line of argument and investigation which weakens the connection between health achievements and a specific health care system. This is the growing weight of evidence that general environmental conditions, which seem to have played a large but undetermined role in reducing the death rate in the 19th and early 20th centuries, may now be playing a substantial role in *increasing* it in the latter third of the 20th century. Thus, Victor Fuchs writes:

> One of the factors contributing to the difficulty of reaching firm conclusions about the relationship between health services and health is the importance of environmental factors. Some . . . are biological, involving the appearance and disappearance of bacteria, viruses, and other sources of disease. Some are tied to the production process, e.g., the factors associated with occupation. Others are part of consumption, e.g., diet, recreation. Major attention has been given to income, partly because many other environmental factors tend to be highly correlated with real income, both over time and cross-sectionally. Examples include housing, education, urbanization, drinking and the use of automobiles.
>
> The prevailing assumption, in some cases with good evidence, has indicated that an increase in real per capita income has favorable assumptions for health, apart from the fact that it permits an increase in health services. *This assumption for the United States at present, except for infant mortality, may reasonably be questioned. This country may have passed the peak with respect to the favorable impact of a rising level of living on health.* [My italics]

For two reasons then, even when we adopt some of the measures that we know will improve our chaotic and frustrating methods of providing health care, we may not do as well as countries that are smaller and poorer. One might conclude with two passages, one from the pediatrician Alfred Yankauer, one from the economist Victor Fuchs. They suggest some of the lines of thought, and the new directions, we are likely to be following in the future.

> The contribution of the traditional personal health services to any measurable improvement of mortality indices may be sharply questioned. It may, in fact, be thoroughly irrational to justify or "sell" a child health care program solely on the basis of its effect upon indices of mortality and morbidity. A more compelling basis is simple compassion and the ideology of service which the professional physician is expected to possess. It is no longer tolerable that the food, or the

quantity, quality, and personalized nature of the health care which an infant receives, should be determined by the income and race of his parents.

Victor Fuchs says:

> My final suggestion — almost plea — is for us to remember that what we are really concerned with is health — not costs as such, and not medical care as such. My reading of the health literature leaves me with the impression that the greatest potential for improving the health of the American people is not to be found in increasing the number of physicians, or in forcing them into groups, or even in increasing hospital productivity, but is to be found in *what people do and don't do, to and for themselves.* With so much attention given to medical care, and so little to health education and individual responsibility for personal health, we run the danger of pandering to the understanding urge to buy a quick solution to a difficult problem. [My italics]

Government Policies for Housing

George Sternlieb

The entangled mesh of ownership patterns, of changes in the form and function of the older city and the folkways of its inhabitants, the great migration patterns which have dominated the demographic considerations in and about the United States metropolitan areas, the rising standards of expectation, all provide the matrix within which our data have taken form. Any efforts at improving attitudes toward slum maintenance and rehabilitation must in turn take this matrix into account, or prove unsuccessful.

The present market situation is one of virtual stagnation in the hardcore slum areas. The combination of risk, decreasing profitability, and loss of potential for capital gains has substantially restricted the kinds of professional owners who are willing to invest in slum properties. It takes a highly insensitive individual to become a professional nonresident owner of slum property, in the light of present societal attitudes. This is not an individual who is easily influenced to invest his money unless an appropriate return can be secured. Given the relative weakness of the

Reprinted by permission from *The Tenement Landlord* by George Sternlieb, Rutgers University Press, New Brunswick, New Jersey, 1969. Copyright © 1969.

slum apartment market, a weakness which has been aided in Newark's case by substantial amounts of public housing, as well as the shifts out of the central city, . . . the professional landlord has been faced with the choice of basically two alternatives: to stand pat and not increase his investment, or to attempt to improve his parcel in order to secure higher rentals.

The pattern that was observed in the course of this study indicates that the choice substantially has been the former. The observer cannot fail to be struck by the "heads you win, tails we lose" nature of this phenomenon. When the apartment market is very strong the landlord need not improve; when the apartment market is very weak the landlord fears for his investment and does not improve. What can municipal authorities use to break this impasse? Code enforcement is the usual reply. Code enforcement, however, must be, as will be noted later in more detail, accompanied by financing help and tax reassurance. Without this accompaniment it will merely lead to wholesale evasion and corruption. Before pursuing these matters in more detail, it is essential that the basic question be resolved — what the city, as a reflection of society, is or should be doing with slums and their occupants.

What Is, or Should Be, the Cities' Attitude Toward Slums and Slum Dwellers?

If this writer may be permitted a gross oversimplification, the problem of the slums is one both of plumbing and morale. It has largely been viewed in the past as consisting solely of plumbing. This is not to denigrate the former; the provision of appropriate housing amenities is certainly an essential step toward improving the outlook and aspiration level of slum dwellers. However, the morale problem cannot be cured merely by providing physical amenities. The relatively limited success of public housing bears testimony on this point.

Government policy towards the slums must have as its primary aim the improvement of the aspiration level and capacity for goal realization of the slums' inhabitants. Tax policy, code enforcement, financing aid, and municipal services; all of these must be viewed within the context of the overall objective.

The community must face the realities of the slum situation fairly, without self-deception or romanticism, and at the same time move for change. A review of slum conditions as they exist in order.

1. In Newark, as in many of other Northern industrial cities, the overwhelming majority of hard-core slum area residents are Negroes. The

whites, who continue to decrease in number, are typically an elderly rem-
nant of earlier immigration.

2. There is little evidence of a substantial return of the white middle
class to the slum areas of the city.

3. A substantial proportion of slum tenements are owned by absentee
white owners. These owners are not merely absentees from the slums per
se, they are also absentees, at least as residents, from the city in which
they own property.

4. The factor of ownership is the single most basic variable which accounts for variations in the maintenance of slum properties. Good parcel
maintenance typically is a function of resident ownership.

5. Dependent upon major programs of land clearance for purposes of
urban renewal and/or highway construction, a population vacuum will
develop in the slums. The tidal wave of Southern Negro migration has
slowed down and is substantially bypassing some of the Northern cities
which were its traditional goals.[1] With virtual stability in the Puerto
Rican population size, there is no new depressed group on the horizon to
fill the older slums.

6. While this population decrease makes the problem of relocation
much simpler, it also tends to limit the landlords' capacity and will to improve parcels.

7. Given a substantial dependence upon land taxes in the face of increased demands upon the municipality for services, taxes have become a
major inhibitor of entrepreneurial activity in the central city. Both in
terms of their impact, and in terms of the uncertainty which surround
their administration, current municipal tax policies are leading to further
degeneration of the slums.

8. The relationship of client and patron, which plays a dominant role
in the dealings between government, both municipal and federal, and
the poor population of the slums, is deleterious to the morale of the individuals concerned.

Within these parameters are there policies which would improve
present slum conditions, both in terms of buildings and of people? Over
the past year a whole armory of enabling legislation has been passed by
Congress. Local authorities have been given the essential weapons for
the fight against blight and for better housing conditions. The Housing

---

[1] The nonwhite population of the United States is continuing to leave the South,
but the outflow has been slowed considerably. Out-migration of Negroes from the
South has averaged little more than seventy thousand per year in the period from
1960 to 1963, or only half that of the 1950 to 1960 period. This is based on a study
done by the Metropolitan Life Insurance Company, See MLIC, *Statistical Bulletin*,
April 1965, p. 3.

and Urban Development Act of 1965 is indicative of the growing sophistication of government policies in rehabilitation. From a direct loan program, which provides long-term 3 percent loans, to the rehabilitation grant procedure under section 115 of Title I of the 1964 act, and to the demolition grant and aid to code enforcement divisions, a vast armory has been supplied to local authority.[2]

It should be stressed that the enabling legislation mentioned above is strictly that — enabling legislation. It remains for local authority to take the initiative in implementing programs which will take advantage of this legislation. There are certain to be many difficulties on the road to implementing this legislation. There is no new legislation that does not require some degree of experience in its utilization. Certainly, however, the community is better armed for rehabilitation than has ever before been the case.

The discussion which follows will focus first on the development of resident landlords, and the ancillary elements which this will require, such as guidance and financing arrangements, as well as tax policy. From this the discussion turns to the question of municipal services and the problem of the hard-core slum and code enforcement.

Boosting the Proportion of Resident
Landlords in Slum Tenements

As all of our data from the Newark survey indicates most forcefully, *there is no question of the significance of landlord residence, particularly of single-parcel landlords, as insurance of proper maintenance of slum tenements.* Given the priority accorded by multiple-parcel owners to tenant problems as an inhibitor . . . the lack of feeling on this score by resident landlords, coupled with their good record in maintenance, is most significant. *It is the resident landlord, and only the resident landlord, who is in a position to properly screen and supervise his tenantry. No one-shot wave of maintenance and paint up–sweep up campaign can provide the day-to-day maintenance which is required in slum areas.* Given the relatively small size of Newark tenement units, and others like them, this can only be accomplished by a resident landlord. The record of these landlords, as we have indicated, is such as to inspire confidence in their future behavior on this score.

By making it feasible for more residents to become owners, we further encourage the development of local leadership which is so sorely

---

[2] See H.H.F.A., *Local Public Agency Letters* 340, 341, 342, 343, 345, & 349 [Washington, 1965].

EXHIBIT 1

Monthly Level Payments Required to Amortize $1,000 over Various Terms and at Various Interest Rates

INTEREST RATE (PERCENTAGE)	TERM (IN YEARS)						
	10	15	20	25	30	35	40
6.0	$11.10	$8.44	$7.16	$6.44	$6.00	$5.70	$5.50
5.5	10.85	8.17	6.88	6.14	5.68	5.37	5.16
5.0	10.61	7.91	6.60	5.85	5.37	5.05	4.82
4.5	10.36	7.65	6.33	5.56	5.07	4.73	4.50
4.0	10.12	7.40	6.06	5.28	4.77	4.43	4.18
3.5	9.89	7.15	5.80	5.01	4.49	4.13	3.87

Source: Ernest M. Fisher, *Urban Real Estate Markets: Characteristics and Financing* (N.Y.C.: National Bureau of Economic Research, 1951) p. 71.

lacking in most slums. The role of resident owners as guides and creators of life patterns for the youth of the slums to follow is clearly evident.[3]

How could this type of development be stimulated? There are several prime requirements. The first of these, obviously, is financing help. In Exhibit 1 is presented a table which indicates cash flow requirements as a function of mortgage term and interest rates. As can be noted in the Exhibit, the term of mortgages is much more significant from a cash flow point of view than are interest rates. For example, a mortgage at 6 percent which is written for a fifteen-year period imposes a smaller cash flow burden than an equivalent size mortgage for ten-year period at 3.5 percent. Given the dearth of available financing, which is currently the case in the slums, there is obviously no alternative but to provide something in the way of long-term FHA guaranteed mortgages for slum tenement purchases *by residents*. The analogy with the early Homestead Act springs readily to mind. In that case, government lands were provided at relatively reasonable rates and with liberal financing to those who would live on them. The same thing must be done in the slums. The 1965 Housing Act is a beginning on the road.

With this must be coupled inexpensive fire and liability insurance for resident owners in slum areas. The expense and difficulty of securing these necessities is rising rapidly and it strikes hardest upon the poor landlord who has limited leverage with an underwriter.

Financing, however, is merely one of the several steps which is required. There is a phenomenon which I call the *storm window syndrome*.

---

[3] Given the lack of a masculine image which has been commented on as a not unfamiliar shortcoming of family upbringing among the poor, the significance of a resident owner *peer unter pares* to slum youth as a potential goal setter is clear-cut.

This is merely one symptom of the frequent victimization of relatively innocent new resident buyers of slum tenements by a variety of home improvement services. The pride of these people in ownership makes them
easy marks for "pay later" operators. The point raised by a money lender
interviewed in the course of this study should be kept in sight here. He
pointed to the fact that commonly when he has to repossess a parcel, the
typical cause is that the owner has burdened the parcel with two or more
home improvement loans. Just as the Agriculture Department provides a
variety of advisory services for the farmer, so the city and/or the Federal
Government must provide equivalent advisory services for the new home
owner in the slum areas. These advisors must be competent not merely
in home improvements, but also in financing and appraising parcels. It
would seem entirely possible that among the ranks of senior savings and
loan people, as well as within the ranks of the present FHA personnel,
such individuals could be found. Technical competence, however, must
be linked with a basic sympathy with the aspiration level of the new
owner and with none of the *deus ex machina* attitude that so often exists
in government relations with the poor.

The question of tax policy is a most significant one on this score, as it
is in terms of the general problem of slums. It may well behoove the city
to continue its policy of full assessment based upon market values. Obviously, where broad-based taxation is available on a basis other than land,
it may reduce some of the strain. Reassessment policy, however, must be
more clearly defined than is presently the case. The landlord should have
no reason to fear city reassessment merely because of painting the outside
of his house.

It is essential that the city not merely adopt a more reasonable attitude toward taxation, but also *sell* the facts of this attitude to those who
may be influenced by misconceptions as to its reality. In addition, in the
long run it may very well pay the city to provide the equivalent of homestead rebates for resident landlords. This is a format (which will be recognized by those readers who are familiar, for example, with tax policy in a
city such as Miami Beach) in which the homesteader, i.e., the resident
landlord, receives either a reduction or a rebate in his real estate taxes.
This might well be coupled with a stipulation that the rebate be employed in the improvement of the parcel in question. The area of uncertainty and suspicion which surrounds current taxing procedures must be
clarified. Its existence clearly inhibits improvements. . . . The reader
may wish to consider the data . . . which indicates the fears of landlords
on municipal tax policy.[4] *This fear has been justified frequently in fact
because of the financial bind of a municipality dependent on realty taxes*

---

[4] [See George Sternlieb, *The Tenement Landlord* (New Brunswick, N.J.: Rutgers University Press, 1966), chapter 11.]

in the face of expanding needs and a static base. In these circumstances, pressure on the landlord's pocket is a constant. While, as has been indicated, tax relief in itself will not generate improvement — it is an essential step toward fostering it. Alternative means of financing municipal needs, therefore, must be found.

Municipal Services

There seems to be ample evidence that the level of municipal services required by the slum areas is higher than that required by nonslum equivalent areas. At the same time there is reason to believe that the actual delivery level of these services is reversed with poorer areas being slighted. The comments of a Negro owner on this subject are most apropos.

> Parcel #330 was purchased in 1935. "You know the neighborhood has really changed terribly since we moved in here. At first it was mostly German and Jewish, and the police in the city took care of things. No trucks parked overnight in the streets and no noise or anything like that. Now there is mostly Negro and they don't seem to come any more. If you complain they want to put you in jail. — Many of the owners here would like to stay, but the neighborhood is run down so that most of them sell just to get away. Since Negroes have become predominant, the city has allowed things that they would not allow when I just first moved here."

One should notice that the parcel was very well maintained. The owner commented that he was sure that continued municipal surveillance would have saved the neighborhood regardless of who moved in. The backyard of this parcel, which has a very handsome garden, looks out upon a sea of debris. The owners complain that they have had to screen their back porches to keep the rats out. Another Negro landlord made the following comment:

> When I went to complain to the police department about overnight truck parking and teenage hoodlums on the block, the cops made me feel like a criminal. I was glad to go home and kind of hide myself behind the door.

These comments mirror attitudes which are most common among current resident landlords.

Every effort must be made by the city to provide an optimum level of services within the slums. Such functions as police protection, street lighting, parking restrictions, garbage collection, and a host of others could be named here. Not least among these is the question of educational facilities. While this is a subject whose depth is beyond the scope of this study, it cannot be omitted. Without substantial efforts on all of these fronts, the efforts at rehabilitating the slums must falter.

The Future of the Hard-core Slum

. . . There are clear-cut indications that new resident buyers are unwilling to move into an area which is as far gone as is Area 1. The dominance of large-scale absentee landlordism in that area is a tribute to the fact that they are the only landlords who are willing to invest in such problem situations. One can seriously question the potential of such an area for rehabilitation. Given the relatively loose housing market, which presently exists in center-city Newark, the bulldozer approach to such hard-core areas would seem to be the only answer. This should not wait upon redevelopers. The existence of such hard-core blight (it should be [noted] that the area in question has less than 25 percent sound housing on the basis of the 1960 Census) can only serve to drag down the neighborhoods peripheral to it.

The loss of tax revenue to the municipality through this process of demolition must be accepted as surgery essential to preserve the surrounding areas from the spread of deep-seated blight. Obviously, the scale of this blight will require considerable discretion on the part of municipal authorities on the phasing and speed of demolition. Given the present functioning of the market, . . . private enterprise cannot be depended on to remove buildings which are no longer usable. Again, new urban renewal legislation to ease this process was adopted in 1965, it must be vigorously utilized.

There is some question whether a change in tax policy to encourage demolition might not be in order. The needs of the city for more open space, the potential of already assembled and cleared substantial size tracts in encouraging further development, must be depended upon to generate future use for the areas in question. The maintenance of the hard-core blight areas, given the facts of alternative housing availability, cannot be justified upon tax income reasons alone.

Code Enforcement

Parallel with all of the suggestions above is the requirement that code enforcement be made much more rigorous. But prior to this, there is required a much more adequate definition of just what the code should be. For example, the requirement of central heat is observed least in some of the better housing areas. . . . It is not uncommon, particularly among members of earlier immigrant groups, that cold-water flats with suitable decentralized heating facilities are preferred to those whose heat supply is subject to the administration of the landlord and of the vagaries of the heating system. *Adequate insect and rodent control, plumbing that works, paint, and general cleanliness may be much more significant to the inhabitants of a tenement both physically and spiritually than the existence of central heat or plaster walls.* Whether the studs used in a repair are 16 inches on center or are 20 inches on center may be completely irrelevant to a tenant. A building which is completely satisfactory on the basis of existing codes may be completely unsatisfactory in terms of its effect upon its occupants.

Code enforcement, therefore, must require a much more subjective approach than has previously been the case. This is particularly the case with those buildings in the hands of landlords who cannot afford repairs. In these cases, it may be necessary to work out a long-term plan of rehabilitating the parcel in question, with major emphasis being given to the paint and cleanliness functions, those most easily encompassed by "sweat equity." Good maintenance and resident landlordism are much more significant than mechanical adherence to a mechanical code. With the legality of multiple housing codes clarified, the city has a new avenue of creative action.

The responsibility of social workers to appreciate the fact that the loose housing market does enable them to move their clients "up" into better quarters is clear, though far from universally acted on. At least one of the major owners interviewed for this study is upgrading his parcels for welfare tenants whose housing allowances have been "opened up" slightly and who have alert social workers as guides.

No False Romanticism!

The self-help capacity of the poor is limited. Some resident landlords are elderly, others are uneducated, and some lack an appropriate aspiration level. The fact remains, however, that as a group, they are presently the best landlords in the slums, and provide probably the major hope for better maintenance in the future. It will require a talented and understanding guidance operation to help generate landlord enthusiasm while restraining over-expenditure. The problems here should not be underestimated. It is essential if this operation is to be truly successful, particularly from a morale standpoint, and also from the standpoint of securing *long-run* improvement, that the advisory service be a guide and an inspiration, not a directorate.

The present and future strains on the municipalities' budget, coupled with limited increases in revenue, will make it most difficult to pay for the services which are required. The alternative, however, of increasing degeneration is all too clear-cut. From a fiscal point of view, the program outlined above is a most burdensome one; this point should not be evaded. There is no other answer, however, from the city's point of view.

Tax policy must be directed toward aiding the good landlord, and penalizing those owners who do not properly maintain their properties. A tax policy based on sales value . . . can easily have the reverse effect. The potential of homestead exemption, of rigorous code enforcement, and of self-help stimulating devices, must be rigorously exploited.

Rehabilitation and Rent Increases

There is a well-founded fear on the part of the tenantry that rehabilitation leads to rent increases. This must be accepted as a fact of the market. Although tax policy can somewhat relieve this factor, particularly when coupled with more adequate financing, this fact should be faced. *The potential of rent subsidies for the underincomed with which to pay better rents is quite clear here. There is no substitute for this approach. This is not to underestimate the value of code enforcement — but rather to add a carrot to the stick. There is more positive achievement by making rehabilitation profitable than in attempting to secure it through punitive measures.* The reward in terms of the aspiration level and general morale of the slum dweller will, I think, outweigh the cost. This is particularly true when the cost/benefits are contrasted with those of institutionalized public housing.

The key to improving the slums from a "people" point of view, is the creation of a resident responsible middle class within those areas — not a middle class which while physically in the area does not belong to it, as is the case with the efforts to create new middle class housing within slum areas cleared by urban renewal. This has no organic unity with the tenements per se, and can only provide frustration rather than leadership and emulation. These goals can best be accomplished and living conditions within the slum areas most enhanced by increasing the number of owner residents of slum tenements. This will require a highly coordinated effort in terms of tax policy, financing help, code enforcement, and advisory services. The rewards of a successful program are very great. The cost of present policies are equally evident.

The New Mythology of Housing

Michael A. Stegman

Good housing can make good people, even out of poor people. Such, cruelly compressed, was the cherished belief of housing reformers as they campaigned 30 years ago for low-rent public housing for the urban poor. By now, needless to say, that belief has been exposed as a myth. It has been shown to rest on faulty assumptions not only with respect to why poor people are poor, but also about what can be done to make them "better." As one student of urban affairs put it:

> Once upon a time, we thought that if we could only get our problem families out of those dreadful slums, then papa would stop taking dope, mama would stop chasing around, and Junior would stop carrying a knife. Well, we've got them in a nice apartment with modern kitchens and a recreation center. And they're the same bunch of bastards they always were.

This is to state the disillusionment rather crudely, to be sure; but that is exactly the trouble, with founding public policy on mythic grounds. The poor are held to be incurable. The reformers who helped spread the faulty gospel are crucified as false prophets or fade away as the public action they helped get going fails to solve the "problems." But, worse than this, their failures never seem to stimulate any attempts to correct the myths or modify the procedures. Rather, they serve only to weaken subsequent efforts to rally political support for further public action. In the case of low-rent public housing, the whole purpose of the program — the provision of decent shelter for the poor — was smeared along with the exposure of its guiding myth.

Today, the public housing program goes without its traditional liberal and intellectual support; it goes without union support; and it goes without any broad demand among the electorate. And as for the poor, they go without decent housing. As John P. Dean wrote 20 years ago in a review of our disappointing efforts in housing reform ". . . in the meantime, the patient has continued to sicken."

What I want to do here is take a hard look at what I believe are the *emerging* myths concerning community development and housing. It is only prudent to acknowledge that it would be much less risky to wait another decade or so to pass judgment. Yet by discussing the emerging

Reprinted by permission from *Trans-action*, January 1970, pp. 55–62. Copyright © 1970 by Transaction, Inc., New Brunswick, New Jersey.

myths before they become crystalized, I may be able to raise some fundamental questions about their utility as a basis for public action. Moreover, the time seems particularly ripe now that the federal government has passed a multibillion dollar housing bill.

The Model Cities program provides a sophisticated example of current thinking about the complexities of the slum housing nexus. Its pronouncements at least indicate a heightened awareness that housing and social service needs are closely interrelated and might best be met simultaneously with a global attack. This is a far cry from the "good housing = good people" theory of years past, but I still get the nagging feeling that the emerging housing reform myths are going to be equally counterproductive.

The old myths developed as justifications for direct federal intervention in an area previously dominated by the private sector. The new myths are rationalizations for particular federal responses to housing problems that have remained unsolved in spite of earlier governmental involvement. These myths, which are concerned more with notions of how the problems can be solved than with their basic causes, can be summarized as follows:

Myths surrounding the nature of the owners of substandard housing.

Mythical explanations of the potential role of nonprofit sponsors in solving the nation's housing problems.

Myths involving the potential value of adopting a systems approach to neighborhood renewal.

Myths surrounding emerging efforts to involve unemployed ghetto manpower in the rehabilitation of slum housing.

Myths explaining why low-income *ownership* programs should be expected to solve those same social problems that the previous low-income minimum *rental* programs could not solve.

Myth #1: Slumlords

> . . . the slumlord, that small body of landlords [who] are out to squeeze every last dollar out of the property as quickly as they can, regardless of the consequences in terms of human life, suffering and sickness. It is against this small minority that battle must be given — constant, unremitting and unrelenting battle — *Former Mayor Robert Wagner of New York.*

Believers in this specimen myth frequently wind up their "argument" with the observation of David Hunter that all owners of substandard housing "look as though they had spent their childhoods drowning their playmates" and then grew up to play that same deadly game as an adult — only now in more subtle and painful ways.

This amateurish personality profile of the "typical slumlord" tends to confuse the real issues and has served to distort our national housing policy since the end of World War II. It has encouraged a myopic view of the housing problem, and it has demonstrably provided an outright faulty basis for public action. The stereotype of the slumlord strongly implies that the owners of substandard housing are largely responsible for our chronic housing problem, simply because they are evil men. This is not so for at least four reasons.

First, the stereotype doesn't stand up statistically. There are upwards of six million substandard housing units in our nation's cities and literally hundreds of thousands of individual landlords. Can *all* their owners match the above grotesque? Surely it is more reasonable to assume that their personal characteristics distribute in a pattern similar to that found in any large sample of population.

Second, slumlords and tenants enjoy, if that's the word, a perfectly symbiotic relationship; that is, they need each other. The owners need the poor and troubled because few others would consider living in depressed housing; and who but the poor and troubled must seek the cheapest possible shelter? Yet, this is no justification for blaming the owners for creating the shortages in decent low-rent housing that mark the inner cores of our cities. The notion that owners of substandard units cause the sickness and suffering that plague the unfortunate families who dwell there sounds suspiciously like an inversion of the "good housing = good people" theory.

Third, the charge that most owners of slum properties are making excess profits may be seriously questioned, both within the real estate industry and in comparison with other major industries. While financial information on slums is extremely scarce, such relatively recent works as Woody Klein's *Let in the Sun* include some economic data that will disconcert liberal believers in the bloated slumlord myth. For example, the 36-unit tenement Klein wrote about grossed nearly one-half million dollars over a 60-year period ending in 1966. The New York City Planning Commission has estimated that such structures generally return around 36 percent of gross revenues on a net basis. With respect to the building in question, then, aggregate net revenues for the 60 years would have amounted to approximately $180,000, or an annual average of $3,000. Since fixed expenses (taxes, water and sewer charges and insurance) of such substandard tenements average 25 percent of gross revenues, it's obvious that when you then add on fuel and minimal maintenance costs, there will be little left over for major repairs. In fact, Klein estimates that in order to bring the tenement up to the standard specified in New

York City's housing code, annual operating expenses would have to increase by $4,000 per year, which means an annual loss of $3,278. Undermaintenance therefore may be not only a rational, but a necessary means of survival in an industry beset with increased unionization and its concomitant, rising costs, as well as tenant incomes that remain either the same or fall over the years and the same or lower levels of occupancy.

Biased View of Landlords

Fourth, it is an incontrovertible fact that almost half (47 percent) of our national housing inventory was built before 1929. Our cities are getting older. And in housing, as in humans, aging causes problems, but it seems naive to place the responsibility for such problems at the feet of the landlord. Old structures are found in old neighborhoods, and more and more of them are becoming slums. Data from the South Los Angeles area show that the proportion of substandard units in that community increased from 18 percent to 34 percent between 1960 and 1965. In New York City the number of slum housing units went from 475,000 in 1960 to an estimated 800,000 in late 1968. The Department of Labor estimates that 600,000 rural and semirural individuals are migrating into large urban areas each year. The housing crisis will surely increase as greater pressures are exerted upon an already aged and obsolete housing stock.

By adopting the myth of the slumlord, the public forecloses any consideration of an alliance with the owner of substandard housing in an attempt to find an enlightened approach to the problem. Also written off is much of the huge investment locked into the existing low-rent private housing stock.

Myth #2: Nonprofit Sponsors

Top housing officials have apparently accepted the myth of the slumlord. They have washed their hands of the individual low-rent property owner. A measure of their disenchantment is the increasing federal attention being paid to such nonprofit institutions as churches, foundations, fraternal organizations and labor unions in their low- and moderate-income housing efforts. In fact, a program was initiated in 1961 which could be interpreted as designed to stimulate such housing efforts. Known by the call letters 221(d)(3), it provides mortgage monies at low interest rates to nonprofit sponsors. Yet at this writing only 1,568 rental units have been rehabilitated under 221(d)(3), while only 46,565 new units have been built.

The meager contributions of 221(d)(3) can be readily explained. First,

there has been an insufficient and uneven flow of federal funds to purchase below-market mortgages. Second, Congress cannot make up its
mind whether the Federal Housing Authority should continue to broaden
its social perspective, or model its role on that of a conservative Back Bay
banker. Third and finally, the federal requirements for obtaining the
financing are so complex and difficult to satisfy, that only the most energetic and well-staffed sponsors can succeed in getting any. The 221(d)(3)
program requires filing forms for preapplication, application, precommit-
ment processing, preinitial closing, initial closing and final closing stages
— more than 40 forms in all. Urban America, Inc., recently published a
guide to the program which is 359 pages long.

Simply put, the concept of nonprofit sponsors such as churches developing housing throughout the nation's urban areas on a scale large
enough to have any measurable impact is basically ill conceived. When
one considers the incredibly large number of steps involved in the residential development process, one has to conclude that the average church
is just not prepared to carry the burden of solving even a fraction of our
national housing problem. And as for the typical Negro church in the
ghetto, the most appropriate potential sponsor for low-income housing, it
unfortunately has even less resources and know-how.

What then is the true purpose of such a policy? Everyone would
agree it is worthwhile to encourage such stable and committed institutions as churches to do their part in easing local housing problems — even
though they are not yet well equipped for the job. But since the policy
has not been enacted on any grand scale, the heart of the matter must lie
elsewhere. It lies in the basic unwillingness of the federal government to
give serious consideration to why private developers are not dealing in
the low- and moderate-income sectors, and in its refusal to provide incentives to encourage such activity. The government has made a tradeoff —
it has accepted the cleaner, less tainted nonprofit sponsor and has given
up housing units.

Myth #3: Aerospace Systems Panaceas

There has been much recent speculation about how efficient community renewal might be if urbanologists and systems analysts planned and
implemented broad programs in our cities. Conceiving the neighborhood
as a subsystem of interrelated physical, economic, social and political
dimensions, which is related in turn to the larger urban system, the integrated approach obviously has value. Yet upon close examination, it reveals serious shortcomings and inaccuracies. The particular advantages of
the aerospace system approach to renewal are more managerial and ad-

ministrative than they are substantive. Thus, the push for employing mutidisciplinary teams and large-scale computers in rebuilding the cities cannot be but one of the most flagrant of the emerging myths of housing reform.

The problem of renewal is money. In the eight major cities recently surveyed by the U.S. Civil Rights Commission, "almost half of the families surveyed received incomes solely from sources such as welfare, AFDC, unemployment compensation or other nonemployment sources." What improvements could come from a sophisticated, fully programmed, multidisciplinary approach to community renewal in those cities? There are hundreds of communities in 42 states where welfare payments fail to meet the states' own standards of the minimum income required for families to live? It is ludicrous to assert that we need a systems approach to reveal that a mother with three children needs $237 a month to live and can be provided through welfare with a maximum of only $126. The basic problem here is lack of money. That is obvious; yet there is no reason to suppose that Congress will show any more willingness to deal with the fundamental problems of poverty than it has in the past.

Another problem is racism. A sophisticated analytical framework cannot be expected to eliminate racial conflict. What could a systems approach accomplish in the Bayside District of Oakland, for example, where the under- and unemployment rate is more than 30 percent? One cannot use a managerial tool and expect to redistribute income. Without basic economic and social reforms, the glamorous aerospace approach to renewal cannot possibly accomplish the ends for which it is intended. Yet Congress has demonstrated that it is far more prepared to sponsor the development of a city technology under the auspices of the aerospace industry than it is to deal with the fact that the poor lack money, that they are the victims of racial discrimination, or that their "assistance programs" are falling apart.

Like the more familiar task forces and blue ribbon commissions empaneled to identify the obvious, the systems approach to community renewal promises to be used as a politically valuable delaying tactic by those who refuse to commit themselves to the necessity of righting wrongs and reversing social or economic injustices. . . .

Myth #4: Self-help Housing

The systems approach is being sold to Congress as the new urban panacea of the 1970s. It is an attractive panacea, suggesting the efficiency and reliability of moon shots and the like. But how well will it work in practice? While it is an obviously intelligent way to go about doing certain things, one may well wonder how well it will function on limited resources. Only time will tell.

As for public service and community facilities, the black ghettos have been the last to get the least. If one peruses a random sample of Model Cities program applications he will quickly learn that cities of all sizes are now quite willing to admit that their policies have been discriminatory. In response, the black community is now demanding direct and meaningful involvement in making policy and running programs designed to improve the quality of life in the ghettos. Most recently they have demanded the inclusion of low-income, low-skilled, unemployed ghetto men as workers in the construction and rehabilitation of low-income housing.

The myth is that housing programs can provide employment for the ghetto resident, and on paper it looks sound. Unemployed ghetto residents would be prepared for jobs in the building trade even as they are helping to alleviate the chronic housing problems in their neighborhoods. It would provide residents with a meaningful experience and a sense of contributing to neighborhood development. And maybe it would even reduce the vandalism in the houses being rehabilitated. All this is fine. Yet it is also, I think, naive to expect that a large share of the greater than six million substandard units in our metropolitan areas can be brought up to standard through such efforts.

Urban self-help housing has not yet assumed the stature of a major myth, but it is gaining increasing exposure and support as Model Cities monies become more available. I do not doubt that such efforts will result in rehabilitated housing; nor that unskilled labor can be trained in the building trades. However, as long as self-help housing is localized in the relatively few communities that have the talent and organizational base to push it, the number of units involved will remain small. And, as long as the rehabilitation efforts are headed by undercapitalized Negro contractors who do not pose overt threats to organized labor, it is a safe bet that direct involvement of black manpower in the rebuilding effort will fail to crack labor's stranglehold on the ghetto.

Localized self-help training programs seem too small a threat to the unions to warrant large mobilization against them. No better evidence need be sought than the fact that black workers themselves recognize the meagerness of these programs. Blacks are now demanding entry into the Chicago, Detroit and Pittsburgh construction unions. This marks the beginning of a much needed and long awaited national confrontation between the blacks and the buildings and trades unions. It also raises the conflict to a level beyond the point where training programs might have been an issue. Even were they to become an issue, the unions seem to have the procedural equipment to appear good guys. Consider the following scenario.

The unions select and deal with relatively small and isolated black contractors in scattered communities. They allow a certain number of trainees to work on the otherwise unionized rehabilitation jobs. If pressures for reform of the union arise, or if blacks make concerted efforts to penetrate the union ranks, the union local can then threaten to slow up or close down the rehabilitation job. As this would spell certain disaster to the usually undercapitalized black contractor, he would find ways to short-circuit the whole procedure. In the end, by permitting a scant few non-union blacks to work on rehabilitation crews in a few ghetto communities, the unions appear progressive while still excluding blacks from where the main action is, in the unions themselves.

Yet, this issue seems to have the potential to escalate into a major conflict. A Negro contractor working in Cleveland's Hough district claims that "a union carpenter brought up in new construction is no better equipped for rehabilitation work than a raw man. . . . We can train a laborer to set up our prefab partitions in two hours. He can learn faster than a veteran carpenter because he isn't set in his ways and has no old work-habits to overcome." If unskilled ghetto labor is capable of being trained to do rehabilitation work in significantly less time than the unions are willing to admit, and this appears to be the case, then massive training programs could be initiated. Such a new labor pool would be highly mobile and a threat to the unions. The unions would probably offer stiff resistance to such a development, so these self-help training programs may prove to be yet another false expectation.

With all these forces eddying around direct involvement in ghetto redevelopment, it is likely that a highly limited program will be enacted, which is tokenism at its worst. The myth is subtle. It plays upon the need and desires of the minority poor for a stake in the action. At the same time it guarantees that institutional changes in organized labor will be minimal or nonexistent, that the buildings and trades unions will not have to open their ranks to black labor on a large scale — because "they" will have their self-help training programs.

Myth #5: Home Ownership for the Poor

Congress recently considered more than 24 low-income home-ownership bills; its action resulted in Section 235 of the Housing Act of 1968. The purpose of the program is to broaden the base of home ownership in an already predominantly home-owning nation through the provision of interest rate subsidies to low- and moderate-income families. The proponents of this program expect it to accomplish all the socially desirable ends that the welfare reformers of 30 years ago had hoped their public housing programs would achieve. Today public housing has come to represent a patronizing dole, they reason, while home ownership involves a stake in a piece of property, a sense of pride in one's home. Belief in this myth persists mainly because the public and the legislators see in home ownership a device to prevent more and greater rioting.

The myth of low-income home ownership is vulnerable on many counts. The most glaring error is that such programs are based on the projection of middle-class values onto a non-middle-class culture. Moreover, it is perceived as a solution, a salve to balm the wounds caused by discrimination, cultural starvation and the structural problems of our national labor market. But there are several difficulties with this romanticized notion of what ownership can accomplish.

There was and is nothing about a publicly supported low-rent housing program that would necessarily rob a man of his pride or sap him of his self-respect. Nor is there anything about owning one's home that guarantees that pride and self-respect will spontaneously spring up in the owner's breast. As far as the actual low-income ownership programs are concerned they may amount to little more than saying that everyone should have a title to his slum.

Realistically speaking, one cannot expect much more than a limited low-income home-ownership program. The entrenched and anachronistic National Association of Real Estate Boards (NAREB) is making visible efforts to avoid opening up the market to Negroes. A recent NAREB circular was distributed to presidents of local real estate boards entitled, "Some Questions (and their answers) suggested by a reading of Title VIII of Public Law No. 90–284 related to forced housing." It was an exploration of means to circumvent the provisions of the federal open-housing bill. In spite of recent federal legislation in this area, and the Supreme Court's ruling that an almost forgotten law enacted in 1866 is effectively a sweeping fair-housing bill, a truly open-housing market seems highly unlikely in the foreseeable future.

Moreover, to stimulate hopes for home ownership without moving toward reducing levels of unemployment and underemployment might be the cruelest hoax yet perpetrated on the low-income population. Let us assume that the program provides for monthly carrying costs equal to 20 percent of monthly income. I feel the average low-income family participating in the program would find it extremely difficult to pay for its housing-related needs (operation, maintenance, taxes, water and insurance) as well as its nonhousing needs from its limited budget. Consequently, such a program might provide the family a piece of middle-class America, but only a little piece — a piece obtained at the cost of accepting the increase pressures that go along with internalizing middle-class values, with only a fraction of the economic resources with which to play the game.

It is of paramount importance to remember that the *style* in which a program is administered has direct impact upon the quality of life of the participants. For example, if a project is administered in a paternalistic manner, that is, if the local authority sits in judgment of the moral suasion of tenant families, the project becomes the enemy. As David Hunter has observed.

> The projects in Harlem are hated. They are hated almost as much as policemen and this is saying a great deal. And they are hated for the same reasons; both reveal, unbearably, the real attitude of the white world. . . .

The way in which the program is administered could conceivably be as important as the housing it makes available to participating families. While the proponents of ownership for low-income families ceremonially chant incantations about the ideals that such an experience instills in one's soul, someone must begin to work out solutions to the many problems. How can the market be opened in the face of organized opposition? How can the low-income family be expected to absorb the hidden costs of ownership on a marginal budget? How can a home-ownership program improve the pride and self-respect of the participants? How can such a program be administered in a fashion that does not duplicate the inexcusably high-handed manner with which we have administered our low-rent housing programs throughout the country?

In the next generation we will have to build as many houses to accommodate population growth and normal replacement needs as we have built in our entire history as a nation. Yet we have seriously underestimated the extent and depth of our current housing crisis.

I cannot recommend a course that can eliminate existing inhuman housing conditions throughout the nation: I do not think that anyone can. The problem is too firmly rooted in our society. It is too much a part of our economic system. It is too closely related to such fundamental issues as the distribution of wealth and income to be dealt with in terms of housing alone. . . .

Strategies for Change: Planning

3

For as long as cities have existed in America, people have been dissatisfied with them. Americans, in the Jeffersonian tradition, have tended to regard urban life as necessarily vice-ridden and un-attractive. Throughout most of the history of this country, the response to urban social and physical disorganization was to ignore it. The city had few defenders to protect it from unbridled capitalist expansion and the unwholesome living conditions caused by mass immigration. Eventually, however, physical planning was advocated by many Progressive reformers as a solution to urban ills. Regulation of existing structures, the use of zoning to channel further expansion, and planning for parks and civic centers became commonplace in American cities. The notion that physical planning could cure social pathology became embodied in the urban renewal programs of the 1950s which razed slum housing in the heart of most American cities.

The original physical planners are attacked by such critics as Victor Gruen for wishing to impose an artificial order and sameness upon the cities, making them both inefficient and uninteresting. Moreover, Gruen accuses planners of being autocratic and argues that only democratic planning can "fit the varied and widely diversified needs of the individuals who make up the city." Gruen contends that the planners' goals must be determined by elected representatives rather than the planners themselves, so that "they will express the will of the people."

Alan Altshuler, however, shows several theoretical and practical problems that make democratic planning very difficult. Most significant of these is whether any single set of goals can be ranked in an order with which a great majority of the community would agree:

> Those who contend that comprehensive planning should play a large role in the future evolution of societies must argue that the common interests of society's members are their most important interest and constitute a large proportion of all their interests. They must assert that conflicts of interest in society are illusory, that they are about

minor matters, or that they can be foreseen and resolved in advance by just arbiters (planners), who understand the total interests of all parties.

Thus, the major theoretical obstacle to democratic planning on behalf of the whole community is the possible absence of a sufficient common interest among different classes and interest groups.

The main practical difficulties are ascertaining the popular will and anticipating the effects of different policies. Altshuler points out that it is very hard for the planner to consult a broad range of interests, because many who would be affected by the plan are not united in any organization and because only people whose jobs require them to spend time on civic affairs are able or willing to maintain an ongoing interest in plan formulation. He notes that even if the planner is able to ascertain public goals, he must be able to discover methods of achieving them which would neither distort them nor produce such harmful side-effects that the gains realized through planning are cancelled out by the losses. The uncertainty surrounding the implementation of any innovation makes predictions of future costs and benefits highly unreliable. There is presumably less uncertainty involved in planned than in unplanned change, but does planning increase the probability of desirable outcomes enough to justify its costs in effort and loss of freedom?

Whereas Altshuler examines the obstacles to physical planning in the public interest, Peter Marris and Martin Rein analyze the dilemmas involved in social planning. Planners, in response to arguments that the physical environment is created by the social one, have attempted since 1960 to eliminate the social causes of urban blight rather than its physical symptoms. Marris and Rein, in the book from which the chapter included here is drawn, examine critically the new assumptions of planning. They chronicle the growth of the Ford Foundation-sponsored programs that provided the model for the federal Poverty Act. The principal aim of the Foundation was to encourage planned social change to benefit the urban poor. The themes of the endeavor were innovation, coordination, and democracy. But the resources for innovation were only available from outsiders, either foundations or the federal government, so that those who controlled funds were not those affected by the programs. As a result, innovation and democracy proved incompatible. Coordination foundered on the question of who should be the coordinator: "The breakdown of coherent social planning had arisen, not so much from a 'vacuum of constructive criticism and leadership,' as from inability to agree on who should fill it." Coordination proved in many respects antagonistic to democracy, particularly if democracy was defined by the ongoing participation of the poor in decisionmaking about programs that vitally affected them. Thus, there were conflicts among the various agencies that supervised the local programs and other participating groups, and further conflicts between the clients of the programs, agency personnel, and the regular municipal political leadership.

Because of the seeming impossibility of identifying an overall public interest and the danger that what planners construe as the public interest might not take sufficient account of the needs of the poor, a number of planners support the model of the planner as advocate. As an advocate the planner gives up the goals of comprehensiveness and coordination and concentrates instead on ascertaining and promoting the interests of the social group that is his client.

Although she does not endorse the older planning goals derived from the conception of the planner as arbiter of the public interest, Frances Piven nevertheless argues against advocacy planning and, in essence, says that rational policymaking will never benefit the poor. She maintains that participation in the planning process diverts the energies of the poor from their most effective uses, and that disruptive behavior rather than rational persuasion offers the only means by which the deprived will ever succeed in extracting benefits from government. The Davidoffs challenge Piven's argument and contend that poor people require the assistance of advocate planners if they are to formulate a coherent set of demands to press on government. Like Piven, however, their perspective is political. They argue that the function of the advocate planner is to polarize issues — he "moves planning decisions from nonpolitical into political forums. . . ." In other words, like Piven they believe that power rather than rational argument prevails.

Clarence Funnyé condemns those advocate planners who assume a paternalistic role in relation to their clients and agrees with Piven that community preoccupation with planning can be diversionary. But he argues that the framing of alternative plans has an important purpose in providing goals that can mobilize a community. "Alternative plans properly prepared can catch the imagination of otherwise hostile or neutral institutions and can serve as a rallying point for a community . . . and as a visible standard against which to measure the official plan." Chester Hartman also stresses the importance of an alternative plan as a focus for community action, as well as an educational device to heighten community consciousness of injustice. Like the Davidoffs, he views the advocate planner as essentially a political actor — he "should employ his professional skills as a node around which political organizing can take place."

In our own article we try to show how the different types of planning discussed here are related to general political theories, particularly as these theories treat social class and political interests. Traditional planning is equated with technocratic thought; democratic or user-oriented planning with democratic theory; and advocacy planning with socialist ideas. Each type of planning suffers from the limitations of the political theory with which it is associated. Traditional planning, based on technocratic elitism, fails to recognize conflicts of interest between the upper and the lower class and is restricted in scope by the unwillingness of upper-class individuals to support reform. Democratic planning assumes that a majority can agree on long-range goals; it must rely on active citizen participation, when most citizens are apathetic. The advocate planner and the socialist theorist agree that social change benefitting the poor will only occur under duress; upper-class elites are never benevolent. But the socialist agitator or propagandist forever runs the risk that he will evoke repression rather than positive action. Unless one accepts Marx's doctrine of the inevitable success of the proletariat, one must see grave dangers in a strategy based only on a conflict view of society. Social polarization can seriously threaten social stability and civic peace without producing any benefits for either side.

We contend that there has been relatively little planning in America; that the very notion of planning is contrary to the dominant American liberal tradition. Lindblom's concept of incremental planning, which we equate with political liberalism, accurately characterizes developments in the United States. Given the dominance of this tradition, it is not to be expected that future changes for the benefit of the urban poor will arise out of rationally devised policies, but rather that such changes will be largely fortuitous.

Planning, then, represents one general strategy for urban social change. It offers the greatest hope for peaceful innovation, but its implementation is limited by social conflict and the absence of general values supporting governmental direction of social development. Advocacy planning has been considered here under the general rubric of rational strategies for change, but in some respects it fits better into the next section of the book — "Strategies for Change: Political Movements." At any rate, advocacy planning forms a link between the two alternatives for effecting change: restructuring of power relationships resulting from popular movements and policies rationally formulated by government.

Planning — Waste or Wisdom?

Victor Gruen

I borrowed the title of this [paper] from a discussion, published in the newspaper *The National Observer*, between Mrs. Jane Jacobs, a writer, and Mr. Robert Moses, who refers to himself as a planner. The fact that Mr. Moses felt that planning was wisdom, while Mrs. Jacobs felt it was waste, holds little significance for me because both were speaking of a specific type of planning, different from the activity and terminology that I wish to employ. They were referring to certain mechanics, to tools and methods of the practitioner which, although necessary in the specific application of the planning process, must be regarded as subservient to the main function of what I may term "creative planning."

Planning is as old as mankind and of divine origin. Let me quote briefly from the Book of Genesis (the italics are mine):

> In the beginning God created the heaven and the earth.
> And the earth was *without form* and void; and darkness was upon the face of the deep. And the Spirit of God moved upon the face of the waters.
> And God said, Let there be light; and there was light;
> . . . and *God separated the light from the darkness.* . . .
> And God said, Let there be a firmament in the midst of the waters, and let it separate the waters from the waters.
> And God made the firmament, and *separated the waters which were under the firmament from the waters which were above the firmament.* . . .
> And God said, Let there be lights in the firmament of the heaven to *separate the day from the night.* . . .

The story of Genesis contains all the elementary tasks of the planning profession. From the very beginning of time, we find the urge to *separate* disparate functions from one another, and to organize them into a meaningful pattern of greatest diversity.

In the beginning was chaos; and the very act of Creation was the conversion of chaos into meaningful order. Out of everlasting, monotonous fog and dusk, the Lord created the wonder of morning, the day, the evening, and then the night, with the sun lending its brilliance to the day, the moon and stars sparkling in the night sky. The Lord *separated* the water from the dry land, and heaven from earth, and on the earth He created mountains and valleys, oceans and continents. He made animals to live in the water and on the ground and in the air; and finally He created man and woman. And when He rested and observed what He had created, He saw that it was good.

Whether one is a believer, taking the Bible literally and asserting that God shaped man in His image, or whether one takes a more liberal outlook and considers the Bible as a beautiful story — believing conversely that man created God as the ideal of his own image — the fact remains that creation, or planning — the making of order out of chaos — appears to man as a most worthy goal.

The separating of elements from each other, endowing each with specific characteristics, defining boundaries between them, the achievement of infinite variety within organic order, whether regarded as divine inspiration or as the highest expression of human aspiration, is accepted in every religion and every philosophic belief as the ultimate achievement.

In spite of this, since the beginning of human history mankind has been busy undoing the divine work; blurring the clean edges of the borders He set up; leveling the differences; watering down characteristics and, in an unholy conspiracy with the powers of evil, nullifying the six days of creative labor and recreating chaos where there was order. Man has, in his perverseness, tried to make day out of night, to create bodies of water where there was dry land and, in a reversal of the usual procedure, to make molehills out of mountains.

For thousands of years of human history, man's struggle to undo the high order of variety met with scant success. Earthquakes, floods and storms, volcanic eruptions and other geological upheavals corrected the situation, reminding him not to tinker with the "divine" order. But nowadays, feeling uppish because of the great and growing size of the human membership roll, we are more hell-bent than ever, especially where we are assembled in large groups, to undo the perfection and rhythm of the act of Creation and re-establish shapelessness, formlessness — in short, chaos.

The concept of hell exists in nearly every religion. There seems to be universal agreement that it is a highly unenjoyable place for sinners in retirement, who suffer there from inescapable sameness. They are further punished by the fact that they are exposed thoroughly to the company of a sociologically undifferentiated group consisting only of devils. There is neither night nor day, neither culture nor artistic pursuits (as opposed to heaven where there are at least such diversions as choral singing or harp playing); only an endless infernal boredom.

Humanity today is using the power of its vast numbers, its scientific and technological "progress," to convert its cities and metropolitan regions into hell on earth. Where once there was an infinite variety of hills and mountains, valleys and forests, streams and lakes, satisfying both the eye and the spirit, an even, cancerous growth of man-made uniformity is being spread. Vast areas are robbed of every last tree, every bush and flower, and covered with an inescapable sameness. Fumes and smoke pervade the day and darken it, while millions of lights illuminate the night. Because we have learned to shrink distances by air travel and by our elaborate means of communication, we are slowly succeeding in wiping out the differences that once existed between individual cities on the various continents, and one man-made hell begins to look like another. Our power to resist natural elements has grown infinitely in the last hundred years; our wisdom in utilizing this power for man's enjoyment has not kept pace.

The human population on this planet is increasing dynamically. We tend more and more to concentrate in already heavily populated areas because modern technology demands such concentration. But unless we learn the true meaning of planning, which is the injection of diversity and variety into a meaningful organic pattern, we will succeed in making our cities unlivable, unworkable places of infernal sameness, plagued by boredom and discomfort — a fate which human fantasy once imagined to be the punishment for those who had sinned against God and man.

The French, with a twinkle in their eyes, say, *"Vive la différence,"* referring mainly to the difference between the sexes. An important difference, indeed. Without it life would be, to say the least, dull, and mankind would die out. But Vive la différence should be the slogan for all expressions of life, and for the planning of our cities. Vive la différence between the new and the old, between the clustered-together buildings in which we work and live, the closely knit city and the openness of the surrounding landscape and countryside, between man-made or man-influenced and natural environment.

What is planning? When we relate planning to the shape of the man-made and man-influenced environment, we find that three main types are being practiced.

The first, which we may refer to as laissez-faire planning, actually is not planning at all. Its advocates — and many thoughtful people must be counted among them — feel that things should be permitted to grow freely as individual wishes, needs and requirements bring them about, with only the most essential policing measures to prevent "criminal" actions in which one individual or group of individuals seriously endangers others. In defense of their attitude, they point to the fact that the powerful United States, with the highest living standard on earth, was created by pioneering individuals, and that any action going beyond the most essential policing methods would be an interference with personal freedom. They also point to the fact that some of the old European cities which we most admire grew without a master plan, and that much of their charm and architectural value is the result of this non-directed free growth.

The second type of planning we might refer to as *autocratic* planning. It is the method that was employed in the past by monarchs and other autocratic rulers; a method which, for example, created the beautiful wide boulevards of Paris, the grand palaces of the Renaissance and baroque periods, and in our own time has been employed by the modern dictators, by Hitler and Mussolini, by Franco, by Stalin, by various Communist states and certain autocratic Latin American governments. It is the method by which large portions of cities can be rebuilt practically overnight, and by which whole new cities like Brasilia can be created in a few years. Autocratic planning, however, is by no means restricted to those countries which are governed by dictators; in many a city in the United States, strong-willed men have pushed through pompous projects for political gain. Some of our monumental but dreary "civic centers," "cultural centers," and "centers for the performing arts" isolate higher urban functions into ghettos, creating sterility within them and impoverishing the remainder of the city outside their boundaries. Some powerful government agencies, run by specialists whose views are shielded by blinders from everything outside their departments, have cut communities to ribbons with highways and freeways. Others have misinterpreted the aims of urban renewal legislation by demolishing whole districts and by replacing lively environments, which could have been rehabilitated, with sterile, inhuman and poorly planned projects.

And then there is a third type, that I will call *democratic planning*, which, although its implementation is the most difficult, most complex and most time-consuming, is, in my view, the only one that holds out real hope for us.

Those who advocate laissez-faire planning deny the existence of historic development. Pioneering days in the United States, and, indeed, in every other part of the world, are irretrievably gone. Independence has been replaced, as the late President Kennedy said, by interdependence. Modern means of communication have shrunk the world, and a shot fired in Korea has repercussions in every American town. Our country has been developed from the Atlantic to the Pacific, and the only "new frontiers" toward which we can strive lie in the direction of planning for better national and international conditions. Our national house, once inhabited by a few who could indulge in the vanishing luxury of living and acting as they pleased without unduly disturbing their neighbors, has filled up and will get even more crowded in the near future.

In the process of laissez-faire planning we have, of course, always taken the way of least resistance. We have concentrated urban development in those areas where basic conditions were most favorable, along the East Coast and the West Coast and in the Great Lakes region in the

Midwest. Those millions of acres which for climatic or geologic reasons are more difficult, though not impossible, to urbanize, we have, in the process of laissez-faire planning, simply neglected.

Those who point to beautiful old cities that have grown without planning must be made to realize that restraints of another type explain their virtues. The need for moving close together was dictated to them not by planning ordinances, but by the threat of enemy attack. Take, for example, the nearly perfect plan of my native town of Vienna. Its inner city, with its small-grained, endless variety of buildings, streets and squares, was once ringed by fortifications. Outside the inner fortification walls stretched, on all sides, a broad area on which nothing could be built, the so-called Glacis, left free of structures so that one could shoot unhindered at the approaching enemy. Beyond the Glacis grew other communities. (These communities, interestingly, are called *Vorstädte*, literally, "before-cities," expressing the idea that these are places one reaches, when coming from the outside, in anticipation of one's arrival in the big city; implying something quite different from our word "suburb," which rather seems to indicate substandard quality.) They in turn were surrounded by a second fortification wall, and it was only in the nineteenth century that other satellite towns grew outside these fortifications. Their spread, however, was halted by the desire of the monarch and the aristocracy for spacious hunting grounds in the forests, hills and meadows that surround the city in a wide arc. As the city became a modern metropolis in the second half of the nineteenth century, as the need for fortification ceased, and as the power of autocratic monarchs was broken, planning did set in, and it was only thanks to planning that the elements of the urban organism, which had been based on stringent needs of the population and on the wishes and desires of the landed gentry, were converted into lasting assets of the city. The inner fortifications surrounding the old town, together with the vacant area of the Glacis, were converted into a pair of concentric roads: the unique Ringstrasse with its broad, tree-lined promenades, parks, private and public buildings of all types; and a secondary ring road called Lastenstrasse, a service road for the hauling of goods. Between those two roads wide-open spaces, parks and plazas were created. The second outlying fortification was converted into an outer ring called the Gürtel or belt, forming not only an excellent distributary road with a rapid-transit system, but also, because of its tree-lined boulevards and parks, a recreation area and a clear division between the inner and outer districts. The former hunting grounds, finally, were declared a permanently protected nature park, in which only agricultural activities, vine growing, and facilities for recreational uses are permitted. They now form the much-sung-about Vienna Woods, an easily accessible area for all Viennese citizens, offering for their *Ausflüge*, or excursions, virgin woods, meadows, hills and mountains. Only beyond this broad ring of nature park does further metropolitan growth take place in the form of satellite towns and villages.

Similar acts of conscious planning which take advantage of city patterns that originally stemmed from the need to guarantee the continued life of the city and its residents against enemy attack, can be observed in many European cities, large and small.

The order and logic that prevail in the city of older origin are derived also from a number of restraints imposed upon them by the technological conditions of the period, the restricted availability of materials, and existence of regional traditions, some of which still endure despite the intense exchange of knowledge and techniques that we enjoy — and suffer under — today. Because building technology had not produced the know-how to build safely higher than five or six stories, there is a unity of building heights. Because only a limited number of building materials was available, and a small number of building methods known, there is harmony, created by the predominant use of brick, stone, wood or stucco, depending on the particular region. Only for a few exceptional buildings were rare materials used and special feats of building technique achieved. Thus landmarks such as towering cathedrals, majestic palaces and city halls form effective accents within the orderly, even appearance of older cityscape.

Today, being deprived of these natural reasons of restraint, we must achieve through planning that measure of harmony which formerly was the result of necessity. Laissez-faire planning is a luxury we can no longer permit ourselves to indulge in. The interdependence of each structure with its neighbor, of each group of structures with its district, of each district with the city, of the city with its neighboring cities (which with it forms the metropolitan area), of one metropolitan area with the other, of all of them with the state, the nation, and indeed the world, has become so great that policing measures alone can no longer work.

The second type of planning, autocratic planning, could effectively regulate this interrelationship if it were guided and implemented by supermen. But inasmuch as men, including planners, are subject to the usual human shortcomings and, in an autocratic society especially, to the lust for power and intense desire for self-expression, the result of autocratic planning is usually deeply disappointing. It suffers from the lack of those balances which lie only within the rules of democracy, and the virtue of their swift accomplishment becomes their downfall. The results are made out of one mold, and that mold may be to the liking of the autocrat who created it, but it does not necessarily fit the varied and widely diversified needs of the individuals who make up the city.

The question is often asked: "Is planning possible in a democratic society, where every single step has to be negotiated, has to be subjected to public hearings, and very often has to be decided upon by vote?" Two issues are involved in this question: The first refers to creative planning for a democratic society, the second to the possibility of practical implementation of such planning.

Creative city planning in a democratic society can undoubtedly be successfully carried out, if one basic condition is met: We must know what our aims and goals are, what we want our cities and urban areas to look like, and why. We need an urban planning philosophy for the second half of the twentieth century. . . .

The problem of implementing these planning efforts can be solved only through improved legislation and its effective administration. Inasmuch as laws and regulations are made by our democratically elected representatives, they will express the will of the people, if it will make itself heard, loud and clear.

Thus if planning in a democratic society, and its implementation, are to succeed, there will have to be creativity, leadership, perseverance and, above all, a consistent philosophy. Planning without these ingredients, piecemeal planning by specialists and special interests — whether they are called economists, real estate experts, traffic engineers, planning officials, zoning administrators, or redevelopment agencies — may indeed be waste. Planning based on philosophical thought and humanitarian principle with experienced and knowledgeable leadership, planning in which the specialists serve the whole (instead of running off in many directions, each with his own little specialty alone at heart) — such planning is not only wise; it is essential if we are to save our culture, which is an urban one.

The Goals of Comprehensive Planning

Alan Altshuler

The Ideal of Comprehensive Planning

Those who consider themselves comprehensive planners typically claim that their most important functions are (1) to create a master plan to guide the deliberations of specialist planners, (2) to evaluate the pro-

Reprinted from Alan A. Altshuler, *The City Planning Process: A Political Analysis.* Copyright © 1965 by Cornell University. Used by permission of Cornell University Press.

posals of specialist planners in the light of the master plan, and (3) to coordinate the planning of specialist agencies so as to ensure that their
proposals reinforce each other to further the public interest. Each of
these functions requires for ideal performance that the comprehensive
planners (a) understand the overall public interest, at least in connection
with the subject matter of their plans, and (b) that they possess causal
knowledge which enables them to gauge the approximate net effect of
proposed actions on the public interest.

This [paper] is concerned with some ways in which city planners
have approached the former of these two requirements, which — contrary
to most students of planning — I consider the more interesting one. If
comprehensive planners deal with a great many more areas of public
policies than specialists, their factual and causal knowledge in each area
is bound to appear shallow — at least by comparison with that of the specialists in it. Hence their claims to comprehensiveness, if they are to be
persuasive, must refer primarily to a special knowledge of the public interest.

Every government planner of integrity, no matter how specialized,
must be guided by some conception of the public interest. And since plans
are proposals of concerted action to achieve goals, each must express his
conception as a goal or series of goals for his community. He will probably conceive these goals, of course, as constantly shifting rather than
highly stable, as always intermediate rather than final, and as more in the
nature of criteria than of concrete destinations. Community goal conceptions are likely to have these characteristics because of the limitations on
collective human foresight and imagination. Nonetheless it is impossible
to plan without some sense of community goals, call them what you will.
Moreover, for the planning process in any community to be democratic
— and I assume in these pages that it should be — the goals must win approval from a democratic political process; they must not be goals simply
prescribed for the community by planners. . . .

Implications of the Ideal

The comprehensive planner must assume that his community's various collective goals can somehow be measured at least roughly as to importance and welded into a single hierarchy of community objectives. In
addition, he must argue that technicians like himself can prescribe courses
of action to achieve these objectives without great distortion or harmful
side-effects of a magnitude sufficient to outweigh the gains achieved
through planning. We may conceive a continuum of faith in the feasi-

bility of comprehensive planning. The "ideal type" defender of comprehensive planning would contend that a serious effort should be made to
plan in detail the future evolution of all important economic and social
patterns. Others would limit their support to the planning-in-general-out-
line of change in particular strategic variables.

Those who contend that comprehensive planning should play a large
role in the future evolution of societies must argue that the common interests of society's members are their most important interests and constitute a large proportion of all their interests. They must assert that
conflicts of interest in society are illusory, that they are about minor matters, or that they can be foreseen and resolved in advance by just arbiters
(planners) who understand the total interests of all parties. Those who
claim that comprehensive planning should play a large part in the future
evolution of any particular economic or societal feature have to assume
similar propositions with regard to conflicts of interest likely to arise in
connection with it.

To the extent, then, that comprehensive planning is possible, the
correct law for a society is something to be discovered, rather than
willed, by public officials. The role of the politician who ignores consistency or obstructs grand schemes to placate interest groups is hard to
defend. So is the concept of majority will, and the idea that party conflict is desirable. It is in this sense that the claims of planners often seem
to be in conflict with those of politicians. Both claim a unique ability to
judge the overall public interest. The politician's claim rests on his popular election, his knowledge of the community, his sensitivity to human
needs, and his personal wisdom. The planner's claim is one of professionalism and research. If it seems somewhat devoid of human warmth, it
also sounds more authoritative, more precise, more modern. As will be
seen shortly, I have no wish to imply that city planners and politicians
must (or, indeed, invariably do) defend their work on the basis of conflicting assumptions. It may well be that the capacities of planners and
politicians are, for many purposes, suited to complement each other.
Here we are not discussing everything that men called planners do, but
rather some implications of the concept "comprehensiveness" in planning.

Few sophisticated American defenders of planning, certainly, believe
that any group of planners can achieve a total comprehensiveness of perspective on any issue. Many do believe, however, that professional planners can come closer to achieving it on numerous vital issues than other
participants in the urban decision process. The explicit claims of practicing planners often seem to suggest that a fair approximation of genuine
comprehensiveness is currently attainable. The problems underlying these
claims may be seen in an examination of planning in Minneapolis and
St. Paul.

Case Study Illustrations

In his introduction to the *St. Paul Land Use Plan,* . . . Herbert Weiland, the St. Paul planning director, described his conception of the planning function in these words:

> The total city planning process, of which land-use planning is but one part, involves a continuing program of deriving, organizing, and presenting a comprehensive plan for the development and renewal of [the city]. . . . The plans must be economically feasible, and must promote the common good, and at the same time [must] preserve the rights and interests of the individual.

Long discussions with every planner involved in the preparation of the St. Paul plan persuaded me that these words were meant literally. City planning was comprehensive and for the common good, not for any lesser objectives.

Several members of the St. Paul planning staff were highly critical of C. David Loeks, Weiland's predecessor, for having offered advice freely to operating agencies without first developing a comprehensive plan. Loeks himself, however, had also conceived his responsibilities broadly, though he had not considered the time ripe for explicitly comprehensive planning during most of his tenure. He had written in the Planning Board's 1957 publication, *The Proposed Freeways for St. Paul,* for example, that while others had considered the cost of freeways and their effect on traffic, the Planning Board had "special responsibilities posed by virtue of its function and status as an advisory representative citizen's group concerned with the development of all facets of the community's life." [1]

In considering the development of [a public hospital], politicians turned finally to city planners to interpret the overall public interest. First the city planners in the St. Paul Housing and Redevelopment Authority, and eventually those in the City Planning Bureau as well, accepted the challenge with confidence. When interviewed, both groups of planners stated without hesitation that they were better equipped to interpret the public interest than the consultant hospital architect, whose primary concern was how best to build a hospital. They believed that because their perspective was broader, their recommendation was highly likely to be wiser, or more rational. [2]

---

[1] *The Proposed Freeways for St. Paul,* Community Plan Report 4, June 1957, p. 30.

[2] Planners tend to use the words "rational" and "wise" interchangeably in evaluating public choices. This is in accord with the usage of natural law philoso-

In formulating the *Central Minneapolis Plan,* Rodney Engelen [the Assistant Director of Planning], with the full support of Planning Director Irvin, cast his arguments in the broadest possible terms. The operational goal of the *Plan* was clearly a limited one: economic growth. Engelen, however, felt that he had to justify the goal itself. He stressed the functions of downtown as bearer of culture, disseminator of news and ideas, haven for unique activities, supplier of taxes to support all public services, and so on. When interviewed, he emphasized that his concern was to enrich the lives of all citizens, not to line the pockets of downtown businessmen. It was merely fortuitous, he believed, that in this case the interests of property owners and those of society coincided. He realized that on many subjects this coincidence did not exist, or was not perceived, and that in such cases the political implementation of the public interest might be impossible.

Engelen admitted freely that no plan or evaluation could be entirely comprehensive, as did all the planners interviewed for this study when pressed. His (and their) disclaimer was perfunctory, however, as if only a minor detail were at stake. Engelen wrote, for example, that the *Central Minneapolis Plan* could not truly be termed comprehensive because "there are and will always be elements — new aspects — yet to be studied and yet to be decided upon." He thus rejected a conception of comprehensiveness that I have suggested is useless: i.e., that the comprehensive plan should deal with everything. In short, he admitted that the object of any decision is necessarily limited, at very least in time, but he preserved the implication that the planner's approach — i.e., his goal orientation — to the object may be comprehensive.

The Search for Planning Goals

All Twin Cities planners agreed that community goals could in the final analysis be discovered only through public discussion. Planners might propose alternative articulations, but goal statements could have

---

phers, but not with that of contemporary economic and social theorists. For the latter, the term "rational" refers to the efficiency of means where ends are known. "Wisdom" refers to deep understanding and the ability to make what are considered "good" judgments on complex human issues, when goals and efficient means are not generally known.

Consequently, the planners use of the word "rational" in the classic sense to defend their distinctly modern "expert" recommendations makes for some confusion of thought. This confusion has a political function, however. It conveys the impression that expert logic or technique can produce "good" decisions on complex human issues.

no claim to represent community thought unless the community or its legitimate representatives ratified them after serious discussion and deliberation. In theory the primary problem was to guide the discussion and to decide when it had gone on long enough. The primary problem in practice, it developed, was to get a discussion going.

St. Paul's planners hoped, for example, that vigorous discussion would follow publication of their *Land Use Plan*. No one showed any interest in discussing it, however. The reason seemed to be that the *Plan's* stated goals were too general. No one knew how the application of these goals would affect him in practice. Those who were not completely uninterested in the *Plan* had learned long ago to be suspicious of high-sounding generalities. The planners had not succeeded in showing opinion leaders the relationship between the *Plan's* stated general goals and its great mass of "standards," or more specific goals. As a result, nonplanners decided with uncoordinated unanimity to ignore the *Plan* until someone proposed specific applications of it. Only at this point, they felt, would there be anything comprehensible — whether or not comprehensive — to argue about.

Minneapolis planners argued that the St. Paul planners' premises were wrong, and would have been wrong even if discussion of their plan had developed. For a discussion truly to influence the planning process, they said, it had to begin before detailed planning got under way. In their view, no one could effectively interpolate changes into a plan after it was complete without upsetting its internal harmony. If one of the goals of a plan were changed, then in theory every specific recommendation should be altered to some extent. No one had the time or intellectual energy to do this when a plan had already taken definite shape, however. The crucial phase in the evolution of any plan, then, was the development of its first draft. Goals should be determined before this phase moved far along.

Minneapolis planners themselves tried to obtain approval for planning goals before developing their central area plan. They decided at the start that they needed a goal statement which would be both "operational" and acceptable to all "reasonable" citizens of the city. By "operational," they meant that progress toward the goal could be objectively measured, and that the broad costs, both tangible and spiritual, of striving toward it could be foreseen. Comprehensive goals, they judged, could not be operational. Therefore, reasonable men could not pass on them intelligently. It followed that goals could win intelligent public approval only if they were partial. The question was: *how* partial? Perhaps it was possible to articulate, and plan to achieve, highly general goals even if not truly comprehensive ones.

They endeavored to bring about a public discussion of essential goal options before preparing the detailed plan. Fortunately, planners and planning consultants throughout the nation had applied themselves to downtown problems in recent years, and had developed a more or less integrated theory explaining characteristic downtown problems. Consequently, Minneapolis planners were able to present their preferred goals with tightly reasoned arguments behind them. The parts were related and mutually reinforcing. The man of affairs with a limited amount of time could quickly grasp the objectives and the main lines of reasoning on which the recommendations were based. The most general operational goal that the planners proposed was "the economic growth of downtown." They recognized that this goal was itself deceptive, however, in that although it sounded noncontroversial the steps necessary to its accomplishment could not keep from being controversial. In their publications on downtown planning goals, therefore, they chose to emphasize what they termed "design goals." These were in fact *types* of projects — rather than project proposals for specific streets and blocks in Minneapolis — that had been tried in other cities. The planners tried to explain the relationship between these types of proposals and the economic problems facing urban downtowns in the current period. It was possible to discuss the types of dislocation that might be expected, and so on, without bringing in specific project proposals. The discussion was really a model of comprehensible argument in favor of middle-range (i.e., operational but still general) planning goals. I strongly doubt that existing theory was sufficiently developed to support comparable justifications of goal recommendations in any other area of city planning activity.[3]

Even in this area, however, the specific financial costs and unintended side-effects that would arise on application in Minneapolis were difficult to foresee. Any intelligent discussion of planning goals had to take these (or their unpredictability) into account. For the discussion to be fully useful, the planners judged, its participants had to be willing to inform themselves about planning detail at some significant expenditure of time and effort. The discussion had to continue throughout the planning process, which itself would have peaks of activity but no final termination. Since the overall goal was partial, the discussants had to be urged to consider the full complexity of its side-effects. This they could not do if they confined themselves to examination of the central economic reasoning behind the "design goals."

---

[3] A major reason for this was probably that in no urban section but downtown did simple economic goals appear entirely plausible. Outside the United States, planners rarely considered them so even for downtown. See, for example, the British Town and Country Planning Association's analysis of central London problems: *The Paper Economy* (London: Town and Country Planning Association, 1962).

The first problem was how to find discussants. The comprehensive planner's search is more complicated than that of any specialist. He cannot be satisfied to consult a narrow constituency. Presumably he should understand every important goal of each of society's members. If he must deal with groups rather than individuals he should not limit himself to constellations of interest that maintain permanent formal organizations. But the planners knew of no way to approach the city's "potential" groups. These would not become actual groups unless some immediate threats activated their potential members; some potential groupings of interests that the observer might identify would not become actual even then. Even those in the first category, however, had no leaders to speak for them. The abstract discussion of goals could seldom seem sufficiently immediate to spur them to organize and choose representatives. It seemed that in no other public endeavor than general goal determination was the disproportion greater between the number of groups that *might* reasonably become involved and the number that *would*.

The planners soon found that they could carry on a continuing discussion only with men whose jobs required them to spend time on the study and discussion of civic affairs. Only a few organizations in the city had such men on their payrolls. All of these fit into a few categories. Most were large downtown business firms or organizations of businessmen. A few good government groups (supported mainly by the contributions of businesses or businessmen) had representatives who took an interest in city planning, but for the most part they were in the same position as planners: they could talk abstractly about the public interest but they could not claim any special qualifications to represent particular interests. The other permanent organizations in the city did not bother to have representatives spending the bulk of their time observing civic affairs. Each had a few continuing interests (racial issues, taxes, city hiring policy, etc.) and became politically active only when immediate threats to these arose.

Making the best of this situation, the planners tried to carry on a discussion of goals with the professional "civic affairs" representatives of downtown business. These professional discussants, however, lacked the power to commit their firms to anything; consequently, as the discussion became more specific they became more and more noncommittal. The businessmen who had the power to commit their firms to specific courses of action had neither the time nor interest to engage in almost endless discussion with the city planners. In a short while, even the professional discussants found that they had no time to study each tentative planning formulation with care. Thus, a major difficulty was revealed. Even had the planners been able to handle all the complexity of life, they would not have found laymen willing or able to evaluate their work.

If it can be so difficult to spur well-informed discussion even of such limited goals as those of the *Central Minneapolis Plan,* the question necessarily arises: what should be considered an adequate discussion of planning goals? Was the discussion in this case adequate although its only participants were businessmen whose interest in the discussion was mild and who were concerned only with direct economic costs and consequences? One might say that it was, because other groups could have entered the discussion to raise additional points had they wished. I did not find any elected officials in Minneapolis, however, who accepted this reasoning. Most were rather inarticulate about their objections, but a few were able to state their views quite precisely.

Downtown businesses are, according to these objectors, "organizations in being." Their owners are accustomed to watching the civic scene and searching for issues likely to affect their interests. They enter the discussion of any proposal at a very early stage and understand its potential impact on their interests relatively early. Other members of the public, however, tend to become aware that something is afoot and then to conceptualize their interests more slowly. After the perception begins to dawn, most take quite some time to organize. The range in the amount of time, and in the degree of immediacy of a threat or opportunity, that it takes to move different types of people with potential interest in a proposal to the threshold of organizational expression is enormous. Government never moves slowly enough or poses issues clearly enough to give everyone his say. It is fair to assume, however, that only when government moves at a snail's pace and deals with issues of rather direct and immediate impact can a significant proportion of the great multitude of interests express themselves. Therefore, comprehensive democratic planning is virtually impossible. No legislature or committee of interest group leaders can rationally evaluate a statement of comprehensive goals. Its members cannot, in the absence of specific project proposals and citizen reactions to them, predict how the countless measures needed to accomplish the goals will affect the overall quality of community life or the interests of their own constituents and organizations. Consequently, they are likely to prefer operating on levels where comprehension and prediction are most feasible, even if this means fragmenting policy choices rather than integrating them. In practice, this means that they will rarely commit themselves to let general and long-range goal statements guide their consideration of lower-level alternatives.

There are no doubt many local politicians in America who would not find the preceding argument a compelling one. In localities lacking a coherent "power elite" firmly committed to a plan, however, it has a high degree of plausibility as a prescription for political survival. Its specific dictates are bound to be, at a minimum, a "project" rather than a "general planning" orientation and a disinclination to deal with controversial issues.

Systematic Criticisms of the
Comprehensive Planning Ideal

The crucial assumptions of those who claim that comprehensive democratic planning is possible and desirable have of course been challenged more systematically than this. Martin Meyerson argued in a 1954 article that the major attacks could be divided into two types.[4] The first is that planning limits the range of individual choice by imposing centrally made decisions. The second is that planning requires "vastly more knowledge . . . about a huge variety of factors" than can be obtained or grasped by any individual or closely integrated group. Meyerson asserted that the few who had tried to answer these criticisms had been more successful in answering the first than the second. They had answered the first by saying that freedom is opportunity, not just the absence of restraint; and that planning agencies are created because people sense a failure of the market and of politics to satisfy their desires. As for the second question: unfortunately, wrote Meyerson, "we all know" that the assertion that planning can provide a rational basis for substantive policy decisions is just a goal today. The danger, he went on, is that planners will become content for it to remain a goal. He left the problem with a call for research.

It is questionable, however, whether planners have answered even the first objection successfully. Though it is certainly true that freedom consists of opportunity as well as the absence of restraint, there is little agreement as to whether planning to date has anywhere in the world produced more opportunity *in toto* than restraint. Only "commonsense" estimates are possible, as any more precise balance sheet would have to be based on determinations of the significance of particular opportunities and restraints. Neither the philosophic (assuming values to be objective) nor the scientific (assuming them to be subjective) foundations for such determinations exist. Second, the fact that people sense a failure of the market and the political process to meet their needs hardly forces one to conclude that they are better satisfied with the planning process. A reading of American city planning publications, not to mention conversations with numerous practicing planners, reveals a preoccupation among city planners with the failure of their work to win popular approval. More-

---

[4] "Research and City Planning," *Journal of the American Institute of Planners,* XX, No. 4 (Autumn 1954), 201–205.

over, the winning of popular approval would itself prove very little. Planners themselves do not hesitate to bemoan the unwisdom of many popular governmental programs. They emphasize that the public must be educated by its leaders to favor comprehensive planning. They admit that the unguided public is likely to prefer an alderman who does petty favors for constituents to one who studies the city's overall needs.

Those who have made this first objection to comprehensive planning have generally emphasized that ambitious plans can only be realized through the generous exercise of public power. They have contended that every grant of power to government increases the chance of its abuse, increases the pervading influence of bureaucracy and red tape in the lives of citizens, decreases the self-reliance of citizens, and, as the habit of delegating tasks to government becomes prevalent, undermines their healthy suspicion of those who wield power. They have said that those charged with taking a comprehensive view of political problems are necessarily charged with safeguarding the complex requisites of the social and political system entrusted to their care. In the case of American society, this means a system in which the rights of individuals to wide spheres of personal freedom are recognized.

If the planner is truly to think comprehensively, in this view, he must consider not only the goals of society, but also the framework within which these goals can be pursued. If all proposals to enlarge governmental power threaten the framework of individual liberty to some degree, the planner must share society's initial bias against them. Those who oppose planning have generally asserted that planners have a professional bias in favor of bigger and bigger government, less and less subject to pressures from interest groups. Planners, they say, are in the business of creating new proposals which call for governmental activity. The planner's own interest is in the success of his plans: that is, in additional governmental activity *ad infinitum.* Most grants of power to government are long-term ones, because the electoral process is ponderous and inflexible. To reverse a major decision once ratified is extremely difficult, though it happens occasionally, as with Prohibition. The general pattern is for public interest to focus on an issue for a short while, and then move on. The planner's bias in favor of ever-larger government should therefore disqualify him from evaluating either his own proposals or those of others. Demands for public action in modern society are so numerous that only by subjecting each to the most searching criticism, based on an initial negative bias, can the trend toward concentration of power (which admittedly cannot be stopped) be slowed to a moderate rate. When government must act to deal with some pressing issue, every effort should be made to define the problem narrowly and to deal with it specifically. The approach should be one of dealing with bottlenecks, not planning the whole production line. In other words, it should be piece-meal, not comprehensive.

.   .   .

Obstacles to Comprehensive Planning in the Twin Cities: An Overview

It seems apparent that the political culture of the Twin Cities has tended to inhibit the development of conditions in which comprehensive planning, even at the level of the city, could have a great deal of impact. Both Minneapolis and St. Paul were run democratically, by politicians who tended to be perceived by their constituents, and to perceive them-selves, as servants rather than leaders. They did not sense any significant demand for comprehensive city planning, nor did they feel any obliga-tion to spur such demand. The pattern of existing city agency jurisdic-tions and services was relatively well fixed. Only infrequently did inter-agency conflicts arise that could not be settled by informal negotiation among the affected officials. This was not to say that more systematic coordination from above could not have produced genuine benefits, but only that official and public perception of these potential benefits was either lacking or had not yet resulted in demands for action. Nor did this mean that the voters of the Twin Cities were ecstatic about the quality of the local government that they had; it meant only that they gave no appearance of believing that a change in the direction of comprehensive planning would improve that quality substantially. Moreover, to politi-cians who obtained reelection with great regularity, it appeared likely that such a change would on balance reduce voter satisfaction as mea-sured in the most meaningful currency they knew — votes. Comprehen-sive planning would probably invite many jurisdictional controversies where few now existed. It would certainly involve additional articulation of city-wide and long-term values that were hard (once articulated) to brush off, but that had less well-organized constituencies than the more narrow and immediate values with which they might often conflict. It was also bound to involve many unusual proposals the ultimate political effects of which were extremely difficult to foresee. So long as the level of voter dissatisfaction, as measured by votes against incumbents, was low, there seemed little reason to advocate substantial change.

We may reasonably ask whether certain special factors may have made the political payoff of planning appear more questionable in the Twin Cities than elsewhere. Several candidates for designation as such factors . . . come quickly to mind. First, the political culture was favor-able to pluralism and the greatest possible autonomy for private groups. Government tended to be perceived by those who shared this culture more as a provider of special services than as a comprehensive designer of the shape of the future.

Second, both cities gave little power — even by American standards — to their chief executives, and party discipline in their city councils was virtually nonexistent. The consequent fragmentation of power discouraged the pursuit of unconventional objectives. No one official or coherent group of officials could reasonably hope to implement such objectives. Moreover, with no one official clearly in the public eye, and with the possibility of dramatization by striking deeds virtually foreclosed, the task of education to make unconventional objectives politically palatable was likely to appear extremely forbidding to anyone who contemplated it. In any event, these political systems did not offer sufficient power or prestige to encourage many men of great independence or imagination to seek elective positions in them. Those who did hold elective positions in them tended to be preoccupied with immediate problems, particularly those of intense concern to their constituents, and in general to be extremely content with things as they were. Not only did they typically believe that the pursuit of ambitious objectives would be politically dangerous; they were also very disinclined to believe that such objectives could be worth pursuing.

Third, it may have been that the level of functional coordination within departments, and that of mutual accommodation among departments, had risen quickly enough over the years to keep pace with public demands for coordination. There had been no proliferation of departments as city budgets had grown in recent decades. Within each department sufficient power was concentrated at the top to impose any desired level of coordination. Coordination by mutual accommodation among the departments was facilitated by the fact that nearly all the highest departmental officers had spent decades in their city's service prior to achieving their current positions. Their capacities for "getting along" within it had been subject to careful observation and informal cultivation during these long apprenticeships. It was true that many high officials were appointed on the basis of written technical examinations alone, but even they were normally quite well "socialized." This is not to say that all strong public demands for improved interagency cooperation were met adequately by mutual accommodation, or that bitter interagency conflicts never developed. It is to hypothesize an explanation, however, as to why such failures were sufficiently rare so that (1) the elective politicians could take time to handle them individually, and (2) perception of the desirability of new coordinating agencies was held to a low level.

Similarly, at the metropolitan area level there were mechanisms for functional coordination in areas where it was widely deemed to be desirable. The state highway department effectively determined the structure of the major highways network. Three single-purpose metropolitan authorities had been created in recent years to deal with sanitation, airports, and mosquito control. A number of other services were provided jointly by two or more local governments in the area under a Minnesota law which authorized all local governments to perform jointly any functions which they were authorized to perform individually. The services that had been dealt with to some extent in this way included fire-protection, water supply, and recreation.

Evaluative Criteria and Factual Perception

To list the factors discussed in the last few paragraphs is to suggest that no evaluation of Twin Cities planning, *circa* 1960 can be very meaningful unless it refers to a carefully specified measure of accomplishment. I have consciously used the traditional ideal of comprehensive planning as my benchmark. It has the virtue of clarity, and the public image of the city planning profession has been built substantially upon it. Despite the fact that most academic planners today recognize the impossibility of achieving it, practicing planners in the Twin Cities constantly referred to it in their public statements. This was not because they lacked awareness of trends in academia. It was rather because they judged that academics had failed to provide substitute ideals which could guide practitioners, inspire supporters, or have very much persuasive impact upon skeptics. . . . The planners' steadfastness in the face of political dangers however was very much reduced by their lack of strong conviction about the comprehensive planning ideal. But they did need some ideal, and they had no other. . . .

The Dilemmas of Guided Reform

Peter Marris and Martin Rein

"In a political system where nearly every adult may vote but where knowledge, wealth, social position, access to officials, and other resources are unequally distributed, who actually governs?" asks Robert Dahl at the outset of his study of New Haven.[1] He concludes that a few profes-

---

Reprinted from Peter Marris and Martin Rein, *Dilemmas of Social Reform* (New York: Atherton Press, 1967); copyright © Peter Marris and Martin Rein 1967.
    [1] Robert Dahl, *Who Governs?* (New Haven: Yale University Press, 1961), p. 1.

sional politicians — who share, despite their competing interests, a common understanding of the rules and procedures of political life — direct affairs within the limits of public tolerance. This tolerance may extend even to policies which, if they gave them thought, most citizens might not approve. The professional therefore holds the initiative, so long as he does not arouse public opinion from its apathy. He can maneuver amongst his peers, who are usually better informed and more coherent in their interpretation of democratic principles than most of their constituents. Government is a sophisticated game of professional players, who abide by the same rules, and react to each other according to the same understanding of the latent democratic constraints upon their freedom of action.

Like the politicians, the Ford Foundation executives who promoted the gray area projects aimed at upgrading impoverished urban neighborhoods, the staff of the President's Committee on juvenile delinquency, and their consultant sociologists were also professionals. Their vocation was reform. And their freedom to initiate reform was similarly circumscribed by an indefinite mandate, whose limits they tested, but which they had ultimately to respect. They too were a small, sophisticated group who knew, or came to know each other, and who — though they did not always agree — thought in the same terms. Within the context of their democratic ideals, and guided by a wary sense of the length to which they could push the authority they represented, they staked their money on a bold initiative. But neither the Foundation nor the Committee was well placed to protect its stake — one because it was unrepresentative, the other because its own standing within the Federal Government was precarious.

The Dilemma of Philanthropy

As the largest of all philanthropic foundations, Ford faces most uncomfortably the crucial dilemma of private giving: it is an exercise of power without responsibility. "With the exception of major governments, the Ford Foundation possesses the largest fund in the world specifically designed for the advancement of mankind. The Foundation therefore should analyze its role . . . with reference to the full depth and breadth of the problems and prospects of mankind." [2] On these terms it is preoccupied with the same broad issues of policy which are already the chief concern of government. How is it to deploy its funds effectively, when — in comparison with government — its resources are, after all,

---

[2] "Directives and Terms of Reference for the 1960's" (Ford Foundation, June 1962).

meager? Since there would be little point in adding marginally to the money government is already spending on a particular policy, it has to find something to do which government does not. How then, as an autonomous organization without a democratic mandate, is it to justify its intervention? Unless it innovates, it wastes its opportunity to advance mankind beyond the scope of political leadership; but whenever it does so, it lays itself open to the charge of unwarranted interference. Philanthropy treads a narrow path between redundancy and presumption.

The Ford Foundation has tried to resolve this dilemma by an emphasis on education, in the broadest sense — demonstrating possibilities, evaluating achievements, but never asserting or institutionalizing purposes of its own. "The Ford Foundation is essentially an Educational Foundation," wrote the President in the 1957 annual report. ". . . In these terms, education extends beyond the academic world, and into the atmosphere of society, which is the composite of the beliefs and ambitions of its members." Even here, he disclaimed any directive influence. "This is where Foundations have an appropriate role to play, not in shaping those beliefs and ambitions but in encouraging competent, serious-minded people to understand, maintain and realize them." Philanthropy is, as it were, a rain-maker — seeding the atmosphere of society to precipitate a latent flood of productive ideas.

In negotiating the gray area projects, the Public Affairs staff tried to act according to this conception of their proper role. They did not begin by putting forward any specific proposals. To impose their own prescription would have seemed both illegitimate and self-defeating. The gray area projects were designed to revitalize community leadership, not to overwhelm it. The Foundation did not want to cut short a thorough reappraisal of the cities' problems by revealing at the outset too much of its own thinking. It defined its aims in very abstract terms — human betterment, opening opportunities, "harnessing the urban-rural reaction." Poverty, unemployment, delinquency were taken as symptoms of a pervasive hardening of the social and bureaucratic structure. The first step, therefore, was to break out of this constricting framework in any promising direction. Once the institutions of the city came together, and saw the problem as a whole; once they examined their performance in the light of this understanding; once the leaders everywhere in the community committed themselves to seek authentic solutions, then the logic of this commitment would drive institutions towards experiment and cooperation. It did not so much matter where they chose to begin.

In principle, then, the Foundation sought to play only a catalytic part. As Paul Ylvisaker wrote modestly of the first gray area grant: "Foundation prospects have expanded and hopefully improved the Oakland project, they did not create it." But in practice, the Public Affairs staff could not seriously pretend to themselves that they were merely crystalizing the ambitions of community leadership. In a less formal memorandum he was franker: "The Foundation is in most cases 'out in front of its customers,'" he admitted, and went on to remark generally on the narrowness of most plans cities had put forward, the vested interests, the lack of hard thinking, the publicity seeking "and worse, the object of human betterment usually gets lost in this morass, replaced by more tangible concerns such as physical monuments and agency survival. . . . If nothing else the Foundation has shown — and temporarily filled — a vacuum of constructive criticism and leadership which exists in most American communities, and in which the problems of the gray areas have thrived."

A note in the file on the original Oakland proposal includes the revealing phrase: "Foundation bargaining position to be agreed upon by September 15th." In the drawn-out negotiations with Oakland, New Haven, Boston, Philadelphia, the Foundation was obliquely setting out terms which it was inhibited from openly declaring. In all its dealings with the cities, it was torn between reluctance to prejudice the communities' own conception of their needs, and insistence on meaningful reform — displaying, according to one's point of view, hypocrisy, humility or inconstancy of purpose.

The Public Affairs negotiators resolved the dilemma by leaving the initiative in drafting proposals to local leadership, while guarding their intentions in the revisions they imposed as a condition of support. In part, this simply reduced the negotiations to a guessing game, in which the cities arrived by elimination at the answer the Foundation had first thought of. Even in the specification of programs, where the Foundation was genuinely open-minded, the fertility of human invention could not match the opportunity. In search of fresh ideas, the drafters of the proposals in the cities could only turn, after all, to the Foundation itself, to discover what it would accept as relevant and new. The programs which gained currency came to look very much alike, and they bore the stamp of the Public Affairs staff's analysis, more than the communities' first thoughts.

But the ambivalence of the Foundation's negotiating posture also gave rise to a confusion of purpose, which damaged its chances of integrating community leadership. By surrendering the initiative, it left the field open to rival interests in the city to compete for the right to coordinate the master plan. And this emphasis upon institutional aggrandisement was the one thing, above all, that the Foundation was trying to prevent.

The breakdown of coherent social planning had arisen, not so much from a "vacuum of constructive criticism and leadership," as from inability to agree on who should fill it. Local reformers in the councils of voluntary agencies, urban renewal authorities, schoolboards and city halls had long recognized their growing problems, and begun to search for solutions. Everyone recognized much the same needs, and the inadequacy of present means to solve them. To Redevelopment Authorities and Health and Welfare Councils alike, to the settlement houses, Youth Commissions, Welfare departments, schools, city managers or universities which in one city or another initiated proposals, more cogent planning, closer coordination and imaginative innovations were unexceptionable aims. But at the same time, everyone was also committed to the interests he represented, and could plausibly argue that urban renewal, or social work, or city hall was the natural focus of a new approach. The Foundation was convinced of the need for a broadly representative coalition of leadership to implement reform. But the institutions which responded most purposefully to the Foundation's invitation were often also those with the most urgent problems of survival, and so least willing to concede any part of their faltering authority. They hoped to reinforce their own functions by assimilating the new resources for social development. They certainly did not expect to subordinate these functions to a new agency.

.   .   .

. . . Although the councils of the voluntary agencies were amongst the most active promoters of the gray area projects, they were also the first to resent them. The health and welfare councils saw their prerogative of social planning usurped. The new organization, with its smart, bustling offices and well-paid staff, flourishing under the patronage of city hall, philanthropy and the Federal Government, became a dangerous rival. Instead of helping the council to reconstruct the pattern of voluntary services, and revive the council's function, the project's staff set about to manipulate public and private agencies to their own design, as if the council were an obsolete and ineffectual body. This was all the more painful since the council, in promoting the project, had indeed confessed its weakness. . . . The voluntary agencies found they had hatched a cuckoo, who swallowed all the grants, grew prodigiously, and left their own starvelings disconsolately chirping at the bottom of the nest.

The disappointment of the . . . voluntary agencies exposes the inherent weakness of the Foundation's position as a disinterested innovator. Whether the response to its invitation originated in concern with relocation or the plight of the United Fund, with the quality of public education, the control of delinquency, or the underlying fiscal crisis of the center city caught between a shrinking tax base and an increasing population in social want, the proposals were all designed to retrieve the viability of the institutions which sponsored them. The needs they described, and the remedies they put forward, did not contradict the Foundation's analysis. But there was a fundamental misunderstanding. The Foundation wanted the plans to arise from a comprehensive review of the problems of gray areas, in which agency services were ruthlessly subordinated to the interests of their users, and reorganized without regard for conventional jurisdictions. But since it was inhibited from taking charge itself, and the authoritative leaders in the cities all had institutional ties, there was no one who could dominate the planning from this detached point of view. Nor did the most active participants represent the most directly relevant institutions. The Public Affairs staff thought in terms of education and vocational training rather than community organization, case work, or the relocation of alcoholics and problem families. At their insistence, the plans shifted their emphasis. But the school system, which now became the center of attention, had not itself taken much part in the initial discussion. In spite of the great cities schools program, the pressure for school reform came from outside the system: in Philadelphia, for instance, from the Citizens Committee on Public Education; in New Haven, from the Mayor, his Redevelopment Administrator, and the School Board they had appointed; in North Carolina, from the Governor. So the proposals came to depend very heavily on an institution whose cooperation was only sought when the planning was already advanced.

The Foundation was also worried by the professional or academic bias of the initial planners, who tended to be recruited from the staff of redevelopment authorities, voluntary agencies and their councils, or from universities. It pressed for a wider involvement of public officials, community and political leaders. So, as boards for the new agencies were set up, and task forces and communities ramified to develop programs, responsibility became shared by people who were less committed to the endeavor, and sometimes only vaguely aware of its aims.

By insisting on a broadly representative coalition of leadership, the Foundation was able to prevent ambitious institutions having their way unchallenged. But the outcome was often . . . a confused compromise in which the issues were unresolved, and the project was left without a constituency of committed supporters. Its originators in the community had been edged from control, while those who displaced them were less sure of their purpose, and less involved.

.   .   .

Hindsight throws the unresolved ambiguities and tenuous assumptions into sharp relief. Yet without this ambiguity, the projects would not

have been negotiable. Neither by its philosophy, nor its posture as a reformer, could the Foundation impose its remedies. At the same time, it
was, in Paul Ylvisaker's phrase, so far "out in front of its customers," that
it had to prepare its own criteria of relevance. It had, then, at once to
seize the initiative, and advertise its aims, and yet to appear responsive
and open-minded. The abstraction of Paul Ylvisaker's conception of the
urban problem, its appeal to moral purpose and the commitment of concern, rather than detailed institutional or social analysis, gave him room
to maneuver. A subtle balance between the exploitation of means, and
the assertion of ultimate ends made the projects possible. And as they
evolved, so the interpretation of the problem evolved with them. But
this saving ambiguity also entangled the projects in a confusion of purpose from which some never fought themselves free.

.   .   .

The Voice of the People

Each of the local projects was forced to choose between its institutional alliances, and its sponsorship of a challenging redistribution of
power within the City. Only Mobilization for Youth in New York dared
to risk antagonizing public agencies, and disastrously miscalculated their
power to exact retribution. It seems unlikely that any program of community action, so dependent upon a consensus of established leadership
and public funds, could be at the same time an effective champion of
radical democracy. If the sponsors of community organization cannot
disclaim responsibility for the organization they create, and if at the
same time they defeat their own purpose in seeking to control it, only a
sponsor free from other commitments can afford to support his organization in whatever course it chooses.

But even had the projects been at liberty to risk the consequences
of aligning themselves with the poor, was it practicable for a sophisticated professional staff to work out programs in equal partnership with
the people they served? Planning with people raised a conflict of intellectual as well as political loyalties. Only one project seriously attempted
it, and the experience suggests the mutually frustrating ambivalence of
such a relationship.

Early in its planning, Harlem Youth Opportunities Unlimited was approached by two young men, President and Vice-President of an organization of young people in Harlem, who wanted "to improve the community in which we live and to better the responsibilities of our youngsters —
you know, fifteen to sixteen." From this initiative grew the HARYOU
Associates, a group of over two hundred young people, who shared for a
year in the development of HARYOU's plans. HARYOU felt the experi-

ment had been a qualified success. But its staff took a lot of punishment, as the Associates adroitly drove them in both mind and body to the wall:

> There were many problems, frustrations, and risks involved in the realities of involving a large group of young people between the ages of fourteen and twenty-one in the day-to-day planning operations of a professional staff. Not the least of these problems was the fact that these young people, encouraged by those staff who were assigned to them, took seriously the invitation to participate and to contribute their ideas in the planning. They understandably interpreted this invitation to mean that they would be welcome in the HARYOU offices not only on Saturdays and Sundays, but also during the work week. The limitations of office space generally made for a type of chaos when groups or committees of Associates were around. They often seemed to take over the HARYOU offices. The patience of some of the members of the professional and secretarial staff was often stretched to the breaking point and beyond. . . . As the interest, excitement, enthusiasm of the Associates increased and reached a crescendo, they tended to dominate more and more of the office and the activities of HARYOU. . . .
>
> During this period, the group held the adult staff team in a "heads I win, tails you lose" bind. A program faltered either because the staff had not given the group its head and had not really shown faith in the group, or because the staff had allowed the group to go off half-cocked.
>
> Alternation between feelings of respect, affection and loyalty, and hostility, suspicion and a contempt for the authority or competence of the adult staff, has characterized not only the youth leaders of the Associates but also some of the rank-and-file members. The adult consultants, on the other hand, have also alternated between over-enthusiastic reliance on the competence and ability of the Associates, and attempts to seize completely the reins of the program at times when it faltered.[3]

If the Associates had been older, no doubt the mutual exasperation would have been less vivid. But if the projects were to plan with the people they served, then they could not ignore the young people with whom their crucial programs were concerned. And even with a more mature group, it is hard to see how a professional staff could divide responsibility with them: one or other must be content with an advisory role. The projects were not only committed to institutional alliances which constricted their freedom of action: they were also committed to an intellectual rationale. They could not unequivocally sacrifice their professional judgment to the inexperienced demands of their public.

In retrospect, it seems evident that the projects could never whole-

---

[3] "Youth in the Ghetto" (HARYOU, 1964), pp. 91–2, 576–7.

heartedly share responsibility for their programs with the people they
served: they had too many other commitments to both theory and practice. They recognized that their manner of reform needed democratic
safeguards, but in trying to build these safeguards into their own organization, they assumed an impossible harmony between different means to
the same fundamental end. The competence of each citizen to uphold his
liberty depends upon political, legal, economic and psychological resources which no one organization can secure. The means to each require
a different emphasis, a different alignment of interests, a different perception of the problem.

The poor can be seen, firstly, as an interest group which like any
other must compete for attention againt rival lobbies. The neglect of
their interests arises from their failure to organize and assert their potential influence. Their economic power is collectively considerable, despite their poverty, as bus boycotts, consumer boycotts and rent strikes
demonstrate. And their political power is greater than their voting
strength, because they can appeal both to an uneasy middle-class conscience and a general fear of open conflict. But to be poor is not itself a
status which defines a common political interest. It is, rather, a humiliating
condition which most people are ashamed to acknowledge, and from
which anyone with the ability to lead has also the ability to escape.
Hence the organization of the poor has to center upon more specific interests which concern them especially, but not them alone — rack-renting,
racial discrimination, education. As tenants, members of a racial minority,
parents, beneficiaries of social services, the poor can act in their own defense without the stigma of inferiority, and their case has a universal
relevance.

But in a highly structured democracy, where every interest tends to
institutionalize its representation, these characteristic concerns of the
poor need to recruit comparable resources of organization and leadership.
Spontaneous protest is too sporadic: soon discouraged by frustration, it
lacks the power of sustained bargaining. If the poor are to attract the
able organizers they need, the defense of their interests must offer a career which rewards the ambitious with growing prestige and power.
Community organization falters because it cannot offer any future to the
neighborhood leaders it promotes but a lifetime of parochial effort. The
real leaders are the professional community organizers, who alone have
the incentive of a career with widening opportunities. No one can fairly
be expected to put the best of his energies, year after year, into the affairs
of his neighborhood without recognition or reward. Political parties understand this: they distribute patronage, curry local favor, and above all,
hold out to every ward leader the opportunity of promotion.

Nor does the neighborhood provide a natural focus of organization, except for those concerns which arise from the immediate environment — garbage collection, police protection, redevelopment plans. Community organization seems to assume that those who live near each other share a community of interest, which ought to find expression in a generalized social cohesion. But unemployment, discrimination, punitive welfare regulations, even the denial of educational opportunity are not neighborhood issues, and only accidently unite the residents of the same block. Community organization, since it provides no hierarchy of affiliation from local to national levels, trivializes major interests by its parochial bias. The pressure for reform becomes fragmented, unsure of itself, and easily patronized.

.　　.　　.

Moreover to mobilize the sanctions which lie within the grasp of the poor, and redistribute power through political action, may not immediately help the individual to secure his rights. The poor are at a disadvantage, not only because their interests are collectively unprotected, but because they are individually less equipped to protect them. They lack money and knowledge to seek redress.

.　　.　　.

The theory of a poverty cycle emphasized the oppression of spirit, the apathy and social disintegration which robbed the poor of any power of initiative in their own interest. The programs had not only to provide opportunities, but regenerate a will to respond to them. In part, then, community organization was a form of treatment for collective depression. Discussion, participation, the devolution of responsibility, the self-analysis of community problems imitated the techniques of group therapy. This conception grew out of a fundamental faith in individual autonomy. But its expression in terms of social health was partly misleading.

The therapeutic analogy breaks down, because the projects approached the community with a preconceived diagnosis, while a doctor waits for a patient to present his symptoms, and can be dismissed at will. A community cannot, like an individual patient, ask for treatment and describe its symptoms. Hence it cannot initiate and ultimately control the relationship with its helper. Social therapy, therefore, tends towards a paternalism which undermines the very qualities it is seeking to promote: self-confidence and self-respect. . . . The dilemma arises whenever the restoration of individual dignity is taken as a psychological problem, inherent in those who are demoralized, rather than as a moral problem, inherent in the society which humiliates them. We derive our sense of worth from the whole context of relationships which define a social being. To restore dignity, you must above all treat people as deserving of respect. The poor cannot respect themselves until the employers, social workers, teachers, doctors, policemen, politicians, and public officials who relate them to the values of society at large respect them. And this means not only politeness and humility, but an honesty of purpose which does not seek to disguise the shortcomings of the services offered. Though community self-help can be useful and satisfying, the projects could probably best meet the psychological need of reassurance and acceptance by their influence on institutional attitudes, and especially by the integrity with which they presented their own program of service.

Symposium on Advocacy Planning

Whom Does the Advocate Planner Serve?

Frances Fox Piven

A new kind of practice, advocacy for the poor, is growing in the professions. The new advocacy has thus far been most vigorous in the legal profession, where the term originates. Traditional legal-defense organizations are challenging in test cases regulations and practices of agencies serving the poor, and new legal agencies offering direct legal services have mushroomed in the slums. Social workers are also stationed in neighborhood storefronts where they act as the advocates of a "walk-in" clientele by badgering public agencies for services. Now planners and architects are offering their services to local groups confronted with neighborhood development proposals.

To account for this new practice, lawyers would probably trace their inspiration to Jacobus Tenbroeck and Charles Reich, two legal scholars who exposed injustices perpetrated on the poor by agencies of the welfare state. Social workers might see their advocacy as a reaction against a "mental hygiene movement" which had come to dominate social agencies, orienting practitioners toward a psychiatrically based therapy and a middle-class clientele amenable to such therapy. And planners and architects would probably say that advocacy reflects their growing unease at the devastations visited on the uprooted poor by a decade and a half of urban

From "Symposium: Whom Does the Advocate Planner Serve?" *Social Policy*, May/ June 1970, pp. 32–37. Reprinted by permission of *Social Policy*, International Arts and Sciences Press, Inc., 901 North Broadway, White Plains, New York 10603.

redevelopment. In other words, each profession sees the emergence of advocacy as the expression of an enlightened professional conscience.

No doubt early volunteer advocates were stirred by the civil rights movement and troubled by the growing concentration of black poverty in the cities. But the efforts of early volunteer advocates were scattershot and ineffective. Nor were their ideas earthshaking. There are always many currents in professional thought.

Advocacy now, however, has become popular and may even become widespread as a form of professional practice because opportunities for advocate practice have been created by the array of federal programs for the inner city launched during the Sixties. Social workers and lawyers were hired by federally funded projects in delinquency, mental health, education, and poverty. Now advocate planning also is becoming both feasible and popular with funds provided by the Model Cities program. In our enthusiasm for the idea, we have tended to see professional advocates as free agents because they are independent of local government, and we ignore the federal dollars which support them and the federal interests they serve.

These federal programs were prompted, as was much else that happened in this nation in the last decade, by the massive migration of blacks into cities. Having been liberated from southern feudal controls without being absorbed into the regulating political and economic institutions of the cities, black were becoming volatile. The new Democratic Administration in 1960 was keenly alert to the key role of this swelling urban black population which had turned increasingly independent at the polls, even as it became a major force in national Democratic politics.

Accordingly, Administration analysts began to explore new programs for the cities that might cement the allegiance of the urban black vote to the national party and stimulate local Democratic organizations to be more responsive to the new voters. What followed was a series of federal programs directed to the "inner city," beginning with the Juvenile Delinquency and Youth Offenses Control Act of 1961 and continuing through the legislation for Model Cities in 1966. However worthy one thinks the social goals attributed to these programs, and whatever their actual social benefits, they also met the political needs of the Democratic Administration in adjusting to population changes in the cities.

Nor should it be surprising that these services were presented as programs to solve such social problems as delinquency and welfare dependency. This, after all, was what urban whites thought the "Negro problem" was all about. By minimizing the resentment of the white working class, who were still the major Democratic constituents in the cities, such definitions helped to lessen opposition — both in Congress and among the general urban population — to new service programs for blacks.

Despite the presumably different social problems to be attacked, the various programs were remarkably similar. Under the broad umbrella of "comprehensive community development," each provided a battery of services not unlike those of old-time political clubs. Equally important, each called for "citizen participation," to be promoted by federal funds under federal guidelines. Whatever the stated goals, these efforts can be understood as a strategy to integrate the new migrants into the political structure of the city by offering them various forms of patronage distributed by local "citizen participants" whom the projects selected and cultivated. To execute the strategy, the projects brought to the ghetto a variety of professionals, many of whom were called "advocates."

There is a minor irony in this, for whatever the variants of the advocacy idea, two elements are essential to it: professional services must be made available to the poor, and these services should be so structured as to assure that professionals are responsive to the interests of the poor as the poor themselves see them. In other words, it is not so much that professionals have been strangers to the slum; rather, it is that those professionals who work with slum people and slum problems are traditionally under hire by, and therefore responsive to, public and private agencies which represent interests other than those of the poor. There is, of course, a dilemma in the ideal, for if professional services are in the end responsive to whoever finances them, where can the poor find the money to pay their advocates? The dilemma, however, concerns the ideal of advocacy, not the realities of advocate practice on the federal payroll.

To point out that advocacy was promoted by national Democratic political interests is not to deny that the poor have benefited from professional advocacy or, put another way, that the poor have gained from federal efforts to integrate them into local and national politics. Overall, it is difficult to dismiss the results. Social workers who pried loose delayed welfare checks, or harassed housing inspectors into taking action, were in a small way easing oppressive conditions, as were lawyers who prevented an eviction or defended a youngster from police harassment. To argue that these small gains diverted the black poor from making greater demands is to set a dubious possibility against a gain that is real, however limited. Furthermore, small material advances, by raising the expectations of blacks, may actually have spurred them to greater demands. In this sense, the federal strategy for the cities, and especially the poverty program, may have contributed to a growing discontent and turbulence in the ghetto, at least in the short run.

But whatever may be said for the tangible accomplishments of social workers and lawyers stationed in the ghettos, the same cannot be said for planning advocates. Planners offer no concrete service or benefit. Rather, they offer their skill in the planning process. The object, planning advocates would say, is to overcome the vast discrepancy in technical capability between local communities and the city bureaucracy, because it is with the bureaucracy that local groups must contend to protect and improve their neighborhoods.

Implicit in this view is the recognition that planning decisions are decisions about who gets what in the city. That is, to determine what kinds of schools, or hospitals, or housing, or recreational facilities will be built, and where they will be located, is to determine who will benefit from the facilities. And to determine which neighborhoods will be demolished to provide space for new facilities or housing is to determine who will lose out. Planning decisions, in other words, are political decisions.

Implicit in the advocate planner's view also is the notion that the urban poor can influence these decisions once they are given the technical help of a planner — or better still, once they actually learn the technical skills of planning. And this is exactly what many neighborhood groups have been trying to do, sometimes with volunteer planners, more often with the help of eager young professionals hired with Model Cities or poverty program funds. The results are worth pondering.

One of the earliest and most dedicated of such efforts began in 1959, in a neighborhood called Cooper Square, on the Lower East Side of New York City. Various neighborhood groups had rallied to fight an urban renewal designation which, familiarly enough, called for demolition of 2,150 existing housing units, half of which were renting for under $40 a month. They secured the services of Walter Thabit, a dedicated New York planner, who set to work in consultation with neighborhood representatives on an "Alternate Plan for Cooper Square." By 1961 the Alternate Plan was presented to the public with much fanfare and the chairman of the city's Planning Commission pronounced it commendable. Then, from 1961 until 1963, the Cooper Square Committee and its advocate planner negotiated with city officials. In 1963 the city prepared once more to move on its own renewal plan. Again the neighborhood rallied, with mass meetings of site tenants. The city withdrew, and new conferences were scheduled to discuss the Alternate Plan. In 1966, however, a new mayor announced indefinite postponement. Then, in January 1968, Walter Thabit was asked to prepare a new, smaller plan, and in 1969 new meetings were conducted between city officials and the Cooper Square Committee.

Early in 1970, the Board of Estimate approved "an early action plan." After ten years of arduous effort on the part of an extraordinary neighborhood group, a small portion of the Alternate Plan had been given formal sanction even though that portion was still far from implementation. The chief accomplishment was that the neighborhood had stopped the early threat of renewal. As Walter Thabit said sourly when it was all over, "Protest without planning could have done as much."

Most advocacy efforts are not yet old enough to provide such over-whelming discouragement. But the signs so far are bleak. In one city after another, local groups in Model Cities neighborhoods are involved in the technical dazzlements of planning, some to prepare plans, others to compete with counterplans. But there is little being built in these neigh-borhoods. Nor are locally prepared plans likely to change the pattern. A plan, of itself, is not force; it is not capable of releasing the necessary federal subsidies or of overcoming the inertia of the city agencies. Quite the contrary, for those people who might otherwise have become a force by the trouble they made are now too busy. As one advocate planner for a Harlem neighborhood that is still without construction funds proudly said, "They are learning how to plan."

What all of this suggests is that involving local groups in elaborate planning procedures is to guide them into a narrowly circumscribed form of political action, and precisely that form for which they are least equipped. What is laid out for the poor when their advocate arrives is a strategy of political participation which, to be effective, requires power-ful group support, stable organization, professional staff, and money — precisely those resources which the poor do not have. Technical skill is only one small aspect of the power discrepancy between the poor and the city bureaucracies.

Not only are low-income groups handicapped when politics becomes planning, but they are diverted from the types of political action by which the poor are most likely to be effective. For all the talk of their powerlessness, the masses of newly urbanized black poor did prompt some federal action long before advocates came to their aid. The threat of their growing and volatile numbers in the voting booth and in the streets exacted some responses from national and local political leaders: the curtailment of slum clearance; the expansion and liberalization of some existing services, such as public welfare; and the new federal pro-grams for the ghetto. But the planning advocates who came with the new programs have not added to the political force of the ghetto. Quite the contrary, for the advocates are coaxing ghetto leaders off the streets, where they might make trouble. The absorbing and elaborate planning procedures which follow are ineffective in compelling concessions, but may be very effective indeed in dampening any impulse toward disrup-tive action which has always been the main political recourse of the very poor.

To be sure, a few neighborhood leaders do gain something from these planning activities. The lucky members of the local "planning com-mittee" become involved in overwhelming and prestigious rites and mysteries, which often absorb them even while action for their neighborhood is going forward without them. In effect, those few selected leaders are drawn away from their base in the community into a lengthy educational program, the end product of which, if all goes well, may be a neighborhood plan. Once produced, that plan is easily stalled by the city, negotiated beyond recognition, or accepted only to be undermined in implementation. In the meantime, the local "planning process" has diverted and confused, and perhaps divided, the community, and surely has not advanced it toward effective political mobilization.

Although the language is new, this kind of advocacy follows a long tradition of neighborhood councils in the slums, through which local residents were encouraged to "participate" in the elaborate rituals of parliamentary procedure as if that were the path of political influence for the very poor. In the past such participation absorbed slum leadership and rendered it ineffective. That may well be the chief result of current planning advocacy. It deflects conflict by preoccupying newcomers to city politics with procedures that pose little threat to entrenched interests. It is a strategy which thus promotes political stability in the city. But if the force of the poor depends on the threat of instability, planning advocacy does little to promote equity.

But Which Advocate Planner?

Sherry R. Arnstein

Frances Piven argues that advocacy planning is a disservice to the poor because it diverts them from street protests. It negates the need for political mobilization of the ghetto, she says, and therefore the poor people's plans can easily be ignored, circumvented or rejected by the powerholders.

I share her jaundiced view of *this model* of advocacy planning, which was conceived and originally promoted by well-meaning, socially oriented city planners and architects. I do not share her view of other more recent models that have emerged as a result of significant input from ghetto leaders and social planners.

Under the original formulation of advocacy, the planners could indeed be playing into the hands of politicians by "coaxing ghetto leaders off the streets." Under the more recent and multidisciplinary models, political mobilization of the poor is viewed as a *sine qua non* for successful negotiation of the ghetto-developed plan.

With the broader conceptualizations of advocacy, communities are obtaining technical assistance from teams of specialists, including social planners, physical planners, lawyers and community organizers, or from one or more generalists with a mix of such technical skills.

These technicians are hired by a community group to work on a three-pronged approach to community development. Simultaneously they help the group (1) to become increasingly more representative and accountable to the neighborhood, (2) to conceptualize what programmatic approaches will benefit the community and to define which trade-offs can be supported at the negotiating stage, and (3) to design the political strategies needed to achieve the group's priorities.

The newer model views the planning process *per se* as only one prong. To teach the have-nots to become physical and/or social planners is not an objective of this process. Rather, the model aims at aiding the poor to reach increased levels of sophistication about what makes the city system (and subsystems) tick, to learn who and where the power-holders are and which levers to press to effect action, and to incorporate such sophistication into concrete programmatic approaches.

In short, the community group develops the capability to design political socioeconomic plans that effectively dent the status quo instead of unwittingly supporting palliative approaches which actually maintain it. In this way the planning process becomes a tactic by which the poor can anticipate the traditional Mickey Mouse games that debase them and prepare a sufficient store of chips to play the game and come out ahead.

Such an advocacy planning model does not preclude street strategies. On the contrary, it incorporates them into a community group's spectrum of possible actions and reactions to be drawn upon when appropriate. It recognizes that the issue is not whether the poor need sticks or pencils to achieve social equity. The fact is that they need both: sticks to gain and hold the attention of the powerholders, and pencils to articulate their priorities and aspirations.

Advocacy Planning Polarizes the Issues

Paul and Linda Davidoff

Advocacy in planning consists in developing and presenting plans that advance the interests of a particular group or class, rather than that of "the public interest" or the "general good," however defined. We have argued that all planning is advocate planning, whether it recognizes itself as such or not; and we feel that the growing movement for advocacy planning on behalf of the poor is a step forward in broadening the process of planning to include formerly unrepresented groups. To the extent that planning is carried on, it should be carried on in behalf of the poor as well as of the rich.

Writing from the perspective of an ideological advocate planner, Frances Piven contributes the worthwhile warning that participation in the planning process may deflect potentially more important or more effective political activity. Piven's view of political activity for the poor and nonwhite seems, however, to lack a sense of the process by which low-income and nonwhite communities reach decisions about appropriate courses of group action.

Assuming that we agree that it is sound practice for those seeking social change to plan the acts required to produce the desired objectives, then planners are required. The planners may exclude, include, or be limited to professional planners. If the planners for minority groups are middle-class white professionals, like Piven and ourselves, then manipulation of the clients by those professionals and imposition of the professionals' ideas upon the clients will always be a potential danger.

Neither of these outcomes need raise problems if we accept the elitist notion that the professional knows best about what the client should do. If we reject the elitist notion of social change, as we do, then a planning process prior to action calls for participation by the group for whose benefit the action is planned, and poor people and blacks must therefore be "planners"; that is, they must have some set of concepts to guide them in making decisions about developing their political power.

In another sense, too, the poor must be planners and must have the assistance of planners. Piven stresses the importance of street demonstrations and "making trouble" as appropriate forms of political expression for the poor. But what are the demonstrations about? A demonstration is an exercise in creating public pressure (power) to implement a series of demands for change in a situation which the demonstrators find intolerable. The formulation and presentation of these demands — as well as the massing of force to support them — are at the heart of mass action for social change. This is where advocacy can be of assistance: to help people draw up their demands on a given part of the power structure. The welfare rights movement, in which Piven has played a key role, provides many examples of the close relationship between the development of demands (rescind certain welfare budget cutbacks, drop work requirements, provide a decent guaranteed minimum income) and the creation of mass demonstrations to back up these demands.

Bringing poor people into the process of preparing and presenting demands is not, as Piven unfortunately seems to imply, involving them in

something that is beyond their intellectual capacity. It is part of building
a movement whose leaders are capable both of seeing what is wrong
with their society and of organizing to do something to change it.

The difficulty Piven perceives — the waste of the limited resources of
the poor and nonwhite on the nonproductive procedures of plan development — should not really be directed against advocacy. It would be far
closer to the mark to attack such programs as Model Cities, which create
elaborate procedural requirements for citizen participation in plan preparation, but which have never received enough money in appropriations
to permit execution of plans created under these requirements. So long as
Congress fails to provide the needed funds, Model Cities' failure to bring
about significant social change will not be caused by the action or inaction
of advocate planners.

Piven sees the process of creating an Alternate Plan for Cooper Square
as a waste of energy. What she fails to consider is that the members of
the Cooper Square Committee, as a result of their ten-year battle, gained
considerable political maturity and sophistication in the ways of New
York City politics. Piven asserts that protest was successful in halting the
original bulldozer plan and, therefore, that the Alternate Plan was unnecessary. This is too glib. It is possible that citizen protest without the
benefit of advocate planning could stop the threat of the neighborhood's
destruction; but what program of affirmative action for decent housing
would have taken its place?

The Thabit Alternate Plan has played an important role in the Cooper
Square area and in other areas of the nation. It signifies an approach to
city rebuilding based on resource allocation to classes of the population
having the greatest economic need, as opposed to perpetuation of traditional renewal policies favoring the rich at the expense of the poor and
the nonwhite.

Still another ground for holding Piven's thesis incorrect is that she
has narrowly defined advocacy planning as wholly client-oriented. In a
number of situations, a clientless advocacy has developed. We are now
engaged in such an advocacy planning program dedicated to changing
public policy about urban development so as to take account of the tre-
mendous land and employment opportunities available in the suburbs. In
this activity, we have no client but work with the support of foundations.[1]

Frances Piven has herself been an active clientless advocate planner.
Along with Richard Cloward, she has presented plans for the way the

---

[1] See Paul and Linda Davidoff and Neil Gold, "Suburban Action: Advocate
Planning for an Open Society," *Journal of the American Institute of Planners,* January 1970.

poor and the nonwhite should act in order to get a fair share of the nation's resources.

Clientless advocacy, ideological advocacy, radical advocacy may work to assist the poor and the black, or they may fail. But the key point is that the professional planner engaged in advocacy tends to polarize issues about urban development policies. He thus moves planning decisions from nonpolitical into political forums, where power of many varieties may be exercised and where the power of the poor to promote greater equity may operate along lines that Piven herself may find effective.

The Advocate Planner as Urban Hustler

Clarence Funnyé

Frances Piven is correct, although overly kind, in assessing the role of early urban advocates as "scattershot and ineffective." They might more accurately be described, at worst, as early urban hustlers. At best, they were well-meaning, but served to tranquilize the poor and "deprived" and, with few exceptions, did very little to alter the quality of the "social contract" between the poor and their keepers — the courts, judges, welfare administrators, etc.

Their efforts were directed largely toward measured accommodation to horrors of the social system. But this was to be expected. They were, after all, Americans and white and the products of essentially racist credentialing machinery. Moreover, their views of what ought to be done for the poor and minorities were necessarily colored by their preconditioning in a society governed by basically racist institutions. This was true irrespective of whether they themselves were, or tended to be, racist in the traditional sense. They just naturally thought in limited, rather short-range terms, and rarely, if ever, gave thought to the condition of the poor and racial minorities as a function of deficiencies in the economic and social system. Like early missionaries, they believed, and to some extent still believe, that blacks and the poor were preordained to a state of permanent slavery or semiservitude, but that, in the interest of Christianity, their condition should be made as bearable as possible. For example, they accepted the notion that the poor, because of their economic station, had to live in ghettos, but at least should have some heat in winter. And while blacks had to rear children in buildings painted with poisonous lead-based paints, it was "only right" that educational programs be devised to minimize the number of children who died or suffered brain damage from eating such paint.

The advocates' education and background had not programmed them
to question why the poor and minorities should not be assured the opportunity of living outside of ghettos in housing and environments equal to
those of other Americans. They could not imagine a serious effort to require removal or neutralization of walls painted with lead-based paint.
Such basic questions, of course, implied a confrontation with the established order.

Piven is right on target in identifying the motives behind poverty
programs and Model Cities. The Democratic Administrations of Kennedy
and Johnson provided an urban gold mine, in both monetary and status
terms, for white social scientists and a variety of urban specialists, who
have become experts on urban problems, do studies, write books, and
give speeches. Blacks and the urban poor by their protests created the
climate and formed the raw material for a very well-paying urban industry.

Piven is again correct when she points out the inherent contradiction
of an "advocate of the poor" being employed by and responsible to agencies whose interests almost always conflicted with those of the poor. She
does not, however, go far enough in this direction. In point of fact, these
new missionaries, including the planners, used their talents to "de-fang"
the poor and create the illusion of progress.

The illustration of Cooper Square as an advocacy planning project is
certainly nontypical. Here the community was well informed and deeply
involved, and the alternative plan did contain sufficient force to save the
community from destruction under the guise of "renewal." The plan was
well reported in a number of local journals and was conceded by several
non-city institutions (for example, *The New York Times* and the New
York Chapter of the American Institute of Architects) to be a fair and
viable alternative to city-proposed renewal. It was clear, cogent, orderly
and based on readily understandable analysis.

The suggestion that the community could have saved itself without
an alternative plan, prepared obviously by an advocate, is, it seems to me,
open to considerable question, since it is extremely doubtful that mere
"protest" could have enlisted the kind of institutional assistance, or acquiescence, necessary to hold up the city for more than ten years. Certainly that little war has not been won, but they did win some battles and
they are still fighting, which is more than can be said for most other
areas which have been subjected to "renewal." Alternate plans properly
prepared can catch the imagination of otherwise hostile or neutral institutions and can serve as a rallying point for a community, as in Cooper
Square, and as a visible standard against which to measure the official
plan.

Piven is right, of course, in decrying the preoccupation of an entire community with the preparation of a plan. This is, pure and simple, deliberate diversion, which works havoc on more-attention-getting forms of protest, such as a thousand people covering City Hall with garbage to get increased sanitation services. But this is to be attributed more to promises, implied or otherwise, by the alleged advocate and to acquiescence by community organizations than to any inherent malfunction or deficiency in the processes of planning. Factually speaking, nearly all the programs involving the new advocates in ghetto areas (Model Cities, etc.) are inherently diversionary and intended to give more of the shadow than the substance of progress. They are designed to buy off meaningful forms of confrontation and provide energy-absorbing make-work procedures that pay people for seeming to do something which the payees know cannot be done.

Sadly, the black counterpart of the urban hustler has fallen into the well-baited trap and can be found, along with the white advocate, mouthing pre-fed clichés as both go marching off into the dead end of the new Nixonism: no funds for people. Certainly not for blacks or for poor, urban or not. However, there is a bright side. The urban hustlers, including the university-based urban think tanks, which spend millions of dollars determining if urban water is wet, now constitute an urban constituency that must be reckoned with. There is already evidence that the fear of being "out of vogue," often worse than being out of work, is causing some of these hustlers to "question basic priorities" and advance the arguments needed to enlist more powerful allies in the "who-gets-what" battle for the tax dollar. This group now sees that their own self-interest (survival as pertinent urban experts) would be better served by a volatile and vocal black-poor constituency, and such realization is certain to dictate a posture that encourages education and mobilization as opposed to diversion and tranquilization. The change, following the Model Cities balloons bursting with the hopes of the ghetto's poor, may galvanize a real urban lobby. Such a lobby will certainly be different from the ideal advocacy environment advocated by Piven but, Model Cities rhetoric notwithstanding, the poor are as much interested in the product as the process.

Piven may be overly pessimistic in not predicting the demise of diversionary Model Cities programs, and in underestimating the tenacity of urban hustlers who have, to their great surprise, begun to eat well and like it. If I am right, and Piven wrong, history may record that Nixon was a President who built while trying to destroy. The Lord moves in mysterious ways.

The Advocate Planner:
From "Hired Gun" to Political Partisan

Chester W. Hartman

Frances Piven has some incisive and valid things to say about social policy, emphasizing the underlying politics of the nascent advocacy planning movement and the critical test of who gets what. It seems to me, however, that she is describing only one kind of advocacy planning and that her observations ought to be considered not as a put-down of advocacy planners generally but as a corrective, at a time when the movement is still in its formative stage, to what clearly can be reactionary results from their work.

Certainly, if "plans" are the end product of the work of advocacy planners, low-income communities will benefit little and the "planning process" can divert real energies for social change. Seen merely as an attempt to firm up the negotiating position of the poor, advocacy planning may serve only to stabilize the system and emasculate any real movement for change.

Advocacy planning for the poor, if it is to have any real meaning, must be planning for power, planning for political and social change. It must serve to organize the community, help the community perceive and understand the workings of the system by which it is oppressed, and direct political energies toward the realization of long-range, as well as tangible short-range, goals. And these goals must be substantive — a larger share of the pie, different kinds and sizes of pies, the acquisition of real political power. My four years of experience working with Urban Planning Aid (at this point, probably the largest advocacy planning group in the country) lead me to a somewhat different set of conclusions from that of Piven about the potentials and problems of this kind of work.

In the first place, I have seen numerous instances where the presence of advocacy planning assistance itself served as a critical catalyst to community organization. The Cooper Square area of New York, which contains a fairly high proportion of middle and lower middle-class families and is fairly sophisticated politically, is not typical of the areas in which we have done our work. In really low-income areas with a rather low level of political organization, the very existence of one's own "hired guns" can serve as an important catalyst. The fact that someone is taking notice of the community's problems, that the neighborhood has its own professionals to counter the establishment's professionals, frequently dispels the prevailing hopelessness, and the advocate professionals become the node around which local organization begins to build.

The critical point of any advocacy work is the building of political organization: where the local group, once organized, moves around the advocacy effort, or (in the Cooper Square type of situation) what a group does with an organization that is already formed. Here the advocate planner can play a very useful function, but there exists at present considerable ambivalence among advocate planners themselves about what their role should be. The "pure" model stresses the "hired gun" notion: we are here to do the community's bidding, to see that it gets what it wants. Since the communities that need advocates are usually those which the present system most neglects and since advocate planners tend to be concerned with issues of social justice, a rough "fit" does prevail. Advocate planners have been terribly concerned not to be or appear manipulative, not to impose their values and political goals on the community. Because of the inherent similarity between the goals of advocate planners and advocate plannees, overt conflict rarely occurs. When it does (e.g., the case of a low-income white community which wants to use planning tools to prevent entry of nonwhites), the planners can always withdraw on principled grounds. However, many of us are beginning to reject the "hired gun" model, although it has taken a good deal of experience, similar to that which Piven describes in Cooper Square, to lead us to a new concept of our role.

That new role is one in which politics and organization are primary. Advocate planners should have a clear political analysis of the way the system works as a whole and the way in which individual elements of the system relevant to their field operate: the housing market, urban renewal, the highway program, etc. If it is accepted that advocate planners can and should have a political analysis that infuses and guides their work, the real question becomes how to make this operational. It is foolish to think that most low-income communities are going to share the same wavelength, and nothing could be more destructive than to apply rigid political tests as a precondition for working in a given community. The process would seem to be one in which the advocacy group deals with the immediate issues that threaten and oppress the community and, in the process of working around these issues, develops an understanding of and organization around a deeper analysis of the nature of the community's problems and the kinds of solutions that are called for.

To give a concrete example. The advocate planner is asked by a tenants' organization to assist in exposing the inadequacies of a much-heralded, large-scale rehabilitation program. Good professional staff work by architects, engineers, lawyers and accountants produces irrefutable documentation of shoddy workmanship, high profits, excessive rents, failure of supervision by FHA and local officials, inadequate relocation assistance, and a host of other defects.

Such a report can lead to different conclusions and levels of analysis. It can be used to create a scandal, a horror-story of corruption, and can lead to immediate patching up of the poor results of this one project. Or it can be used to educate the community and the public about the workings of the system: that the system of profit-motivated developers, surrounded by government aids but few government controls, without any meaningful participation of the community itself in this rebuilding process, will inevitably lead to the results described. If the advocate planners understanding of the situation leads him to analyze the system as a whole, it is his responsibility to frame his findings in broader systematic terms and to attempt to persuade the community that this analysis is correct. The action implications are, of course, quite different, depending on the analysis.

That analysis should also lead to a consistent program of action which can provide guidance as to whether the planning group works with certain communities or not. For example, the group, convinced of the destructive impact of the interstate highway program and its failure to meet metropolitan transportation needs, is working with a community threatened by the program in an effort to stop construction of a new highway. Clearly, it should not work at the same time with a community group which wants assistance in changing to a depressed route a planned elevated segment of the highway. It may be possible to persuade the second community to join the fight against the overall construction program, but both the analysis underlying the work of the planning group and the need to build strong community organization dictate a consistent policy.

With regard to the second critical issue of community political organization, the style of advocacy planning which Piven so rightly criticizes is that of professional-speaking-to-professional. The community goes through all the standard procedures and attempts to persuade the powers-that-be of the superiority of its plan, using all the accepted tools and terminology. It would seem clear from both our sets of experiences that unless the community develops political muscle which can cover the entire spectrum, from sophisticated conventional organizations to disruption and rebellion, there is no certainty that its plans will be implemented. The process of developing a plan of action must be a process of political organizing. It may be that the rehabilitation report described above could produce some improvements without concomitant political organization among the tenants, because of the outrageous nature of the case and the clear documentation provided by the investigation. But the improvements would be minimal and short-lived in the absence of underlying organization. If that entire system is to be changed into one which is controlled by the community to insure maximum economic benefits from the millions of dollars expended on the project, to produce low rents and a high quality of work, and to create a system by which the community controls its own housing stock, such change can come about only through political action.

Above all, the advocate planner should employ his professional skills as a node around which political organizing can take place. His job is to persuade those for whom he works that the necessary course of political action derives from a radical analysis of the reasons why the system has not produced adequately.

City Planning and Political Values

Susan S. Fainstein and Norman I. Fainstein

City planners have increasingly come to interpret their mandate as a broad demand for social planning. In response to the many criticisms of master planning and urban renewal design as naive attempts to change society through manipulation of the physical environment, city planners have begun to seek wide training in the social sciences and to produce grand designs for social change. The recent New York Master Plan is an archetypal example. Moreover, the requirements of much federal urban legislation mean that cities must produce plans or forfeit aid.

As the breadth of planning increases, as it affects more and more aspects of the urban environment, and as a growing number of cities enact plans of various sorts, it becomes important to understand the political implications of different kinds of planning. While the planner himself may not be a political figure, an enacted urban plan constitutes the substance of a political decision — it determines who gets what. Thus, even though many aspects of the planning process are technical and "nonpolitical," the way in which a plan is formulated and implemented can be treated in the same terminology as political decision-making.

For the purposes of this paper, we shall define planning as future-oriented, public decision-making directed toward attaining specified goals. Although a plan once enacted constitutes a politically determined public policy, it differs from other kinds of political decisions in that it is based

"City Planning and Political Values" by Susan S. and Norman I. Fainstein is reprinted from *Urban Affairs Quarterly*, Volume 6, Number 3 (March 1971), pp. 341–362, by permission of the publisher, Sage Publications, Inc.

on formal rationality and is explicit about ends and means. This is in sharp contrast to many other public decisions which are left purposefully vague and ambiguous so as to mitigate controversy. While a decision need not be labeled a plan in order to fit our definition, political decisions directed at long-term goals are rarely made except under the auspices of a planning group.

It is possible to set up a typology of planning methods on the basis of who determines the plan's goals and who determines its means. While one can conceive of a number of different bases for typologies of planning, that of policy determination is politically the most important. For once planning is viewed as a political process, and once a typology is established which is based upon the location of authoritative decision-making, it becomes possible to equate each planning type with a particular model of decision-making developed in political theory.

These analogies between kinds of planning and political theories serve two distinct and important purposes: First, they show the implications of each type of planning in terms of political benefits; that is, they make clear which social groups each form favors. Second, they point toward an explanation of why certain kinds of planning have been favored by particular societies. An examination of the political thought which underlies each planning type reveals the political values embodied in planning procedures. In this way, planning methods can be related to political culture, and it can be seen why the United States has been willing to adopt certain planning procedures and not others.

The Planning Typology

The categories that follow are derived from the points of view presented in discussions of planning and are not necessarily either exhaustive or mutually exclusive. Like the political doctrines to which they will be related, they contain internal contradictions and elements in common with one another. Thus, the planning typology which we are establishing is an empirical rather than a strictly logical one. But, as we shall attempt to show later, the differences among the types make a great deal of sense within the history of political thought.

The four kinds of planning which we will discuss are:

1. traditional;
2. user-oriented;
3. advocacy;
4. incremental. (We shall attempt to demonstrate that incrementalism, while a logical fourth category, is not truly planning.)

Traditional Planning

In this type of planning, the planner prescribes both the goals of the plan and the means of attaining them:

> Planning began as a reform movement, not a client-centered service, and when predispositions [of the population being planned for] conflicted with the requirements of planning ideology, they were rejected.[1]

The principal objective of traditional planners is the orderly development of the urban environment, and the proximate goals of the plan are derived from standards which supposedly measure desirable physical arrangements. Thus, for example, the amount of land to be devoted to parks would be calculated on the basis of a fixed ratio between green space and population density. Traditional planning asumes that its goal of orderly development of the environment is in the general public interest and that planners are in the best position of any group to determine the plan's intermediate goals. The use of general standards permits the designation of planning objectives without reference to groups within the general population.

Thomas A. Reiner summarizes the traditional outlook as follows:

> An appealing and plausible idea attracts planners the world over: we are scientists, or at least capable of becoming such. As scientists, or technicians, we work with facts to arrive at truth, using methods and language appropriate to our tasks, and our ways of handling problems are not subject to outsiders' criticism.[2]

The conception of scientific planning assumes that the planner's special qualifications free him from class or special-interest biases when he is formulating the contents of the plan. Gans, however, correctly points out that

> generally . . . the planner has advocated policies that fit the predispositions of the upper-middle class, but not those of the rest of the population. For example, his advocacy of high-density urban housing has so far found favor only with the cosmopolitan upper-middle class. His proposal for increasing suburban density to cut down urban sprawl is rejected by people who feel that row housing lacks privacy and that it is less desirable for other reasons than the single-family house. The

---

[1] Herbert Gans, *People and Plans* (N.Y.: Basic Books, 1968), p. 20.

[2] Thomas A. Reiner, "The Planner as Value Technician: Two Classes of Utopian Constructs and their Impact on Planning," in H. Wentworth Eldredge (ed.), *Taming Megalopolis*, I (N.Y.: Anchor, 1967), pp. 232–247. See also William Alonso, "Cities and City Planners," *ibid.*, II, pp. 580–595.

planner's advocacy of more open space has also received little support, partially because the kind of open space he favors is not very
important to the people who are supposed to use it.[3]

Like the entire movement for municipal reform, the planning movement was based on the assumption that efficiency and orderly administration in government were general public goals which did not serve particular social interests. Proponents of planning failed to see that the
apolitical planning process which they supported tended to embody
values that were particularly those of the upper-middle class. One element within the planning movement did concern itself with the plight of
the poor. The advocates of parks, playgrounds, and other urban amenities
were attempting to improve the welfare of slum dwellers and showed
more concern with the lot of the deprived than did less elitist policy
makers. But even the overall goal of an orderly physical environment for
both rich and poor reflected a class bias against the disorderliness of the
lower classes and an assumption that physical neatness went along with
rational patterns of social behavior. The much criticized replacement of
Boston's West End [4] by a group of neatly arranged, high-rise apartments
for upper-income residents marked the apogee of the movement to up-
grade the urban environment through the imposition of physical orderli-
ness. The different kinds of order that observers such as Gans found in
the West End were not apparent to the planners whose criteria for demar-
cating slums rated the number of "standard" dwelling units present in an
area.

Hence, traditional planning has as its principal goal the original aim
of the planning movement: the creation of an orderly urban environment. Traditional planners, through the use of accepted standards and
professional methods, translate this overall goal into programs designed
to fit individual communities and their needs.

User-Oriented Planning

Herbert Gans employs the term "user-oriented" planning to describe
planning which takes as its goals the desires of the clients of the facility
being planned. In discussing planning for the public library, he argues
that "the planning of its facilities ought to be determined by whatever
goal or goals the community considers important vis-à-vis books and the
value of reading." Once the planner discovers the community's desires,

---

[3] Gans, *op. cit.*, p. 21.
[4] See Marc Fried, "Grieving for a Lost Home," in James Q. Wilson (ed.), *Urban
Renewal* (Cambridge, Mass.: MIT Press, 1967), pp. 359–379; and Herbert Gans,
"The Failure of Urban Renewal," *ibid.*, pp. 540–542.

it becomes his duty to "implement them in relation to the available resources." [5] The phrases democratic planning, collaborative planning, and
citizen participation in planning are often also used to describe this type
of planning. According to David R. Godschalk, "What is needed is a
modus operandi which brings governmental planners face-to-face with
citizens in a continuous cooperative venture. Such a venture could not
only educate and involve the community in planning, but could also
educate and involve the planners in their community." [6]

As a pure type, the democratic planner relies on the public as the
ultimate authority in the formulation of plans. His outlook is basically
majoritarian: "The client is clearly the public rather than special interests or the power structure." [7] The planner does not recognize the interests or values of one particular segment of society as more important
than any other, and he attempts to attain the general welfare through
satisfying the individual needs of as many people as possible.

While exponents of user-oriented planning generally agree that the
public should determine the ends of the plan, they disagree on the extent
to which citizens should be involved in the day-to-day planning process.
In general, however, there is an acceptance of at least some citizen participation in the formulation of specific programs and policies. On the
whole there is confusion over which clienteles should be involved in the
formulation of plans; as Gans puts it in his discussion of the public library, "The question is, which users should be planned for?" [8]

While the problem is not insurmountable in the planning of a library,
it becomes much more difficult in cases where there are fewer possibilities for serving a plurality of interests simultaneously. For example,
should urban renewal planning involve primarily present or future occupants of the site? Should it involve businessmen and other groups
which, although they do not occupy the site, may be profoundly affected
by the consequences of renewal? Should zoning regulations be aimed at
perpetuating the character of the district as it is, or should they respond
to the desires of outsiders who might wish to move into the district?

The democratic planner must contend with the problem of conflicting interests and must judge the legitimacy of the representatives of various clienteles. By accepting the right of other actors to participate in the
planning process, the user-oriented planner finds himself forced to make
political judgments which the insulated, traditional planner never had to

---

[5] Gans, *People and Plans*, pp. 102–103.
[6] David R. Godschalk, "The Circle of Urban Participation," in Eldredge, *op.
cit.*, II, p. 972.
[7] *Ibid.*
[8] Gans, *op. cit.*, p. 103.

confront. Yet, in making these judgments, he evades admitting that he is advancing the particular values or interests of some segment of society; rather, he claims to be acting in the public interest, or, at the least, following the will of the majority.

Advocacy Planning

The concept of advocacy planning contains an explicit recognition of a multitude of conflicting social interests, some of which may be irreconcilable. Rather than attempting to plan for society as a whole, the advocate planner would:

> be responsible to his client and would seek to express his client's views. This does not mean that the planner could not seek to persuade his client. In some situations persuasion might not be necessary, for the planner would have sought out an employer with whom he shared common views about desired social conditions and the means toward them.[9]

> The advocate planner would devote much attention to assisting the client organization to clarify its ideas and to give expression to them. . . . But the advocate's most important function would be to carry out the planning process for the organization and to argue persuasively in favor of its planning proposals.[10]

While the advocate planner can theoretically work for any social group, the term has generally been interpreted to mean "advocates for the poor." In fact, private planning and consulting firms have always acted as advocates for various interests that could afford to buy their services. Advocacy planning differs from what Lindblom calls partisan mutual adjustment only when it is defined as planning for the poor by planners who are accountable solely to their clients. While Davidoff does not limit advocacy planning to this function in his formulation of the concept, we shall use this meaning exclusively in our typology. . . .

Thus, in advocacy planning a particular client group determines the goals of the plan, and the planner is in principle subservient to that group rather than to the majority of citizens. As in user-oriented planning, the extent to which the client participates in the formulation of planning specifics may vary. Davidoff portrays the planner as an educator, attempting to persuade his client to his own diagnosis of the client's best interest. In real life, however, there may be significant conflict between the ad-

---

[9] Paul Davidoff, "Advocacy and Pluralism in Planning," in Eldredge, *op. cit.*, II, p. 602.
[10] *Ibid.*, p. 604.

vocate planner and his client. For example, Judith May describes the conflict between Oakland officials and citizens in the West Oakland Model Cities planning area as a dispute between advocate planners and their clients over who should deal with the city administration. Miss May summarizes the profesional viewpoint as follows:

1. Although community residents in the past had been unable to insert their views into the policy-making process, they are able to do so if they are supervised by an established organization . . . and assisted by professional advocates.

2. Planning itself is a job for professionals who possess both technical skill and political sensitivity; plans for the Model Cities program are to be hammered out in negotiations between the city's planners and the community's advocates.[11]

The community, however, did not trust the planners to be its guides and mediators; West Oakland residents wanted to control the planning process themselves. According to Miss May:

Oakland's experience suggests that both planners and community residents view the new federal interest in urban problems as an opportunity to reduce their past ineffectiveness in influencing urban policies; and each has invented an ideology which justifies this new route to communal upward mobility: "advocacy" in the case of planners, and "community control" in the case of community residents.[12]

Advocacy planning differs fundamentally from traditional planning in that the plan need not be justified as being in the general public interest. Moreover, the planner enlists the participation of his clients in determining the plan's goals and explicitly accepts planning as a political rather than a strictly scientific endeavor. Traditional planning was part of the old movement for municipal reform; advocacy planning is part of the new movement for urban change which calls for greater representation of the lower classes in the governmental process and for the decentralization of governmental policy-making.

Advocacy planning is not necessarily incompatible with user-oriented planning and, in fact, both doctrines result from an increasing concern among planners with citizen participation in the planning process. User-oriented planning, however, assumes an equality among citizens and pre-

11 Judith V. May, "Two Model Cities: Development on the Local Level," paper presented at the annual meeting of the American Political Science Association, New York, September 2–6, 1969, p. 13.
12 *Ibid.*, p. 4.

sents the planner as an impartial arbiter who seeks the plan which will
be most satisfying to the largest number of people. Advocacy planning
has the planner find that policy which is most in the interest of a single
social group. If the democratic planner is working within a restricted
locale such that his clients constitute a homogeneous group, he becomes
identical with the advocate planner. If, however, he is working for a city-
wide planning commission and he must take into account the effects of
the plan on a large number of groups, then his approach must differ from
that of the advocate planner.

Incremental Planning

In incremental planning, the policy maker comes to a decision by
weighing the marginal advantages of a limited number of alternatives.
He does not work in terms of long-range objectives but rather moves
ahead through successive approximations:

> Decision makers typically consider, among all the alternative policies
> that they might be imagined to consider, only those relatively few
> alternatives that represent small or incremental changes from existing
> policies. In this sense . . . decision-making is incremental. In short,
> policy makers and analysts take as their starting point not the whole
> range of hypothetical possibilities, but only the here and now in
> which we live, and then move on to consider how alterations might
> be made at the margin.[13]

Planning is not done by a single agency: "That society requires conscious control and manipulation is one assertion; that an 'organizing cen-
tre' is required is quite another." [14]

Like Davidoff, Lindblom recognizes a multitude of interests. But
where the advocate planner sees irremediable conflict, the incrementalist
sees an ultimate harmony:

> On an immensely larger scale coordination also is often achieved
> through mutual adjustment of persons not ordered by rule, central
> management, or dominant common purpose. An American consumer
> of coffee and a Brazilian supplier are so coordinated. The market
> mechanism is, both within many countries and among them, a large-
> scale, highly developed process for coordinating millions of economi-
> cally interdependent persons without their being deliberately coordi-
> nated by a central coordinator, without rules that assign to each person

---

[13] Charles Lindblom, *The Intelligence of Democracy* (N.Y.: Free Press, 1965),
p. 144.
[14] *Ibid.*, p. 5.

his position relative to all others, and without a dominant common purpose. Market coordination is powered by diverse self-interests. Scholars can hardly fail to note the possibilities of coordination through mutual adjustment of partisans in the market, for a long tradition of theory has produced an increasingly refined explanation of the process.[15]

In terms of our definition of planning incrementalism is not really planning at all. Policy outcomes are not arrived at through formal rationality, and there is no specifying of ends and means. But Lindblom claims that the mechanism of "partisan mutual adjustment" — the working out of different claims through compromise, adherence to procedural rules, and the market process — results in rational decision-making: "The concern of this study has been . . . with partisan mutual adjustment as a method for *calculated, reasonable, rational, intelligent, wise* . . . policy making." [16] Even though ends and means are not formulated, decision makers work out ways to reach socially desirable goals:

> Behind the incremental and disjointed tactics we have just summarized is a concept of problem solving as a strategy. In this view public problems are too complex to be well understood, too complex to be mastered. One develops a strategy to cope with problems, not to solve them.[17]

Therefore, while incrementalism embodies the opposite of planning in its methods, it produces the fruits of planning in its results. Like an economic system of numerous buyers and sellers, a political system of atomized decision makers working at cross-purposes can rely on the invisible hand to produce orderly progress toward social goals — in fact, to produce the very goals themselves.

Lindblom attempts to show that seemingly ad hoc methods of arriving at public policies result in a hidden rationality. The ultimate decision-making power does not lie with a single group, and it is not desirable that any one social interest should prevail. Political interaction causes the clash of interests to be resolved in a Pareto optimum such that no group can benefit further without some other group losing out.[18] Lindblom assumes that such an optimum, which implies the preservation of the existing arrangement of social power,[19] is desirable.

---

[15] *Ibid.*, p. 4.
[16] *Ibid.*, p. 294; italics added.
[17] *Ibid.*, p. 148.
[18] *Ibid.*, p. 223.
[19] If a Pareto optimum exists, any redistribution of social power would require some other group to suffer a loss equal to the benefit received by the gaining group.

Four Types of Political Theory

Planners have mainly been satisfied to contain within narrow bounds their debate over who should make planning decisions. To a large extent, they have attempted to justify their arguments by evaluating the merits of the policies each type of planning is likely to produce rather than looking at the fundamental questions of social power and legitimacy which each type raises.

In contrast, political theorists have addressed themselves to a broad range of fundamental questions. Because the basis of our planning typology comprises two of these questions, it initially struck us that planners who theorized were really political theorists, though de facto and often unaware. Furthermore, given its political basis, the planning typology might well be a reflection of a fragment of a typology of political theories. This we argue is, indeed, the case.

What is so striking about the typology of political theories, once constructed, is the extent to which it corresponds to the typology of planning. It is, in fact, this correspondence which makes the exercise worthwhile, by baring the value skeletons upon which planning theories have been built, and by permitting us to apply generalizations about the political culture in America to the nature of American planning.

One may distill from the tangle of political thought in the modern world — i.e., in the period since Locke — four major types of political theory. These are technocratic, democratic, socialist, and liberal. Each type of theory is historically significant; its ideas have been advanced by men of power and have affected the actual development of political and social institutions. Virtually all *modern* political controversy may be fitted into these categories, and may be understood in terms of clashes among these theories.[20]

---

[20] It is important to italicize the word modern. There are states even in the industrial West where premodern thought appears to play a significant role. Indeed, our use of the word may seem a bit of hand-waving designed to cover up a rather glaring omission, for there is no mention in our typology of truly conservative thought — that, for example, associated with Edmund Burke in England, with Ronald and de Maistre in France.

We have purposely ignored conservative thought for two reasons. The first is that conservative thinking stands antithetical to the whole idea of rational policy-making. If we took the time to discuss it, it would only be to dismiss it. Second, there is in America a total absence of conservative thinking, of the conservative desire to maintain a feudal past. What genuine conservatism exists is combined with praise of industrialism and thus fits under our classification of technocratic thought. What is sometimes called conservatism in the United States is nothing more than liberalism at its extreme — the liberalism of Spencer and the Social Darwinists; as such, we treat it in our section on liberalism.

Technocratic Theory and Traditional Planning

Technocratic thinking is a product of the industrial era. It represents an effort to come to grips with the central social problems created by the Industrial Revolution — the miserable condition of the lower classes and the breakdown in the old structure of authority which seemed previously to have maintained order. Like the conservatives, the technocrats desire to restore the order of the preindustrial world, but unlike the conservatives they accept industrialization, welcoming technology as the cure for the ills of mankind. Their motto is "order and progress." Their most significant thinkers are Comte, Saint-Simon, and, to a lesser extent, Owen and Fourier.[21]

The technocrats stand in opposition to the social anarchy they see created by capitalism. In their eyes, capitalism dissolved the bonds of the *ancien régime,* replacing community with the marketplace, and the paternalism of the old elite with the laissez faire of the new. But rather than intending a return to the days before industrialization — an impossibility — they wish to harness the power of technology to create a new society, and thereby to ameliorate the condition of the lower classes, as well as the threat to social order posed by proletarian restlessness. The technocrats desire to unleash the power of reason and science, to transpose the old, theological religion into a modern, positivist one. The power of the state, through rational planning, will be employed to regulate the economy and to advance the lower classes, as well as to ensure the position of the productive ones. All of this will be possible only when the scientific and industrial classes control the state and do away with politics in the name of science and reason.

In the words of Comte:

> Since the abolition of personal servitude, the lowest class has never been really incorporated with the social system; the power of capital . . . has become exorbitant in daily transactions, however just is its influence through its generality and superior responsibility. . . . This philosophy will show that industrial relations, instead of being left to a dangerous empiricism and an oppressive antagonism [among the classes], must be systematized according to moral laws. The duty [of the upper classes] to the lower classes will not consist in alms-

---

[21] The reader may note that the last three names are usually associated with the category "utopian socialism." The use of this term is, we feel, misleading and almost entirely a result of Marx having the label stick. Louis Hartz calls them "feudal socialists," which is a better choice of words, since it makes any simplistic association of their names with socialism more difficult. By choosing to emphasize Comte and the elements in the thought of the others most closely related to his theories, we have even further loosened the connection between technocratic and socialist thought.

giving. . . . The obligation will be to procure for all, suitable education and employment — the only condition that the lower classes can
justly demand.[22]

The Saint-Simonians echo Comte's faith in science, and his concern
for the condition of the lower classes, and stress equally the positive
quality of power as a tool in remolding society.

> The most direct method of improving the moral and physical welfare
> of the majority of the population is to give priority in State expendi-
> tures to ensuring work for all fit men, to secure their physical exis-
> tence. . . .
>   We must add to this the measures necessary to ensure that the
> national wealth is administered by men most fitted for it, and most
> concerned in its administration, that is to say, the most important in-
> dustrialists.[23]

The technocrats visualize a hierarchical society in which the lower
orders are secure and happy, but strictly subordinate to the managerial-
scientific elite. In this respect, as in others, technocratic theory, while
more detailed and explicit than discussions of traditional planning, presents a picture of society which is quite compatible with traditional planning ideas and useful in baring their hidden foundation.

Underlying traditional planning is the technocratic faith in progress
through science and rationality tied to the constructive use of power in
the form of *le plan*. The technocrats make explicit the planner's belief
that there is indeed some unitary public interest which men of science
and good will can identify and maximize. Like the traditional planner,
they seek to replace politics with scientific administration.

Social change for the technocrats must be engineered from the top,
by social strata that command the economy, and in the public interest,
indeed in the interest of the lower classes; for they see a harmony of
interests between themselves and the masses. Here again, technocratic
theory makes clear an assumption of traditional planning: that social
change for the benefit of all society must be initiated paternalistically by
the upper classes. Because all classes benefit from increasing productivity
and public order, the interests of the upper classes become identical with
the public interest. If the natural rulers fail to play their roles, sometimes
even resist change, it is only because they remain as yet insufficiently
enlightened.

---

[22] August Comte, *The Positive Philosophy of August Comte*, trans. by Harriet
Martineau (N.Y.: Peter Eckler, n.d.), p. 781.
[23] Henri de Saint-Simon, "On Social Organization," in F. Markham (ed. and
trans.), *Henri de Saint-Simon: Social Organization, The Science of Man and Other
Writings* (N.Y.: Harper Torchbooks, 1964; orig. pub. 1825), p. 77.

The traditional planners, much more limited in their expectations than the technocrats, did manage to see some of their programs carried out. Parks were built, building codes passed and sometimes enforced, transit lines planned and constructed, slums razed; land use zoning became a commonplace. Social change was initiated from the top, in the name of the public good, sometimes in the interest of the lower classes, and with the ultimate necessity of legislative sanction. But it was always limited in its scope by the willingness of the upper strata to support reform. In fact, traditional planners have long been perplexed by the all-too-common refusal of the bearers of political and economic power to recognize the importance of rational planning as a means for the improvement of life. Yet traditional planning, like the technocratic movement, continues to press for change from the top, not understanding why change should be so difficult, should often be resisted so obstinately in the face of its apparent rationality.

Democratic Theory and User-Oriented Planning

User-oriented planning stands squarely within the mainstream of democratic thought. The premises which underlie its arguments are essentially those of democratic political theory. Our task, then, must be to analyze the theoretical substructure of such planning. Doing so, however, immediately presents us with a difficulty: it is impossible to find anywhere a pure theory of democracy. Democratic theory has typically been created as a foil by its opponents; to use their formulations would then be to start off with a flimsy straw man. On the other hand, we *can* distill from the disparate works of several men the basic elements of the democratic "type," although in doing so we must realize that we commit a disservice to the complexity of, and differences among, their ideas. The argument which follows represents elements from the thinking of Locke, de Tocqueville, and J. S. Mill. It is, we feel, democratic, even though it has been derived from thinkers who are to very different degrees democrats.

Democratic theory begins with the sanctity of the individual and the primacy of his interests. Not only does all sovereignty emanate from the people, they are also the only source of public values. "Everyone is the best and sole judge of his own private interests." [24] Everyone is equal and has an equal right to advance his cause. There is no interest in society which cannot be related to that of its members. Thus, the democrat starts with equal individuals and their desires — rather than by exploring the

---

[24] Alexis de Tocqueville, *Democracy in America* (N.Y.: Vintage, 1957; orig. pub. 1848), p. 67.

social origin or intrinsic merit of these desires – and goes on to equate the public interest with the interests of the public, or at least, with those of the majority.[25]

Having accepted individual sovereignty as his basic axiom, the democrat then goes on to deal with the problem of government, of how public power is to be distributed. Some form of differentiation between the government and the citizenry becomes immediately necessary – unless, of course, the size of the polity is severely limited. Recognizing this, the democrat attempts to keep as much political power in the hands of the citizenry as is feasible. He does so through the rule of the majority which, if it cannot actually be the government, must control the government. For "the very essence of democratic government consists in the absolute sovereignty of the majority." [26] The governors must be forced to remain the delegates of the governed. Unless they do – and they only *will* if power remains within the hands of the citizenry – government cannot be expected to advance the interests of the majority. Government by men freed from the control of the majority, government by an independent aristocracy of wealth or even merit, is likely to act in its own interests, which are necessarily at odds with those of the sovereign people.

> Democratic laws generally tend to promote the welfare of the greatest possible number; for they emanate from the majority of the citizens, who are subject to error, but [who] cannot have an interest opposed to their own advantage. The laws of an aristocracy tend, on the contrary, to concentrate wealth and power in the hands of the minority; because an aristocracy, by its very nature, constitutes a minority.[27]

> Under aristocratic governments public men are swayed by the interest of their order, which, if it is sometimes confused with the interests of the majority, is very frequently distinct from them.[28]

User-oriented planning accepts the democratic conception of the public man – or, in this case, the planner acting as delegate of the citizenry. It implicitly accepts the democratic veneration of the individual and his interests. But this is not to say that the user-oriented or democratic planner must be a passive figure blindly following his instructions. Rather, the democratic planner, like the democratic governor, both responds to his constituents and attempts to educate them, to show them

---

[25] This formulation is that of the liberal democratic tradition and ignores the sociological insights of Rousseau, as well as his attempt to equate morality with liberty by means of the monolithic rule of the General Will.

[26] *Ibid.*, p. 264.

[27] *Ibid.*, p. 247.

[28] *Ibid.*, p. 249.

alternatives and the relation between particular policies and their interests. Indeed, the reason that citizens must participate in government and retain power in their hands is not only to prevent governmental outcomes contrary to their interests, but also so that they themselves may grow, may learn from participation, becoming ever more knowledgeable and better able to govern themselves.

There are three major criticisms of democratic theory, which apply equally to user-oriented planning. First, democratic policy makers are immediately confronted with the short-term relative ignorance of the citizenry, and the fact that "education through participation" is a slow process which public policy cannot await. Participating citizens are thus unlikely to accept very readily the planner's conception of how means are related to goals, or of how particular policies may be derived from their interests. In addition, most men are unwilling to make long-run decisions, i.e., to plan, when doing so necessitates the deferment of immediate gratification, the result being that democracies are less likely to plan than aristocracies.

Second, it is difficult for democratic theory to explain why men should bother to participate in public policy-making or planning at all, for a rational calculus of the costs and benefits of participation often makes apathy quite compatible with the private interests of individuals. The costs in time and effort to the individual, given his minimal impact, outweigh any real benefits which could accrue to him personally. So most citizens are apathetic most of the time, and the democratic planner has only a small minority with whom to plan. Democratic planning under these circumstances either becomes impossible, or the planner must take upon himself the task of divining the will of the majority, in which case the planning process can hardly be called democratic.

The final criticism of democratic theory suggests that the rule of the majority leads to social mediocrity, for there are any number of values and institutions which civilized men should want to preserve, toward which the majority is indifferent or even hostile. It is the duty of the aristocracy, of which the planner is a member, to defend these values of civilization, though doing so may be directly antagonistic to the interests of the majority. Where there is no elite planning, civilization may decline to the common denominator of the mass and its taste. In de Tocqueville's classic statement:

> Do you wish to give a certain elevation to the human mind and teach it to regard the things of this world with genuine feelings, to inspire men with a scorn of mere temporal advantages? . . . Is it your object to refine the habits, embellish the manners, and cultivate the arts, to promote the love of poetry, beauty and glory? . . . If you believe

such to be the principal object of society, avoid the government of
the democracy, for it would not lead you with certainty to the goal.[29]

Socialist Theory and Advocacy Planning

Socialist theory cannot readily be molded into a single type. While all
socialists — from Marx and Lenin to Bernstein, Laski, and the Webbs —
accept premises which clearly distinguish their thought from each of our
other three types, they also differ sharply among themselves on some very
basic issues. Socialism has forked many times since the days of Marx and
Engels. So we should recognize that by picking out only those elements
of socialist thought which parallel our conception of advocacy planning,
we fail to do justice to the complexity of the movement. The aspects of
the theory of socialism that we will develop here are concerned entirely
with winning power for the poor in a capitalist society rather than with
the operation of socialist government. Thus, we have been forced to look
at the question of who decides ends and who decides means at a different
level than we have in the other sections of this paper. Here we assume
that ultimate authority continues to remain in the hands of present decision makers and concern ourselves with who is responsible for setting
strategies and objectives for lower-class groups.

Socialism begins with a conflict analysis of society. It emphasizes the
divergence of interests among different social strata, and the extent to
which the upper strata maintain control of a disproportionate share of social resources through their use of power. Socialism sees the interests of
individuals as determined by the objective circumstances of their lives.
Precisely because the circumstances of life are dissimilar at different
positions in the social hierarchy, the interests of the various social strata
conflict. The conflict of interests is real and unavoidable so long as social
inequality endures.

Socialist theory identifies the general good of society with the advancement of deprived classes. Its fundamental value is equality; it goal
is an egalitarianism which can be achieved only through the elevation of
the lowest social strata. Thus, the socialist, like the advocate planner we
have described, throws his lot in with those at the bottom of the social
order. He claims that furthering the interests of the lower classes — in our
epoch the *lumpenproletariat*, comprised mostly of blacks and the poorest
whites — will further the social good. But he also recognizes that doing so
conflicts with the particular interests of the upper strata. Until the day we
have a just society, deprived groups will gain only to the extent that

---

[29] *Ibid.*, p. 262.

privileged groups lose. Any other analysis is the product of wishful thinking.

From the argument that interests are class- or stratum-based, it follows that what is generally called "the public interest" must not be such at all. Rather, it is merely a reflection of the values and programs of the politically and economically dominant groups. Only these groups are in a position to define that which is particularly beneficial to them as generally beneficial to the whole society. "The ideas of the ruling class are in every epoch the ruling ideas: i.e., the class which is the ruling material force of society, is at the same time its ruling intellectual force." [30]

> Each new class which puts itself in the place of one ruling before it, is compelled, merely to carry through its aims, to represent its interest as the common interest of all the members of society, put in an ideal form; it will give its ideas the form of universality, and represent them as the only rational, universally valid ones.[31]

Thus, in American society today the "public interest" which we find described in the press and lauded by politicians is actually the particular class interest of the upper bourgeoisie, the class which controls the government, and in whose interest it acts. On the other hand, the real welfare of our society is tied to the class interests of the poor.

Those who wish to improve America, argue the socialist and advocate planner alike, must work for social change to benefit the poor. But real social change never takes place from the top. It does not result from the persuasive power of reasonable argument directed toward those who control our government and economy, for the upper classes are willing to redistribute their power or wealth *only* when under duress from those beneath them. Social change, in fact, can be initiated only by a social force. Such a force results from the collective action of a deprived group whose interests are in conflict with the conditions of the status quo.

The obligation of the socialist intelligentsia, to which our advocate planners belong, is then to work for social change in two related ways. First, it acts as the spokesman for the poor, articulating their interests and demands to those in positions of power, prodding the political institutions of society in order to benefit the poor wherever possible. Second, and more important, the intelligentsia becomes the vanguard of the poor, seeking to educate them, to develop their consciousness so as to make them into a coherent political group capable of the collective action required to pressure the governing elite into making concessions.

---

[30] Karl Marx and Friedrich Engels, *The German Ideology* (N.Y.: International, 1947; orig. pub. 1846), p. 39.
[31] *Ibid.*, p. 41.

Socialist theory has much merit as a guide to action for the would-be social reformer. Yet it also demands a good deal of faith on his part. There is no certainty that the egalitarian society desired by socialists will not be a relatively unproductive one where men have lost some of their motivation, and perhaps also some of their liberty. Is socialism justified in equating the interests of one group with the social good? Marx deduced the norms of equality and proletarian advancement from his theory of historical development, claiming that facts imply values, equating what will be with what should be. If we reject this analysis, the argument about the universality of proletarian interests rests on a shaky foundation than this role of umpire. There is, however, another strand of liberal theory when the latter elevates above all else the rule of the majority. Equality may imply mediocrity and a sacrifice of the elitist aspects of society which maintain high culture.

But in spite of the flaws in socialism as an integrated political theory, it seems to us quite tenable to hold a socialist perspective, and to work to advance the interests of the poor in America today. After all, success is not so assured that the advocate planner need be overly concerned with the problems of a truly egalitarian society.

Liberal Theory and Incrementalism

Incremental decision-making is the form of planning logically implied by liberal political theory. Lindblom's model is nothing more than the particular application of the general premises of liberal thought, as formulated by Locke and developed by Bentham, Spencer, and a number of other thinkers in the last century. Liberalism begins with an atomistic conception of human society, seeing men as rational actors who are the best judges of their own private interests. "Society has no right to control a man's actions unless they are prejudicial to the common weal or unless the common weal demands his help." [32] The public interest is accepted as real, but is regarded as resulting from the interplay of a multiplicity of private interests within the confines of the political marketplace.

The obligation of liberal government is first and foremost to guarantee the rule of law, to defend agreed-upon procedures; as Locke puts it, to act as an impartial judge or umpire. Liberalism in its Spencerian form — which we identify as the pure type — gives government no other function than this role of umpire. There is, however, another strand of liberal thought — often called "positive liberalism" and associated with Green and Hobhouse — which does give to government the additional function of trying to advance its own conception of the public interest, which usu-

---

[32] Tocqueville, *op. cit.*, p. 67.

ally implies governmental aid for certain private interests who are ill-treated in the marketplace. Thus, positive liberalism weds the technocratic conception of constructive governmental action to the mainstream of liberal thought.

Liberalism in all its forms emphasizes the prime importance of a diffusion of power within society. Neither the democrat's majority, nor the socialist's deprived class, nor the technocrat's elite should have absolute power. No group or institution should have so much power that it can corner the political market. The most "positive" liberal conception of government still sees it only as being *primus inter pares*. The largest role played by the governmental decision maker is to add another input to the market of alternative policies – a government may create plans and attempt to implement them, but it can never be assured of their being carried out.

Thus, the general direction in which society is to move, or the way in which political benefits are to be distributed, is not decided explicitly at all. Rather, it is the result of a large number of decisions, some of which may be made by government. Overall social policy is not made deliberately but results from a mechanism which acts like an invisible hand, producing outcomes that are ultimately rational.

Significance of the Typology

Our discussion of the relationship between planning types and political theories shows the concepts of planning to be not just analogous to certain strains in modern political thought but actually fragments of these political formulations. The fuller articulation of the planning types in terms of value assumptions and justifications of social power permits us to understand why America has largely rejected the programs of city planners – with certain exceptions, to be sure, in the area of parks, zoning, and urban renewal.

The United States for a variety of historical and cultural reasons [33] has been dominated by the liberal tradition. This tradition values individualism, accepts the primacy of private interests, and prefers minimal government. Thus, the very notion of planning, which assumes an overriding and ascertainable public interest *that can be maximized through the positive actions of government* is antithetical to general American

---

[33] For extensive arguments in support of this interpretation, see Louis Hartz, *The Liberal Tradition in America* (N.Y.: Harcourt, Brace & World, 1955); Daniel Boorstin, *The Genius of American Politics* (Chicago: University of Chicago Press, 1953); and Seymour Martin Lipset, *The First New Nation* (N.Y.: Basic Books, 1963).

STRATEGIES FOR CHANGE: PLANNING

political values. As Lindblom correctly argues, most decision-making in this country follows his description of partisan mutual adjustment. Policy is determined incrementally; it is arrived at through the clash and compromise of opposing views within the political marketplace. But this incrementalism itself marks the absence of planning. Incrementalism and partisan mutual adjustment maximize liberal values: they restrict the role of government to that of umpire in the political maketplace, guaranteeing the enforcement of procedural rules, but oblivious to outcomes, to which groups win and which lose in the process of politics. At a maximum, government becomes another actor in the political process, offering its own solutions to social problems, with the proviso that its solutions must compete with those offered by private decision makers.

Because incrementalism is based on a procedural value of laissez faire, it benefits primarily those social strata — the entrepreneurial and corporate classes — already most privileged under present conditions. These are the strata which command the greatest share of power resources,[34] enabling them to take a disproportionate amount of social rewards. The most acceptable form of governmental activity for these groups is that which ensures their present position — hence, the acceptability of zoning ordinances and the like. Because they have favored government as an arbiter rather than as a positive actor, they have rallied behind the values of efficiency and economy in municipal government rather than those of welfare and innovation.

America's political tradition is, of course, democratic as well as liberal. Why then has there been an absence of democratic planning in the United States? For, to the extent that we have had planning, it has not involved the vast working-class/middle-class majority of voters. To see this, one may look at housing policy in America.

Perhaps no sector of public policy has been so subject to the unimpeded workings of the market as the area of middle-class housing. Government has provided the stimulus of FHA subsidies for single-family dwellings, resulting in a gigantic, unplanned expansion of the housing supply — beneficial to the majority in terms of its bounty, but costly in waste and ugliness. Although it can be argued that builders planned in accordance with the demands of the public as registered through its willingness to pay, there was no democratic participation in planning, no continuous, conscious involvement of the public in the formulation of specified means and goals.[35]

Indeed, democratic planning involving conscious participation of a mass public in specifying means and ends may be infeasible, not because

---

[34] See Robert Dahl, *Who Governs?* (New Haven: Yale University Press, 1961), esp. p. 94, for use of the term.

[35] Herbert Gans, *The Levittowners* (N.Y.: Pantheon, 1967), p. 335.

it is antithetical to American values but because it is institutionally impossible to attain. Institutional theories of large-scale democracy — that is, those theories which actually spell out the mechanisms such as voting, representation, and parliamentary deliberation through which the public can register its will — all provide opportunities for public expression only through the election of representatives or the vetoing or accepting of already specified policies. Continuous participation only makes sense within a relatively small political unit — hence, democratic planning becomes a meaningful goal only when it is combined with decentralization of policy-making. Since in the United States "positive" government has been associated with the centralization of power, it is not surprising that in those areas were government *has* planned, it has done so without the active involvement of the general public.

Moreover, democracy requires an equal weighting of each person's vote; it assumes a radical equality among citizens which does not exist in the United States. Permitting each person to have an equal voice in policy-making would mean legitimizing his right to demand an equal share of social output. It was not for want of vision that the propertied classes of the nineteenth century feared the broadening of the franchise. But as institutionalized democracy has actually worked itself out in America, policy has come to be made "incrementally"; the mass public has no opportunity to formulate policy alternatives that differ greatly from those under governmental consideration. Thus, while the public possesses an ultimate veto, it has no power to *create* plans which alter fundamentally the distribution of social benefits.

Unlike democratic planning, traditional planning has been inhibited neither by a lack of institutional mechanisms nor by the absence of supportive social conditions. As in Europe, there is in the United States a powerful scientific-industrial class. But technocratic thought has largely been rejected by this group in America in favor of liberalism. Thus, planning has been much more successful in Europe, where the industrial elite has consciously visualized itself as an aristocracy of talent, attempting to supplant the old aristocracy of birth. The technocratic idea has been embodied in the European planned city, the mixed public-private corporation, the whole *dirigiste* tendency of the modern Western European economies.

American industrialists have tended to see themselves as individual entrepreneurs rather than as members of an aristocratic class. They have supported laissez faire instead of *dirigisme*. It is extremely significant that the great successes of traditional planning in the United States have been in those cases where businessmen have acted in a coalition with government to improve the central city. The most notable instances have been the Logue-engineered coalitions in New Haven and Boston. The elements of technocracy and their results are quite apparent in these two locales.

Planning was carried on in the name of the general good, but its principal beneficiaries were downtown business interests and upper-middle-class residents. Although there were also closely allied attempts at benefiting the poor, the major resources of the effort were directed at physical improvements. It was assumed that the creation of new jobs and a more beautiful and dynamic city would be to everyone's benefit, even though the people who received specific advantages in terms of governmental subsidies were primarily those already well-off.

The relative absence of advocacy planning for the poor, like the limited extent of traditional planning, can be attributed largely to American political values. There are two prerequisites for socialist planning: the first is a crystallized consciousness among at least part of the poor, of the social basis of their deprivation and of the need for collective action for their advancement; the second is the existence of a political spectrum broad enough to permit the presentation of a radical ideology by spokesmen for the poor. Except perhaps for a brief period during the 1930s, these conditions did not exist in the United States at all until today. The poor accepted the individualist bias of the general political culture. The middle-class sympathizers who constituted the intellectual leadership of European socialist movements were unable to escape from the dominant American liberal ideology. Thus, they stumbled into technocratic reformism rather than socialist radicalism. It is only the rise of black militance, based on the premise that the interests of lower-class blacks are fundamentally opposed to those of middle-class white America, that has led to a new consciousness on the part of a segment of the lower class. This change in the consciousness of the lower class in combination with the movement toward the left among young American intellectuals has laid a foundation for the development of advocacy planning and other "socialistic" strategies for achieving social change.

Until the present time, social change in America has largely been unplanned. While the poor may have benefited from increasing material prosperity, they have not been the particular beneficiaries of change, and the improvement of their lot — to the extent that it has taken place — has been largely accidental. The planner who intends to ameliorate the conditions of the deprived must recognize that redistribution of social goods will not take place without social conflict. As an advocate for the poor, he must admit, at least to himself, that he is acting in support of the particular interests of a particular social group. Realistic planners must give up the delusion that they can serve the whole public equally well, that there is an indissoluble social good which they are particularly well circumstanced to ascertain. They must, in short, reject many of the technocratic biases underlying the professional rhetoric of planning, and construct a new rationale for themselves.

Strategies for Change:
Political Movements

4

The increasing American consciousness of poverty and racial discrimination has precipitated a search for political means to redress the social inequities that affect the urban poor. Two overall strategies have characterized this search. The first, or policymaking strategy, relies on politicians and administrators who are aware of racial and class grievances to devise programs aimed at their elimination. The second, or political movement strategy, calls for members of affected groups to threaten established interests, forcing society to respond to their needs. Many would argue that the two approaches are complementary — that political and administrative elites will only attend to the interests of the poor when they are forced to do so. Even the reliance on policymaking may therefore require the development of political power among the poor.

Effective mobilization of the poor, however, is no easy matter. The principal power resources of the lower class are its numbers and potential for organization based on shared status and common grievances. But utilizing these resources requires an organizational capacity that is often lacking among the deprived. One approach to this problem has been to emphasize the client status of the poor, to create solidarity by waging a battle against a common enemy such as the urban renewal authority, the school system, or the police. In recent years, client-based political movements have raised the banner of "community control."

The political mobilization of poor people may require the initial help of some outside agent. Charles Silberman describes the strategy of perhaps the most successful of such agents, Saul Alinsky and his Industrial Areas Foundation. Alinsky attempts to advance community solidarity — itself a prime power resource — by intensifying conflict between the community and locally salient institutions. He first helps indigenous leaders to educate residents to the actual nature of their grievances and their enemies. Then he chooses a target against which an attack can be waged with some hope of success. The fruits of political activity must be seen early in the campaign if more people are to feel that "supporting the cause" is worth the personal costs it entails. Alinsky recognizes that the perception of success increases the potential for mobilization, hence for later successes. Thus, the initial targets must be highly visible. Because poor people have few resources, the main tactic employed against these targets is symbolic. As Silberman puts it, "the emphasis is on such dramatic actions as parades and rent strikes." Once the neighborhood organization has achieved some successes and is able to stand alone, Alinsky withdraws, leaving a politically more powerful community.

The question, however, is how much more powerful the poor community is likely to become. Silberman tells us that the problems of Woodlawn — the Chicago neighborhood in which he studied Alinsky at work — cannot be solved by community organization alone. Rather, he feels, "enormous resources must be poured into Woodlawn." Indeed, the community organization's greatest contribution is to give residents "the sense of dignity that makes it possible for them to accept help." But how much help is likely to be provided? How resistant are local institutions to the kind of symbolic warfare waged by the community political movements of the Alinsky model?

Michael Lipsky suggests that they are quite resistant. Leaders in poor communities do not have the resources to force concessions by bargaining with governmental bureaucracies. Instead, they mobilize their constituents and engage in demonstrations, strikes, sit-ins, and other forms of public behavior whose impact is primarily symbolic. Protests and other symbolic acts, says Lipsky, can be used both to mobilize more followers — i.e., to strengthen the community organization or political movement — and to appeal to more powerful third parties (liberals, labor unions, the church) which may intervene on behalf of the poor. But, as Lipsky points out, movement leaders are appealing to distinct constituencies whose aims are likely to conflict. A particular action, such as an inflammatory speech, may rouse the movement's followers, temporarily gain the attention of the media (which craves the unusual yet is likely to picture movement leaders as irresponsible), but frighten off third parties and elicit a counterattack from the target bureaucracy.

Moreover, the bureaucracy under attack is itself far from helpless. So long as the community organization or movement has nothing tangible to trade for concessions, the bureaucracy may be able to defend itself with a symbolic counterattack. This is possible because it is concerned primarily with its own reference groups, among whom clients are usually not included. It can employ numerous tactics that make the protesting clients appear to be irresponsible, show the good intentions of the bureaucracy, emphasize its limited resources to correct unfortunate situations, and so forth. In short, the bureaucracy attempts to appease those groups upon which it depends for resources or support; if it succeeds, it need not actually meet the demands of the protestors.

Lipsky is therefore less sanguine than Silberman about the possibilities of symbolic action for bringing about tangible gains. He documents the numerous obstacles in the way of creating and maintaining organizations that "get results." He sees no substitute however, for grassroots organizational power, which, like Alinsky, he believes is necessary for changing the dependent status of the urban poor.

The goal of the movement for community control of education in New York City was to change the political relationships that keep school clients in a subject position and protect the bureaucracy from having to innovate and improve educational output. Marilyn Gittell shows how the clients of the system, as well as the larger public, operate within a framework of interpretation — "professionalism"; "keeping the schools nonpolitical" — which supports the interests of the educational establishment. Here we see another obstacle to effective political action by the poor: their own inability to break through the frame of reference that conserves extant institutions and practices.

The case of community control of schools also provides examples in support of Lipsky's analysis. The advocates of community control had few resources at their disposal. The more they protested, the more "irresponsible" or "politically motivated" they appeared. The media ignored educational innovations in the demonstration districts, and instead concentrated on confrontations and disorder. The United Federation of Teachers and the educational bureaucracy succeeded in discrediting the advocates of community control in the eyes of the third parties upon whom they depended for help. But perhaps the most important insight to be drawn from Gittell's depiction of events in New York is how issues are framed and manipulated in political conflict to favor one side or the other — here the professional defenders of the schools.

In contrast to the general acceptance by Silberman, Lipsky, and Gittell of the importance of grassroots mobilization, Daniel Bell and Virginia Held are wary of a conflict strategy and see dangers in the movement for community control. They feel in particular that the increasing politicization of previously administrative — presumably nonpolitical — decision areas threatens to impair the effectiveness and efficiency of the very agencies on which the poor depend. The effect of agitation and mobilization of urban communities by indigenous leaders is ever more unrealistic popular demands. Rather than a revolution of rising expectations among the urban poor leading to effective political mobilization, Bell and Held foresee polarization, white resistance, and black frustration. The emphasis of ghetto movements on group solidarity and advancement and their rejection of the procedural norms and professionalization of government for which liberals have long fought, may ultimately threaten political stability and decency. In that case "rational politics" will be impossible and, the authors hold, the best hope for the poor will unwittingly be destroyed.

Black Power shifts the emphasis of political action from movements organized principally around the status of client to those which emphasize common racial identity. The effort to build local organizations and attain community control is a significant part of Black Power. But Black Power as a strategy must ultimately take on a national perspective. Its goals are the creation of racial solidarity among black people, the mobilization of power at the national level (through the creation of a black political party), and finally the restructuring of American institutions to permit the inclusion of black people in our social, economic, and political life as equals.

To many Americans Black Power has revolutionary implications. This is especially true because it involves a denial of racial integration as a meaningful goal for black people. In the words of Carmichael and Hamilton,

> The concept of Black Power rests on a fundamental premise: *Before a group can enter the open society it must first close ranks. . . .* The values of this society support a racist system; we find it incongruous to ask black people to adopt and support most of those values. We also reject the assumption that the basic institutions of this society must be preserved.

Although Carmichael and Hamilton recognize that Black Power implies the destruction of the coalition between blacks and liberal whites and the strategy of moral appeal which were associated with the Civil Rights Movement in the fifties and early sixties, they see racial solidarity and group power as essential to further progress for black people. For, as the movement has shifted its attention from legal discrimination in the South to social and economic inequality in the entire country, further concessions from the larger society depend upon the use of political power by blacks. Black mobilization will threaten the stability of the American system, but blacks can make significant gains, they say, only by raising a revolutionary threat.

The most important organizational manifestation of Black Power in its most radical form has been the Black Panther Party. The Panthers combine racial militance with a Marxian class analysis. Their goal is to end racism, which they see as possible only if capitalism too is transformed or destroyed. The actual programs of the Panthers, through which they have attempted to solidify and educate black communities, have included providing free breakfasts to ghetto children, hiring lawyers to defend black people against police repression, and sponsoring organizing efforts. Some observers have concluded that the Panthers are "reformist" rather than genuinely "revolutionary." Yet, as Bobby Seale's statements show, the Panthers have used an inflammatory rhetoric that sounds revolutionary. They have also armed themselves.

To white law enforcement officials the Panthers have become a symbol of revolutionary threat to American society. Whether they have actually been, as Ronald Steel suggests, "a force for stability in the ghetto" may by now be a moot point. The Panthers have been the targets of police activity, sometimes instigated by illegal acts on their part. Panthers have been killed in gun battles with the police; others have been imprisoned for long periods awaiting trials for "conspiracy," and a number of Panther leaders have taken exile abroad. In short, the Panthers have been significantly hurt by white attack — or counterattack, as the case may be. Their situation shows both the difficulty of mounting a radical attack on American institutions, and the extent to which they (and other American radical activists) have been ambivalent about the implications of their own analysis. Although the party has argued that America is racist and corrupt, it has nonetheless attempted to exercise freedom of speech, remaining visible and above ground. As a result, the Panthers have made themselves vulnerable to the kinds of suppression predicted by their own analysis.

What then are the possibilities for political movements leading to major changes in the distribution of power and wealth in our society? Richard Rubenstein suggests that we free ourselves from the simple either-or model of violent revolution (storming of the Bastille) countered by peaceful evolution (Congressional debates, etc.). In fact, he argues, America *has* undergone a number of political changes of revolutionary proportion. A great deal of conflict and violence was associated with these periods of upheaval. The protagonists were usually ethnic groups (rather than the classes expected by Marxian analysts). In each case, Rubenstein suggests, the crucial preconditions to change were the formation of an alliance among power-seeking groups and a split within the governing elite.

One implication of Rubenstein's analysis is that collective political action by blacks could provide the basis for revolutionary change. Whether blacks can form an alliance with other groups and force major concessions from the governing elite remains unknown, however. Rubenstein sees both social improvement and "domestic fascism" as possible outcomes; as yet one can neither foresee the consequences of black militance nor determine if America is today in a historical period ripe for revolutionary change.

The Potential for Community Organization

Charles E. Silberman

The Woodlawn section of Chicago, which in the 1920s was a pleasant middle-class neighborhood, has in 1960 become a virtually all-Negro slum.[1] Although nearly 25 per cent of the area's residents receive some form of welfare, they pay an average of $84 a month in rent — more than $10 *above* the city average — for which they occupy an average housing unit of 2.2 rooms. A birth rate 25 per cent above the city's average has put pressure on the capacity of the local public schools. There is a flourishing traffic in gambling, narcotics, and prostitution, especially in one stretch under the elevated subway tracks; the commercial business district is active but declining, with large numbers of stores vacant. In short, Woodlawn is precisely the sort of obsolescent, decaying, crowded neighborhood which social workers and city planners assume can never help itself — the sort of neighborhood in which even such advocates of social action as S. M. Miller assume that "directed, concerted action toward political or any other kind of goals is extremely unlikely."

But Woodlawn *is* helping itself; it is taking concerted action toward a wide variety of goals. The impetus for TWO [The Woodlawn Organization] came from three Protestant ministers and a Catholic priest who had come together through their concern with the spiraling decline of their neighborhood and the indifference of both the city and the Univer-

---

Condensed from *Crisis in Black and White* by Charles E. Silberman. Copyright © 1964 by Random House, Inc. Reprinted by permission of Random House, Inc.
    [1] The change in the color of Woodlawn's residents seems to have changed the area's history as well; thus, a 1962 city report on "Key Social Characteristics of the Woodlawn Community" suggests, in contradiction to the 1946 report, that as a result of "almost planless growth since the 1893 Columbia Exposition," the community had been deteriorating for more than a half-century.

sity of Chicago, located just to the north of Woodlawn. The clergymen had "worn out the seats of several good pairs of trousers attending an uncountable number of meetings held to 'do something about Woodlawn'" — meetings which seemed only to lead to still more meetings. "We were watching a community dying for lack of leaders, a community that had lost hope in the decency of things and people," one of the founders, Dr. Ulysses B. Blakeley, co-pastor of the First Presbyterian Church and Moderator of the Chicago Presbytery, explains. "Outsiders consider a place like this a kind of zoo or jungle; they may mean well, but they choke us. It seemed to us that any effort would be futile unless our own people could direct it, choose their own goals, and work for them, grow in the process, and have a sense again of the rightness of things."

After investigating various approaches to community organization, therefore, the clergymen "took the plunge," as Dr. Blakeley and his copastor, Dr. Charles T. Leber, Jr., described it in *Presbyterian Life:* they called on Saul D. Alinsky, executive director of the Industrial Areas Foundation, and invited him to help organize the Woodlawn community. A sociologist and criminologist by training, Alinsky is a specialist in creating mass organizations on a democratic basis "in order that the so-called 'little man' can gather into his hands the power he needs to make and shape his life." His organizing career began in the late 1930s, when he was one of the principal architects of Chicago's much admired Back of the Yards Neighborhood Council, which turned the stockyards area — the locale for Upton Sinclair's *The Jungle* — into one of the most desirable working-class neighborhoods in Chicago.[2] When his success in organizing the Back of the Yards evoked requests to do the same in other cities, Alinsky organized the Industrial Areas Foundation, a non-profit institution which has organized some forty-four groups across the country. The most notable of these, until the formation of The Woodlawn Organization, were in California, where the IAF organized some thirty communities of Mexican-Americans and welded them together in the Community Service Organization. . . .

---

[2] Critics of Alinsky now point to Back of the Yards and suggest that *anyone* could have organized the area, since the residents are virtually all Catholics. But when Alinsky began his organizing work, the stockyards area quite literally was a jungle. The residents were Catholic, all right — but they belonged to an incredible number of churches, each representing a different nationality or ethnic group at war with all the others. Animosity between them was so great that Catholic priests ministering to one ethnic group literally were not on speaking terms with priests from other ethnic backgrounds. Alinsky managed to unite all the Catholics — and then to forge a working alliance between the local Churches, the Chicago Archdiocese, and the Packinghouse Workers Union — at the time (though no longer) under communist domination. Paradoxically, the Back of the Yards organization has become very conservative in recent years: e.g., it has been quite effective in keeping Negroes out of the neighborhood.

"Took the plunge" is an apt way of describing what the Woodlawn ministers did in approaching Alinsky, however — for he is nothing if not controversial. Indeed, he delights in controversy; one of his basic premises, he likes to say, is that *all* important issues are controversial. . . .

. . . Alinsky really believes in democracy: he really believes that the helpless, the poor, the badly-educated can solve their own problems if given the chance and the means; he really believes that the poor and educated, no less than the rich and educated, have the right to decide how their lives should be run and what services should be offered to them, instead of being ministered to like children. "I do not believe that democracy can survive, except as a formality," he has written, "if the ordinary citizen's part is limited to voting — if he is incapable of initiative and unable to influence the political, social and economic structures surrounding him."

The individual can influence these structures only if he has power, for power means nothing more or less than the capacity to make one's interests felt in the decisions that affect him. There are two sources of power, in Alinsky's view: money and people. Since the residents of Woodlawn and of areas like it obviously have no money, their only source of power is themselves — which is to say the creation of an effective organization. Alinsky's frankness about power is upsetting to a good many people who regard open discussion of power as somehow lacking in taste — the equivalent, almost, of discussing one's marital life in public. For power, as John Kenneth Galbraith has written, plays a curious role in American life. "The privilege of controlling the actions or of affecting the income and property of others is something that no one of us can profess to seek or admit to possessing. No American ever runs for office because of an avowed desire to govern. He seeks to serve. . . . The same scrupulous avoidance of the terminology of power," Galbraith adds, "characterizes American business. The head of the company is no longer the boss — the term survives only as an amiable form of address — but the leader of the team. No union leader ever presents himself as anything but a spokesman for the boys." [3]

Alinsky takes delight in violating this etiquette. "The only reason people have ever banded together," he baldly states, "and the only reason they ever will, is the fact that organization gives them the power to satisfy their desires or to realize their needs. There never has been any other reason." In his view, people join a trade union to develop enough power to force a change in their working conditions; they join a political party in order to have a power instrument that can win an election and carry

[3] John Kenneth Galbraith, *American Capitalism* (Boston: Houghton Mifflin Company, 1956).

out their political objectives; they organize a church as a power instrument to convert others to their religious belief. "Even when we talk of a community lifting itself by its bootstraps," Alinsky says, "we are talking of power. It takes a great deal of power to lift oneself by one's own bootstraps."

To create such a power structure in an area like Woodlawn, however, requires enormous skill and effort, and a break with convention. The reason most efforts at organizing slum neighborhoods fail, Alinsky argues, is not the nature of the community but the objectives of the organizers and of the methods they use. Most approaches to community organization, as Professor Dan W. Dodson has written, involve "more of an emphasis on how to get the different vested interests together to slice up areas of 'service' than . . . a consideration of how to get people genuinely organized in fighting for the things which would bring them dignity and respect." The conventional appeal to homeowners' interests in conserving property values is useless in a community in which the majority of people rent, and in which the homeowners would have to sell if forced to comply with the building code. A call for civic pride falls flat in a community which hates its neighbors and which is convinced it is going to be bulldozed out of existence sooner or later; neighborhoods like Woodlawn are too drab and dismal to cause anyone to rally around them. Even civil rights is too much of an abstraction. "The daily lives of Woodlawn people," an early Alinsky memo on Woodlawn suggested, "leave them with little energy or enthusiasm for realizing principles from which they themselves will derive little practical benefit. They know that with their educational and economic handicaps they will be exceptions indeed if they can struggle into a middle-class neighborhood or a white-collar job." Instead of these appeals of the conventional neighborhood organizer and group worker, Alinsky uses the classical approach of trade union organization: he appeals to the self-interest of the local residents and to their resentment and distrust of the outside world, and he seeks out and develops a local, indigenous leadership.

While indigenous leadership is crucial if the organization is to mean anything in the lives of its members, the initial impetus must come from the outside, and the mean and difficult job of building the organization must be handled by full-time organizers who know how to conquer the apathy of the slum and how to weld its disparate fragments into a unified whole. For the indigenous leaders of the slum area are not in touch with each other; without training, they lack the skills needed to keep a large organization running; and in most cases it has never occurred to any of them to lead a mass organization. (If any one thing is known in the Negro slum — or the white slum, for that matter — it is that you can't fight City Hall.) Just as no factory would ever be organized without stimulus and guidance from the outside, so no slum can be organized without a good deal of help.

But the Industrial Areas Foundation insists that help be used to make the local community self-sufficient, not to keep it dependent. Alinsky will not enter a community unless he is invited by something like a cross-section of the population, and he usually insists, as a condition of entering, that the community itself, no matter how poor, take over the full responsibility for financing the new organization within a period of three years.[4] . . .

Once the Industrial Areas Foundation enters a community, the process of building an organization follows a fairly standard pattern:

> Organizers from the Industrial Areas Foundation filter through the neighborhood, asking questions and, more important, listening in bars, at street corners, in stores, in peoples' homes — in short, wherever people are talking — to discover the residents' specific grievances;
>
> At the same time, the organizers try to spot the individuals and the groups on which people seem to lean for advice or to which they go for help: a barber, a minister, a mailman, a restaurant owner, etc. — the "indigenous" leaders;
>
> The organizers get those leaders together, discuss the irritations, frustrations, and problems animating the neighborhood, and suggest the ways in which power might be used to ameliorate or solve them;
>
> A demonstration or series of demonstrations are put on to show how power can be used. These may take a variety of forms: a rent strike against slum landlords, a cleanup campaign against a notorious trouble spot, etc. What is crucial is that meetings and talk, the bedrock on which middle-class organizations founder, are avoided; the emphasis is on action, and on action that can lead to visible results.

In this way, the new organization begins to take form as a super-group comprising many existing member groups — churches, block clubs, businessmen's associations — and of new groups that are formed purely as a means of joining the larger organization. As the organization begins to move under its own steam, the IAF men gradually phase themselves out and local leaders take over. This does not mean that volunteers take over the whole work load, however. One of the cardinal principles of the IAF is that a full-time paid staff is necessary if a community organization is to continue to function; volunteers, especially in a slum neighborhood, simply do not have the time. But the local leaders take on the responsibility for making decisions and for meeting the budget; sometimes they

---

[4] Because of the poverty of Woodlawn, and even more because of the long tradition of Negro dependence, Alinsky has found it necessary to stretch that period by a year or two. TWO is on its way to financial independence, however; as of January, 1964, it had $10,000 in its treasury.

hire one of the IAF organizers as a permanent staff head, sometimes they come up with their own organizers.

So much for general principles and procedures. The actual work of creating The Woodlawn Organization was begun in the spring and summer of 1960, eighteen months after the four ministers had called on Alinsky for help. (He had told them he would not come into Woodlawn until a representative committee had extended the invitation.) By this time, the invitation was being extended by the Greater Woodlawn Pastors Alliance with support from most other organized groups in the community. The organizing effort was made possible by grants from the Catholic Archdiocese of Chicago, the Presbyterian Church of Chicago, and the Schwarzhaupt Foundation, a private philanthropy which has supported Industrial Areas Foundation projects elsewhere in the United States.

How do you begin to organize an area like Woodlawn? As Nicholas von Hoffman, then chief organizer for the IAF . . . put it with studied casualness, "I found myself at the corner of Sixty-third and Kimbark and I looked around." It did not take much looking or listening to discover, as might be expected in a Negro slum, that one of the things that "bugged" residents the most was cheating and exploitation by some of the businessmen of the area. In most low-income areas, credit-purchasing is a trap; naïve and semi-literate customers are high-pressured into signing instalment contracts without reading the fine print or having it explained. According to Dr. Leber, there were instances of customers being charged effective interest rates as high as 200 per cent; second-hand merchandise was represented as new; and prices bordered on outright piracy: a $6 diamond chip in a gaudy ring setting would be sold for $250, with a "Certificate of Guarantee" that it was a real diamond. (It *was* a real diamond — but one worth only $6.) Credit-purchasing aside, many merchants took unfair advantage of their customers' ignorance; food stores, for example, gave short weight, overcharged, and in a few cases actually rigged their cash registers to give false totals.

Hence, when the IAF organizers started fanning through the community, complaints began to pile up. Here was an issue, moreover, on which the legitimate businessmen in the area could unite with the consumers, for the crooked merchants hurt business for everyone else. As a result, TWO — bringing together the leaders of the Businessman's Association, some of the ministers, and some of the indigenous leaders who were being turned up — worked out a Code of Business Ethics covering credit practices, pricing, and advertising. To implement the Code, TWO set up a Board of Arbitration consisting of four representatives from the Businessman's Association, four from consumer groups, with an impartial chairman from outside the community elected by the eight Board members.

If this had been all, however, TWO would have been stillborn. To publicize the code, and to publicize the new organization, a big parade was staged in which nearly a thousand people marched through the business section carrying signs, singing, and creating enough of a stir to make the front pages of most Chicago newspapers. The next Saturday, a registered scale was set up at a nearby Catholic church, along with an adding machine; people who shopped at the markets suspected of giving false weights and improper totals brought their packages directly to the church, where they were weighed, and cash register slips checked and the false weights and false totals publicized. Most of the offending merchants quickly agreed to comply with the "Square Deal" agreement. To bring recalcitrant merchants to terms, leaflets were distributed through the community accusing them of cheating and urging residents to stay away.

The Square Deal campaign served its purpose. It eliminated a considerable amount of exploitation and chicanery on the part of Woodlawn merchants. More important, it made the residents of Woodlawn aware of the existence of the new organization and drove home the fact that through organization they *could* improve some of the circumstances of their lives. Two years later, a TWO vice-president recalled that it was the Square Deal campaign that brought him into the organization, and that really put TWO on a solid footing. "We showed people that they don't have to accept everything, that they can do something about it," he said — "but they have to be organized to do it."

To capitalize on the enthusiasm this campaign created, the IAF staff men moved next to organize rent strikes in a number of Woodlawn buildings. Wherever a substantial majority of the tenants could be persuaded to act together, a tenants' group was formed which demanded that the landlord, within some stated period of time, clear up physical violations that made occupancy hazardous or uncomfortable — broken windows, plumbing that did not work, missing steps from staircases, inadequate heat, etc. When the landlords ignored the ultimatum, TWO organized a rent strike: rents were withheld from the landlord and deposited in escrow in a special bank account. To dramatize the strike on one block where several adjoining buildings were involved, residents spelled out "This Is A Slum" in huge letters on the outside of the building. If the landlord remained recalcitrant, groups of pickets were dispatched to march up and down in front of the landlord's own home, carrying placards that read "Your Neighbor Is A Slumlord." The picketing provided a useful outlet for the anger the tenants felt, and gave them an opportunity, for the first time in their lives, to use their color in an affirmative way. For as soon as the Negro pickets appeared in a white suburban block, the landlord was deluged with phonecalls from angry neighbors demanding that he do something to call the pickets off. Within a matter of hours landlords who were picketed were on the phone with TWO, agreeing to make repairs.

Landlords were not the only ones who were picketed; over-crowded and segregated schools became a target, too. When William G. Caples, president of the Board of Education, refused to meet with TWO to discuss their complaints — he denounced the organization as "the lunatic fringe" — a delegation of eighteen Protestant and Catholic pastors staged a sit-in at the executive offices of Inland Steel, where Caples was public relations vice-president; at the same time, TWO rank-and-filers circled the building on the outside, carrying placards denouncing Caples as a segregationist. (Caples resigned the following month "because of the pressure of company business.") And when Superintendent of School Benjamin Willis denied that overcrowding could be relieved by transferring Negro students to all-white schools, TWO sent "truth squads" of mothers into neighboring white schools to photograph empty and half-empty classrooms. (In one elementary school, which was 81.5 per cent Negro, classes averaged 48.4 students per room; a school nine blocks away, but 99 per cent white, had an average of 28.4 pupils per room.) TWO members also staged a "death watch" at Board of Education meetings: a large group would attend each meeting wearing long black capes, to symbolize the "mourning" of Negro parents over the plight of their children.

It is precisely this sort of tactic that leads some of Alinsky's critics to denounce him as an agitator who deals in hate and who incites to conflict, a troublemaker whose stated goal is to "rub raw the sores of discontent," as an early TWO memorandum put it. "The fact that a community may be stirred and organized by 'sharpening dormant hostilities' and 'rubbing raw the sores of discontent' is not new," says Julian Levi, executive director of the South East Chicago Commission and mastermind and director of the University of Chicago's urban renewal activities. "The technique has been proved in practice in the assembling of lynch mobs." (Levi and the University have been trying alternately to discredit Alinsky and to ignore him since he began organizing Woodlawn.) As an example of the methods to which he objects, Levi cites a TWO leaflet naming a local food store and warning people to "watch out" for short weights, spoiled food, and short-changing. "If this is what this merchant is really doing," Levi says, "he should be punished by the court — but with all the safeguards the law provides. This is not the way people should be taught to protect themselves," he argues; they should be taught to register complaints with the Department of Health (about spoiled food), and Department of Weights and Measures (about short weights), and the Police Department (about short change). Levi similarly deplores the use of rent strikes. If landlords were violating the building code, he argues, TWO should have brought action through the Building Department, the way the South East Chicago Commission does, instead of taking the law into its own hands.

But slum dwellers, as Levi surely knows, have been complaining to the Building Department and to other city agencies for years, to no avail. The reason the South East Chicago Commission is able to get rapid action on complaints it registers with the Building Department or any other city agency is that it has what politicians call "clout": the Commission is the urban renewal arm of the University of Chicago, whose board of trustees includes some of the most influential businessmen and politicians in the city. As Professors Peter H. Rossi and Robert A. Dentler said in their study of the University's urban renewal program in the Hyde Park-Kenwood area, Levi "could in effect represent the most powerful community interests in demanding protection from the Chicago Department of Buildings and the Mayor's Housing and Redevelopment Coordinator. Pressure on real estate speculators was also channeled through the University's strong connections with the business community. Banks and insurance companies were warned that their funds were in jeopardy when invested as mortgages on illegally converted property in the area. Insurance companies were persuaded to suspend policies written on badly maintained properties. Publicity about the ownership of notorious slum properties was given to the press, which published unflattering accounts of the abuse of housing decency." [5] TWO had none of these gentlemanly weapons at its disposal — hence its need to use cruder tactics.

.   .   .

Moreover, Levi's criticisms miss the point — that the tactics he deplores are designed to serve more than one end. In the case of the fledgling Woodlawn Organization, the most urgent need was to persuade the local population that it could solve some of its problems through organization. It is impossible to understand Alinsky's tactics, in fact, without understanding the basic dilemma inherent in organizing any slum area, and particularly a Negro slum. The basic characteristic of slum — its "life style" so to speak — is apathy; no organization can be created unless this apathy can be overcome. But slum residents will not stir unless they see a reasonable chance of winning, unless there is some evidence that they *can* change things for the better. This reluctance to act is perfectly understandable; it is not true that the very poor have nothing to lose. Quite the contrary. In some respects, they have more to lose than the middle class; they face the danger of having their relief checks cut off, of losing an unskilled patronage job, of having a son on probation remanded to jail — of suffering any one of a host of reprisals a politically-oriented bureaucracy

---

[5] Peter H. Rossi & Robert A. Dentler, *The Politics of Urban Renewal* (Glencoe, Ill.: The Free Press, 1961).

can impose. (One of the differences between the lower-class Negro communities and middle-class white communities is that the latter clamor
for more protection *by* the police, while the former frequently demand —
and need — protection *from* the police. Certainly the traffic in narcotics,
gambling, and illicit sex that is omnipresent in every Negro slum could
not go on without the active cooperation of the local police.)

Quite frequently, therefore, the apathy that characterizes the slum
represents what in many ways is a realistic response to a hostile environment. But realistic or not, the adjustment that is reached is one
of surrender to the existing conditions and abdication of any hope of
change. The result is a community seething with inarticulate resentments and dormant hostilities repressed for safety's sake, but which
break out every now and then in some explosion of deviant or irrational
behavior. The slum dwellers are incapable of acting, or even of joining,
until these suppressed resentments and hostilities are brought to the sur-
face where they can be seen as problems — i.e., as a condition you can do
something about.

And so Alinsky pleads guilty to the charge of being an agitator, of
arousing dormant hostilities or rubbing raw the sores of discontent: that
is precisely the point of what he is doing! "The community organizer," he
writes, "digs into a morass of resignation, hopelessness, and despair and
works with the local people in articulating (or 'rubbing raw') their resentments." In telling them over and over again, "You don't have to take
this, and you can do something about it,' he becomes a catalytic agent
transmuting hidden resentments and hostilities into open problems." His
job is to persuade the people to move — to be active, to participate, in
short to develop and harness the power necessary to change the prevailing patterns. "When those prominent in the status quo turn and label
you an agitator, they are completely correct, for that is, in one word, your
function — to agitate to the point of conflict."

But agitation by itself is not enough; the inhabitants of a slum like
Woodlawn must be convinced not only that a solution is possible but
also that it is probable; they must see some tangible evidence that band-
ing together will give them the capacity to alter the circumstances of
their lives. To use the language of war (for that is what it is), the only
way to build an army is by winning a few victories. But how do you
gain a victory before you have an army? The only method ever devised
is guerilla warfare: to avoid a fixed battle, where the forces are arrayed
and where the new army's weakness would become visible, and to concentrate instead on hit-and-run tactics designed to gain small but measurable victories. Hence the emphasis on such dramatic actions as
parades and rent strikes whose main objective is to create a sense of
solidarity and of community.

Once this guerilla warfare begins, the best organizing help of all frequently comes from "the enemy" — the established institutions who feel themselves threatened by the new organization. What really welded the Woodlawn community together, for example, was the University of Chicago's announcement, on July 19, 1960, that it planned to extend its "South Campus" into Woodlawn by annexing an adjacent strip a block wide and a mile long. Woodlawn residents had no particular attachment to the area in question, which was filled with an amalgam of warehouses, rooming houses, empty lots, and old hotels that served mainly as centers of prostitution. But they suspected that annexation of this strip was simply the prelude to bulldozing a large part of Woodlawn itself for middle- and upper-income apartment and town houses. There was ample basis for their fears; urban renewal projects had been going on for some time under University sponsorship in the Hyde Park-Kenwood district north of the University, designed in good measure to clear Negroes out.[6] Unless they acted quickly to establish the principle that no plan be adopted for Woodlawn without active participation by Woodlawn residents in the planning itself, the community might be faced with a *fait accompli.* ("The characteristic mode of action of the University and of the South East Chicago Commission," Rossi and Dentler wrote, "was to develop plans quickly, announce proposals in general terms, and then obtain quick approval through political leverage downtown.") And so TWO immediately and loudly demanded that the city defer approval until University and city planning officials sat down with TWO and negotiated a long-term plan for Woodlawn. Otherwise, the organization warned, Woodlawnites would lie down in front of the bulldozers and wrecking equipment to prevent them from moving in. Some three hundred TWO members crowded into a City Plan Commission hearing and succeeded in blocking the quick approval the University had expected.

The Negro tenants and homeowners were not the only ones alarmed by the University's announcement. Having seen the small businessmen of Hyde Park-Kenwood area destroyed by the University's urban renewal program, the Woodlawn merchants became concerned over the way in which the University's plans might affect them. Conversations with University and city officials only served to increase their apprehension. For example, Julian Levi appeared at a meeting of the Woodlawn Businessman's Association; according to George Kyros, a local restaurant pro-

---

[6] There is ample documentation of this fact in Rossi and Dentler's *The Politics of Urban Renewal.* For example, "Asked by our interviewer why the University did not consider expansion to the east (which in many ways seemed more plausible than expansion in Hyde Park), a respondent high in the University administration replied that the area to the east contained 'our people.' . . . Whether one liked it or not, neighborhood conservation and renewal meant the preservation of Hyde Park-Kenwood as a primarily *white* middle-class residential neighborhood."

prietor, Levi "said we could either accept the plan and help it or sit back and watch it go through." Phil Doyle, head of the Land Clearance Commission, was even less reassuring. "He said the biggest investment he would advise us to make in our business was one coat of paint," Kyros recalls. "I've never seen people feel so bad." The upshot was that the businessmen voted unanimously to join TWO in fighting the University's program.

And so the University of Chicago obligingly supplied the whipping boy — itself — that was needed to unite tenants, homeowners, and businessmen in a common cause. Even before the South Campus proposal, the University was generally hated in Woodlawn — in part because it was white, in part because of its "Negro removal" tactics in the Hyde Park-Kenwood area, and in part because of a barbed-wire fence the University had put up to protect its campus against the Woodlawn community.

Woodlawn's dislike for the University was returned in kind. "Woodlawn is a terrible neighborhood," a University spokesman exclaimed, "and if these people want to preserve it, I don't know what's become of American values." Not every University official saw the dispute in quite such simple terms, but few, if any, seemed to have any doubt that right was on their side. "The University of Chicago is one of the few really first-rate things in the city of Chicago," Julian Levi told this writer in the spring of 1963, when the dispute was coming to a head, "and it needs more land if it's going to continue to be first rate." Levi's job, as he defined it, was to get the land the University needed, and if possible, to create a compatible community as well. But getting the land came first. A certain degree of conflict seemed inevitable — for the University, as Levi explained it, would be there thirty, fifty, a hundred years from now, whereas the people in the surrounding community would long since have departed. It was understandable that the local residents might want to put their short-run interests first; but the University had to keep its eyes fixed on the long run.

.   .   .

The controversy over the South Campus plan has been revealing in another respect. There has been a great deal of talk, in recent years, about ways of increasing "citizen participation" in city planning, especially urban renewal planning; federal legislation now requires local citizen participation in the formulation of renewal plans as a condition of federal aid. The Woodlawn experience indicates that "participation" means something very different to planners and to the academic researchers on whom they lean, than it does to the people being planned for. To the former, "citizen participation" means that the local residents are given a chance to air their views *after* the plans have been drawn, not before; planning, in this view, is a matter for experts, and "participation" is really thought of as "acquiescence." Thus Rossi and Dentler hail the Hyde Park-Kenwood Community Conference as the outstanding example of citizen participation in urban renewal planning — but they also point out that the organization did not play a significant role in influencing the specific details of the plan. Its achievement was to create popular acceptance for a plan which, at least in part, was inconsistent with the organization's stated objectives. Hence the two scholars concluded that "the maximum role to be played by a citizen-participation movement in urban renewal is primarily a passive one." Professor James Q. Wilson is even more blunt: "If one's goal is urban renewal on any really large scale in our cities," he writes, planners would be well-advised to eschew any real citizen participation. For "the higher the level of indigenous organization in a lower-class neighborhood, the poorer the prospects for renewal in that area. . . . Perhaps this explains," Professor Wilson adds, "why most local urban renewal directors made no effort to encourage citizen participation except on a city-wide basis — with little or no representation from the affected neighborhood." [7]

Certainly the Chicago city planners showed no eagerness to engage the Woodlawn residents in any active role. Indeed, the planners' response to Woodlawn's demand that it be given responsibility and allowed to exercise initiative in planning for its own future was a proposal to inundate the area with paternalism. Thus, the City Plan Commission, in March of 1962, presented a comprehensive plan for Woodlawn which included a huge program of urban renewal clearance, conservation, and rehabilitation; a massive investigation of illiteracy, ill-health, crime and unemployment; and a pilot attack on these problems to be financed by large government and foundation grants. In response to a question as to whether the planning committee had been guided by opinions from the community, the committee's Coordinating Consultant replied, "There is nobody to speak for the community. A community does not exist in Woodlawn." And Professor Philip Hauser, another consultant, volunteered his view that "The people there have only one common bond, opposition to the University of Chicago," and added gratuitously, "This is a community that reads nothing."

The two consultants were quickly disabused of their view. TWO responded with rhetoric ("We don't want to be planned for like children"; "We're tired of being pawns in sociological experiments"). But it did something unique in the annals of urban renewal: in conjunction with

---

[7] *Cf.*, James Q. Wilson, "Planning and Politics: Citizen Participation in Urban Renewal," *Journal of the American Institute of Planners* (November 1963).

the Businessman's Association, it hired a firm of city planners to make a detailed critique of the city's proposal and to come up with alternate proposals. The critique pointed out a number of glaring contradictions between the City Plan Department's evaluation of Woodlawn in 1946, when it was all-white, and in 1962, when it was virtually all-Negro; for example, the 1946 report found that "land coverage in the community is not excessively high," while the 1962 report complained of dangerous overcrowding of both land and buildings, although no new construction had taken place in the interim. The critique also pointed out that the city's program would demolish a substantial number of attractive, well-kept homes in an area of relatively high owner-occupancy, but left untouched the bulk of the area classified as the most blighted.

To the discomfiture of the planners, TWO attacked the city's "social planning" as vigorously as it attacked the urban renewal planning. "Self-determination applies in the field of social welfare," the organization resolved at its 1962 convention. "Therefore the best programs are the ones that we develop, pay for and direct ourselves. . . . Our aim is to lessen burdens in practical ways, but in ways that also guarantee we will keep our personal and community independence. We go on record as unqualifiedly opposing all notions of 'social planning' by either government or private groups. We will not be planned for as though we were children." Far from pleasing them, Woodlawn's desire for independence seemed only to anger the planners, whose "Papa knows best" attitude was being attacked on all sides. "Some of their resolutions against welfare are singularly unfortunate," Professor Hauser observed. "What would they do without welfare?" Others called the resolutions "revolutionary" and even "subversive." The Woodlawnites were puzzled. "They've been calling us 'welfare chiselers' and 'dependent' and everything else in the book," said one TWO Negro. "Now they distrust us for trying things for ourselves." "Do you think it's possible," a TWO organizer asked Georgie Ann Geyer, a reporter for the *Chicago Daily News*, "that someone other than the Negro has a vested interest in welfare?"

The distinguished University of Chicago sociologists and the professional planners may not have gotten the message (they have scrupulously ignored TWO's existence), but the politicians did. Concerned for his political life, Mayor Richard Daley forced the reluctant Chancellor of the University of Chicago to meet with TWO representatives in the Mayor's office; the negotiators agreed on a compromise which called for construction of low-income housing on vacant land *before* any existing buildings were torn down. For the first time in the history of urban renewal in the United States, people displaced by demolition will have new homes waiting for them in the same neighborhood. Instead of the usual wholesale replacement of lower-class housing by "middle-income" units,

Woodlawn will be renewed in steps. Only houses beyond salvage will be torn down; units to be rehabilitated will be repaired without evicting tenants. And city officials agreed to give TWO majority representation on the citizens planning committee that will draw up further plans and supervise their execution; Mayor Daley personally called Dr. Blakeley to ask him to serve as chairman.

Forcing the University of Chicago and the city planners to take account of the desires of the community is not the only victory The Woodlawn Organization has won. Before TWO was formed, every school in Woodlawn save one was on either double shift or overlapping session, and Board of Education members had announced that they saw no possibility of eliminating the double shift in their lifetime. By the spring of 1963, the double shift had been dropped and overcrowding substantially reduced. TWO has persuaded a number of Chicago firms to open up jobs for Negroes; it has stimulated a number of local block organizations to clean up and maintain their neighborhoods, and has forced landlords to repair their property. TWO's attacks on "the silent six" Negro aldermen of the Dawson machine has forced an unaccustomed militancy on them, and thereby changed the whole complexion of Chicago politics. . . .

What makes The Woodlawn Organization significant, however, is not so much what it is doing for its members as what it is doing *to* them. "The most important thing to me about the forty-six busloads of people who went to City Hall to register," Alinsky commented at the time, "was their own reaction. Many were weeping; others were saying, 'They're paying attention to us'; 'They're recognizing that we're people.' " Eighteen months later, an active member observed, "City Hall used to be a forbidden place, but we've made so many trips there and seen so many people that it's beginning to feel like a neighborhood store." Other members expressed themselves in much the same way: "We've lost our fear of standing up and expressing ourselves"; "We don't have to go hat in hand, begging, anymore. It's a wonderful feeling." What is crucial, in short, is not what the Woodlawn residents win, but that *they* are winning it; and this makes them see themselves in a new light — as men and women of substance and worth.

Besides giving its members a sense of dignity and worth, the Woodlawn Organization has given a good many people a sense of direction and purpose and an inner discipline that has enabled them to overcome the "floundering phenomenon." "This has been the most satisfying and rewarding period of my life," one TWO officer remarked in the spring of 1963. 'The organization has given me a real sense of accomplishing something — the only time in my life I've had that feeling." Indeed, activity in TWO has completely reshaped this man's life; he remembers the date and even the hour of the first TWO meeting he attended; he dates events from that time, the way a happily married couple dates events from their wedding day. But TWO has done more than just give purpose and meaning to his life, important as that is. Like so many other Woodlawnites, he had been accustomed to waste enormous amounts of time and energy through sheer inefficiency, i.e., personal disorganization. This made the initial organizing work more difficult than anything the organizers had ever encountered in white slums; at first, every little venture seemed to fail because of the personal disorganization. Even such an apparently simple matter as rounding up a half-dozen people to hand out leaflets at a particular time loomed as a major task: the six selected would turn up at different times, the leaflets would be lost or misplaced, the volunteers would get bored before they had finished distributing the leaflets, etc., etc., etc. Bit by bit, however, the members learned how to accept orders, how to carry out a simple task and follow through on it; then they began to learn how to give orders, how to organize a rent strike or a rally, how to handle a meeting, how to talk on their feet and debate an issue, how to handle opposition. The result, for those who have been actively involved in the organization, has been to transform their existence, for the discipline of the organization gradually imposes itself on their own lives. And as the individual learns to organize his own life, he learns how to relate to others. "We've learned to live together and act as a community," another TWO activist says. "Now I know people all over Woodlawn, and I've been in all the churches. Two years ago I didn't know a soul."

It would be inane to pretend that Woodlawn has become a model community; it remains a poverty-stricken, crime-ridden slum, though a slum with hope — a slum that is developing the means of raising itself by its own bootstraps. Most of the problems that make Woodlawn what it is — high unemployment, lack of education, family disorganization, poor health, bad housing — cannot be solved by a community organization alone. Help is needed; enormous resources must be poured into Woodlawn in the form of compensatory education, job retraining, advice on child-rearing, preventive medicine, etc. But experience in every city in the nation demonstrates that any paternalistic program imposed from above will be resisted and resented as "welfare colonialism." *TWO's greatest contribution, therefore, is its most subtle: it gives Woodlawn residents the sense of dignity that makes it possible for them to accept help.* For help now comes (or seems to come, which amounts to the same thing) not as the result of charity but as the result of their own power; they have decided what services they need and what services they would like to have. Hence programs which the community, in the past, would have avoided with contempt as one more instance of "Mr. Charlie's brainwashing," are now eagerly sought after. Thus, negotiations between TWO and the University of Chicago have led to development of a nursery school

program designed to reverse the effects of cultural deprivation. Negotiations between TWO and a team of psychiatrists enabled the latter to
set up some promising experiments in group therapy: the psychiatrists
and social workers work through TWO's network of block clubs to bring
people into the program. When a program enters Woodlawn with TWO's
endorsement and recommendation, it carriers a cachet that greatly multi-
plies its chances of success.

Rent Strikes: Poor Man's Weapon

Michael Lipsky

The poor lack not only money, but power. Low-income political
groups may be thought of as politically impoverished. In the bargaining
arena of city politics the poor have little to trade.

Protest has come to be an important part of the politics of low-
income minorities. By attempting to enlarge the conflict, and bring outside pressures to bear on their concerns, protest has developed as one
tactic the poor can use to exert power and gain greater control over their
lives. Since the sit-in movement of 1960, Negro civil-rights strategists
have used protest to bring about political change, and so have groups
associated with the war on poverty. Saul Alinsky's Industrial Areas
Foundation continues to receive invitations to help organize low-income
communities because it has demonstrated that it can mobilize poor people around the tactics of protest.

The Harlem rent strikes of 1963 and 1964, organized by Jesse Gray,
a dynamic black leader who has been agitating about slum housing for
more than 15 years, affected some tenants in approximately 150 Harlem
tenements. Following the March on Washington in August, 1963, the
rent strikes played on the liberal sympathies of New Yorkers who were
just beginning to re-examine the conditions of New York City slums.
Through a combination of appeal and threat, Jesse Gray mounted a
movement that succeeded in changing the orientation of some city services, obtained greater *legal* rights for organized tenants, and resulted in
obtaining repairs in a minority of the buildings in which tenants struck.
Along with rent strikes conducted by Mobilization for Youth, a pre-war

Reprinted by permission from *Trans-action*, February 1969, pp. 10–15. Copyright
© February 1969 by Transaction, Inc., New Brunswick, New Jersey.

poverty program, the rent strikes managed to project images of thousands of aroused tenants to a concerned public, and to somewhat anxious reform-oriented city officials.

The rent strikes did not succeed in obtaining fundamental goals. Most buildings in which tenants struck remained in disrepair, or deteriorated even further. City housing officials became more responsive to housing problems, but general programs to repair slum housing remained as remote as ever. Perhaps most significant, the rent strike movement, after a hectic initial winter, quickly petered out when cold weather again swept the Harlem streets. Focusing upon the rent strikes may help explain why this protest failed, and why protest in general is not a reliable political weapon.

Protest Has Long-Range Limits

Protest as a political tactic is limited because protest leaders must appeal to four constituencies at the same time. A protest leader must:

1. nurture and sustain an organization composed of people who may not always agree with his program or style;

2. adapt to the mass media — choose strategies and voice goals that will give him as much favorable exposure as possible;

3. try to develop and sustain the protest's impact on third parties — the general public, sympathetic liberals, or anyone who can put pressure on those with power; and

4. try to influence directly the targets of the protest — those who have the power to give him what he wants.

The tensions that result from the leader's need to manipulate four constituencies at once are the basic reason why protest is an unreliable political tactic, unlikely to prove successful in the long run.

Protest activity may be defined as a political activity designed to dramatize an objection to some policies or conditions, using unconventional showmanship or display and aimed at obtaining rewards from the political system while working within that system. The problem of the powerless is that they have little to bargain with, and must acquire resources. Fifteen people sitting in the Mayor's Office cannot, of themselves, hope to move City Hall. But through the publicity they get, or the reaction they evoke, they may politically activate a wider public to which the city administration is sensitive.

The tactic of activating third parties to enter the political process is most important to relatively powerless groups, although it is available to all. Obviously any organization which can call upon a large membership to engage in political activity — a trade union on strike, for example — has some degree of power. But the poor in individual neighborhoods frequently cannot exert such power. Neighborhood political groups may not have mass followings, or may not be able to rely on membership participation in political struggles. In such cases they may be able to activate other political forces in the city to enter the conflict on their behalf. However, the contradiction of the protest process suggest that even this tactic — now widely employed by various low-income groups — cannot be relied upon.

Take, for example, the problem of protest leaders and their constituents. If poor people are to be organized for protest activities, their involvement must be sustained by the symbolic and intangible rewards of participation in protest action, and by the promises of material rewards that protest leaders extend. Yet a leadership style suited to providing protesters with the intangible rewards of participating in rebellious political movements is sometimes incompatible with a style designed to secure tangible benefits for protest group members.

Furthermore, the need of protest leaders to develop a distinctive style in order to overcome the lack of involvement of potential group members diffuses as well as consolidates support. People who want psychological gratification (such as revenge or public notice and acknowledgment), but have little hope of material rewards, will be attracted to a militant leader. They want angry rhetoric and denunciation. On the other hand, those people who depend on the political system for tangible benefits, and therefore believe in it and cooperate with it to some extent, are likely to want moderate leadership. Groups that materially profit from participation in the system will not accept men who question the whole system. Yet the cohesion of relatively powerless groups may be strengthened by militant, ideological leadership that questions the rules of the game, that challenges their morality and legitimacy.

On the other hand, the fact that the sympathies and support of third parties are essential to the success of protesters may make the protesters' fear of retribution, where justified, an asset. For when people put themselves in danger by complaining, they are more likely to gain widespread sympathy. The cattle-prod and police-dog tactics of Alabama police in breaking up demonstrations a few years ago brought immediate response and support from around the country.

In short, the nature of protesters curtails the flexibility of protest leadership. Leaders must limit their public actions to preserve their basis of support. They must also limit protest in line with what they can reasonably expect of their followers. The poor cannot be expected to engage in activities that require much money. The anxieties developed throughout their lives — such as loss of job, fear of police, or danger of eviction — also limit the scope of protest. Negro protest in the South was limited by such retributions or anxieties about facing reprisals.

Jesse Gray was able to gain sympathy for the rent strikers because he was able to project an image of people willing to risk eviction in order to protest against the (rarely identified) slumlords, who exploited them, or the city, whose iceberg pace aided landlords rather than forced them to make repairs. In fact, Gray used an underutilized provision of the law which protected tenants against eviction if they paid their rent to court. It was one of the great strengths of the rent strikes that the image of danger to tenants was projected, while the tenants remained somewhat secure and within the legal process. This fortunate combination is not readily transferable to other cases in which protest activity is contemplated.

Apart from problems relating to manipulation of protest group members, protest leaders must command at least some resources. For instance, skilled professionals must be made available to protest organizations. Lawyers are needed to help protesters use the judicial process, and to handle court cases. The effectiveness of a protest organization may depend upon a combination of an ability to threaten the political system and an ability to exercise legal rights. The organization may either pay lawyers or depend on volunteers. In the case of the rent strikes, dependence on volunteer lawyers was finally abandoned — there were not enough available, and those who were willing could not survive long without payment.

Other professionals may be needed in other protest circumstances. A group trying to protest against an urban-renewal project, for example, will need architects and city planners to present a viable alternative to the city's plan.

Financial resources not only pay lawyers, but allow a minimum program of political activity. In the Harlem rent strikes, dues assessed against the protesters were low and were not collected systematically. Lawyers often complained that tenants were unwilling to pay incidental and minor fees, such as the $2 charge to subpoena departmental records. Obtaining money for mimeo flyers, supplies, rent, telephones, and a small payroll became major problems. The fact that Jesse Gray spent a great deal of time trying to organize new groups, and speaking all over the city, prevented him from paying attention to organizational details. Furthermore, he did not or could not develop assistants who could assume the organizational burden.

Lack of money can sometimes be made up for by passionate support. Lawyers, office help, and block organizers did come forth to work voluntarily for the rent strike. But such help is unreliable and usually transient. When spring came, volunteers vanished rapidly and did not return the following winter. Volunteer assistance usually comes from the more educated and skilled who can get other jobs, at good salaries. The diehards of ad hoc political groups are usually those who have no place to go, nothing else to do.

Lack of money also can be overcome with skilled nonprofessionals; but usually they are scarce. The college students, Negro and white, who staffed the rent-strike offices, handled paper work and press releases, and served as neighborhood organizers, were vital to the strike's success. Not only could they communicate with tenants, but they were relatively sophisticated about the operations of the city government and the communications media. They could help tenants with city agencies, and tell reporters that they wanted to hear. They also maintained contacts with other civil rights and liberal organizations. Other workers might have eventually acquired these skills and contacts, but these student organizers allowed the movement to go into action quickly, on a city-wide scale, and with a large volume of cases. One of the casualties of "black power" has been the exclusion of skilled white college students from potentially useful roles of this kind.

Like the proverbial tree that falls unheard in the forest, protest, politically speaking, does not exist unless it is projected and perceived. To the extent that a successful protest depends on appealing to, or perhaps also threatening, other groups in the community, publicity through the public media will set the limits of how far that protest activity will go toward success. (A number of writers, in fact, have noticed that the success of a protest seems directly related to publicity outside the immediate protest area.) If the communications media either ignore the protest or play it down, it will not succeed.

When the protest *is* covered, the way it is given publicity will influence all participants including the protesters themselves. Therefore, it is vital that a leader know what the media consider newsworthy, and be familiar with the prejudices and desires of those who determine what is to be covered and how much.

Media's Demands May Be Destructive

But media requirements are often contradictory and hard to meet. TV wants spot news, perhaps 30 seconds' worth; newspapers want somewhat more than that, and long stories may appear only in weekly neighborhood or ethnic papers. Reporters want topical newsworthiness in the short run — the more exciting the better. They will even stretch to get it. But after that they want evidence, accuracy, and reliability. The leader who was too accommodating in the beginning may come to be portrayed as an irresponsible liar.

This conflict was well illustrated in the rent strike. Jesse Gray and the reporters developed an almost symbiotic relationship. They wanted fresh, dramatic news on the growth of the strike — and Gray was happy to give them progress reports he did not, and could not, substantiate.

Actually, just keeping the strikes going in a limited number of buildings would have been a considerable feat. Yet reporters wanted more than that — they wanted growth. Gray, of course, had other reasons for reporting that the strike was spreading — he knew that such reports, if believed, would help pressure city officials. In misrepresenting the facts, Gray was encouraged by sympathetic reporters — in the long run actually undermining his case. As a *New York Times* reporter explained, "We had an interest in keeping it going."

Having encouraged Gray to go out on a limb and overstate the support he had, the reporters later were just as eager for documentation. It was not forthcoming. Gray consistently failed to produce a reliable list of rent-strike buildings that could withstand independent verification. He took the reporters only to those buildings he considered "safe." And the newspapers that had themselves strongly contributed to the inflation of Gray's claims then helped deflate them and denied him press coverage.

The clash between the needs of these two constituencies — the media and the protesters — often puts great strain on leaders. The old-line leader who appeals to his followers because of his apparent responsibility, integrity, and restraint will not capture the necessary headlines. On the other hand, the leader who finds militant rhetoric a useful weapon for organizing some people will find the media only too eager to carry his more inflammatory statements. But this portrayal of him as an uncompromising firebrand (often meant for a limited audience and as a limited tactic) will alienate him from people he may need for broad support, and may work toward excluding him from bargaining with city officials.

If a leader takes strong or extreme positions, he may win followers and newspaper space, but alienate the protest's target. Exclusion from the councils of bargaining or decision-making can have serious consequences for protest leaders, since the targets can then concentrate on satisfying the aroused public and civic groups, while ignoring the demands of the protesters.

What a protest leader must do to get support from third parties will also often conflict with what he must do to retain the interest and support of his followers. For instance, when Negro leaders actually engage in direct bargaining with politicians, they may find their supporters outraged or discouraged, and slipping away. They need militancy to arouse support; they need support to bargain; but if they bargain, they may seem to betray that militancy, and lose support. Yet bargaining at some point may be necessary to obtain objectives from city politicians. These tensions can be minimized to some extent by a protest organization's having divided leadership. One leader may bargain with city officials, while another continues rhetorical guerilla warfare.

Divided leadership may also prove useful in solving the problem that James Q. Wilson has noted: "The militant displays an unwillingness to perform those administrative tasks which are necessary to operate an organization." The nuts and bolts of administrative detail are vital. If protest depends primarily on a leader's charisma, as the rent strikes did to some extent, allocating responsibility (already difficult because of lack of skilled personnel) can become a major problem. In the rent strike, somebody had to coordinate court appearances for tenants and lawyers; somebody had to subpoena Building and Health Department records and collect money to pay for them; and somebody had to be alert to the fact that, through landlord duplicity or tenant neglect, tenants might face immediate eviction and require emergency legal assistance. Jesse Gray was often unable, or unwilling, to concentrate on these details. In part failures of these kinds are forced on the protest leader, who must give higher priority to publicity and arousing support than to adminis-trative detail. However, divided leadership can help separate responsi-bility for administration from responsibility for mobilization.

Strain between militancy to gain and maintain support and reason-ableness to obtain concessions can also be diminished by successful "pub-lic relations." Protest groups may understand the same words differently than city officials. Imperatives to march or burn are usually not the com-mands frightened whites sometimes think they are.

Bargaining Is for Insiders

Protest success depends partly upon enlarging the number of groups and individuals who are concerned about the issues. It also depends upon ability to influence the shape of the decision, not merely whether or not there will be a decision. This is one reason why protest is more likely to succeed when groups are trying to veto a decision (say, to stop construction of an expressway), than when they try to initiate projects (say, to establish low-cost transportation systems for a neighborhood).

Protest groups are often excluded from the bargaining arena because the civic groups and city officials who make decisions in various policy areas have developed relationships over long periods of time, for mutual benefit. Interlopers are not admitted to these councils easily. Men in power do not like to sit down with people they consider rogues. They do not seek the dubious pleasure of being denounced, and are uneasy in the presence of people whose class, race, or manners are unfamiliar. They may make opportunities available for "consultation," or even "confrontation," but decisions will be made behind closed doors where the nature of the decision is not open to discussion by "outsiders."

As noted before, relatively powerless protest groups seldom have enough people of high status to work for their proposals. Good causes sometimes attract such people, but seldom for long. Therefore protest groups hardly ever have the expertise and experience they need, including professionals in such fields as law, architecture, accounting, education, and how to get government money. This is one area in which the "political impoverishment" of low-income groups is most clearly observed. Protest groups may learn how to dramatize issues, but they cannot present data or proposals that public officials consider "objective" or "reasonable." Few men can be both passionate advocate and persuasive arbiter at the same time.

Ultimately the success of a protest depends on the targets.

Many of the forces that inhibit protest leaders from influencing target groups have already been mentioned: the protesters' lack of status, experience, and resources in bargaining; the conflict between the rhetoric that will inspire and hold supporters, and what will open the door to meaningful bargaining; conflicting press demands, and so on.

But there is an additional factor that constrains protest organizations that deal with public agencies. As many students of organizations have pointed out, public agencies and the men who run them are concerned with maintaining and enhancing the agency's position. This means protecting the agency from criticism and budget cuts, and attempting to increase the agency's status and scope. This piece of conventional wisdom has great importance for a protest group which can only succeed by getting others to apply pressure on public policy. Public agencies are most responsive to their regular critics and immediate organizational allies. Thus if they can deflect pressure from these, their reference groups, they can ease the pressure brought by protest *without meeting any of the protest demands*.

At least six tactics are available to targets that are inclined to respond in some way to protests. They may respond with symbolic satisfactions. Typical, in city politics, is the ribbon-cutting, street-corner ceremony, or the Mayor's walking press conference. When tension builds up in Harlem, Mayor Lindsay walks the streets and talks to the people. Such occasions are not only used to build support, but to persuade the residents that attention is being directed to their problems.

City agencies establish special machinery and procedures to prepare symbolic means for handling protest crises. For instance, in those New York departments having to do with housing, top officials, a press secretary, and one or two others will devote whatever time is necessary to collecting information and responding quickly to reporters' inquiries about a developing crisis. This is useful for tenants: It means that if they can create enough concern, they can cut through red tape. It is also useful for officials who want to appear ready to take action.

During the New York rent strikes, city officials responded by: initiating an anti-rat campaign; proposing ways to "legalize" rent strikes (already legal under certain conditions); starting a program to permit the city to make repairs; and contracting for a costly university study to review housing code enforcement procedures. Some of these steps were of distinct advantage to tenants, although none was directed at the overall slum problem. It is important to note, however, that the announcement of these programs served to deflect pressure by reassuring civic groups and a liberal public that something was being done. Regardless of how well-meaning public officials are, real changes in conditions are secondary to the general agency need to develop a response to protest that will "take the heat off."

Another tactic available to public officials is to give token satisfactions. When city officials respond, with much publicity, to a few cases brought to them, they can appear to be meeting protest demands, while actually meeting only those few cases. If a child is bitten by a rat, and enough hue and cry is raised, the rats in that apartment or building may be exterminated, with much fanfare. The building next door remains infested.

Such tokenism may give the appearance of great improvement, while actually impeding real overall progress by alleviating public concern. Tokenism is particularly attractive to reporters and television news directors, who are able to dramatize individual cases convincingly. General situations are notoriously hard to dramatize.

To blunt protest drives, protest targets may also work to change their internal procedures and organization. This tactic is similar to the preceding one. By developing means to concentrate on those cases that are most dramatic, or seem to pose the greatest threats, city officials can effectively wear down the cutting-edges of protest.

As noted, all New York City agencies have informal arrangements to deal with such crisis cases. During the rent strikes two new programs were developed by the city whereby officials could enter buildings to make repairs and exterminate rats on an emergency basis. Previously, officials had been confined to trying to find the landlords and to taking them to court (a time-consuming, ineffective process that has been almost universally criticized by knowledgeable observers). These new programs were highly significant developments because they expanded the scope of governmental responsibility. They acknowledged, in a sense, that slum conditions are a social disease requiring public intervention.

At the same time, these innovations served the purposes of administrators who needed the power to make repairs in the worst housing cases. If public officials can act quickly in the most desperate situations that come to their attention, pressure for more general attacks on housing problems can be deflected.

The new programs could never significantly affect the 800,000 deteriorating apartments in New York City. The new programs can operate only so long as the number of crises are relatively limited. Crisis treatment for everyone would mean shifting resources from routine services. If all cases receive priority, then none can.

The new programs, however welcomed by some individual tenants, help agencies to "cool off" crises quicker. This also may be the function of police review boards and internal complaint bureaus. Problems can be handled more expeditiously with such mechanisms while agency personnel behavior remains unaffected.

Target groups may plead that their hands are tied — because of laws or stubborn superiors, or lack of resources or authority. They may be sympathetic, but what can they do? Besides, "If-I-give-it-to-you-I-have-to-give-it-to-everyone."

Illustratively, at various times during the rent strike, city officials claimed they did not have funds for emergency repairs (although they found funds later), and lacked authority to enter buildings to make emergency repairs (although the city later acted to make emergency repairs under provisions of a law available for over 60 years). This tactic is persuasive; everyone knows that cities are broke, and limited by state law. But if pressure rises, funds for specific, relatively inexpensive programs, or expansion of existing programs, can often be found.

Targets may use their extensive resources and contacts to discredit protest leaders and organizations: "They don't really have the people behind them"; they are acting "criminally"; they are "left-wing." These allegations can cool the sympathies of the vital third parties, whether or not there is any truth behind them. City officials, especially, can use this device in their contacts with civic groups and communication media, with which they are mutually dependent for support and assistance. Some city officials can downgrade protesters while others appear sympathetic to the protesters' demands.

Finally, target groups may postpone action — time is on their side. Public sympathy cools quickly, and issues are soon forgotten. Moreover, because low-income protest groups have difficulty sustaining organiza-

tion (for reasons suggested above), they are particularly affected by de-
lays. The threat represented by protest dissipates with time, the difficulty
of managing for constituencies increases as more and more information
circulates, and the inherent instability of protest groups makes it unlikely
that they will be able to take effective action when decisions are finally
announced.

Survey Research as Procrastination

The best way to procrastinate is to commit the subject to "study."
By the time the study is ready, if ever, the protest group will probably
not be around to criticize or press for implementation of proposals. The
higher the status of the study group, the less capable low-status protest
groups will be able to effectively challenge the final product. Furthermore, officials retain the option of rejecting or failing to accept the reports of study groups, a practice developed to an art by the Johnson
administration.

This is not to say that surveys, research and study groups are to be
identified solely as delaying tactics. They are often desirable, even necessary, to document need and mobilize public and pressure group support.
But postponement, for whatever reason, will always change the pressures
on policy-makers, usually in directions unfavorable to protest results.

Groups without power can attempt to gain influence through protest.
I have argued that protest will be successful to the extent that the protesters can get third parties to put pressure on the targets. But protest
leaders have severe problems in trying to meet the needs and desires of
four separate and often conflicting constituencies — their supporters, the
mass media, the interested and vital third parties, and the targets of the
protest.

By definition, relatively powerless groups have few resources, and
therefore little probability of success. But to survive at all and to arouse
the third parties, they need at least some resources. Even to get these
minimal resources, conflicting demands limit the leader's effectiveness.
And when, finally, public officials are forced to recognize protest activity,
it is not to meet the demands, but to satisfy other groups that have influence.

Edelman has written that, in practice, regulatory policy consists of
reassuring mass publics symbolically while at the same time dispensing
tangible concessions only to narrow interest groups. Complementing
Edelman, I have suggested that public officials give symbolic reassurances
to protest groups, rather than real conceptions, because those on whom
they most depend will be satisfied with appearances of action. Rent

strikers wanted to see repairs in their apartments and dramatic improvements in slum housing; but the wider publics that most influence city officials could be satisfied simply by the appearance of reform. And when city officials had satisfied the publics this way, they could then resist or ignore the protesters' demands for other or more profound changes.

Kenneth Clark, in *Dark Ghetto,* has observed that the illusion of having power, when unaccompanied by material rewards, leads to feelings of helplessness and reinforces political apathy in the ghetto. If the poor and politically weak protest to acquire influence that will help change their lives and conditions, only to find that little comes from all that risk and trouble, then apathy or hostility toward conventional political methods may result.

If the arguments presented in this article are convincing, then those militant civil-rights leaders who insist that protest is a shallow foundation on which to build longterm, concrete gains are essentially correct. But their accompanying arguments — the fickleness of the white liberal, the difficulty of changing discriminatory institutions as opposed to discriminatory laws — are only part of the explanation for the essential failure of protest. An analysis of the politics involved strongly suggests that protest is best understood by concentrating on problems of managing diverse protest constituencies.

It may be, therefore, that Saul Alinsky is on soundest ground when he recommends protest as a tactic to build an organization, which can then command its own power. Protest also may be recommended to increase or change the political consciousness of people, or to gain short-run goals in a potentially sympathetic political environment. This may be the most significant contribution of the black power movement — the development of group consciousness which provides a more cohesive political base. But ultimately relatively powerless groups cannot rely on the protest process alone to help them obtain long-run goals, or general improvements in conditions. What they need for long-run success are stable political resources — in a word, power. The American political system is theoretically open; but it is closed, for many reasons suggested here, to politically impoverished groups. While politicians continue to affirm the right to dissent or protest within reason, the political process in which protest takes place remains highly restricted.

Community Control of Education

Marilyn Gittell

While political scientists and sociologists research who has power, we tend to ignore the powerless. While we study decision-making, we are reluctant to expose nondecision-making. Satisfied to rationalize a multiple-elite stucture as pluralism,[1] we depreciate the relevance of public participation in the political process.[2] The scope of our research and concerns is reflected in our limited views of institutional and social change in the cities.[3]

Reprinted by permission from *The Politics of Urban Education*, Marilyn Gittell and Alan Hevesi (eds.). Copyright © 1969 by Frederick A. Praeger, Inc.

[1] Robert A. Dahl, *Who Governs? Democracy and Power in an American City* (New Haven: Yale University Press, 1961); Edward C. Banfield, *Political Influence* (New York: The Free Press of Glencoe, 1961); Wallace S. Sayre and Herbert Kaufman, *Governing New York City: Politics in the Metropolis* (New York: Russell Sage Foundation, 1960); and Nelson W. Polsby, *Community Power and Political Theory* (New Haven: Yale University Press, 1963).

[2] Lester W. Milbrath, *Political Participation: How and Why Do People Get Involved in Politics* (Chicago: Rand McNally Co., 1965); Gabriel A. Almond and Sidney Verba, *The Civic Culture: Political Attitudes and Democracy in Five Nations* (Boston: Little, Brown & Co., 1963); and Robert E. Lane, *Political Life: Why and How People Get Involved in Politics* (Glencoe, Ill.: The Free Press, 1959), particularly chap. vi. The data in these studies are generally supportive of the correlation between Socio-Economic-Status and participation, concluding that middle-class, educated people are more likely to participate. Participation is largely defined as voting and there are only limited surveys of other types of participation and/or differences among such culture groups under different circumstances. The general assumption that moderate or low participation indicates consensus has undoubtedly conditioned the character and limited scope of research on participation.

[3] The critics of the democratic elitist theories have thus far been notably unsuccessful in their efforts to undermine the rationalization for replacing concepts of participatory democracy. There are obvious reasons for that failure; most important is that they have not developed empirical data to support their position. The bulk of the studies in political behavior are oriented to the reinforcement of the newly defined concepts of pluralism, as reflected in multiple-elite structure. Political scientists have generally avoided research on participation. The democratic elitists, after all, structured their defense of a new definition of pluralism on findings from the most current behavioral research. Such studies, from voting-behavior analysis to decision-making, indicated an increasingly limited role for public participants. How then could one justify a traditional concept of participatory democracy in the face of a declining participatory system? The democratic elitists have stressed simplistic pluralistic elements in the system, i.e., the existence of many elites within a political system and the lack of overlapping of these groups. In addition, they have stressed the varied sources of recruitment of elites and the potential ability of anyone to enter those elites. Few have addressed themselves to the issue of the effects of increasing noninvolvement. Certainly the cities are a significant laboratory for gathering supportive empirical evidence to begin to challenge the democratic elitist theories. See Peter Bachrach, *The Theory of Democratic Elitism* (Boston: Little, Brown & Co., 1967); Jack L. Walker, "A Critique of the Elitist Theory of Democracy," in Gittell

The ghetto community, in the meantime, has exposed the insulation of the political system and challenged its irrelevance to their demands for "a piece of the action." These communities are struggling daily with a political structure in the cities that combines two oppressive elements: bureaucratic centralization and specialization, and professionalism. In the face of these obstacles, ghetto leaders are necessarily concerned with restructuring to form a participatory system. They are forced to consider, and force all of us to consider, new mechanisms for increasing public participation. Unless they and we can find the channels for such participation, our political system may be in serious difficulty. The city school system is one of the battlegrounds and, in many respects, it reflects the larger problem in microcosm.

City Schools and Public Education

There are those who suggest that educational institutions cannot correct the maladies of the society that reflect larger social problems. In the 1930's, when educators similarly rejected George Counts's plea for using education as a vehicle for social change, they presaged a period of thirty years of insulation of the school system from social needs.[4] It should by now be evident that educational systems are a vital component of the constructive adjustment of urban institutions to the changing needs of our society.

The public education systems in our large cities are paralyzed. Their failure is political as well as educational. The educational failure is relatively easy to substantiate: There is sufficient hard data in test scores, dropout rates, the number of academic diplomas produced, and so forth, to establish the nature of that failure. Rationales developed to relate the cause of this failure to the problems of a disadvantaged community, while they may be valid, do not in any way negate the responsibility of the school system to educate its clientele. The inability of school professionals to cope with this problem must still be labeled an educational failure.[5]

---

and Hevesi, *The Politics of Urban Education* (New York: Praeger, 1969); and Robert A. Dahl, "Further Reflections on 'The Elitist Theory of Democracy,'" *American Political Science Review*, LX (June, 1966), 296–305.

[4] George Counts, *Decision-Making and American Values in School Administration* (New York: Teachers College, Columbia University, 1954). Published for the Cooperative Program in Educational Administration, Middle Atlantic Region, by the Bureau of Publications.

[5] Peter Schrag, "Boston: Education's Last Hurrah," in Gittell and Hevesi; Herbert Kohl, *36 Children* (N.Y.: New American Library, 1967); Peter Schrag, *Village School Downtown* (Boston: Beacon Press, 1967); Jonathan Kozol, *Death*

It is unfortunate that we do not have enough reliable information to measure comparatively the success or failure of the school systems in meeting the needs of immigrant populations over the years. Too often it is assumed that the education of the disadvantaged in previous decades was somehow successful. Nonetheless, while the data are limited, there is some evidence to suggest that educational institutions in large cities have traditionally been unable to meet the needs of the ghetto community. The difference in the current problem is that dropouts in the black community are unemployable because of racial barriers and automation, whereas earlier dropouts were hidden in an expanding work force.

The Political Failure of City School Systems

The political failure of the school system cannot be measured quantitatively except in the sense that educational failings can be traced to the environment of the total system. From my own research, I am convinced that the political failure of the school system is fundamental.[6] It can best be described in terms of the development within the city of a political subsystem whose policy process is wholly controlled by a small professional elite at headquarters. The policies emanating from this elite support an educational establishment that maintains a status quo orientation in all areas of education policy.

The lack of innovation in city school systems, except as periodically stimulated by outside funding, is indicative of this status quo orientation. Over the last sixty years, city school systems have experienced a high degree of professionalization combined with extensive centralization of the educational bureaucracy. In every large city, an inbred bureaucratic supervisory staff sits at headquarters offices holding a tight rein on educational policy. Their vested interests are clear: Any major shift in educational policy might well challenge their control of the system. Perhaps the only new agent to enter the domain of school affairs in recent years is the teacher organization or union. Unfortunately, these groups have concentrated their attention on salary and related issues; on all other questions, they have supported establishment pol-

---

at an Early Age: The Destruction of the Hearts and Minds of Negro Children in the Boston Public Schools (Boston: Houghton Mifflin Co., 1967); and Bel Kaufman, Up the Down Staircase (Englewood Cliffs, N.J.: Prentice-Hall, 1964).

  [6] Marilyn Gittell, Participants and Participation (New York: Frederick A. Praeger, 1967); and Marilyn Gittell and T. Edward Hollander, Six Urban School Districts (New York: Frederick A. Praeger, 1967).

icies.[7] Additionally, we have seen the abdication of responsibility for education by civic groups, businessmen, labor unions, and parents. The result is a closed political system, which, if measured against our ideological commitments to public participation, falls far short of any standards for a pluralistic society.

The Rationale for Community Control

The initial thrust that followed on the *Brown v. Board of Education* decision in 1954 was directed at achieving quality integrated education. It met not only with public opposition to change but also with bureaucratic inaction. In every large city, school segregation has increased in the last decade. Residential patterns explain part of the problem, but, beyond this, many plans for integration have simply been sidetracked. The integration movement, however, provided the ghetto community with insights into their exclusion from the school decision-making process. It was the struggle for integration that spotlighted the political failure of large-city school systems. How could the ghetto communities be assured of quality education and a participatory role in the system? The response has been clear. Those who now control the schools have been unable to produce results; they have excluded the public from its rightful role in the policy process; the structure, therefore, must be adjusted to give the community a measure of control over educational institutions. Participation in itself provides an involvement with the system that can not only diminish attitudes of alienation but also serve to stimulate educational change. This new role for the community is not conceived of as an abandonment of professionalism but, rather, as an effort to achieve a proper balance between professionalism and public involvement in the policy process. The definition of community includes parents of school children, as well as those segments of the public that have been excluded from a role in public education. Hence, community control implies a redistribution of power within the educational subsystem.[8] It is directed toward achieving a modern mechanism for participatory democracy. It attempts to answer the political failure in educational systems, and, as regards the educational failure, community

---

[7] Marilyn Gittell, "Teacher Power and Its Implications for Urban Education," *Theory Into Practice* (April, 1968).

[8] The redistribution of power is an important element in social change. The further enhancement of new power sources in a political system in turn provides the opportunity for achieving other changes in the system and related institutions. See Marilyn Gittell, "A Typology of Power for Measuring Social Change," *American Behavioral Scientist*, IX (April, 1966), 23–28.

control is intended to create an environment in which more meaningful educational policies can be developed and a wide variety of alternative solutions and techniques can be tested. It seems plausible to assume that a school system devoted to community needs and serving as an agent of community interests will provide an environment more conducive to learning.

Community Control as an Instrument for Social Change

Support for community participation is voiced by the educational establishment and the professionals, but their concept of community participation is more closely related to the traditional parent-association concept and has nothing to do with community control of decision-making. It is essential that community control be defined in clear and precise terms. As one critic has noted, "participation without power is a ritual." Community control of the schools must involve local control over key policy decisions in four critical areas: (1) personnel, (2) budget, (3) curriculum, and (4) pupil policy. Local governing bodies must be locally selected, and mechanisms for encouraging broader community participation must be thoughtfully developed.

Properly instituted, community control is an instrument of social change. The redistribution of power is in itself an aspect of that change. If adequate provision is made for giving the community the technical resources to carry out this new role, community control has the potential for offering new insights into our concept of professionalism and our general theories of educational expertise. If community boards have the resources to engage a variety of professionals and nonprofessionals in the policy process, institutional changes of all kinds can be anticipated. The business community as well as university faculties and research centers may become more actively involved in the schools. Flexible staffing policies and innovative institutional arrangements are more likely to be developed. The scope of other community resources will be greatly expanded as well.

Demonstration School Projects in New York City

The three demonstration projects established in New York City, in July, 1967, to experiment with community participation offer some experience on which to base predictions. Although these three demonstration districts (Ocean Hill-Brownsville, Two Bridges, and the 201 complex) suffered from an almost total lack of delegated power and resources, they did prove that community involvement can and does expand the scope of professional and public participation. Teacher and administrative recruitment in these districts was innovative even within the constraints of established central procedures and the union contract. In Ocean Hill-Brownsville, seven new principals were appointed by the Local Governing Board, drawing on people from outside the regular bureaucratic hierarchy. For the first time, a Puerto Rican and a Chinese principal were appointed to head local schools.[9] A unit administrator (equivalent to a district superintendent) appointed by another of the local boards was trained in public administration rather than in the traditional professional education area. His insights and approach differed markedly from the usual school administrator. Another district, in the process of recruiting a unit administrator, established community orientation as a *sine qua non* for the candidates. . . . The districts drew on the expertise of professionals in fields not previously involved in the schools; anthropologists, political scientists, and sociologists were used. In addition, community people were viewed as a new and special kind of resource. . . . Members of the local boards were, largely, parents of school children in the district; many were from lower-income groups and their involvement in community affairs began in poverty programs; several had never been involved in school affairs prior to the creation of the demonstration districts. . . .

The Bundy Plan

The first significant general proposal for community control was the Bundy Plan, presented to the mayor of New York City in the autumn of 1967.[10] The plan called for city-wide decentralization and rather extensive community control. It suggested a city-wide education structure for special schools, for establishing minimum standards, for control of capital construction, and for provision of voluntary services at the request of local districts. By its provision for local selection of a majority of the members of local school boards and for community control of the expense budget, student policy, curriculum, and personnel, the Bundy Plan met the test of redistributing power in the system. Perhaps the plan's

---

[9] A recent court action has held that these appointments were illegal since they were made in violation of state law. The case is presently on appeal.

[10] Mayor's Advisory Panel on Decentralization of the New York City Schools, *Reconnection for Learning: A Community School System for New York City* (November, 1967).

obvious commitment to community control explained the opposition to it. The outcry surrounding the Bundy Plan suggested the general alignment of forces to be faced by any proposal for decentralization and increased community control in cities throughout the country. It also reflected the current education power structure and its failure to respond to the pressing demands of the community.

.   .   .

Viewing the decentralization controversy as it has developed around the Bundy Plan and the experimental demonstration districts, it is possible to mark out three phases. In the first place, a rhetoric related to the concept of community control was developed to defeat the Bundy Plan.

.   .   .

This phase in the controversy culminated in the spring of 1968 in a concerted attempt by opponents of decentralization to prevent legislative action. The thrust of the attempt was directed against the Regents' bill that had been introduced into the State Legislature during that spring. Neither the United Federation of Teachers (UFT) nor its new-found ally the Principals' Association (CSA) spared any expense in trying to defeat the passage of this decentralization bill, which had been based on the Bundy Plan. The UFT reportedly spent upward of $500,000 in a public relations campaign that included hundreds of school meetings, newspaper ads, and radio spots; the CSA assessed its members nearly $1 million for a war chest, though it actually spent less money and expended less effort than did the UFT.

The pro-decentralization forces, lacking tight organizational direction and unlimited funds, were hampered in their attempts to press for a meaningful bill. The two most influential civic educational organizations, for example, the United Parents Association and the Public Education Association, in presenting their own drafts of a decentralization bill, departed significantly from the Bundy model. The net effect of the various ideological differences among black and reform white groups was to enfeeble their collective strength. A loose umbrella coalition was finally formed in the early spring of 1968, under the chairmanship of RCA President Robert Sarnoff, to lobby for the mayor's amended version of the Bundy Plan. At the same time, it appears that the mayor did not play as forceful a role as he could have in pushing for passage of the bill. It has been said that the mayor did not feel the white community, already divided in its support, backed his efforts sufficiently to enable him to push harder.

.   .   .

The UFT successfully coupled a threat of political vengeance with the fear of extremism over the involuntary transfer of nineteen educators from the Ocean Hill-Brownsville experimental district. As a result, the legislators, all up for re-election in the fall, merely postponed action for a year, empowering a hostile city school board to draw up another decentralization plan. In order to placate the pro-decentralization forces, the legislature increased the membership of the nine-member city board to thirteen. Although the legislative battle was postponed to the 1969 session, a new campaign was begun by the UFT in the fall of 1968.

The defeat of both the Bundy Plan and the Regents Plan ended the first phase of the political decentralization struggle. The escalation of the Ocean Hill-Brownsville controversy by the UFT into a city-wide strike marked the beginning of the second phase, which pitted white and black against each other in a racial confrontation.

The opening thrust was a not-too-subtle CSA–UFT campaign that charged the Ocean Hill–Brownsville district with encouraging racial extremism and anti-Semitism; it proved very successful. The Jewish community in the city became supportive and grew increasingly militant in its demands for redress. Leaflets and flyers, distributed throughout the city by the UFT and the CSA, quoted from materials purported to have been circulating in the Ocean Hill–Brownsville district. Some of the material was later proven to have been falsified; none of it was ever proven to have come from the district. Mass circulation of this propaganda fed existing fears and latent racism, as the atmosphere in the city became more charged with the passing of each day of the strike.

Although the mayor attempted to balance the interests of both sides during the strike, he was committed to the preservation of the Ocean Hill–Brownsville district and of decentralization, and this pitted him against the UFT–CSA, creating a political stalemate. The solid alignment of labor in support of the UFT was a major element in the controversy. The Central Labor Council threatened a general strike and forced the mayor to make a series of concessions to the union. The mayor appeared to have no political leverage in dealing with the union and was unable to use any of his normal political powers to de-escalate the union's demands or to force a settlement. Additionally, new efforts to develop institutional muscle for decentralization through the Committee to Save Decentralization and Community Control were slow in getting off the ground, although several sources of support, particularly church groups, were successfully tapped.

[The passage of the 1969 School Decentralization Law by the New York State Legislature marked the third, and perhaps final, phase of the dispute. Legislators who were merely ill-informed in 1968 became solidly opposed to community control. Thus, while the law provided certain elements of administrative decentralization, it forbade the establishment of small community school boards, gave only limited powers to the large local boards which it mandated, and set up election procedures for local board members designed to prevent domination of the boards by militant parents.]

Reformism and Community Control

It is apparent from this brief rundown of the politics of community control in New York City that traditional reform concepts developed in the first half of the twentieth century are a source of much of the opposition rhetoric. The failure of neo-reformers to challenge these outdated concepts has allowed their opposition to use the rhetoric of reform against them. These traditional concepts are reflected in the professionals' defense of their role and in the white middle-class reactions to community control. Historically, the reform movement distrusted machine politics. The movement was a reaction to widespread corruption in government, and professionalism was the panacea that it developed to replace "political" or public decision-making. Citizen participation was to be satisfied by public voting in referenda and the creation of watchdog civic groups. Consequently, any challenge to professionalism, or any attempt to strengthen community control, would be an anathema to middle-class and professional attitudes. Neo-reformers in the city have not been emphatic enough in arguing that much has happened in the last two decades to prove that the traditional reform mechanisms and battle lines are no longer meaningful. Because of the radical changes in the character of large-city populations and the ever increasing expansion of city functions and responsibilities, with a concurrent growth in city bureaucracy, reform must take on a new character. We cannot ignore the fact that increasingly large segments of our city population are alienated from formal policy-makers as well as from old-style civic reformers. Consequently, they have been unable to use the traditional and limited mechanisms for public participation and influence.

The Ghetto and Community Control

The ghetto communities and their leaders are not "hung-up" on professionalism. They have adequate proof that the school system and the professionals who run it have failed. In fact, the frustrations engendered by the unwillingness of the educators to yield power within the system has led to more broad-based demands for fundamental change. In two recent conferences, the Five State Organizing Committee for Community Control reaffirmed as one of its objectives absolute community control of school administrative and fiscal policies.[11] It rejected the idea of a subsystem within the city school system; such a subsystem would be a violation of self-determination because "basic control remains with the white establishment." . . .

Opposition to the Concept

The arguments against community control tend to center around two themes — the parochialism that might result from neighborhood districts' controlling the schools and the lack of qualifications of community people and their inability to cope with the highly technical problems in education.

The concern with the dangers of parochialism usually relates to fears of the emergence of black racism and separatism. State legislation and administrative regulations now prescribe certain limitations, but it is possible that new protective controls will prove necessary; these could be worked out as the need suggests. The concern with black racism is more often a misinterpretation of the movement toward creating a sense of community identity; it is evidence of a lack of understanding of the ghetto community's desire to increase the number of black teachers and administrators in local schools. In fact, there is no evidence in any of the three demonstration projects that there is any unusual stress in this area.

Local rivalries and ethnic conflicts may be intensified by local control and this should be anticipated. However, the ability to deal with, and resolve or compromise, these conflicts locally may well be an important part of the participatory process. Conflict does not necessarily have to be viewed as dangerous; rather, it may stimulate increased public and group participation in the affairs of the community. The advantages to be gained from encouraging community identity and consciousness, particularly in the ghetto, may well outweigh any negative aspects of parochialism. There is empirical evidence that participation and involvement increase when group identity is stronger: Alinsky identified greater worker participation in a worker-identified community; the experience in Norway with a workers' party showed similar results.[12]

---

[11] Five State Organizing Committee for Community Control to the Office of Metropolitan Educational Sub-systems, *Position Statement* (January 25, 1968), p. 3.

[12] Lane, *op. cit.* A Norwegian study indicated higher turnout in elections where socio-economic status of an area is more homogeneous; see Stein Rokkan, "The Comparative Study of Political Participation: Notes Toward a Perspective on Current Research," in Austin Ranney (ed.), *Essays on the Behavioral Study of Politics*

The group identity factor probably supersedes Socio-Economic-Status (SES) and racial background as an influence on the kind and extent of community participation. In fact, from the reactions and responses in the three demonstration school projects, it appears that community control stimulated wider local participation. Election returns in governing-board elections, although somewhat influenced by lack of publicity, inability to attain registration lists from the Board of Education, and absence of experience in conducting political campaigns, were higher than the responses in other local political elections in the same districts. Estimates of eligible parent voters who participated in the three districts were, approximately, 20 per cent in the 201 complex, 30 per cent in Ocean Hill–Brownsville, and 50 per cent in the Two Bridges district. There were also indications of wider parent interest and involvement in school meetings and school organizations in these three communities. The background of governing-board members suggests that low SES has not deterred extensive participation in the policy process — when the group can exercise power. This experience may offer important evidence to suggest that low participation by level of income or SES reflects the failure of our political system to provide either the means for participation or direct power to lower-class groups. Given both a political structure with which the ghetto resident can identify and a delegation of effective power in decision-making, his involvement is substantially increased.

Participation should be defined in two general categories: first, as involvement or expressed interest, as reflected in attendance at meetings or voting; second, as direct engagement in the policy-making process and in the exercise of power. The latter experience should provide the basis for testing the effect of community control as a mechanism for achieving social and institutional change in the system. The limited evidence in the three demonstration projects strongly supports the hypothesis that community control in the ghetto is a source of social change.

Serious opposition to community control stems from a lack of confidence in the ability of community people to make decisions that may require some technical competence. A corollary to that position is the fear that community control denies or negates professionalism. In fact, public attitudes often attribute far too much to the ability of the professionals to come up with answers to problems. Community control must embody decision-making power vested in community representatives. Those representatives, however, must, to some extent, still rely on both professionals and nonprofessionals for inputs into the policy process.

(Urbana, Ill.: University of Illinois Press, 1962), pp. 47–90. See also Herbert J. Gans, *The Urban Villagers. Group and Class in the Life of Italian Americans* (New York: The Free Press of Glencoe, 1965), pp. 106–10.

In addition, technical resources must be made readily available to the community, to be used at its discretion. Such resources should be integral to any projected plan for community control. It should also be noted that there is advantage to injecting the dimension of community nonprofessional experience and expertise, which is now excluded from the policy process; in many ways, the parents of school children have insights into needs and values that can contribute significantly to a more viable educational program.[13] A broader concept of education, one that goes beyond the four-walls classroom concept and extends into the larger community, can gain particularly from that experience.

Again, the experience of the three demonstration projects suggests that community control does not deny professional involvement; rather, it broadens it, tapping new professional resources. However, achieving the proper balance between a professional and public role is a continuing process that can only be defined in a practical setting.

Community control of education is only one aspect of the general movement toward expanded community involvement. Underlying the effort toward this goal is the desire to guarantee a meaningful redistribution of power in our cities. Although the community-at-large has suffered from the insulation of the policy process in the bureaucratic structure, it is the ghetto population that has recognized the problem and pressed for change. The ends that they seek and the thrust of their actions may benefit the political system and the larger community as a whole.

The Community Revolution

Daniel Bell and Virginia Held

A number of extraordinary changes are taking place in American life which we can deal with only schematically here.

There is, first, the increasing "politicalization" of society, particularly in urban affairs. Activities which were once allocated through the mar-

---

13 Curriculum experts now suggest the value of wider participation in the development of school curriculum; see George A. Beauchamp, *Planning the Elementary School Curriculum* (Englewood Cliffs, N.J.: Allyn and Bacon, 1956), p. 10.

Reprinted with permission from *The Public Interest*, Summer 1969, pp. 173–177. Copyright © 1969 by National Affairs, Inc.

ket are now subject to political decisions or political controls. Previously
the question of who was to be housed where, would be settled through a
"rationing by purse." Today, the decisions as to where housing is to be
sited, what tax abatements are to be given, what proportion is to be re-
served for low income or for municipal housing, etc. are made politically.
And this carries over into many other areas as well. The sociological
question is whether a society, this society, can carry such an increasing
burden. The classical effects of politicalization are clear: the decision
points are visible, rather than dispersed. The consequences are plain, for
people know "whose ox will be gored." There is an overconcentration on
law and legislation, and an increasing burden on administration. All of
this, inevitably, increases the potential for group conflict. One of the
chief reasons why in the last twenty years New York has been deemed
to be "ungovernable" is the increasing politicalization of decision-making.

Second, a group of "new men" have come into the political system,
specifically among the blacks. They are angry and they feel deprived.
Their goal, in many instances, is not integration or the sharing of power
but the control of their "own" institutions and enclaves. Yet two things
are remarkable about this movement. The projects in which a large number of the new leaders are employed are federally-funded. And second,
other than schools and a few local services such as health and the like,
there is little possibility that the blacks will achieve control of major economic or political resources, for the locus of these resources are not in the
neighborhood or community. To this extent, a whole series of unrealistic
expectations are being generated in black communities which may
boomerang badly. What the black leadership may be able to achieve is a
significant bargaining power, or even a veto in many instances, of city
policies, but the talk of the ultramilitants about gaining control of the
"major" institutions of society is unreal. The outcome will either be some
accommodation or an increase in senseless rage. Despite the ultramilitant
talk, the likelihood, still, is of accommodation.

Finally, we have seen the emergence, in a formal way, of the idea of
"group rights" as the means whereby disadvantaged groups, particularly
the blacks, can establish their claims in the system. The focal point here
is education and it lies in the demands of the blacks for control of the
schools in black districts, and for a quota or some preferential system in
the colleges. In New York this demand has brought the militant blacks
squarely into conflict with the teachers union, which has felt its position
threatened by the demand. It has raised the ugly spectre of anti-Semitism because a number of the blacks, particularly those in the leadership
of the Afro-American Teachers Association, have deliberately made anti-
Semitic statements in order to frighten away Jewish teachers and particularly Jewish principals from schools in the ghetto.

Three issues are involved in the argument for group rights. One is that of merit: the question whether a person should or should not achieve a position on the basis of his demonstrated ability, or whether a proportion of posts should be allotted on the basis of group membership. The second, allied to it, is that of common culture. The argument, made by Rhody McCoy at Ocean Hill, for example, was that any principal from the civil service list would be white, but that a white principal could not understand or guide a black child. Such an argument strikes at the traditional understanding of a common education and raises the question whether, in the future, all education in the major American cities may not be parochial or segmented by class or race. Third is the question of representation. Should there be majority rule or proportional representation; and if the latter, by geography or by group? When the New York State legislature proposed the election of a city Board of Education by boroughs, the Rev. Milton A. Galamison cried that the bill "deprives the blacks and Puerto Rican people of representation. . . . Whenever we get into this nose-counting business, it's to the disadvantage of blacks and Puerto Ricans." And the administrator of Harlem's IS 201 district, Charles Wilson, agreed, saying: "The notion that the elected board will democratize the system is not so." What are the appropriate answers?

These divisive questions of political rights and political philosophy conjoin with a different set of problems that arise out of the nature of the size of the polis in a modern society. In a brilliant essay in the *American Political Science Review,* for December 1967, "The City in the Future of Democracy," Robert A. Dahl raised the question, "which is no longer a subject of discussion among political scientists," of what "is the optimum size for a city." And, he remarks, "the evidence seems to me . . . that the all-round optimum size for a contemporary American city is probably somewhere between 50,000 and 200,000, which, even taking the larger figure, may be within the threshold for wide civic participation." [1]

---

[1] Dahl says further: "There is, for example, no worthwhile evidence that there are any significant economies of scale in city governments for cities over about 50,000. The few items on which increasing size does lead to decreasing unit costs, such as water and sewerage, are too small a proportion of total city outlays to lead to significant economies; and even these reductions are probably offset by rising costs for other services such as police protection.

"Per capita city expenditures increase with the size of city, at least in the United States. In 1960 the mean expenditure for U.S. cities over 150,000 was $123 per capita compared with $70 per capita for cities in the 35–50,000 range. Yet there is no evidence that these higher costs per capita provide residents of large cities with a better life, taking it in the round, than the life enjoyed by residents of smaller cities. If it costs more in a city of a million than in a city of 25,000 to build, maintain and police a park within walking distance of every citizen, then

Not only has there been little discussion on the optimum size of a city or a "quarter" of a large city, but there has been little thought as to what is the appropriate size and scope of the appropriate social unit to handle what problems: i.e., what services and functions can be left to a neighborhood or community, what has to be handled on a borough or city level, what has to be conducted in a region, and what has to be federalized? All that we have are shibboleths. We have the traditional decentralizers such as Paul Goodman, or the regionalists, or the federalizers. But nowhere is there a detailed examination of what functions of government are best handled at what levels of government.

A few suggestions may be hazarded, but they must be tentative. They involve ways of separating kinds of decisions in such a way that some are best decided at the periphery by participatory discussion and voluntary agreement, and some are best decided at more central levels, not only in order to arrive at such decisions with dispatch, but also to be able to bring local interests into line with wider, more regional considerations. An example of such a division of decision-making power is the way the Human Resources Administration divides antipoverty funds between the various poverty areas according to impartial, mathematical calculations of the areas' poverty index. But then, once the amounts have thus been centrally fixed on the basis of such formulas, decisions on how to spend these funds are allowed to reflect the ebbs and flows of local sentiment and preference. Another example is the way the central Council Against Poverty decided [in 1969], also on the basis of general and quantifiable criteria, to establish priorities to which all Community Corporations would be expected to allocate 70 per cent of their funds. These priorities [were] "Education Action, Manpower Action, Economic Development and Consumer Education, and Housing." Within the bounds of these general requirements, the localities can then pursue these objectives in ways that satisfy the particular moods, tastes, and nonquantifiable enthusiasms of their members. In the field of housing, central and long-range decisions on appropriate relative proportions of low and middle-income housing units can be recommended, within which communities can develop the housing projects that seem to them most humane and habitable. And central decisions on the allocation of funds for education according to fairly abstract principles of justice can

---

higher per capita expenditure for parks in big cities hardly signify that their residents have better public services than residents of smaller cities. . . .

"The oft-cited cultural advantages of metropolis are also largely illusory. On the basis of his research on American cities, [Otis Dudley] Duncan estimates that the requisite population base for a library of desirable minimum professional standards, 50,000–75,000, for an art museum, 100,000, with a somewhat higher figure for science and historical museums. . . ."

still make possible neighborhood determination of the particular ways to spend such funds.

Behind the notion of optimum level is not just the question of administrative efficiency. There is the larger question . . . of participation. One virtue of participation is a simple one. It not only creates a basis of community, by allowing people to share in decisions that affect their lives, it is also a deeply conservatizing institution for, like property, it gives people a stake in the decision which becomes binding on all.

Participation, however, is not the end of politics, as it seems to be in some of the rhetoric of the new left. It is the beginning, for politics arises in the first instance when one realizes that there is no such thing as *the* people — that no single decision can please all people. There are only *peoples,* with contradictory and conflicting ideas and interests. Suggest a jetport near some builtup area and a committee will arise to save "our" community; locate an airport on a swamp, and there will be a committee to protect the wildlife; suggest a floating airport and a group will form to keep our lakes and waters clear of pollution.

A rational politics, to the extent there can be one, is bounded by economics, that is, the recognition of the principle of relative scarcity and the necessity, therefore, of bargaining as a means of allocation and adjudication within some principle of justice. If in a multigroup society, within which there is to be effective participation, social conflict is to be regulated within bounds, then, just as mechanisms for economic bargaining were worked out in the 1940's and 1950's which brought the trade unions in the society, so mechanisms for political bargaining have to be established which allow for a tradeoff of objectives between groups. This means a more formal recognition of political groups, just as there was recognition of trade unions, and the establishment of rules of the game, within boundaries of defined communities within which the bargaining can take place.

But if economics deals with relative scarcity; politics includes the effort to gain relative advantage; and this is a never-ending process in human affairs. The political problem is to make sure that the process takes place within bounds and does not tear the society apart. And this possibility can only be realized if one strengthens that most fragile of social relations — the trust that each person has in the other that the rules of the game will be observed and that each will have his chance to participate.

Black Power

Stokely Carmichael and Charles Hamilton

Black people must redefine themselves, and only *they* can do that. Throughout this country, vast segments of the black communities are beginning to recognize the need to assert their own definitions, to reclaim their history, their culture; to create their own sense of community and togetherness. There is a growing resentment of the word "Negro," for example, because this term is the invention of our oppressor; it is *his* image of us that he describes. Many blacks are now calling themselves African-Americans, Afro-Americans or black people because that is *our* image of ourselves. When we begin to define our own image, the stereotypes — that is, lies — that our oppressor has developed will begin in the white community and end there. The black community will have a positive image of itself that *it* has created. This means we will no longer call ourselves lazy, apathetic, dumb, good-timers, shiftless, etc. Those are words used by white America to define us. If we accept these adjectives, as some of us have in the past, then we see ourselves only in a negative way, precisely the way white America wants us to see ourselves. Our incentive is broken and our will to fight is surrendered. From now on we shall view ourselves as African-Americans and as black people who are in fact energetic, determined, intelligent, beautiful and peace-loving.

There is a terminology and ethos peculiar to the black community of which black people are beginning to be no longer ashamed. Black communities are the only large segments of this society where people refer to each other as brother — soul-brother, soul-sister. Some people may look upon this as *ersatz,* as make-believe, but it is not that. It is real. It is a growing sense of community. . . .

More and more black Americans are developing this feeling. They are becoming aware that they have a history which pre-dates their forced introduction to this country. African-American history means a long history beginning on the continent of Africa, a history not taught in the standard textbooks of this country. It is absolutely essential that black people know this history, that they know their roots, that they develop an awareness of their cultural heritage. Too long have they been kept in submission by being told that they had no culture, no manifest heritage, before they landed on the slave auction blocks in this country. If black people are to know themselves as a vibrant, valiant people, they must know their roots. And they will soon learn that the Hollywood image of man-eating cannibals waiting for, and waiting on, the Great White Hunter is a lie.

. . . Only when black people fully develop this sense of community, of themselves, can they begin to deal effectively with the problems of racism in *this* country. This is what we mean by a new consciousness; this is the vital first step.

The next step is what we shall call the process of political modernization — a process which must take place if the society is to be rid of racism. "Political modernization" includes many things, but we mean by it three major concepts: (1) questioning old values and institutions of the society; (2) searching for new and different forms of political structure to solve political and economic problems; and (3) broadening the base of political participation to include more people in the decision-making process. . . .

The values of this society support a racist system; we find it incongruous to ask black people to adopt and support most of those values. We also reject the assumption that the basic institutions of this society must be preserved. The goal of black people must *not* be to assimilate into middle-class America, for that class — as a whole — is without a viable conscience as regards humanity. The values of the middle class permit the perpetuation of the ravages of the black community. The values of that class are based on material aggrandizement, not the expansion of humanity. The values of that class ultimately support cloistered little closed societies tucked away neatly in tree-lined suburbia. The values of that class do *not* lead to the creation of an open society. That class *mouths* its preference for a free, competitive society, while at the same time forcefully and even viciously denying to black people as a group the opportunity to compete.

We are not unmindful of other descriptions of the social utility of the middle class. Banfield and Wilson, in *City Politics*, concluded:

> The departure of the middle class from the central city is important in other ways. . . . The middle class supplies a social and political leavening in the life of a city. Middle-class people demand good schools and integrity in government. They support churches, lodges, parent-teacher associations, scout troops, better-housing committees, art galleries, and operas. It is the middle class, in short, that asserts a conception of the public interest. Now its activity is increasingly concentrated in the suburbs.[1]

---

[1] Edward C. Banfield and James Q. Wilson, *City Politics* (Cambridge: Harvard University Press and M.I.T. Press, 1963), p. 14.

But this same middle class manifests a sense of superior group position in regard to race. This class wants "good government" *for themselves;* it wants good schools *for its children.* At the same time, many of its members sneak into the black community by day, exploit it, and take the money home to their middle-class communities at night to support their operas and art galleries and comfortable homes. When not actually robbing, they will fight off the handful of more affluent black people who seek to move in; when they approve or even seek token integration, it applies only to black people like themselves — as "white" as possible. *This class is the backbone of institutional racism in this country.*

Thus we reject the goal of assimilation into middle-class America because the values of that class are in themselves anti-humanist and because that class as a social force perpetuates racism. We must face the fact that, in the past, what we have called the movement has not really questioned the middle-class values and institutions of this country. If anything, it has accepted those values and institutions without fully realizing their racist nature. Reorientation means an emphasis on the dignity of man, not on the sanctity of property. It means the creation of a society where human misery and poverty are repugnant to that society, not an indication of laziness or lack of initiative. The creation of new values means the establishment of a society based . . . on "free people," not "free enterprise." To do this means to modernize — *indeed, to civilize* — this country.

Supporting the old values are old political and economic structures; these must also be "modernized." We should at this point distinguish between "structures" and "system." By system, we have in mind the entire American complex of basic institutions, values, beliefs, etc. By structures, we mean the specific institutions (political parties, interest groups, bureaucratic administrations) which exist to conduct the business of that system. Obviously, the first is broader than the second. Also, the second assumes the legitimacy of the first. Our view is that, given the illegitimacy of the system, we cannot then proceed to transform that system with existing structures.

The two major political parties in this country have become nonviable entities for the legitimate representation of the real needs of masses — especially blacks — in this country. Walter Lippmann raised the same point in his syndicated column of December 8, 1966. He pointed out that the party system in the United States developed before our society became as technologically complex as it is now. He says that the ways in which men live and define themselves are changing radically. Old ideological issues, once the subject of passionate controversy, Lippmann argues, are of little interest today. He asks whether the great urban complexes — which are rapidly becoming the centers of black population in the U.S. — can be run with the same systems and ideas that derive from a time when America was a country of small villages and farms. While not addressing himself directly to the question of race, Lippmann raises a major question about our political institutions; and the crisis of race in America may be its major symptom.

Black people have seen the city planning commissions, the urban renewal commissions, the boards of education and the police departments fail to speak to their needs in a meaningful way. We must devise new structures, new institutions to replace those forms or to make them responsive. There is nothing sacred or inevitable about old institutions; the focus must be on people, not forms.

.   .   .

Essential to the modernization of structures is a broadened base of political participation. More and more people must become politically sensitive and active (we have already seen this happening in some areas of the South). People must no longer be tied, by small incentives or handouts, to a corrupting and corruptible white machine. Black people will choose their own leaders and hold those leaders responsible to *them*. A broadened base means an end to the condition described by James Wilson in *Negro Politics*, whereby "Negroes tended to be the objects rather than the subjects of civic action. Things are often done for, or about, or to, or because of Negroes, but they are less frequently done *by* Negroes." [2] Broadening the base of political participation, then, has as much to do with the quality of black participation as with the quantity. We are fully aware that the black vote, especially in the North, has been pulled out of white pockets and "delivered" whenever it was in the interest of white politicians to do so. That vote must no longer be controllable by those who have neither the interests nor the demonstrated concern of black people in mind.

As the base broadens, as more and more black people become activated, they will perceive more clearly the special disadvantages heaped upon them as a group. They will perceive that the larger society is growing more affluent while the black society is retrogressing. . . . Black people will become increasingly active as they notice that their retrogressive status exists in large measure because of values and institutions arraigned against them. They will begin to stress and strain and call the entire system into question. Political modernization will be in motion. We believe that it is now in motion. One form of that motion is Black Power.

---

[2] James Q. Wilson, *Negro Politics* (N.Y.: Free Press, 1960), p. 133.

The adoption of the concept of Black Power is one of the most legitimate and healthy developments in American politics and race relations in our time. The concept of Black Power speaks to all the needs mentioned in this chapter. It is a call for black people in this country to unite, to recognize their heritage, to build a sense of community. It is a call for black people to begin to define their own goals, to lead their own organizations and to support those organizations. It is a call to reject the racist institutions and values of this society.

The concept of Black Power rests on a fundamental premise: *Before a group can enter the open society, it must first close ranks.* By this we mean that group solidarity is necessary before a group can operate effectively from a bargaining position of strength in a pluralistic society. Traditionally, each new ethnic group in this society has found the route to social and political viability through the organization of its own institutions with which to represent its needs within the larger society. Studies in voting behavior specifically, and political behavior generally, have made it clear that politically the American pot has not melted. Italians vote for Rubino over O'Brien; Irish for Murphy over Goldberg, etc. This phenomenon may seem distasteful to some, but it has been and remains today a central fact of the American political system.

.   .   .

. . . Black people must lead and run their own organizations. Only black people can convey the revolutionary idea — and it is a revolutionary idea — that black people are able to do things themselves. Only they can help create in the community an aroused and continuing black consciousness that will provide the basis for political strength. In the past, white allies have often furthered white supremacy without the whites involved realizing it, or even wanting to do so. Black people must come together and do things for themselves. They must achieve self-identity and self-determination in order to have their daily needs met.

Black Power means, for example, that in Lowndes County, Alabama, a black sheriff can end police brutality. A black tax assessor and tax collector and county board of revenue can lay, collect, and channel tax monies for the building of better roads and schools serving black people. In such areas as Lowndes, where black people have a majority, they will attempt to use power to exercise control. This is what they seek: control. When black people lack a majority, Black Power means proper representation and sharing of control. It means the creation of power bases, of strength, from which black people can press to change local or nationwide patterns of oppression — instead of from weakness.

It does not mean *merely* putting black faces into office. Black visibility is not Black Power. Most of the black politicians around the country today are not examples of Black Power. The power must be that of a community, and emanate from there. The black politicians must start from there. The black politicians must stop being representatives of "downtown" machines, whatever the cost might be in terms of lost patronage and holiday handouts.

Black Power recognizes — it must recognize — the ethnic basis of American politics as well as the power-oriented nature of American politics. Black Power therefore calls for black people to consolidate behind their own, so that they can bargain from a position of strength. But while we endorse the *procedure* of group solidarity and identity for the purpose of attaining certain goals in the body politic, this does not mean that black people should strive for the same kind of rewards (i.e., end results) obtained by the white society. The ultimate values and goals are not domination or exploitation of other groups, but rather an effective share in the total power of the society.

Nevertheless, some observers have labeled those who advocate Black Power as racists; they have said that the call for self-identification and self-determination is "racism in reverse" or "black supremacy." This is a deliberate and absurd lie. There is no analogy — by any stretch of definition or imagination — between the advocates of Black Power and white racists. Racism is not merely exclusion on the basis of race but exclusion for the purpose of subjugating or maintaining subjugation. The goal of the racists is to keep black people on the bottom, arbitrarily and dictatorially, as they have done in this country for over three hundred years. The goal of black self-determination and black self-identity — Black Power — is full participation in the decision-making processes affecting the lives of black people, and recognition of the virtues in themselves as black people. The black people of this country have not lynched whites, bombed their churches, murdered their children and manipulated laws and institutions to maintain oppression. White racists have. Congressional laws, one after the other, have not been necessary to stop black people from oppressing others and denying others the full enjoyment of their rights. White racists have made such laws necessary. The goal of Black Power is positive and functional to a free and viable society. No white racist can make this claim.

.   .   .

In the end, we cannot and shall not offer any guarantees that Black Power, if achieved, would be non-racist. No one can predict human behavior. Social change always has unanticipated consequences. If black racism is what the larger society fears, we cannot help them. We can only state what we hope will be the result, given the fact that the present situation is unacceptable and that we have no real alternative but to

work for Black Power. The final truth is that the white society is not entitled to reassurances, even if it were possible to offer them.

We have outlined the meaning and goals of Black Power; we have
also discussed one major thing which it is not. There are others of greater
importance. The advocates of Black Power reject the old slogans and
meaningless rhetoric of previous years in the civil rights struggle. The
language of yesterday is indeed irrelevant: progress, non-violence, integration, fear of "white backlash," coalition. Let us look at the rhetoric
and see why these terms must be set aside or redefined.

One of the tragedies of the struggle against racism is that up to this
point there has been no national organization which could speak to the
growing militancy of young black people in the urban ghettos and the
black-belt South. There has been only a "civil rights" movement, whose
tone of voice was adapted to an audience of middle-class whites. It
served as a sort of buffer zone between that audience and angry young
blacks. It claimed to speak for the needs of a community, but it did not
speak in the tone of that community. None of its so-called leaders could
go into a rioting community and be listened to. In a sense, the blame
must be shared — along with the mass media — by those leaders for what
happened in Watts, Harlem, Chicago, Cleveland and other places. Each
time the black people in those cities saw Dr. Martin Luther King get
slapped they became angry. When they saw little black girls bombed to
death *in a church* and civil rights workers ambushed and murdered, they
were angrier; and when nothing happened, they were steaming mad. We
had nothing to offer that they could see, except to go out and be beaten
again. We helped to build their frustration.

We had only the old language of love and suffering. And in most
places — that is, from the liberals and middle class — we got back the old
language of patience and progress. The civil rights leaders were saying
to the country: "Look, you guys are supposed to be nice guys, and we are
only going to do what we are supposed to do. Why do you beat us up?
Why don't you give us what we ask? Why don't you straighten your-
selves out?" For the masses of black people, this language resulted in
virtually nothing. In fact, their objective day-to-day condition worsened.
The unemployment rate among black people increased while that among
whites declined. Housing conditions in the black communities deteriorated. Schools in the black ghettos continued to plod along on outmoded
techniques, inadequate curricula, and with all too many tired and indifferent teachers. Meanwhile, the President picked up the refrain of
"We Shall Overcome" while the Congress passed civil rights law after
civil rights law, only to have them effectively nullified by deliberately
weak enforcement. "Progress is being made," we were told.

Such language, along with admonitions to remain non-violent and
fear the white backlash, convinced some that that course was the *only*

course to follow. It misled some into believing that a black minority could bow its head and get whipped into a meaningful position of power. The very notion is absurd. The white society devised the language, adopted the rules and had the black community narcotized into believing that that language and those rules were, in fact, relevant. The black community was told time and again how *other* immigrants finally won *acceptance:* that is, by following the Protestant Ethic of Work and Achievement. They worked hard; therefore, they achieved. We were not told that it was by building Irish Power, Italian Power, Polish Power or Jewish Power that these groups got themselves together and operated from positions of strength. We were not told that "the American dream" wasn't designed for black people. That while today, to whites, the dream may *seem* to include black people, it cannot do so by the very nature of this nation's political and economic system, which imposes institutional racism on the black masses if not upon every individual black.

.   .   .

When the concept of Black Power is set forth, many people immediately conjure up notions of violence. The country's reaction to the Deacons for Defense and Justice, which originated in Louisiana, is instructive. Here is a group which realized that the "law" and law enforcement agencies would not protect people, so they had to do it themselves. If a nation fails to protect its citizens, then that nation cannot condemn those who take up the task themselves. The Deacons and all other blacks who resort to self-defense represent a simple answer to a simple question: what man would not defend his family and home from attack?

But this frightened some white people, because they knew that black people would now fight back. They knew that this was precisely what *they* would have long since done if *they* were subjected to the injustices and oppression heaped on blacks. Those of us who advocate Black Power are quite clear in our own minds that a "non-violent" approach to civil rights is an approach black people cannot afford and a luxury white people do not deserve. It is crystal clear to us — and it must become so with the white society — *that there can be no social order without social justice.* White people must be made to understand that they must stop messing with the black people, or the blacks *will* fight back!

Next, we must deal with the term "integration." According to its advocates, social justice will be accomplished by "integrating the Negro into the mainstream institutions of the society from which he has been traditionally excluded." This concept is based on the assumption that there is nothing of value in the black community and that little of value could be created among black people. The thing to do is siphon off the "acceptable" black people into the surrounding middle-class white community.

The goals of integrationists are middle-class goals, articulated primarily by a small group of Negroes with middle-class aspirations or status. Their kind of integration has meant that a few blacks "make it," leaving the black community, sapping it of leadership potential and know-how. . . . Those token Negroes — absorbed into a white mass — are of no value to the remaining black masses. They become meaningless show-pieces for a conscience-soothed white society. Such people will state that they would prefer to be treated "only as individuals, not as Negroes"; that they "are not and should not be preoccupied with race." This is a totally unrealistic position. In the first place, black people have not suffered as individuals but as members of a group; therefore, their liberation lies in group action. . . . Helping *individual* black people to solve their problems on an *individual* basis does little to alleviate the mass of black people. Secondly, while color blindness *may* be a sound goal ultimately, we must realize that race is an overwhelming fact of life in this historical period. There is no black man in this country who can live "simply as a man." His blackness is an ever-present fact of this racist society, whether he recognizes it or not. It is unlikely that this or the next generation will witness the time when race will no longer be relevant in the conduct of public affairs and in public policy decision-making. To realize this and to attempt to deal with it does not make one a racist or overly preoccupied with race; it puts one in the forefront of a significant *struggle*. If there is no intense struggle today, there will be no meaningful results tomorrow.

"Integration" as a goal today speaks to the problem of blackness not only in an unrealistic way but also in a despicable way. It is based on complete acceptance of the fact that in order to have a decent house or education, black people must move into a white neighborhood or send their children to a white school. This reinforces, among both black and white, the idea that "white" is automatically superior and "black" is by definition inferior.

·   ·   ·

The racial and cultural personality of the black community must be preserved and that community must win its freedom while preserving its cultural integrity. Integrity includes a pride — in the sense of self-acceptance, not chauvinism — in being black, in the historical attainments and contributions of black people. No person can be healthy, complete and mature if he must deny a part of himself; this is what "integration" has required thus far. This is the essential difference between integration as it is currently practiced and the concept of Black Power.

·   ·   ·

The Search for New Forms

We are aware that it has become commonplace to pinpoint and describe the ills of our urban ghettos. The social, political and economic problems are so acute that even a casual observer cannot fail to see that something is wrong. While description is plentiful, however, there remains a blatant timidity about what to *do* to solve the problems.

Neither rain nor endless "definitive," costly reports nor stop-gap measures will even approach a solution to the explosive situation in the nation's ghettos. This country cannot begin to solve the problems of the ghettos as long as it continues to hang on to outmoded structures and institutions. A political party system that seeks only to "manage conflict" and hope for the best will not be able to serve a growing body of alienated black people. An educational system which, year after year, continues to cripple hundreds of thousands of black children must be replaced by wholly new mechanisms of control and management. We must begin to think and operate in terms of entirely new and substantially different forms of expression.

It is crystal clear that the initiative for such changes will have to come from the black community. We cannot expect white America to begin to move forcefully on these problems unless and until black America begins to move. This means that black people must organize themselves without regard for what is traditionally acceptable, precisely because the traditional approaches have failed. It means that black people must make demands without regard to their initial "respectability," precisely because "respectable" demands have not been sufficient.

The northern urban ghettos are in many ways different from the black-belt South, but in neither area will substantial change come about until black people organize independently to exert power. As noted in earlier chapters, black people already have the voting potential to control the politics of entire southern counties. . . . These people should concentrate on forming independent political parties and not waste time trying to reform or convert the racist parties. In the North, it is no less important that independent groups be formed. It has been clearly shown that when black people attempt to get within one of the two major parties in the cities, they become co-opted and their interests are shunted to the background. They become expendable.

We must begin to think of the black community as a base of organization to control institutions in that community. Control of the ghetto schools must be taken out of the hands of "professionals," most of whom have long since demonstrated their insensitivity to the needs and problems of the black child. These "experts" bring with them middle-class biases, unsuitable techniques and materials; these are, at best, dysfunctional and at worst destructive. . . . Virtually no attention is paid to the wishes and demands of the parents, especially the black parents. This is totally unacceptable.

Black parents should seek as their goal the actual control of the public schools in their community: hiring and firing of teachers, selection of teaching materials, determination of standards, etc. This can be done with a committee of teachers. The traditional, irrelevant "See Dick, See Jane, Run Dick, Run Jane, White House, Nice Farm" nonsense must be ended. The principals and as many teachers as possible of the ghetto schools should be black. The children will be able to see their kind in positions of leadership and authority. It should never occur to anyone that a brand new school can be built in the heart of the black community and then given a white person to head it. The fact is that in this day and time, it is crucial that race be taken into account in determining policy of this sort. Some people will, again, view this as "reverse segregation" or as "racism." It is not. It is emphasizing race in a positive way: not to subordinate or rule over others but to overcome the effects of centuries in which race has been used to the detriment of the black man.

.   .   .

The tenements of the ghetto represent another target of high priority. Tenants in buildings should form cohesive organizations — unions — to act in their common interest vis-à-vis the absentee slumlord. Obviously, rents should be withheld if the owner does not provide adequate services and decent facilities. But more importantly, the black community should set as a prime goal the policy of having the owner's rights forfeited if he does not make repairs: forfeited and turned over to the black organization, which would not only manage the property but own it outright. The absentee slumlord is perpetuating a socially detrimental condition, and he should not be allowed to hide behind the rubric of property rights. The black community must insist that the goal of human rights take precedent over property rights, and back up that insistence in ways which will make it in the self-interest of the white society to act morally. Behavior — in this case, the misuse of property — can be regulated to any extent the power structure wishes. No one should be naïve enough to think that an owner will give up his property easily, but the black community, properly organized and mobilized, could apply pressure that would make him choose between the alternatives of forfeiture or compliance. Thousands of black people refusing to pay rents month after month in the ghettos could have more than a salutary effect on public policy.

. . . Virtually all of the money earned by merchants and exploiters of the black ghetto leaves those communities. Properly organized black groups should seek to establish a community rebate plan. The black people in a given community would organize and refuse to do business with any merchant who did not agree to "reinvest," say, forty to fifty percent of his net profit in the indigenous community. This contribution could take many forms: providing additional jobs for black people, donating scholarship funds for students, supporting certain types of community organizations. An agreement would be reached between the merchants and the black consumers. If a merchant wants customers from a black community, he must be made to understand that he has to contribute to that community. If he chooses not to do so, he will not be patronized, and the end result will be *no* profits from that community. Contractors who seek to do business in the black community would also be made to understand that they face a boycott if they do not donate to the black community.

Such a community rebate plan will require careful organization and tight discipline on the part of the black people. But it is possible, and has in fact already been put into effect by some ethnic communities. White America realizes the market in the black community; black America must begin to realize the potential of that market.

Under the present institutional arrangements, no one should think that the mere election of a few black people to local or national office will solve the problem of political representation. There are now ten black people on the City Council in Chicago, but there are not more than two or three (out of the total of fifty) who will speak out forcefully. The fact is that the present political institutions are not geared to giving the black minority an effective voice. Two needs arise from this.

First, it is important that the black communities in these northern ghettos form independent party groups to elect their own choices to office when and where they can. It should not be assumed that "you cannot beat City Hall." It has been done, as evidenced by the 1967 aldermanic elections in one of the tightest machine cities in the country: Chicago. In the Sixth Ward, an independent black candidate, Sammy Rayner, defeated an incumbent, machine-backed black alderman. . . .

The cynics will say that Rayner will be just one voice, unable to accomplish anything unless he buckles under to the Daley machine. Let us be very clear: we do not endorse Rayner nor are we blind to the problems he faces. It is the job of the machine to crush such men or to co-opt them before they grow in numbers and power. At the same time, men like Rayner are useful only so long as they speak to the community's broad needs; . . . black visibility is not Black Power. If Rayner does not remain true to his constituents, then they should dislodge him as decisively as they did his predecessor. This establishes the principle that the black politicians must first be responsive to his constituents, not to the white machine. The problem then is to resist the forces which would crush or co-opt while building community strength so that more of such men can be elected and compelled to act in the community's interest.

.   .   .

Let no one protest that this type of politics is naïve or childish or fails to understand the "rules of the game." The price of going along with the "regulars" is too high to pay for the so-called benefits received. The rewards of independence can be considerable. It is too soon to say precisely where this new spirit of independence could take us. New forms may lead to a new political force. Hopefully, this force might move to create new national and local political parties — or, more accurately, the first *legitimate* political parties. Some have spoken of a "third party" or "third political force." But from the viewpoint of community needs and popular participation, no existing force or party in this country has ever been relevant. A force which is relevant would therefore be a first — something truly new.

The second implication of the political dilemma facing black people is that ultimately they may have to spearhead a drive to revamp completely the present institutions of representation. If the Rayners are continually outvoted, if the grievances of the black community continue to be overlooked, then it will become necessary to devise wholly new forms of local political representation. There is nothing sacred about the system of electing candidates to serve as aldermen, councilmen, etc., by wards or districts. Geographical representation is not inherently right. Perhaps political interests have to be represented in some entirely different manner — such as community-parent control of schools, unions of tenants, unions of welfare recipients actually taking an official role in running the welfare departments. If political institutions do not meet the needs of the people, if the people finally believe that those institutions do not express their own values, then those institutions must be discarded. It is wasteful and inefficient, not to mention unjust, to continue imposing old forms and ways of doing things on a people who no longer view those forms and ways as functional.

We see independent politics . . . as the first step toward implementing something new. Voting year after year for the traditional party and its silent representatives gets the black community nowhere; voters then get their own candidates, but these may become frustrated by the power and organization of the machines. The next logical step is to demand more meaningful structures, forms and ways of dealing with long-standing problems.

We see this as the potential power of the ghettos. In a real sense, it is similar to what is taking place in the South: the move in the direction of independent politics — and from there, the move toward the development of wholly new political institutions. If these proposals also sound impractical, utopian, then we ask: what other real alternatives exist? There are none; the choice lies between a genuinely new approach and maintaining the brutalizing, destructive, violence-breeding life of the ghettos as they exist today. From the viewpoint of black people, that is no choice.

Black Panther Party Programs — Serving the People

Bobby Seale

. . . The Black Panther Party [has] tried to reach millions of people both to organize resistance to fascism and to find out about, and receive service from, the basic community programs that we have already set up and will be setting up in the future. This is what we call a broad, massive, people's type of political machinery. It developed out of the rising tide of fascism in America, the rapid attempt on the part of the power structure to try to wipe out the Black Panther Party and other progressive organizations, and the use of more troops and more police forces to occupy our communities.

The cops in Los Angeles and several other places have walked in on the Free Breakfast for Children Program to try to intimidate the children and the Party. They come down there with their guns, they draw a gun or two, say a few words and walk all over the place, with shotguns in their hands. Then the little kids go home and say, "Mama, the police came into the Breakfast for Children Program." This is the power structure's technique to try to destroy the program. It's an attempt to scare the people away from sending their children to the Breakfast Program and at the same time, trying to intimidate the Black Panther Party.

Meanwhile, through the politicians and the media they try to mislead the people about the value of such a program and the political nature of such a program. We say that we want that program, not just right now for some political purpose — we say that the program should survive right into the future for years and years. The Party's community programs are the peoples' programs that we define as revolutionary, community, socialistic programs.

A lot of people misunderstand the politics of these programs; some people have a tendency to call them reform programs. They're not reform programs; they're actually revolutionary community programs. A revolutionary program is one set forth by revolutionaries, by those who want to change the existing system to a better system. A reform program is set up by the existing exploitative system as an appeasing handout, to fool the people and to keep them quiet. Examples of these programs are poverty programs, youth work programs, and things like that which are set up by the present demagogic government. Generally they're set up to appease the people for a short period of time, and then are phased out and forgotten about.

The objective of programs set forth by revolutionaries like the Black Panther Party is to educate the masses of the people to the politics of changing the system. The politics are related to people's needs, to a hungry stomach, or to getting rid of the vicious pigs with their revolvers and clubs. The revolutionary struggle becomes bloody when the pig power structure attacks organizations or groups of people who go forth with these programs.

We started the Free Breakfast for Children Program by asking businessmen in the black community and outside of it, to donate food and money. We also moved to get as many other people in the community as possible to work on these programs and take over running them. The programs are generally started off in churches. In one case we actually got a Free Breakfast for Children going in the school itself, which was very, very good, because the school cafeteria facilities and everything were used; this was over in Marin County, north of San Francisco. We generally work out of churches because the churches all have facilities, like a large hall, a kitchen, tables and chairs, etc. Members of the Party get up early in the morning, at 6:00 A.M. to get down and begin preparing the food so when the kids start coming at 7:00 and 7:30, everything is ready. We also try to get as many people from the community to schedule themselves, for one or two days out of the week to come in and work on the Breakfast for Children Program. It has to be a very organized thing so that it's speedy and at the same time the children get good, wholesome breakfasts.

There are millions of people in this country who are living below subsistence; welfare mothers, poor white people, Mexican-Americans, Chicano peoples, Latinos, and black people. This type of program, if spread out, should readily relate to the needs of the people. Donations of food and money can be gotten from churches, stores, and companies. When the stores and milk companies don't donate, people should leaflet the community. Any particular chain foodstores that can't donate a small, small percentage of its profits or one penny from every dollar it makes from the community, to Breakfast for Children and other community programs, should be boycotted. We don't ever threaten or anything like that, but we tell the people in the community that the businessman exploits them and makes thousands and thousands of dollars, and that he won't donate to a Breakfast for Children Program that's actually tax deductible. This is exposing the power structure for what it is, the robbery of poor oppressed people by avaricious businessmen. Black, brown, and red people, and poor whites can all have the same basic program, and that means we're breaking down racism and focusing in on the power structure.

Another program that we're setting up is free medicine and free medical care. We'll be setting those up in community centers. If we start off with nothing more than a doctor and his bag, and some aspirin, this is the beginning of a free health clinic, the beginning of free medicine for the people in the communities. We work to serve the people in the communities on a very practical level.

Right in the Bay Area we have some twenty-five doctors and medical students who've pledged their time to be scheduled in different community centers that we're putting up and this will be free of charge. We have free health clinics all over the country and we are putting more up. . . .

In addition, Charles R. Garry is contacting a lot of lawyers who are opening their eyes and beginning to see that the black community needs more legal aid. So we're putting together free legal services, which will also be set up in the community centers. The poverty programs that have free legal service are always told that they can't get funds if they're at all political. That's done so they won't expose the power structure and the injustices of the system. They only handle civil cases. Our legal aid will handle both civil and criminal cases.

Another thing we'll be doing is heavy voter registration. The purpose of this registration will be to get more black and poor people on the juries so we can really be tried in courts by juries of our peers. The D.A.'s will try to get all white racist juries or maybe to put one jive Uncle Tom on them, but it'll be much harder if a lot of blacks are registered and are on the jury panel that they pick from. Black people have to understand the experience of serving on juries because black people are railroaded in these courts. Poor oppressed people are railroaded in courts because they don't have funds to obtain lawyers. A lot of the older people are frightened or allow themselves to be frightened away from being jury

members, and a lot of black people move around so much that they
don't bother to re-register. It's a real problem, but we've got to educate
the people to the fact that they should be on the rolls for jury duty. Then
we can begin to get some revolutionary justice. Right now the type of
so-called justice that's being meted out to a majority of the poor oppressed people is the "injustice" of racism and capitalistic exploitation.

The Black Panther Party has black caucuses, Black Panther caucuses
in a number of unions, and we definitely are working with the union
people. We're not putting in Black Panther caucuses as racist groups.
We're talking about a caucus that works in conjunction with the union to
help educate the rest of the members of the union to the fact that they
can have a better life, too. We want the workers to understand that they
must control the means of production, and that they should begin to use
their power to control the means of production to serve all the people.

Workers have high taxes taken away from their wages, but they
should begin to understand that they have to move not only for a 15 or
20 percent wage raise, because taxes have gone up, and not only for
better working conditions, but also because they have to realize the
need to use their working power for the benefit of all the other poor
oppressed people.

They should use their union power to create employment for more
of the poor people throughout the country. We're advocating that
workers begin to move to control the means of production by first demanding thirty-hour work weeks with the same forty-hour pay. By doing
this, they will automatically open up more jobs. These jobs can be filled
by poor, unemployed people. This would be part of the program of educating the masses of the workers to be a political force against the three
levels of oppression — the avaricious, big-time, greedy businessmen, the
demagogic politicians who lie and use the unions, and also the fascist pig
cops who have been used in the past and are used today to break up the
workers' constitutional rights to strike and redress their grievances.

Employed or unemployed, workers must unite with each other and
with the community. They should be registered voters, too, and serve on
jury panels and circulate the community control of police petition, too.

Another Black Panther Party program is the Liberation Schools.
These schools are held in the afternoons, along with the free breakfasts
and free lunches. They're held in churches and the community centers.
We see the Liberation Schools as a supplement to the existing institutions, which still teach racism to children, both white and black. The
youth have to understand that the revolutionary struggle in this country
that's now being waged is not a race struggle but a class struggle. This
is what the Liberation Schools are all about.

We are working to show children that a person's skin color is not important, but in fact it's a class struggle against the avaricious business-man and the small ruling class who exploit us and perpetuate the racism that's rampant in our communities. When we teach Black American History, we teach it in terms of the class struggle, not in terms of a race struggle.

In New York we also started a free clothing program. Black Panther Party members went out and asked businessmen to donate sets of clothes, for school children on up to teenagers. We tried to get brand new clothing, because black people are tired of hand-me-downs. Some of the clothing was very good clothing that people never came back and picked up from dry cleaners. We got all kinds of clothing together, but our primary objective was to get free clothing for the people by asking the businessmen to donate two complete changes of clothes for children. This is especially important before school begins in September and in mid-term around January. When this free clothing program got kicked off, some five or six hundred black people in Harlem, mothers and welfare people, came down and got the clothing for their kids.

It takes a lot of work, and a lot of people donating time and funds to run these programs. The programs are not run by the fascist government at all. Naturally, these programs spread and as they begin to reach more and more people, the Party is moving closer and closer to implementing the ten-point platform and program of the Black Panther Party. When we have community socialistic programs such as these, and move them to a real level where people actually begin to receive help from them, it shows the people that by unity, by working and unifying around such programs, we can begin to end the oppressive conditions.

The Black Panther Party is not stupid at all in understanding the politics of the situation. We understand that the avaricious, demagogic, ruling class will use racist police departments and mass media to distort the real objectives of the Black Panther Party. The more we're successful with the programs, the more we'll be attacked. We don't take guns with us to implement these programs, but we understand and know from our own history that we're going to be attacked, and that we have to be able to defend ourselves. They're going to attack us viciously and fascistically and try to say it was all justifiable homicide, in the same manner they've always attacked black people in the black communities.

We also go forth to advocate the right to self-defense from unjust attack by racist, fascist pigs. Even when the policemen come into our communities with guns and tanks and the National Guard, we have the right to self-defense. Brothers and sisters shouldn't riot in large numbers. They should work in small groups of three, four, and five, to fight back when they attack our communities with tanks and start blasting buildings away and killing people. When they come and occupy our community and start killing people, those brothers running in threes, fours, and fives are going to have to know how to stop those tanks and those guardsmen from brutalizing and killing and murdering us.

We aren't hungry for violence; we don't want violence. Violence is ugly, guns are ugly. But we understand that there are two kinds of violence: the violence that is perpetrated against our people by the fascist aggression of the power structure; and self-defense — a form of violence used to defend ourselves from the unjust violence that's inflicted upon us. The power structure metes this violence upon the Black Panther Party because we've implemented programs that are actually exposing the government, and they're being implemented and put together by a revolutionary political party.

The freeing of political prisoners is also on the program of the Black Panther Party, because we have now, at this writing, over 300 Black Panthers who have court cases that are pending. In addition there have been hundreds of arrests, unjust arrests of Party members, who were exercising their constitutional rights. We believe in exercising our constitutional rights of freedom of assembly, of freedom of the press (the Black Panther Party newspaper), our constitutional right to bear arms, to be able to defend ourselves when attacked, and all the others. So we've been arrested.

What has to be understood is that they intend to destroy our basic programs. This is very important to understand. The fact that they murder Black Panther Party members, conduct attacks and raids on our offices, arrest us and lie about us, is all an attempt to stop these basic programs that we're putting together in the community. The people learn from these programs because they're clear examples, and the power structure wants to stop that learning.

We do not believe in the power structure controlling these programs, but we do believe in making the power structure admit that it has to change the system, because we, the people, united and together, can begin to change our conditions ourselves. We have to move with the power of the people, with the workers and the laboring masses of the people, to have control of the means of production and make the power structure step back. We're going to have to defend ourselves with guns because we know we're going to be attacked and we know they're going to attempt to make more political prisoners.

Community control of police is the key. We've got to have community control of the police in every city where there exists police brutality, in every metropolis in America where black people, Latino people, and Chinese people live in large numbers. In all these cities, and where there are progressive and liberal white people who are protesting, police forces have been doubled, tripled, and quadrupled, and fascist oppression has been meted out upon the heads of all of us. The workers too are attacked and threatened by police when they strike and protest over their conditions.

Our community control of the police campaign is a petition drive. Registered voters will sign the petition and will vote into their city charters a new legal structure for the police department. The people will be voting in a law that says that all policemen who patrol the community, must live in the community. They will be voting in a decentralized police department.

We will have neighborhood divisions with neighborhood councils, who are duly elected in the particular neighborhoods. We'll have two, three, four, and five police departments that work in conjunction together through the commissioners of particular neighborhood divisions, so there will not be a single police chief. These commissioners can be removed by the duly elected neighborhood councils. The fifteen-man neighborhood councils will be able to appoint and fire a commissioner, will be able to discipline police officers who are unjust, or who get out of hand, and will be able to set salaries and pay the police officers. The people throughout the city will control the police, rather than the power structure, the avaricious businessmen, and demagogic politicians who presently control them. The point of community control of police is that those people living in those neighborhoods will actually do the hiring and firing of the policemen who patrol that area, and those policemen will be people from those neighborhoods — black police for a black neighborhood, Chinese for a Chinese neighborhood, white for a white neighborhood, etc. The tax money which used to be given to the central police department will be divided up among the neighborhood divisions. All the facilities, all the cars, all the equipment for the police that the city now owns, will be in the hands and in the control of the people in the community.

Now when this begins to move, the power structure is gonna say, "OK, you can have civilian review boards." But all that does is allow the same old fascist power structure to keep control of the police while you have a front civilian review board, and this is not what we're talking about at all. What we're talking about is righteous community control, where the people who control the police are elected by the people of the community. Those people who are elected have to live in the community. They can be removed by circulating petitions for re-elections if they go wrong. We know that such a program is very positive and necessary in order for the people to have power in this country and to stop the avaricious businessman from ruling us with guns and violating our constitutional rights.

Everybody knows that they lied about the way they murdered

brother Fred Hampton, and then tried to justify it. Mitchell, Agnew, and Nixon are running an operation to wipe out the Black Panther Party behind the scenes, when they send the Civil Rights Division of the Justice Department in to investigate the slaying of brother Fred Hampton and Mark Clark. We don't want them to investigate anything. We want the civilian and people's investigation to come forth. Thousands of people went into the brothers' apartment and investigated, and found out that it was outright murder; that there was no shoot-out, but the brothers in fact, were shot in their bedrooms while they slept. This is outright murder, this is outright fascism. The next attack was on the Los Angeles office, a few days later. Community control of police is where it's at. The only other choice is guerrilla warfare.

Guerrilla warfare is going to exist if the power structure is not stopped with community control of the police. One of the reasons the people have to work on the community control of police campaign is to curtail civil war in America, because it's at that point right now. Community control of police is one of the most functional and most necessary programs to make all the other basic community programs work.

The Panthers

Ronald Steel

I went to Oakland, dead end of the westward course of empire, and home of the Black Panthers, to take a look at a conference of the revolutionary Left. Oakland, where the American dream ends at the Pacific, and the nightmare begins, is a familiar kind of industrial city: high-rise office buildings and apartments downtown, plasticene shopping centers on the fringe, and slowly decaying wooden houses in between. West Oakland, facing the Bay and the gleaming hills of San Francisco beyond, is the ghetto were the Black Panthers were born. It is a California-style ghetto, with one-family houses and neglected yards, where poverty wears a more casual face and despair is masked by sunshine.

The Panthers . . . summoned their friends — a mixed bag of revolutionaries, radicals, pacifists, and liberals — to assemble in Oakland to form what they called a "united front against fascism." The phrase itself had a defensive ring, reminiscent of the ill-fated Popular Fronts of the 1930s, and it seemed to indicate that the Panthers were in trouble. . . .

Like so many other gatherings of the radical Left, the conference produced little unity but a great deal of dissatisfaction. Most of the sessions were disorganized and, with a few exceptions, the speeches were little more than an interminable series of spot announcements denouncing the evils of rampant fascism. No one seemed interested in discussing whether fascism had indeed arrived in America. This, like so much of the other rhetoric of the revolutionary Left, was simply taken for granted.

When the three-day conference finally rambled to an end, the dwindling band of white radicals drifted away in dismay, wondering what kind of bag the Panthers had got themselves into. . . .

Why did the Panthers call such a conference in the first place? At least in part because they have been under increasing harassment and intimidation by the police and the FBI. . . . The Panthers see a concerted plot by the federal government, with the assistance of local police, to destroy them. Recently Spiro Agnew has described them as a "completely irresponsible, anarchistic group of criminals," and J. Edgar Hoover has called them, among black militants, the "greatest threat to the internal security of the country."

.   .   .

Now that the federal government has joined the local police in operations against the Panthers — Attorney-General Mitchell is trying to get the courts to admit wiretap evidence against the Panthers and other groups ostensibly threatening "national security" — the strengthening of their links with white radical groups is more important than before. This is partly a question of ideology, for the Panthers insist they are not racist. Indeed, they are virtually the only black militant group that actually welcomes white allies. It is also a question of survival, for without support from the white community they fear they will be picked off and destroyed.

Vilified and distorted by the press, which has little understanding of their program, they are generally viewed as an anarchistic band of gun-toting, white-hating thugs. This allows the police and federal officials to abridge their constitutional rights in a way they would not dare to use against whites. Provocation, false arrests, trumped-up charges, illegal detention, barbaric treatment, excessive bail, and even legal murder — this is everyday treatment for the Panthers. They have been defined as threatening to white society, and therefore beyond the normal protection of the law.

Is it likely that members of a white political organization, even the

Ku Klux Klan, would be rounded up in the middle of the night, thrown into jails dispersed around the city, kept under maximum security and even solitary confinement, detained in prison for months on exhorbitant bail for a crime that was never committed, and charged with plotting irrational actions, without the liberal press voicing its indignation? Yet this is precisely what has happened to the New York twenty-one. If you let it happen to us, the Panthers are saying to white liberals, it will happen to anyone who dissents. After the lessons of Chicago and Berkeley, white radicals, at least, are beginning to believe the Panther contention that we're all niggers now.

The Panthers are convinced that those in power are out to get them as much for their socialist ideology and their efforts to organize the black community into an effective political force as for their defensive actions against the police. Heavily into the economics and sociology of Marxism, the Panthers see racism in this country as an integral part of the capitalist system. "Capitalism deprives us all of self-determination," Huey Newton has said. "Only in the context of socialism can men practice the self-determination necessary to provide for their freedom."

The Panthers are absolutely serious when they talk of the need for "socialism"; and this is what distinguishes them from the other black militant and black power groups. They see themselves as "revolutionary nationalists," as opposed to "cultural nationalists," who seek black pride in separatist movements, religious cults, and emulation of ancient African culture. "The revolutionary nationalist," according to Huey Newton, "sees that there is no hope for cultural or individual expression, or even hope that his people can exist as a unique entity in a complex whole as long as the bureaucratic capitalist is in control." On the other hand, "cultural nationalism," explained David Hilliard, "is basically related to the physiological need for a return back to Africa in the culture, and we don't see that that is really relevant to any revolution, because culture never frees anyone. As Fanon says, the only culture is that of the revolution."

The reference to Fanon is instructive, for the Panthers, as can readily be seen from the writings of Huey Newton and Eldridge Cleaver, have been deeply influenced by the black psychiatrist from Martinique who died in the service of the Algerian revolution. *The Wretched of the Earth* is a kind of revolutionary Bible for them, and one with far more emotional impact than the Little Red Books which are so often quoted. Both Newton and Cleaver, freely acknowledging their debt to Fanon, have described black people as forming an oppressed colony within the white mother country, the United States. The colony is kept in line by an occupying army — white policemen who live outside the ghetto — and is exploited by businessmen and politicians.

The exploiters can be black as well as white, for the enemy, they insist, is not so much racism as capitalism, which creates and nourishes it. As would be expected of socialist revolutionaries, the Panthers are opposed to black capitalism, which Huey Newton has described as a "giant stride *away* from liberation . . ." since ". . . the rules of black capitalism, and the limits of black capitalism are set by the white power structure." Explaining his opposition, Newton has written:

> There can be no real black capitalism because no blacks control the means of production. All blacks can do is have illusions. They can dream of the day when they might share ownership of the means of production. But there is no free enterprise in America. We have monopoly capitalism which is a closed society of white industrialists and their protectors, white politicians in Washington.

According to the Panthers, black power has been absorbed into the establishment, shorn of its horns, and transformed into innocent black capitalism, which even Richard Nixon can praise because it poses no threat to the white power structure.

As an alternative they offer "revolution," to liberate oppressed minorities in the United States and break the stranglehold of capitalism on the economically underdeveloped countries of the Third World. Until there is some form of socialist "revolution" in America, they believe, small countries will remain prey to neo-colonialism and imperialism. The revolutionary in America, therefore, carries the world upon his shoulders. The black man in America will not be free until the white man is free, and until the white man is free, until America is transformed by a socialist revolution, the underdeveloped countries of the world will remain in economic chains.

Such a comprehensive theory clearly has its inadequacies. Although blacks can be described as forming an internal colony within the United States, they do not supply raw materials, labor, or markets to capitalism in the same way as the colonies did. There is, moreover, no evidence at present that the United States is entering a revolutionary crisis that will involve the mass of workers. Nor can the Panthers have much success in breaking away into a separate state. What happens, as has been asked, when there's a border dispute? (It is not fair, however, to charge the Panthers with advocating political separatism. They claim neither to favor it nor to discourage it; they simply demand that a UN-supervised plebiscite be held on the issue in the black colony. In any case, this is not an immediate problem, and certainly not a major objective for them.)

The Panthers' Marxist-Leninist language, combined with their Fanonist theories of psychological alienation and Third World solidarity, makes them particularly appealing to middle-class white militants, who share their ideology but lack their discipline. White radicals also lack the black man's non-reducible commitment to black liberation: the fact that he is black. A white radical can cop out any time he wants by cutting his hair and behaving like a square. A black man cannot escape. In fighting against the system he becomes, by his very act of resistance, a hero to white radicals. As Huey Newton has explained:

> Black people in America, in the black colony, are oppressed because we're black and we're exploited. The whites are rebels, many of them from the middle class, and as far as any overt oppression this is not the case. So therefore I call their rejection of the system somewhat of an abstract thing. They're looking for new heroes. . . . In pressing for new heroes the young white revolution found the heroes in the black colony at home and in the colonies throughout the world. . . .

While Newton favors alliances with white radicals, he points out that "there can be no black-white unity until there first is black unity." Only blacks can decide the proper strategy for the black community.

White radicals, divided on tactics and ideology, and split into a plethora of competing, often hostile, groups, have only recently begun to deal with some of the problems of "black liberation." There has always been sympathy for the black struggle, and even participation when it was permitted during the civil rights movement. But things have changed greatly since Stokely Carmichael kicked the whites out of SNCC and the Panthers moved into the streets with guns. Unable to lead the black movement, white radicals are no longer even sure how they can aid it. Uncertain of their tactics, and confused about their goals, they revert to ready-made formulas, like "revolution," to deal with a multitude of complexities that are too difficult to analyze right now. Some assert that groups like the Panthers are the "vanguard" of the revolution — as though this justified white radicals' inability to work out a coherent theory or strategy.

The Vietnam war no longer serves as the great rallying point for the Left that it used to. Radicals have a good deal to protest about, but they seem to focus their energies on largely symbolic issues, such as the People's Park, or on the predictable seizure of university administration buildings. The radical Left is hung up on revolution, but doesn't seem to have the vaguest idea of how it should be organized, or how the country would be run if such an event ever took place.

For the time being the Left is divided, confused, and hopelessly weak and inept, and there is no more telling sign of the insecurity of those who hold power in America than that they are seriously worried about its activities. The McClellan committee solemnly listens to the "threats to national security" posed by campus agitators, while Congress debates unconstitutional limitations on dissent and hysterical punishments against demonstrators. Not only do conventional politicians fear the Panthers, who at least carry guns and who can be described as a para-military organization, but even the scholastic debaters of the Students for a Democratic Society. In spite of all the spies and *agents provocateurs* it planted at the SDS convention in Chicago this past June, the politicians and the police apparently failed to learn that the Left is too schismatic and ego-centered to threaten anybody.

.   .   .

Never very comfortable with SDS, the Panthers feel much more at home with the "brothers off the block," the street people, the lumpenproletariat, to use another phase they are fond of, than with the guilt-ridden children of the white bourgeoisie. With a few exceptions, such as Huey Newton and Bobby Seale, they have had little formal education beyond high school, and some of the most intelligent do not even have that. . . .

"We relate to the Young Patriots" (a white, recently radicalized Chicago group that is organizing nationally), David Hilliard stated, "because they're operating on the same class level as the Black Panther Party." They also share a similar rhetoric.

.   .   .

The Young Patriots started out as a street gang and gradually developed a political consciousness that led them in the direction of the Panthers. A similar attempt at radicalizing organized labor is being made with the creation of the League of Revolutionary Black Workers, a federation of several Detroit-based workers' groups such as the Dodge Revolutionary Union Movement (DRUM) and its equivalents at Ford (FRUM), Chrysler (CRUM), and elsewhere. The all-black League was started, according to John Watson, one of its founders, "because the working class is already divided between the races, and because it is necessary for black workers to be able to act independently of white workers."

White workers have been encouraged to form radical organizations of their own to work out a common strategy with black union revolutionaries, but progress has been slow. Speaking of such a group at the Detroit *News*, Watson observed, ". . . although a number of the white guys who were down there had risen above the levels of racism and understood the exploitative nature of the company and of the system, they had very little experience in organizing to fight oppression and exploitation." As with the Panthers, these black workers consider themselves to be in the "vanguard of the revolutionary movement," and see most whites still on the fringes of the real struggle.

These "revolutionary" union groups were started to protect black workers who felt they were being treated unfairly and even victimized by racist white union leaders. Also, they believed, together with like-minded white workers, that union chiefs were in collusion with the bosses to speed up work schedules and ignore grievances over intolerable working conditions. The radical union groups are, first of all, self-protective associations for people unprotected or abused by the regular, bureaucratized unions. Secondly, they hope to stimulate a political awareness that will lead to a revolutionary situation in America.

For the time being, however, it is clear that the ghettos are potentially the most explosive places in the country. This is where the Panthers are organized (although they are trying to establish closer contacts with the revolutionary union movements, as well as with student groups) and where they draw their main support. Much of their appeal for ghetto youths (shared by many whites) is their image of a powerful black man with a rifle. In his recent book of essays [1] Eldridge Cleaver describes his own first encounter with the Panthers at a meeting in the Fillmore district ghetto of San Francisco: "I spun round in my seat and saw the most beautiful sight I had ever seen: four black men wearing black berets, powder blue shirts, black leather jackets, black trousers, shiny black shoes — and each with a gun!"

Since then Cleaver has learned that there is more to being a Panther than carrying a gun. But the image of power and violence is still the basic one created by the Panthers. When ghetto youths learn that party membership is not like joining a street gang but more like taking religious vows, many of them become disillusioned and turn away from the Panthers. They are put off by the strict discipline,[2] the political indoctrination, the discouragement of racism, and such community service projects as the Panther program to provide free breakfast to ghetto children. . . .

---

[1] *Eldridge Cleaver*, Random House, 211 pp. $5.95.

[2] There are twenty-six rules of discipline that all members must follow, of which the first is "no party member can have narcotics or weed in his possession while doing party work." In addition, there are eight "points of attention":

1. Speak politely.
2. Pay fairly for what you buy.
3. Return everything you borrow.
4. Pay for anything you damage.
5. Do not hit or swear at people.
6. Do not damage property or crops of the poor, oppressed masses.
7. Do not take liberties with women.
8. If we ever have to take capitives, do not ill-treat them.

Unlike many of the ghetto youth, who want action, retribution, and loot, some black idealists are drawn to the Panthers' philosophy of social justice and equality through power. Where there have been spontaneous black riots, such as those following the assassination of Martin Luther King, the Panthers have tried to cool it, to discourage violence that could lead only to further repression without any political gains. Unfortunately the political leadership in most cities is too dense to realize that the Panthers are actually a force for stability in the ghettos. An intelligent white ruling class would encourage the Panthers rather than try to destroy them; that it has failed to understand this does indeed argue for its own inherent instability.

Lately the Panthers have been emphasizing programs directly related to the needs of the ghetto community, such as free breakfasts and health clinics. This summer they have also been setting up black "liberation schools," where children between two and sixteen are taught some things about American history, economics, and politics that they never learn in the public schools. Clearly much of this is indoctrination, although the Panthers claim that they are correcting the distorted image that black children receive of themselves and their society.

White middle-class revolutionaries tend to patronize such activities as reformist. But the breakfasts, the schools, and the clinics have won the Panthers support within the ghetto that they never could have gained by guns alone or by Marxist-Leninist analyses of the internal contradictions of capitalism. In Oakland, where the party has existed for nearly three years, it is an important element of the black community, respected even though it is not often fully understood. Just as the police have been forced to respect the power of the Panthers, so the white power elite has had to deal with an organized, politically conscious force within the black community. Throughout much of the Bay area, where the Panthers are particularly well organized, they are an articulate, alert defender of black people's interests. The Panthers are there when the community needs them, and they are there when no one else seems to be listening.

An example that comes to mind, simply because it occurred while I was in San Francisco, concerned a sixteen-year-old boy who was shot in the back by a member of San Francisco's Tactical Squad while he was fleeing the scene of an alleged auto theft. The shooting occured near his home and was heard by his mother, a practical nurse, who was thrown to the ground by the police when she ran to his side screaming, "Don't shoot my boy again." The wounded boy was thrown into a police truck and nearly an hour elapsed before he actually reached the hospital. It is the sort of thing that happens every day in Hunter's Point and a hundred other black ghettos around America. The only difference is that, miraculously, the bullet was deflected by a rib bone and the boy was not killed, and that the Panthers brought it to the attention of the public by calling a press conference which Bobby Seale, David Hilliard, and Masai, the party's three top leaders, attended.

.   .   .

What followed was . . . a lawsuit under the 1964 Civil Rights Act, followed by press coverage — which of course could never have occurred had the Panthers not been called in.

The cynical would say that the Panthers have something to gain from this publicity, which indeed they have. But that is to miss the point, which is that by such actions they are establishing themselves, in the eyes of the black community, as the defenders of the black man too humble to interest anyone else. They can sink their roots in the black community and win its allegiance partly because no one else is fulfilling that role. This is one of the things that the Panthers mean by "educating" the people, informing them of their rights and making them activist defenders rather than passive victims. This education is carried on through meetings, discussions, leaflets, and the party newspaper. While their tactics have shifted several times since the formation of the party in October 1966, their objectives remain the ones set out in their ten-point program of black liberation.[3]

------

[3] 1. We want freedom. We want power to determine the destiny of our Black Community.

2. We want full employment for our people.

3. We want an end to the robbery by the CAPITALIST of our Black Community. [N.B. Recently changed to "capitalist" from "white man."]

4. We want decent housing, fit for shelter of human beings.

5. We want education for our people that exposes the true nature of this decadent American society. We want education that teaches us our true history and our role in the present day society.

6. We want all black men to be exempt from military service.

7. We want an immediate end to POLICE BRUTALITY and MURDER of black people.

8. We want freedom for all black men held in federal, state, county and city prisons and jails.

9. We want all black people when brought to trial to be tried in court by a jury of their peer group or people from their black communities, as defined by the Constitution of the United States.

10. We want land, bread, housing, education, clothing, justice and peace. And as our major political objective, a United Nations-supervised plebiscite to be held throughout the black colony in which only black colonial subjects will be allowed to participate, for the purpose of determining the will of black people as to their national destiny. [Followed by an explanatory paragraph taken from the United States Constitution: "When in the course of human events. . . ."]

Looking at this program and talking to the Panthers, as well as reading their newspaper, *The Black Panther* (which everyone interested
enough to read this essay ought to do in order to gain, if nothing else, an
idea of what is going on under the name of law and order), make one
realize that the "revolution" they talk about is not necessarily the cata-
clysmic upheaval that sends the white middle class into spasms. Rather,
it is the achievement of constitutional guarantees and economic justice
for black people. These gun-carrying, Mao-quoting revolutionaries want
what most middle-class Americans take for granted. As Huey Newton
has said, if reformist politicians like the Kennedys and Lindsay could
solve the problems of housing, employment, and justice for blacks and
other Americans at the bottom of the social heap, there would be no
need for a revolution. And, it goes without saying, little support for such
groups as the Black Panther Party.

The Panthers have a voice in the black community (although not
necessarily so large as many whites imagine) because they offer hope for
change to ghetto people whom the civil rights movement and the poverty
program bureaucrats have been unable to touch. They walk proudly
through the streets of Oakland in their black leather jackets, and they
hold mass rallies for the liberation of Huey Newton in the shadow of the
Alameda County Court House where he was sentenced. They speak to
the black man's image of himself. They tell him that he is no longer
powerless against the forces that oppress him, and that his struggle for
freedom is part of a world-wide liberation movement. In this sense they
fulfill a real psychological need.

While they have not yet shed white blood, except in self-defense,
does this mean that they never will, that their talk of guerrilla warfare is
simply rhetoric? It would be rash to say so, for the Panthers have declared that they are ready to kill anyone who stands in the way of "black
liberation." And they are convinced that racism in this society is so pervasive and deeply rooted that there can be no freedom for black people
until it is extirpated by some form of revolution. Even Gene Marine,
who, in his highly informative book, *The Black Panthers*,[4] freely admits
his admiration for the Panthers, confesses, "I am frightened by them."
Like some of the white revolutionaries who emulate them, the Panthers
seem to have over-learned *The Battle of Algiers*, and have tried to apply
its lesson to a society where the situation is totally different. The United
States today is not Algeria of 1954, nor Cuba of 1958, nor even France of
1968. It is a deeply troubled, but nonetheless largely stable society which
is capable of putting down an insurrection ruthlessly and quickly.

Don't the Panthers realize this? They seem to, at the present moment

[4] Signet, 1969, 224 pp., $.95 (paper).

anyway. This is why they are serving free breakfasts to ghetto children; attempting to form alliances with white radicals, liberals, workers, and pacifists; and urging people to sign petitions for the decentralization of the police. They may be going through a temporary stage, but the direction in which they are heading is clearly marked reformism. Right now they seem interested in maximum publicity, which is why they hold meetings and press conferences, and complain about the way the mass media ignores or distorts their actions. Some of their sympathizers fear that the Panthers are pushing themselves too much in the public eye, and that this only aids the enemies who are trying to destroy them. But since the police and politicians are out to get the Panthers in any case, perhaps such an effort to convince the public that they are not really monsters is their only chance for survival.

.   .   .

Mention of the word "revolution" is enough to send most politicians and police officers into a rage. Like radicals in general, the Panthers naturally talk a good deal about revolution, and use such other catchwords as fascism, imperialism, and the dictatorship of the proletariat. They connect racism with the evils of capitalism, and quote freely from the sacred texts of Marx, Lenin, and Mao. Walk into any Panther office and you are likely to find not only Little Red Books lying about, but the officer of the day with his nose buried in the works of Mao, or one of Lenin's many pamphlets. Slogans, often vague and even meaningless in the context in which they are used, become part of the revolutionary vocabulary. This is true not only of the Panthers, who use such slogans to reach an audience with little formal education, but of young radicals generally. The deliberate inflation and distortion of language is a disease of the Left.

The Panthers, however, realize that racism is deeply embedded in the cultural history of Europe and America and is not, as certain Marxists still argue, simply a by-product of class society. As Huey Newton has said, "Until you get rid of racism . . . no matter what kind of economic system you have, black people will still be oppressed." What revolution seems to mean for the Panthers is the transformation of the ghetto and the "liberation" of black people, and of all oppressed people, from lives of poverty, degradation, and despair. The steps by which this will take place are not specified precisely, but they need not be violent ones unless every other road to radical change is closed. Having defined the problem, the Panthers now ask white America what kind of solution it proposes. So far as the Panthers are concerned, the answer has been harassment, repression, and even murder.

The Panthers [insist they] are not racist, but they refuse to take any instructions from their white sympathizers. Indeed, this may be what makes it possible for them to be anti-racist. Commenting on the anti-white sentiment in SNCC before it became an all-black organization, Huey Newton recently said, "We have never been controlled by whites, and therefore we don't fear the white mother-country radicals." Their willingness to work with allied white radicals is not shared by most black militant groups. When Stokely Carmichael recently left the Panthers, his stormy letter of departure centered on just this issue.

As the Carmichael-Cleaver exchange indicated, the black militants are just as fragmented into feuding factions as are the whites. Their rivalry, however, is a good deal more violent, and the struggle between the Panthers and the "cultural nationalist" US group of Ron Karenga led to the murder of two Panthers in Los Angeles last year. The Panthers are serious about wanting to carry on programs of education, and in spite of the terrible repression they are now facing have an enduring faith in the democratic system of petitions and ballots — far more than do the young white radicals. But like most revolutionaries, they are highly authoritarian and want loyal and unquestioning followers (as Stokely Carmichael rightly pointed out in his letter) rather than critical colleagues.

Unlike the white revolutionaries, however, the Panthers do have some fairly clear ideas of what they want — even though they are uncertain about the best way to get it. Whatever their shortcomings, they did not seem to me self-indulgent, romantic, or part-time players at revolution. They are in this struggle for keeps. Anyone who is a Panther today, or who contemplates joining the party, knows that there is a good chance that he will be jailed or die a violent death. Panthers have already been murdered by the police, many have been beaten and wounded, and others are almost certain to be killed in the months and years ahead. It takes courage to join the party, to submit to its discipline, and to face the likely prospect of imprisonment or death. But for some there is no other way. As Eldridge Cleaver has written, "A slave who dies of natural causes will not balance two dead flies on the scale of eternity."

Revolution in America

Richard E. Rubenstein

Logic compels us to consider the question of revolution. For if the solution to the problem of group revolt is a social and political transformation which admits the powerless to power, we are already talking about a kind of revolution. The discussion will be brief and, of necessity, speculative. Nevertheless, it is at precisely such times that historical perspective is needed. Does the social and political disorder of the 1960s betoken a subsequent period of even greater disorder and more rapid change? Are we living in a revolutionary era? The answer depends to a large extent upon one's perspective on the American past.

First, however, one must grapple with a loaded word: revolution. When historians say (as they so often do) that the United States has never experienced a revolution, one is entitled to know what they mean. For example, Barrington Moore, Jr., maintains that the American struggle for independence was *not* a true revolution, because it was not accompanied by significant social change; the bourgeoisie which had run the pre-revolutionary show continued to run it after 1781.[1] J. Franklin Jameson and other historians think that it *was* a revolution because it *was* accompanied by genuine social change — the elimination of a domestic aristocracy and a transference of power to small businessmen, artisans, and farmers.[2] Charles Beard thought that it started out to be a revolution, but was undone by the reaction of 1789;[3] whereas Hannah Arendt believes that it *was* a true revolution although *not* accompanied by genuine social change, since the struggle brought into the world a brand new type of constitutional democracy.[4] Similarly, when social scientists or political figures state, as is their wont, that revolution in the United States is impossible, again we are entitled to know what they mean. According to Charles Beard, the Civil War was a revolution; does

Reprinted with permission of The Macmillan Company from *The New American Revolution* by Roderick Aya and Norman Miller. Copyright © 1971 by The Free Press, a Division of The Macmillan Company.

[1] Barrington Moore, Jr., *Social Origins of Dictatorship and Democracy* (Boston, 1966), pp. 111–113. See also "Revolution in America?" *The New York Review of Books*, Vol. XII, No. 2 (January 30, 1969), pp. 6–12.

[2] J. Franklin Jameson, *The American Revolution Considered as a Social Movement* (Princeton, 1926).

[3] Charles A. Beard, *An Economic Interpretation of the Constitution of the United States* (New York, 1913; 1935).

[4] Hannah Arendt, *On Revolution* (New York, 1965).

the statement then mean that civil war in the United States is now impossible? According to Arthur Schlesinger, Jr., the ages of Jackson and Roosevelt were revolutionary ages; are we to conclude that further political transformations are now impossible in America?

Although dispute continues about the facts of the American Revolution, the age of Jackson, the Civil War, and the New Deal (e.g., was there really a Tory aristocracy? Did small farmers really exercise power under Jackson?), the disagreements among the authorities noted above would not disappear even if all of them accepted the same facts. Such agreement would not prevent Moore, for example, from holding that the transfer of power from the large to the petit bourgeoisie is not a revolution (and perhaps not even a power transfer); nor would it prevent Arendt from asserting that whether or not the colonial bourgeoisie maintained its position is irrelevant in the light of the political significance of the American Revolution. Perhaps, then, the problem is one of definition. Hannah Arendt suggests as much when she states that one ought to distinguish French-style social revolutions from American-style political ones (and, one might now add, from Algerian- or Vietnamese-style wars of national liberation). But such definitional disputes are only symptoms of a more profound disagreement. At issue is the fundamental question: What kind of change makes a revolution? Amid the welter of political changes that characterize any rapidly developing society, which changes alter the political system so rapidly, drastically, and permanently as to be called revolutionary?

Note that this question itself implies a definition, but it is a definition based upon what political analysts seem to mean when they use the word — that is, change occurring over a fairly short period of time which replaces an old political system (not just a regime) with a new one. Like all definitions, this one begs substantive questions: What is meant by political system? How does one tell when a new system has come into existence? All I want to do here, however, is to establish some principles of exclusion and clarification. We are *not* concerned with evolutionary change, although we will come back to the evolutionist posture, common among American scholars, which assumes that revolutionary change in the United States is a fiction. Nor are we concerned with non-political revolutions, such as those in science and technology, except insofar as they affect politics. Finally, we do not adopt as a matter of definition the concept of revolution as inevitably violent, but leave the relationship of violence to revolution for later formulation. With this by way of background, *has* America ever experienced a revolution?

To begin with, it is clear that America has not had a revolution in the Marxist sense, unless one believes that the Civil War was a capitalist revolution against a seigneurial slave system. In Marxist terms, the

United States remains at present, and has always been, a bourgeois society characterized by private ownership and control of the means of
production and distribution, an exploited proletariat, bourgeois trade
unions dedicated to strengthening rather than replacing the capitalist
system, individual rather than collective farming, and so forth. Many reasons have been advanced to explain the non-occurrence of a revolution
of the proletariat, among them the prior absence of a feudal aristocracy
to set in motion the Marxist dialectic, the availability of cheap land as a
safety valve, America's bountiful natural resources, and the ability of the
capitalist class to save itself periodically via reforms, cooptation of dissidents, and destruction of radical movements. All these factors help to
explain what did *not* happen. As a springboard for discussion of what
did happen to change the American political system between 1776 and
1970, an idea of Richard Hofstadter's may be more useful: in America,
"ethnic animosities . . . have been at times almost a substitute for the
class struggle. . . ."[5]

America does lack a revolutionary tradition in the Marxist sense, but
she has . . . experienced revolts aplenty, from Indian and slave rebel-
lions, farmer revolts, and nativist terrorism through labor-management
warfare, race rioting, and ghetto revolts and campus confrontations of
the present time. Many of these rebellious out-groups have been homogeneous sub-nations, whose rebellious actions have been aimed at redeem-
ing territory, jobs, and lives from control by outsiders. The dynamics
of internal colonialism generate such movements for group liberation;
and those in authority have often responded to such revolts ineffectu-
ally, rather than participating in the system-transformation required
to satisfy the demands of large excluded groups. The existence of
this tradition of group insurrection suggests that group consciousness
in America supersedes or inhibits the development of class consciousness.
But if this is so, perhaps we have been looking for the wrong sort of
revolution in American history. Perhaps domestic revolution is merely
sub-nation revolt writ large.

Generally, movements which begin as single-group revolts end as revolts. A group which comes to conceive of itself as an oppressed nation
or sub-nation distinguishes itself in the process from those who are outsiders and tends to move in the direction of local autonomy or independence rather than seizure of central power. For this reason, although
such movements are often *locally* revolutionary, they seem profoundly
non-revolutionary with regard to the political system as a whole. On the
other hand, in at least three situations, insurrectionary movements may

---

[5] Richard Hofstadter, *The Paranoid Style in American Politics* (New York, 1965),
p. xii.

become revolutionary, in the sense that they require a rapid transformation of the entire system:

1. when those defining themselves as a group are so numerous, in control of such a large geographical area, and so nation-conscious as to attempt secession with some hope of success;

2. when a single group excluded from power at all levels attempts to force a system-transformation by resort to aggressive violence (since the group may be threatened with extinction, such violence is not necessarily aggression; the term is used here to describe attacks outside rebel territory); and

3. when similarly-situated groups conducting separate revolts join forces for the purpose of gaining power simultaneously through radical change in the political system.

The best known instances of revolutionary secessionism are, of course, the American Revolution and the southern rebellion which precipitated the Civil War. (Many Indian revolts may also fall into this category, since they aimed at independent control of large geographical areas, although most tribes found collaboration for the purpose of joint rebellion impossible.) A key to the development of major secessionist movements is the growth of nation-consciousness among groups which may be extremely diverse economically, politically, and even culturally. Those who came to consider themselves Americans began as Virginia planters or Boston traders; to a great extent the unifying group definition which they eventually adopted was forced upon them by British mercantilists. Similarly, southerners originally owing primary loyalty to a state or class were driven together by simultaneous northern attacks upon all classes of white southerners. Such movements have been revolutionary in effect rather than in intent, for no matter what form of government the secessionists adopted, the effect of the separation itself would have been to alter the original system immediately and profoundly. Imagine the northern United States confronted on its southern border by an expansionist slave power ambitious to conquer Central and South America — a North without a southern investment outlet, deprived of the free land of the West, forced to trade as a foreign nation for cotton, oil, natural gas, etc. — and the revolutionary implications of southern secession become apparent.

At present there exists only one serious domestic secessionist movement: the movement to establish an independent black state somewhere within the continental United States (probably within the South, where selective black immigration might make it possible to gain legal control of certain states). As white oppression of all black economic and social classes continues to generate black nationalism, polls show independence sentiment gaining substantial support among northern ghetto-dwellers. The movement deserves more serious study than it has so far received, particularly since the most obvious objections — that the numbers of people involved are too small, that the new nation could not support itself economically, that it could never happen, etc. — prove on analysis to be unfounded. Like white nationalism in the South after 1865, black nationalism is not revolutionary in effect except as to the territory claimed. It is therefore possible to imagine the United States Government several years and race wars hence permitting a black state to become independent (at least with regard to domestic affairs) as a way of ridding the nation of an "insoluble" problem. The more cogent objection is not that such a development is impossible, but that it is probably fruitless, since the fate of small neighbors of the United States is to be dominated either by the U.S. or some countervailing foreign power. The use of local power bases to forge, with other dissident groups, a new domestic alliance would seem to be better designed to maximize black power.

Black nationalism could become revolutionary under the circumstances described in category 2, however, whether or not secession were a goal. Continued exclusion from collective power at all levels produces widespread fear of permanent exclusion and possible group extinction. Under the circumstances, from the point of view of the excluded group, terrorism directed against the enemy wherever he may be found is justifiable self-defense; the fact that massive counterforce may destroy the group is no deterrent, since the rebels prefer a brave death to perpetual dependence and elimination of their militant members. The United States has not experienced this type of revolution before, for at least two reasons: First, the nation has never before been so centralized and so integrated (politically and economically) as to permit the members of a ruling coalition to collaborate in maintaining power at all levels. Earlier insurgent groups found it possible to take power locally; later groups benefitted from the growth of federal power under the New Deal and its successors; present-day blacks find both roads blocked, except where they constitute a majority or near-majority in the cities. (Even here, there is talk of instituting "metropolitan-regional governments," which would operate to nullify such black majorities.) Second, never before has the excluded group been a racial caste with revolutionary-nationalist potential. As a result, failing a radical redistribution of power under her present political system, America must face the prospect of a new type of domestic revolutionary movement which would seek to generate the necessary transformation by force.

It is very difficult, of course, to identify outright revolutionaries presently active within or without the ghetto, or to measure the extent of such activity or the degree to which it commands mass support. Even criminal convictions, such as those obtained against members of the Revolutionary Action Movement for alleged conspiracy to assassinate certain political leaders, indicate little about the nature and extent of revolutionary activity; the probability of frameups in such cases is at least fifty percent. What seems clear, however, is that there *are* organizations with some standing in the black community that will initiate revolutionary activity if the situation deteriorates further — for example, if the police are unleashed upon ghetto activists, or if there is an attempt at forced relocation of the black population. The largest and best organized of these is the Black Panther Party, with establishments in many large cities. However, despite occasional shoot-outs with police, the imprisonment of West Coast leader Huey Newton, and the exile (to escape imprisonment) of Minister of Information Eldridge Cleaver, the Panthers are not yet revolutionary activists. Along with other black organizers (for example, certain large street organizations in New York, Chicago, Detroit, and Los Angeles) they stand in the wings of the revolutionary theater, waiting to enter if whites decide upon the forcible suppression of black militancy. A dangerous game? Certainly. But, to many blacks, no more dangerous than waiting passively for the blow to fall.

If the United States is now entering a revolutionary period, however, racial conflict alone will not explain what is happening to the present political system. For this purpose we must consider a more characteristic type of revolutionary movement in America — the alliance of militant out-groups with dissidents in power that radically alters both the distribution of power and its mode of exercise throughout the system. Three examples of such alliance come to mind: the Jeffersonian alliance, which isolated New England business interests, brought the two-party system into existence and the "little man" into the electoral process, and opened up the West for mass settlement; the Northern Republican alliance, which united eastern businessmen and native workers with western farmers and abolitionists on a new ethnic-sectional basis, unleashed the energies of northern capitalism, and doomed the slave system to violent extinction; and the New Deal alliance, which joined elements of organized labor, immigrant groups, farmers, and the business community in a new coalition, expanded the federal government beyond the Founding Fathers' wildest dreams, and created a mixed economy and a welfare-warfare state.

None of these alliances was revolutionary in the sense that capitalists were prevented from dominating them: each contained powerful elements of the business and commercial communities while attacking others. None came to power by formally overthrowing a pre-existing political system, although in each case, the opposition claimed that the

methods used to take and exercise power (e.g., creation of political parties, expansion of Presidential power, election by a minority of a sectional
party candidate, expansion of federal government) were illegitimate or
illegal. Similarly, none succeeded by force of arms alone, although, as
explained in a moment, violence played an important role in each case.
In what sense, then, were these alliances revolutionary?

The difficulty is that most Americans are accustomed to thinking about political systems on the basis of two contrasting models: the
revolutionary model, in which a society characterized by rigid class distinctions, extremist ideologies, and a suppressive political apparatus is
regularly ripped apart; and the *evolutionary model,* in which a permissive
political apparatus permits free play among interest groups in an essentially classless society, thus making possible change which is peaceful and gradual rather than violent and sudden. (A further assumption
implicit in the contrast is that change in the revolutionary society is
cyclical, and ultimately to no avail, while change in the evolutionary
society is linear, and therefore progressive.) Americans who deny that
their nation has experienced a revolution generally have in mind images
drawn from the experiences of revolutionary societies: since the *canaille*
have never stormed the White House and the Bolsheviks have never
subverted the Army, and since America has never passed an election nor
General Motors a dividend, therefore there has been no revolution. (In
this respect, domestic Marxists and bourgeois moderates are in agreement.) But the distinction between revolutionary and evolutionary societies is a gross exaggeration, if not entirely false. France, the Soviet
Union, and China have known peaceful change and progress, *while most
significant alterations of the American political system have been revolutionary in character.* That is, drastic alterations both in the distribution
of power and the mode of exercising it have been made rapidly, extra-
legally, and — in a sense now to be explained — violently.

Consider two contrasting scenarios: (a) Armed peasants surround
the palace. Their leader breaks into the throne room, kills the king, and
promulgates a new constitution. This is called "violent revolution." (b)
The same peasants surround the palace. Their leader is granted an audience with the king. The king counts up the number of peasants, compares
it with the number of his troops, and promulgates a new constitution.
This is "peaceful change."

Facetious though it may seem, the second scenario comes closer to
the truth about political change in the United States than does the theory
of peaceful evolution. Despite the fact that, in America, sub-national
group consciousness has often superseded class consciousness, major
alterations of the political order have taken place against a background
of civil disorder and potential revolution or civil war. The admission of

new group alliances to power has been accomplished through redefinition of the system itself, involving both the improvisation of new institutions and the exercise of powers formerly held to be unconstitutional. And new alliances, with their new constitutions, have frequently consolidated power violently:

1. Jefferson and his new party came to power at the conclusion of two decades of farmer uprisings and urban riots, and after a serious attempt at counterrevolution had been made by the ruling Federalists. Naturally enough, the Federalists considered the idea of competitive political parties to be seditious and unconstitutional, especially since Jefferson himself was a self-declared French sympathizer and revolutionary. If the Alien and Sedition Acts, which filled the jails with political prisoners, had not been repealed and Jefferson elected in 1800, the farmer-planter-worker coalition would probably have become an armed alliance (Jeffersonians had been active among the Whiskey Rebels and were prepared to nullify offensive legislation), or else the West would have attempted to secede (up to the time of the Louisiana Purchase, such attempts were still being made). Jefferson's Presidency was considered by John Marshall to be little more than a series of attacks on the U.S. Constitution, and Federalist New England continued to plot against "the anti-Christ" in office until the Jeffersonians fomented a war with England and Canada. The war ruined New England shipping, drove that section to threaten secession, and utterly destroyed the Federalist Party. Jeffersonians therefore held power, with the exception of John Quincy Adams' freak election, from 1800 until 1840.

2. The Northern Republican Alliance was forged in an era of national distintegration, as civil disorder rose in the 1850s toward the level of civil war. The Republican Party itself was founded in the year the Kansas-Nebraska civil war began; six subsequent years of violence polarized pro-slave and anti-slave sentiment both North and South, driving the Whig Party into the Republican coalition and splitting the Democratic Party in two. As in the case of the Jeffersonian revolution, the law clearly favored the *ancien régime;* Congressional legislation in the 1850s reflected the conservative views of Stephen Douglas, while the Supreme Court, even more reactionary, committed itself to the Dred Scott decision of 1856. The election of Lincoln — a minority President — deprived the system of its last ounce of legitimacy from the southern point of view, and the bloodiest war of the nineteenth century commenced. Civil disorder continued in the North throughout Lincoln's first administration (the New York Draft Riot was the most serious of numerous anti-Republican riots and disturbances), and the Republicans would probably not have remained in power in 1864 but for the dubious

soldiers' vote and the absence of southern voters. In fact, as Milton Viorst suggests, Republican power rested for a long time on sheer force:

> Relying on a minority faction as their base of support, the Republicans never quite managed to find a majority that was consistent and reliable. In 1868 and 1872, Grant won respectively by 300,000 and 750,000 votes, but in both elections virtually all of the white voters of the South were disfranchised. In 1876 and 1888, the Republican candidate actually polled fewer popular votes than the Democratic while achieving victory in the electoral college. . . . Thus, of seven elections from 1868 to 1892, the Republicans won five, but in only one — Benjamin Harrison's narrow victory in 1888 — could they claim a nationwide majority.[6]

Thus, for a second time, a revolutionary coalition was formed against the backdrop of civil disorder and went to war to consolidate its gains, ruling a virtual one-party state for a long while thereafter.

3. In the mid-1930s, with homeless farmers afoot and workers staging bloody sit-down strikes, domestic fascists and communists gaining broad support, and the nation filled with a fear of violent revolution, Franklin Roosevelt made his famous "left turn" and rode to triumph on the shoulders of a new alliance. Again, the new alliance exercised power through instrumentalities that were denounced as un-American and that for a long time were held to be illegal by the United States Supreme Court. Again, changes in the political system were rapid and profound. And again, although Roosevelt can hardly be said to have fomented World War II, it was war, rather than politics-as-usual, that silenced the domestic opposition, solved the problems of unemployment and underproduction, and made possible FDR's four terms. Postwar militarization and prosperity insured the continuing hegemony of the coalition which ruled through both political parties without serious challenge until civil disorder began anew in the 1960s.

Perhaps these movements were not revolutionary in the Marxist sense; perhaps a capitalist alliance is simply a capitalist alliance. Very well, but the moral is clear: how much civil disorder there has been, how much turmoil, and how much blood spilled, just to obtain the relatively minor structural changes represented by the alliances of Jefferson, Lincoln, and Roosevelt!

We have drawn attention to modern manifestations among black Americans of secessionism and violent revolt, and we have noted that such movements are not at present revolutionary, although their revolu-

---

[6] Milton Viorst, *Fall From Grace* (New York, 1968), p. 92.

tionary potential increases with the passage of time and the continuation of black powerlessness. The matter of revolutionary alliances, however, generates additional questions for the contemporary analyst. Is the period of mass protest and civil disorder which began in the 1960s the modern equivalent of the 1790s, 1850s, or 1930s? Against the backdrop of this disorder, is a new political alliance in the process of formation? If so, will it take power non-violently or resort to violence? In either case, will there be the equivalent of a counterrevolution? Obviously, when one is deeply involved in the events of the day, answers to such questions come hard. Nevertheless, it is worthwhile to speculate on the possible persistence of the pattern elucidated thus far.

As mentioned earlier, one factor inhibiting mass revolutionary movement in the United States has been the inclination of oppressed groups sharing a common cultural heritage to define themselves as nations, thus making it initially very difficult to work with outsiders. On the other hand, we have also seen that prolonged revolt can produce a political awakening in which the insurgent group, increasingly aware of its goals and impatient for power, seeks like-minded allies from without. The result may be expressed as a dialectical process through which several domestic groups are now proceeding: (a) cooperation with a broad cross-section of similarly situated groups and groups in power for purposes of gaining quick access to the system through moderate reform: (b) disillusionment and withdrawal from multi-group activity, selection of new leaders, redefinition of goals, and solidification on the basis of group nationalism; and (c) collaboration with carefully selected groups in and out of power as part of a broader strategy for radical change.

It is interesting to note, in this regard, that it is now the most militant black leaders who speak of a black-white alliance — men like the late Malcolm X and Eldridge Cleaver. Similarly, militant black students, both in high schools and in colleges, have established patterns of cooperation with members of other minority groups and with white radicals. Meanwhile, the latter move through the same three-stage process, beginning with indiscriminate collaboration (e.g., the civil rights and McCarthy-for-President movements), continuing into withdrawal and the development of group nationalism, and ending in selective collaboration based upon a redefined group interest.

Implicit in the idea of revolutionary group alliances rather than economic class alliances is the notion that the unit of revolt in America is the sub-nation, and that before there can be an alliance there must be conscious and coherent sub-national groups. This is why it is so difficult at present to plot the development of new alliances; not all potential members have yet experienced the process described above. For white radicals, for example, the most important question is whether their group

identity will be stabilized and maintained beyond college and after termination of the Vietnam War. Young radicals clearly do *not* fit easily into
the tradition of group insurgency represented by Appalachian farmers,
white southerners, and urban blacks, since in one sense they are not a
sub-nation; and in another, being predominantly middle-class in origin,
they are not an out-group at all. In an almost Darwinian response to
these requirements for group survival, they are in the process of creating
an *ethos* — an amalgam of cultural tastes, political attitudes, ethical
norms, and social mores — which is the analogue of ethnicity, or perhaps
even a new form of it. (One piece of evidence supporting this thesis is
the growth of a racist stereotype that pictures all radicals as dirty, over-
sexed, foul-smelling, addicted to drugs, incurably violence-prone, etc. —
in fact the whole battery of anti-Irish and anti-black prejudices!) Additionally, as they emerge from college without returning to the family
fold or entering the world of the great corporations and traditional professions, their movement develops an economic base comprising selected
traditional occupations (such as high school and college teaching), newly
created occupations (community organizing, international development
work, and service in independent institutes or foundations), and new
branches of traditional occupations (legal services for the poor, group
medical practice, community-owned businesses, etc.)

Additionally, like their rebellious predecessors, today's young leftists
seek territory on which group life may be sustained and strengthened.
Hence, they occupy existing communities *en masse* (e.g., the East Village
in New York, Old Town in Chicago, and the Telegraph Area and People's Park in Berkeley), participate in community control movements
elsewhere, attempt to create rural communes, etc. Violent confrontations
on college campuses become somewhat more comprehensible when one
keeps in mind that the student activists and their supporters are not
merely reformers attempting to improve their lot during a four-year
hitch, or young folks raising youthful hell; they are members of an
emerging social and political group with hopes of permanence, whose
principal economic, political, and territorial base is, and will remain for
some time, the university community. Those colleges experiencing the
most intense conflict are therefore those located in cities where a radical
community is forming both on and off campus, and where control of
territory is an issue. It comes as no surprise that the most explosive confrontations are taking place in San Francisco, Boston, New York, and
Chicago.

As the pace of political change quickens, other out-groups are experiencing a process of revolt and awakening similar to that undergone
by urban blacks and white radicals. In some cases, the process is tele-
scoped: the militant organization of labor leader Cesar Chavez, for example, has had an electrifying effect on the Mexican-American farm

workers of California. Mexican-Americans in the Southwest have begun to fight for their lost land. A new cadre of American Indian leaders now preaches the doctrine of Red Power to willing ears, and at several universities, American Indian students have joined black and Third World students in confrontations with police. In other cases, the initial period of collaboration has barely begun. Despite awakening outside interest in the rural poor and their unemployed brethren in the cities, the masses of rural poor people and poor urban whites remain voiceless. Yet, even here, there are signs of stirring — the "Black Lung" revolt of West Virginia miners, the participation of Appalachian Whites and Puerto Ricans in the Poor People's March of 1968, and the formation of community unions and street organizations among urban "hillbillies" are evidence of the new consciousness.

The formation of a new out-group alliance with revolutionary political potential has therefore not yet occurred. It would be rash, however, to predict that it could not occur in a fairly short time — say by 1975 — given the speed of the spreading wave of political awakening. Before this can take place, however, the historical material suggests that one other change is necessary: a falling out among members of the present ruling coalition. In the past, no significant alteration of the political system occurred without the development of serious divisions among groups in power; all successful past alliances split the middle and upper middle classes, attaching elements of each to the new coalition. It seems fairly clear that the disintegration of the present ruling coalition has already begun. The development of a radical group identity among large elements of the young has already split the suburban middle class, at least generationally. Equally important, organized labor is now entering a period of widespread discontent with the established leadership groups, political polarization, competition between dissidents of Right and Left, and growing schismatic movements at both local and national levels.

That in 1968 the established union leadership kept much of the labor vote in line for Hubert Humphrey is widely misinterpreted as a sign that no significant changes are taking place in that movement. Political scientists have an unfortunate tendency to interpret electoral behavior as the key to a group's politics when, for a variety of reasons, how men vote may bear little relationship to their deepest political desires and clearest intentions. It seems likely that labor voted for Humphrey not because the rank-and-file trusted George Meany or shared his political philosophy, but because there was no viable candidate of the Right (George Wallace being a southerner with a lifelong record of opposition to labor) or of the Left (Robert Kennedy being dead, and the other candidates of the Left were black socialists) to which they could turn. Although the vote for Nixon-Humphrey, the candidates of the Center, may have reflected a widely felt wish for peace and order, such wishes are historically consistent with action *at the local level* to overthrow the established order. In any event, developments since the 1968 election — including a formal schism between the conservative AFL-CIO and the more liberal United Auto Workers and Teamsters unions, the formation of radical and black caucuses in dozens of labor unions, the organization of white block clubs and support-your-local-police associations in blue-collar neighborhoods, and the formation of new unions (both right-wing and left-wing) outside the established labor structure — make it clear that the processes of change within the labor movement are accelerating rather than slowing down.

The same is true (although not often recognized by radical critics of the establishment) of other traditionally capitalist or managerial groups, many of which are in the process of being "declassed" as the result of a growing socio-economic gap between lower middle and upper middle classes. As the technological revolution proceeds and industrial concentration continues, as costs of living and of doing business rise without letup, Horatio Alger begins to disappear even as myth. Small businessmen know that they will never be big businessmen — they will be lucky to be able to educate their children. Small farmers know that their days on the land are numbered, and that the only successful farmer is the agricultural corporation. Even within the corporate world, lower management personnel are aware that they have plateaued out — that survival, rather than advancement, is now the goal. In other words, lower management jobs, like those of teachers and many professionals, are being industrialized. All of these groups and more have common complaints based upon powerlessness and boredom in a technocratic state. And, it may be, they will discover that they have common enemies. When this happens, a revolutionary alliance will be in existence.

The turmoil of the 1960s may well herald the beginning of another revolutionary phase in American history. Sooner or later — and probably sooner — the inability of the present ruling coalition to satisfy the human needs and political demands of its subjects will become clearly apparent, and the processes of political disintegration and reconstruction will accelerate. Hopefully, as the necessity for systemic change is accepted, political violence will be reduced even as political controversy intensifies.

A Note on the Possibility of
Domestic Fascism

One must directly confront a question that plagues any analyst of contemporary social change, particularly if his sympathies are with the dispossessed. We have seen on several occasions that although working-class and middle-class discontent may catalyze a revolutionary alliance, it may also be directed socially downward, against those out-groups which are in direct competition for jobs and living space with workers and members of the lower middle class. The specter of domestic reaction — the formation, out of the wreckage of the present political system, of a right-wing alliance that would annihilate moderates and radicals alike — is frequently invoked to prevent those out of power from agitation. "If you think what you have now is bad, just wait until your real enemies take over!" runs the refrain, with appropriate references to the philosophy of the German Communists of the early thirties: "After the Nazis, us!" In effect, defenders of the status quo contend that the only alternative to rule by the present coalition is a police state — an argument which rests upon the assumption that what most workers, small businessmen, farmers, housewives, and professionals really want is an authoritarian government to establish order at all costs. Therefore, the argument concludes, increasing political agitation, which produces increasing disorder, is the surest road to domestic fascism.

To this line of reasoning there is no easy answer. The possibility of a realignment dominated by a right-wing coalition is one of the risks to be weighed by any group which seeks to alter the distribution of political power. One would be worse than a fool to adopt the slogan of the German Communists as an article of faith or as a corollary of historical necessity. There is, however, a more complex and persuasive answer.

It is erroneous to assume that what any group really wants is either stability or change; most groups want both, simultaneously. By measuring reactions and testing group responses at a time when existing political configurations are beginning to break up — at an early stage in the process of political polarization and alliance formation — one will almost always find a vast majority of those polled leaning towards stability. There are several reasons for this: the inevitability of change is not yet accepted; initial reactions to conduct that seems unusual and disorderly are usually negative. And since new alliances are not yet formed, each group desires change for itself and stability for everyone else. Thus, at the beginning of what we might call the revolutionary process, the Right always seems extremely strong. As the process continues, however, initial reactions to social disorder are qualified (this may be seen, for example, by comparing the results of polls of urban blacks taken immediately after ghetto riots with those taken somewhat later). The society becomes conditioned to accept a higher degree of political militancy and social turbulence (compare the front-page newspaper coverage of the 1964 disturbances at Berkeley with the minimal reporting of the more serious disturbances of 1968–1969). The irreversibility of change is increasingly accepted, and the question is then not *whether* there shall be change or order, but what *kind* of change shall prevail. At this point, diverse groups realize that they cannot fight alone, new alliances are formed, and, eventually, a new national consensus may come into being.

This analysis reveals little about the shape and content of the new consensus; nor does it negate the possibility of domination by the extreme Right. What it *does* show, however, is that sampling public opinion prematurely is not only useless but misleading, particularly when such samples are used to predict the probable outcome of a period of revolutionary change. If a rightist coalition eventually takes power, it will not be composed of sentimental opponents of change but of the apostles of a new order — for example, overt racists and militarists. But the ultimate Right is no more identifiable at present than the ultimate Left. No group in American society is inherently right-wing or left-wing, especially since the meaning of these terms continues to change. The shape of the future political system therefore depends upon how groups come to perceive their interests as the revolutionary process continues — whom they deem to be their friends and whom their enemies.

Will the labor movement five to ten years hence follow the successors of George Wallace or the successors of Robert Kennedy? Will members of the lower middle class support existing business and professional elites or attempt to depose them? Will professors align themselves with boards of trustees or students? No one knows the answer to such questions, since even such supposedly hard-core conservative groups as big business and the military are riven by internal dissension and debate.

It is entirely incorrect to assume, however, as many analysts do, that increasing political turbulence will inevitably push "doubtful" groups to the Right. In the turbulent disorderly 1850s, the Northern business community found its way into the arms of abolitionists and Free Soilers, just as American farmers moved in the turbulent, disorderly 1930s from a brief flirtation with proto-fascism into alliance with organized labor and urban immigrant groups. There was, of course, nothing inevitable about these developments. Indeed, what they demonstrate is the *non-inevitability* of specific political realignments and the critical importance, therefore, of continuing ideological competition, political agitation, and organization during revolutionary periods. At such times, radical change *is* possible.